American ENGLISH FILE

Teacher's Book

Christina Latham-Koenig
Clive Oxenden

with Anna Lowy
Beatriz Martín García

Paul Seligson and Clive Oxenden are the original co-authors of *English File 1* and *English File 2*

OXFORD
UNIVERSITY PRESS

198 Madison Avenue
New York, NY 10016 USA

Great Clarendon Street, Oxford, OX2 6DP, United Kingdom

Oxford University Press is a department of the University of Oxford. It furthers the University's objective of excellence in research, scholarship, and education by publishing worldwide. Oxford is a registered trade mark of Oxford University Press in the UK and in certain other countries.

© Oxford University Press 2014

The moral rights of the author have been asserted.

First published in 2014
2018 2017 2016 2015 2014
10 9 8 7 6 5 4 3 2 1

All rights reserved. No part of this publication may be reproduced, stored in a retrieval system, or transmitted, in any form or by any means, without the prior permission in writing of Oxford University Press, or as expressly permitted by law, by licence or under terms agreed with the appropriate reprographics rights organization. Enquiries concerning reproduction outside the scope of the above should be sent to the ELT Rights Department, Oxford University Press, at the address above.

You must not circulate this work in any other form and you must impose this same condition on any acquirer.

Links to third party websites are provided by Oxford in good faith and for information only. Oxford disclaims any responsibility for the materials contained in any third party website referenced in this work.

Photocopying

The Publisher grants permission for the photocopying of those pages marked "photocopiable" according to the following conditions. Individual purchasers may make copies for their own use or for use by classes that they teach. School purchasers may make copies for use by staff and students, but this permission does not extend to additional schools or branches.

Under no circumstances may any part of this book be photocopied for resale.

Director, ELT New York: Laura Pearson
Head of Adult, ELT New York: Stephanie Karras
Publisher, Adult Coursebooks: Louisa van Houten
Development Editor: Hana Yoo
Executive Art and Design Manager: Maj-Britt Hagsted
Design Project Manager: Michael Steinhofer
Image Manager: Trisha Masterson
Image Editor: Liaht Pashayan
Electronic Production Manager: Julie Armstrong
Production Coordinator: Brad Tucker

ISBN: 978 0 19 477576 2 teacher's book (pack component)
ISBN: 978 0 19 477636 3 teacher's book (pack)
ISBN: 978 0 19 477660 8 testing program cd-rom (pack component)

Printed in China

This book is printed on paper from certified and well-managed sources.

ACKNOWLEDGEMENTS

The authors would like to thank all the teachers and students around the world whose feedback has helped us shape American English File.

The authors would also like to thank: all those at Oxford University Press (both in Oxford and around the world) and the design team who have contributed their skills and ideas to producing this course.

Finally very special thanks from Clive to Maria Angeles, Lucia, and Eric, and from Christina to Cristina, for all their support and encouragement. Christina would also like to thank her children Joaquin, Marco, and Krysia for their constant inspiration.

The Publishers would like to thank the following for their kind permission to reproduce photographs and other copyright material: Alamy Images pp.162 (Portrait of man/Juice Images), 162 (Couple smiling/PhotoAlto sas), 165 (Police officer at crime scene/Cultura Creative), 169 (Kiwi/Life on white), 173 (Extreme free climbing/Prisma Bildagentur AG), 176 (Boy with grandfather/moodboard), 178 (*Gone with the Wind*/AF Archive), 190 (Stethoscope/Michael Willis), 196 (Road sign/Vikki Martin), 196 (Snowboarder/StockShot), 196 (Bear/FLPA), 203 (Stockholm, Sweden/Sweden and Swedish), 203 (Fruit and vegetables/Image Source Plus), 207 (Lightning/Dorset Media Service), 207 (Eye/Medical-on-Line), 208 (Kisumu Lake/Images of Africa Photobank), 208 (Astronaut Buzz Aldrin/NASA Archive), 216 (Woman eating chocolates/Blend Images), 222 (Stack of newspapers/Johnny Greig), 222 (Woman using tablet computer/Anatolii Babii), 236 (Final edition of the News of the World newspaper/Richard Saker); Corbis pp.152 (Business people talking/Dan Bannister/Image Source), 170 (Russia, Moscow/Andrey Petrosjan/FotoS.A.), 178 (Furious manager/Wavebreak Media Ltd.), 196 (Rioting on the streets of Belfast/Michel Philippot/Sygma), 204 (Microphone/Beau Lark), 217 (Tropical storm/Marc Serota/Reuters); Getty Images pp.150 (Mother carrying son/Image Source RF/InStock), 162 (Smiling woman/dibrova), 170 (Climbing mountain/Damiano Levati), 196 (Great white shark/Fuse), 234 (Crowd/Mat Hayward), 235 (Sad couple/Eric Audras); Oxford University Press pp.169 (Penguin/Ingram), 174 (Tennis player after defeat/StockbrokerXtra), 175 (Friends at beach/Image Source), 196 (Brazilian snake/Photodisc), 203 (Recycling box/Marnie Burkhart); Rex Features p.230 (Pink/Sipa Press); Shutterstock pp.160 (Moody girl/CarlaVanWagoner), 160 (Smiling teen boy/RyFlip), 160 (Portrait of man/Goodluz), 160 (Portrait of woman/Oleg Golovnev), 169 (Ostrich/Aaron Amat), 189 (Maldives/Patryk Kosmider), 203 (Dog at training centre/lightpoet), 203 (Man driving car/Minerva Studio), 223 (Business meeting/dotshock), 231 (Man at airport/Tyler Olson), 233 (Man with acoustic guitar/Jose AS Reyes), 237 (Couple at restaurant/Peter Bernik).

Illustrations by: Paul Boston/Meiklejohn Illustration Agency pp.151, 171; Astushi Hara/Dutch Uncle Agency p.159; Anna Hymas/New Division pp.153, 163, 177; Adam Larkham/Illustration Ltd pp.168, 191; Tim Marrs pp.229, 232; Roger Penwill pp.155, 156, 164, 192, 194, 238; Lucy Truman/New Division pp.193, 202.

The authors and publishers are grateful to those who have given permission to reproduce the following extracts and adaptations of copyright material: p.229 "Unbelievable" words and music by Ian Alec Harvey Dench, James Saul Atkin, Zachary Sebastian Rex James Foley, Mark Simon Decloedt and Derrangene Brownson © Warner/Chappell Music Ltd (PRS) All Rights Administered by Warner Chappell Music Australia PTY LTD. p.230 "Just Like a Pill" Words and Music by Alicia Moore and Dallas Austin © 2001, Reproduced by permission of EMI Music Publishing Ltd, London W1F 9LD. p.233 "Same Mistake" Words and Music by James Blunt © 2006, Reproduced by permission of EMI Music Publishing Ltd, London W1F 9LD. p.235 "My Girl" Words and Music by Michael Barson © 1979, Reproduced by permission of EMI Music Publishing Ltd, London W1F 9LD. p.236 "News of the World" Words and Music by Bruce Foxton © 1978, Reproduced by permission of And Son Music Ltd/EMI Music Publishing Ltd, London W1F 9LD. p.238 "World" Words and Music by John Ondrasik © 2006, Reproduced by permission of EMI Music Publishing Ltd, London W1F 9LD. p.234 "Sing" Words and Music by Gerard Way, Michael Way, Frank Iero and Ray Toro © 2010, Reproduced by permission of Blow The Doors Off The Jersey Shore Music Publishing Inc/EMI Music Publishing Ltd, London W1F 9LD. p.231 "The Airplane Song" Words and Music by Roy Neville Francis Stride © 2007, Reproduced by permission of EMI Music Publishing Ltd, London W1F 9LD. p.237 "The Truth" Words and Music by Joel Madden, Benji Madden and John Feldmann © 2004, Reproduced by permission of Dead Executives Publishing/Vegan Boy Publishing/EMI Music Publishing Ltd, London W1F 9LD. p.232 "(Love Is Like a) Heatwave" Words and Music by James Edward Holland Jr., Herbert Lamont Dozier and Brian Holland © 1963, Reproduced by permission of Jobete Music Co Inc/EMI Music Publishing Ltd, London W1F 9LD

All rights reserved. Any unauthorised copying, reproduction, rental, or communication to the public of the material contained in this product is a violation of applicable laws.

Photocopiables designed by: Stewart Grieve

Grammar photocopiable activities written by: Carol Tabor, Brian Brennan

Contents

Syllabus checklist

Pronunciation	Speaking	Listening	Reading
friendly intonation, showing interest	Q&A interviews *Extreme interviews*	Strange questions in job interviews	Q&A Extreme interviews
intonation and sentence rhythm	What do you think? Paranormal experiences Signature analysis	*The coffee cup reading* What your signature says about you Song: *Unbelievable*	Hard to believe? But it happened to me...
/s/, /dʒ/, /tʃ/, and /k/; word stress	First aid questionnaire Health and well-being	Radio interview about cyberchondria Song: *Just Like a Pill*	Confessions of a cyberchondriac
vowel sounds	Teenagers and elderly people Clothes – do you agree with the statements?	Radio program about dressing your age	Trading ages
regular and irregular past forms, sentence rhythm	Asking and answering questions about flying *Flight stories*	Radio program with an airline pilot and air traffic controller Song: *The Airplane Song*	*Air Babylon*
word stress and intonation	*Reading habits* questionnaire	*The Gift of the Magi*	*The Gift of the Magi*
vowel sounds	*How eco-guilty are you?* questionnaire Extreme weather	Extreme weather experiences in the US Song: *Heatwave*	*How eco-guilty are you?* Don't know what to say? Talk about the weather!
sentence stress and rhythm	Taking risks	Are you a risk taker? The risks of driving	I'm John, I'm a speedaholic
word stress	Discuss what you would do in hypothetical situations	*Lost in the Jungle*	How to eat an elephant *Lost in the Jungle*
sentence rhythm and intonation	Situations where you felt a particular way Discussing statements about regret Things you wish you...	Top five regrets Five people talking about regrets Song: *Same Mistake*	Regrets, we've had a few Some of the top 20 regrets

Pronunciation	Speaking	Listening	Reading
words that come from other languages	Your music Asking and answering questions about music	John Sloboda – why we listen to music and how it affects the way we feel Song: *Sing*	What music would you play to an alien?
sentence stress and linking	Asking and answering questions about sleep Discussing issues from the text Sleepwalking	Sleeping problems Radio program about sleepwalking	Three things you (probably) didn't know about sleep
weak form of *have*	How men and women argue Do you agree?	Psychologist's tips for disagreeing Sentences with missing words Song: *My Girl*	How men and women argue
silent letters	Describing someone Two photos	Tim Bentinck interview	What every body is saying
the letter *u*	Asking and answering questions about crime Discussing what should / shouldn't be illegal	Interview with an ex-burglar	How not to get robbed on the street Crime online
word stress	How you find out about news Discussing how news is produced	Radio news Jennifer Buhl interview Song: *News of the World*	24 hours in journalism
changing stress on nouns and verbs	Advertising and marketing The economic situation in your country	Radio program about the tricks of advertising Paul Feldman's experiment Song: *The truth*	Four of the most misleading ads of all time *What the Bagel Man Saw*
word stress with prefixes and suffixes	What is a "megacity"? Cities or regions in your country Asking and answering questions about where you would like to travel	Interview with Miles Roddis	*Andrew Marr's Megacities*
stress in word families	*Scientific facts... or myths?* Science questions	Scientists discussing facts and myths	Suffering scientists
pausing and sentence stress	Presentation experiences Giving a presentation	Disastrous presentations Song: *World*	Famous inspirational speeches

Introduction

American English File is an integrated skills series that gets students talking – in class and everywhere.

Our aim with *American English File* Second Edition has been to make every lesson better and more student-friendly and teacher-friendly. We've created a blend of completely new lessons, updated texts and activities, and refreshed and fine-tuned some favorite lessons from *New English File*.

In addition to Student Book Lessons A and B, there is a range of material that can be used according to your students' needs and the time and resources you have available.

- **Colloquial English video and exercises (also available on the audio CD, class DVD for home-study)**
- **Review & Check pages, with reading and listening (also available on the audio CD for home-study)**
- **Photocopiable Grammar, Vocabulary, Communicative, and Song activities (in the Teacher's Book).**

STUDY LINK Online Practice, Workbook, iChecker, and the Pronunciation app provide multimedia review, support, and practice for students outside of class.

The Teacher's Book also suggests different ways of exploiting many of the Student Book activities depending on the level of your class.

What do Upper-intermediate students need?

Upper-intermediate students justly feel that they are now high-level learners of English, and are ready to advance to become very proficient users of the language. To achieve this, they need motivating materials and challenging tasks. They need to set clear course goals from day one in terms of language knowledge, fluency, and accuracy in speaking. Finally, they need classes to be as fun and dynamic as they were at lower levels: there is no reason why higher-level teaching should become dry and over-serious. Students still want to enjoy their English classes – roleplays, language games, challenges, quizzes, and songs are still as valuable pedagogically as they were, and can often be exploited even better at this level.

Grammar, Vocabulary, and Pronunciation

At any level, the basic tools students need to speak English with confidence are Grammar, Vocabulary, and Pronunciation (G, V, P). In *American English File* Second Edition, all three elements are given equal importance. Each lesson has clearly stated grammar, vocabulary, and pronunciation goals. This keeps lessons focused and gives students concrete learning objectives and a sense of progress.

Grammar

Upper-intermediate students need

- to review their knowledge of main structures.
- to learn more sophisticated grammar structures.
- opportunities to use instinct.

American English File 4 Second Edition puts as much emphasis on consolidating and putting into practice known grammar as learning new structures. It provides contexts for new language that will engage students, using real-life stories and situations, humor, and suspense. The **Grammar Banks** give students a single, easy-to-access grammar reference section, with clear rules, example sentences with audio, and common errors. There are at least two practice exercises for each grammar point.

Mini Grammar focuses on smaller grammar items. There is a photocopiable activity to give more practice of each point.

The oral grammar practice exercise in the Student Book and the photocopiable Communicative speaking activities in the Teacher's Book encourage students to use grammatical structures in controlled and freer contexts.

The photocopiable Grammar activities in the Teacher's Book can be used for practice in class or for self-study.

Vocabulary

Upper-intermediate students need

- systematic expansion of topic-based lexical areas.
- opportunities to put new vocabulary into practice.
- to further develop their ability to "build" new words by adding prefixes and suffixes.

At this level, expanding students' vocabulary is the most visible and motivating measure of their progress. Every lesson has a clear lexical aim. Many lessons are linked to the **Vocabulary Banks** which help present and practice high-frequency, topic-based vocabulary. The stress in multi-syllable words is clearly marked, and both phonemic script and an audio model of each word is provided.

Pronunciation

Upper-intermediate students need

- "fine-tuning" of pronunciation of difficult sounds.
- to be able to use appropriate rhythm and intonation.
- to continue to develop their instinct for spelling, pronunciation rules, and patterns.

The objective is to make students totally *intelligible* to other speakers of English (native and non-native). However, it's also important to make clear that perfection is not the aim.

Students who studied with previous levels or editions of *American English File* will already be familiar with *American English File*'s unique system of sound pictures. *American English File 4* Second Edition integrates this focus on individual sounds with a regular focus on words and sentence stress. Pronunciation is also integrated into Grammar and Vocabulary activities, offering more practice for students and often preparing students for a speaking activity.

Speaking

Upper-intermediate students need

- up-to-date, stimulating topics to get them talking and exchanging opinions.
- the key words and phrases necessary to discuss a topic.
- practice in more extended speaking, e.g., role plays and debates.
- to improve accuracy as well as developing their fluency.

We believe that a good topic or text is very important in motivating students to speak in class. Every lesson in *American English File 4* has a speaking activity that enables students to contribute their own knowledge or experience.

Photocopiable Communicative activities can be found in the Teacher's Book. These include pairwork activities, small-group discussions, and speaking games.

For students who have time to do further practice, there are extra speaking activities available in **Online Skills**.

Listening

Upper-intermediate students need

- motivating, integrated listening material.
- achievable tasks but with an increasing level of challenge.
- exposure to longer listenings and a wide variety of accents.
- exposure to authentic and colloquial spoken language.

For most students listening is still the hardest skill, and it is vital that listening material is both interesting and provides the right level of challenge. *American English File 4* Second Edition has motivating listening texts and activities that are challenging, but always achievable, and that expose students to a wider variety of language and speed of speech.

The Colloquial English lessons give students practice in listening to unscripted authentic speech when speakers are interviewed in a studio and on the street.

There are also ten songs that we hope students will find enjoyable and motivating.

For students who have time to do further practice, there are extra listening activities available in **Online Skills**.

Reading

Upper-intermediate students need

- engaging topics and stimulating texts.
- exposure to a wide variety of authentic text types.
- challenging tasks that help them read better.

Many students need to read in English for their work or academic studies, and reading is also important in helping to build vocabulary and to consolidate grammar. The key to encouraging students to read is to give them motivating but accessible material and tasks they can do. In *American English File 4* reading texts have been adapted from a variety of real sources (newspapers, magazines, news websites) and have been chosen for their intrinsic interest, which we hope will stimulate students to want to read them and will help spark classroom discussion.

For students who have time to do further practice, there are extra reading activities available in **Online Skills**.

Writing

Upper-intermediate students need

- practice in planning, organizing, writing, and checking.
- an awareness of register, structure, and fixed phrases.
- a focus on "micro" writing skills, e.g., paraphrasing.

The growth of the Internet, email, and social networking means that people worldwide are writing in English more than ever before, both for business and personal communication. *American English File 4* provides guided writing tasks that consolidate grammar and lexis taught previously.

There is also always a focus on a "micro skill" in each Writing lesson, for example writing headings, paragraphing, and using connecting expressions.

For students who have time to do further practice, there are extra writing activities available in **Online Skills**.

Colloquial English

Upper-intermediate students need

- to get used to listening to authentic colloquial speech.
- to be able to deal with different speeds and accents.
- exposure to high-frequency colloquial phrases and idioms.

Most listening material in the main lessons is controlled and graded in terms of language and level of difficulty. However, in these five *Colloquial English* lessons, students listen to completely unscripted and authentic English. The lessons consist of an interview with a person who is an expert in his / her field. In the second part of the lesson, students hear street interviews where people answer questions related to the lesson topic. There is also a "Looking at Language" focus that looks at a particular aspect of functional language as used by the speaker.

The *Colloquial English* lessons are on the ***American English File 4* DVD** and **iTools**. Teachers can also use the *Colloquial English* Student Book exercises with the class audio CD.

Review

Upper-intermediate students need

- regular review.
- motivating reference and practice material.
- a sense of progress.

Upper-intermediate students need to feel they are increasing their knowledge, improving their skills, and using English more fluently. After every two Files there is a two-page Review & Check section. The left-hand page reviews the grammar, vocabulary, and pronunciation of each File. The right-hand page provides a series of skills-based challenges, including a short documentary film. These pages are designed to be used flexibly. Students can also review and consolidate after each lesson using the Workbook exercises and accompanying tests on iChecker.

Student Book Files 1-10

The Student Book has ten Files, or units. Each File is organized as follows:

A and B lessons

Each File contains two two-page lessons that present and practice **Grammar**, **Vocabulary**, and **Pronunciation** with a balance of reading and listening activities and lots of opportunities for speaking. These lessons have clear references to the Grammar Bank, Vocabulary Bank, and Sound Bank at the back of the book.

Colloquial English

Every two Files (starting from File 1) there is a two-page lesson where students develop their ability to listen to authentic English and look at functional language in use. Integrated into every *Colloquial English* lesson is an interview with an expert in his / her field, and *On the street* interviews, which can be found in the *American English File 4* DVD and on iTools.

Review & Check

Every two Files (starting from File 2) there is a two-page section reviewing **Grammar**, **Vocabulary**, and **Pronunciation** of each File and providing **Reading**, **Listening**, and **Speaking** *Can you…?* challenges to show students what they can achieve. There are also videos in Review & Check: short documentary films that extend the Student Book topics and that are filmed specially for *American English File*.

The audio versions of the Review and Check short movies, and the Irregular verbs list, are available as MP3s on CD 1 of the class audio CDs. To access these tracks, play CD 1 in your computer.

The back of the Student Book

The lessons contain references to these sections: Communication, Writing, Listening, Grammar Bank, Vocabulary Bank, and Sound Bank.

STUDY LINK

Workbook

For practice after class

- All of the Grammar, Vocabulary, Pronunciation, and Colloquial English
- Extra reading
- A listening exercise for every lesson
- Pronunciation exercises with audio
- Useful words and phrases
- Audio for Pronunciation and Listening exercises (on **iChecker**)
- Available with or without an answer key

iChecker CD-ROM

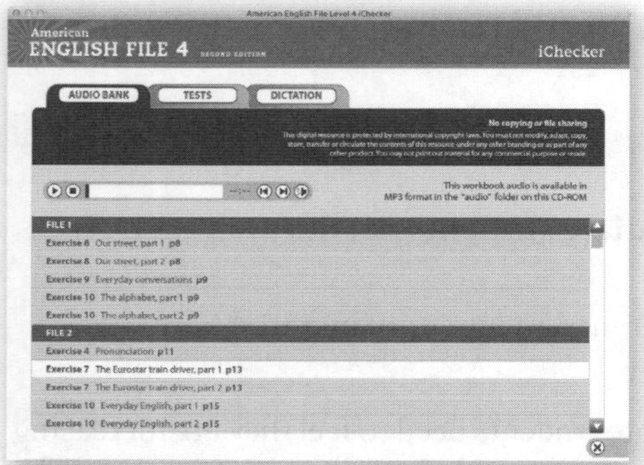

Each workbook is packaged with an iChecker CD-Rom for students to check their progress and receive immediate feedback.

- A Progress Check with 30 multiple-choice questions for each File
- A Dictation exercise for each File
- All of the audio from the Workbook lessons

Online Practice

There is an access card on the inside back cover of each Student Book. Students register for engaging LMS-powered practice with immediate feedback.

- A flexible and extensive program of extra skills practice to support students

Pronunciation app

Students can purchase an engaging app through the iTunes or Google Android online stores for tablet- or phone-based practice. Students can learn and practice the sounds of English:

- Individual sounds
- Sounds in useful phrases
- Speak and record

For teachers

Teacher's Book

4

SECOND EDITION

American ENGLISH FILE

Teacher's Book

Christina Latham-Koenig
Clive Oxenden
with Anna Lowy
Beatriz Martín García

OXFORD

Detailed lesson plans for all the lessons, including:

- an optional "books closed" lead-in for every lesson
- **Extra idea** suggestions for optional extra activities
- **Extra challenge** suggestions for ways of exploiting the Student Book material in a more challenging way if you have a stronger class
- **Extra support** suggestions for adapting activities to make them work with students who need extra support

Extra activities are in **red type** so you can see at a glance what is core material and what is extra when you are planning and teaching your classes.

All lesson plans include keys and complete audioscripts.

Seventy pages of photocopiable activities are in the Teacher's Book.

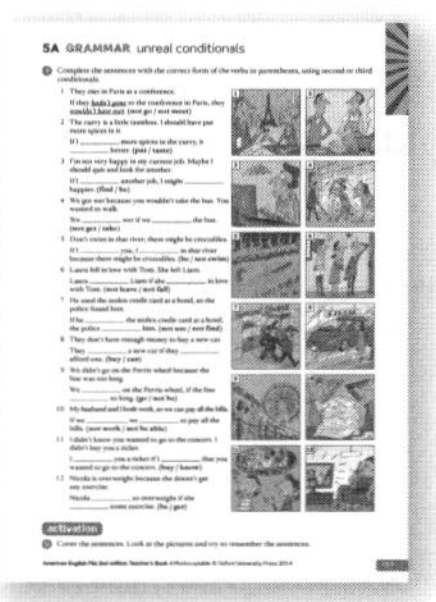

Grammar

see pages 150–178

- An activity for every Grammar Bank that can be used in class or for self-study extra practice
- An Activation section to help students use the new language in class

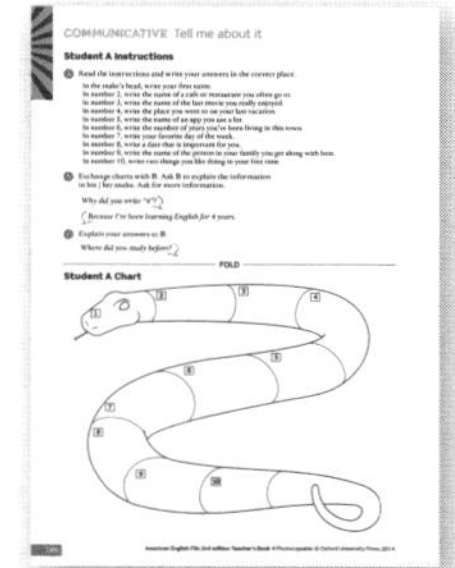

Communicative

see pages 179–209

- Extra speaking practice for every A and B lesson
- "No cut" alternatives to reduce preparation time

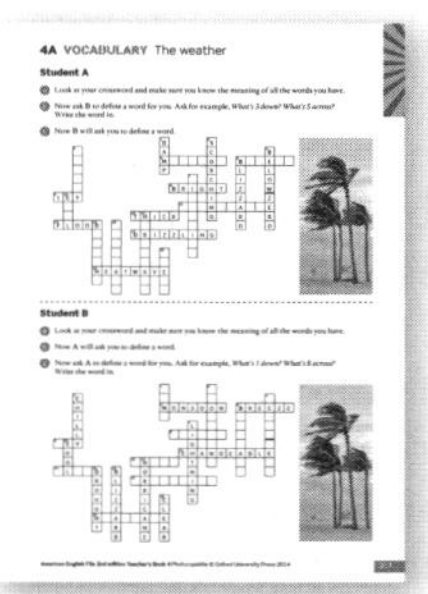

Vocabulary

see pages 210–225

- Extra practice of new vocabulary in every Vocabulary Bank

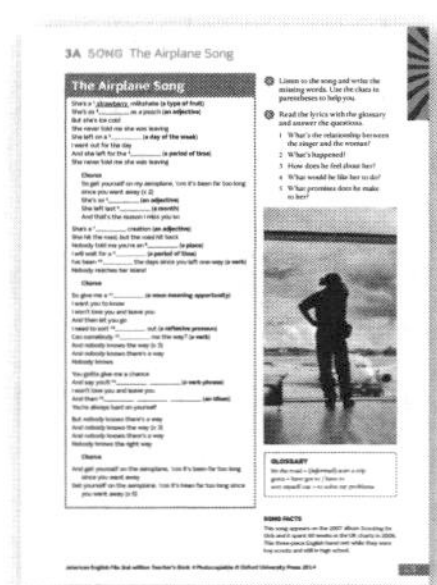

Songs

see pages 226–238

- A song for every File
- Provides the lyrics of the song, with tasks to do before, during, or after listening

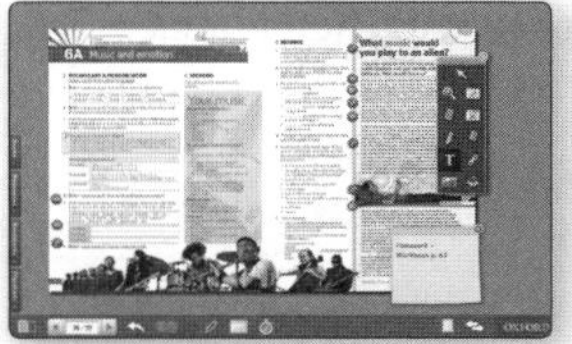

iTools - bring your classroom to life

- The Student Book, Workbook, and Teacher's Book (photocopiables only) onscreen
- All class audio (including songs) and video, with interactive audioscripts
- Answer keys for Student Book, Workbook, and Teacher's Book
- Resources including Grammar Bank PowerPoints, maps, and CEFR Mapping Guide

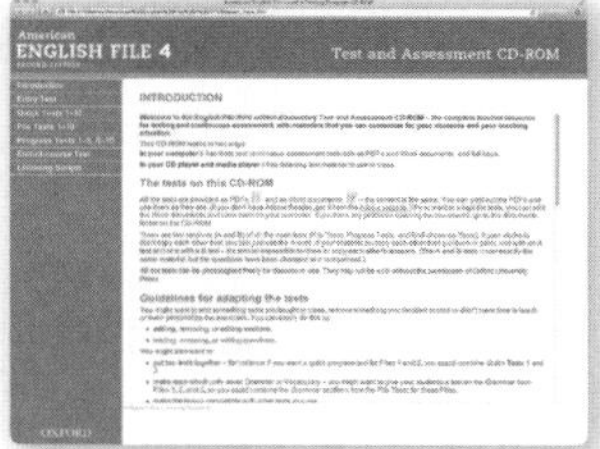

Testing Program CD-ROM

- A Quick Test for every File
- A File test for every File covering G, V, P, Reading and Listening, and Speaking and Writing
- An Entry Test, two Progress Tests, and an End-of-course Test
- A and B versions of all the main tests
- Audio for all the Listening tests

Class Audio CDs

- All of the listening materials for the Student Book

DVD

Colloquial English

- A unique teaching video that goes with the Practical English lessons in the Student Book

On the street

- Short real-world interviews to accompany the Colloquial English lessons

Short movie

- Short documentary movies for students to watch for pleasure after the Review & Check section

G question formation
V figuring out meaning from context
P friendly intonation, showing interest

1A Questions and answers

Lesson plan

Even at the Upper-intermediate level, many Sts still need support forming questions correctly. This lesson aims to review all aspects of question formation, including indirect questions, negative questions, and questions which end with a preposition. By the end of the lesson, Sts should be forming questions more accurately and more confidently, and we suggest that from then on you set ground rules for Sts that questions are always formed correctly.
The lesson has two distinct sections. In the first section, Sts read two interviews from Q&A, a regular feature in *The Guardian* newspaper. They then focus on the grammar of question formation and this is followed by Pronunciation, which reviews friendly intonation in questions and showing interest.
In the second section, the topic is extreme interviews and Sts read an article about the kind of "extreme" questions which some companies now use at job interviews. The vocabulary focus is on figuring out the meaning of new words in a text from context. This is followed by a listening, where Sts hear various speakers talk about strange or unusual questions they have been asked in interviews, and the lesson ends with speaking, where Sts role-play extreme interviews and write some questions of their own.
If you would like to begin the first lesson without the book, there are two photocopiable "first day" activities on *page 150* and *pages 186–187* (instructions *page 179*).
There is an Entry Test on the *Testing Program CD-ROM*, which you can give the Sts before starting the course.

STUDY LINK
- **Workbook** 1A
- **Online Practice**
- **iChecker**

Extra photocopiable activities

- **Grammar** Introduction *page 150*
  question formation *page 151*
- **Communicative** Introduction: Tell me about it *pages 186–187* (instructions *page 179*)
  Ask me a question *page 188* (instructions *page 179*)

Optional lead-in – the quote

- Write the quote at the top of *page 4* on the board (books closed) and the name of the person who said it, or get Sts to open their books and read it.
- You could point out / elicit that Harrison Ford (1942–) is famous in particular for his performances as Han Solo in *Star Wars* and the title character of the Indiana Jones film series. Elicit / explain what *a lightsaber* and *a whip* are.
- Ask Sts why they think Harrison Ford said this. (He gives it as an example of silly questions he is sometimes asked in interviews.)

1 READING & SPEAKING

a Focus on the photos of the two actors and ask Sts if they know anything about them. Don't worry if they don't.

Give Sts time to read about who they are.

Elicit answers to the two questions and tell Sts if you have seen these actors before and what you think of them.

b Focus on the two interviews and ask Sts what the title, *Q&A*, means (Questions and Answers).

Then give Sts time to read the interviews and match questions A–G with the numbered blanks. Point out the **Glossary** to Sts.

Get Sts to compare with a partner and then check answers.

Extra support

- Before Sts read the article, check it for words and phrases that your Sts might not know and be ready to help with these.

Benedict Cumberbatch
2 F 5 B 9 E
Elisabeth Moss
1 C 4 D 6 G 8 A

Help Sts with any vocabulary questions that come up.

c Quickly go through questions 1–8 with Sts, making sure they understand all the lexis in them.

Now tell Sts to read the interviews again and to answer the questions with the actors' initials.

Get Sts to compare with a partner and then check answers.

1 BC 3 EM 5 EM 7 EM
2 BC 4 BC 6 BC 8 EM

Extra challenge

- You could get Sts to close their books and then call out some of the answers (or parts of the answer) from the two *Q&A* questionnaires to see if Sts can remember the questions, e.g.,
  T *Jasmine*
  Sts *What is your favorite smell?*
  T *I say "Um" too much.*
  Sts *Which words or phrases do you most overuse?*

d Put Sts in pairs to decide which question is the most interesting, the most boring, and too personal to ask a person who you don't know well. You might want to tell Sts that they don't have to agree with each other.

Get feedback from the class.

e Focus on the task and put Sts in pairs. Give Sts time to choose their six questions.

Extra support

- Demonstrate the activity by getting Sts to choose questions to ask you. Give reasonably full answers and encourage Sts to ask follow-up questions.

Get Sts to ask and answer their questions. Encourage "questioners" to ask for more information where possible.

Get feedback by asking Sts for any interesting / funny answers and help with any vocabulary problems that come up.

2 GRAMMAR question formation

a Focus on the task and go through questions 1 and 2. Make sure Sts remember what, for example, an auxiliary verb is (*do*, *have*, etc.).

Get Sts to do the task in pairs or do it as an open-class activity.

Check answers.

1 a subject question where there is no auxiliary verb: D
a question that ends with a preposition: G
a question that uses a negative auxiliary verb: B

2 The question becomes *What do you think you would change?* It becomes an indirect question and there is no inversion of *you* and *would* (the subject and auxiliary).

b 1 2)) 1 3)) Tell Sts to go to **Grammar Bank 1A** on *page 132*. Focus on the example sentences and play the audio for Sts to listen to the sentence rhythm. You could also get Sts to repeat the sentences to practice getting the rhythm right. Then go through the rules with the class.

Additional grammar notes

- The **Additional grammar notes** in this Teacher's Book aim to add more information to the notes and rules on the **Grammar Bank** pages in the Student Book. There is a direct link between the number of each rule in the Teacher's Book and the Student Book. If there is no extra information about a rule in the Teacher's Book, this is either because we assume that Sts at this level should already know it or because all the information needed is on the Student Book page.

question formation

rule 1: basic word order in questions

- Sts at this level should be familiar with basic rules regarding question formation, though they may still be making mistakes, especially when they speak.

rule 2: word order in negative questions

- The word order is the same as in affirmative questions, i.e., just add ***n't*** to the auxiliary verb, e.g., *Are**n't** you going to come? Why did**n't** you tell me?*
- You may want to point out when full forms are used you have to put the *not* between the subject and verb, e.g., *Are you not going to come? Why did you not tell me?*
- You should point out to Sts that it is much more common to use the contracted negative, especially in spoken English.

indirect questions

- You may want to highlight that in this kind of question the second question "disappears."

Other expressions followed by the word order of indirect questions

- Highlight that we only use a question mark when the introductory phrase is a question, e.g., *Could you tell me…? Do you have any idea…?* Where the introductory phrase is not a question, e.g., *I'm not sure… I wonder…*, then the sentence ends with a period.

Focus on the exercises and get Sts to do them individually or in pairs.

Check answers, getting Sts to read the full questions.

a
1 Should I tell her how I feel?
2 How long have you known your best friend?
3 Could you tell me when the next train leaves?
4 Who does the housework in your family?
5 What are you thinking about?
6 What don't you like doing on the weekend?
7 What kind of music does Jane like listening to?
8 Do you know what time the movie ends?
9 How many students came to class yesterday?
10 Do you remember where the restaurant is?

b

1	do you usually do	6	does your sister do
2	wrote	7	ate
3	this book costs	8	the swimming pool opens
4	I parked	9	Didn't / Doesn't your sister like
5	Did you enjoy	10	Do you have to

Tell Sts to go back to the main lesson **1A**.

Extra support

- If you think Sts need more practice, you may want to give them the Grammar photocopiable activity at this point or leave it for later as consolidation or review.

3 PRONUNCIATION

friendly intonation, showing interest

Pronunciation notes

- Non-native speakers can unintentionally sound unfriendly or uninterested if they use very flat intonation. The first two exercises focus on encouraging Sts to use a wide voice range when asking questions and on stressing the right words.
- These exercises do not focus specifically on distinguishing between the different intonation patterns for *yes* / *no* questions and question-word questions (*yes* / *no* questions usually have a rising intonation and question-word questions a falling intonation). In practice, we think it is very hard for Sts to notice this distinction. However, when they are asked to copy the rhythm and intonation of a question, they can usually produce the correct pattern.
- In exercises **c**, **d**, and **e**, Sts focus on using friendly intonation to respond to what someone says. This is another context in which using flat intonation (e.g., when responding *Really?*) can unintentionally convey a lack of interest.

a 1 4 Focus on the task. Tell Sts they are going to hear someone asking each question twice – once with friendly intonation and once without – and they must decide which one has the friendlier intonation.

Play the audio once all the way through for Sts just to listen.

Now play the audio again, pausing after each question if necessary, to give Sts time. If necessary, play again.

Check answers.

1 a 2 a 3 b 4 b 5 a

1 4
See questions in Student Book on *page 5*

b 1 5 Tell Sts they will hear the five questions again with friendly intonation. They must listen and then repeat the question, copying the intonation.

Play the audio, pausing after each question for Sts to listen and repeat.

1 5
See questions in **a** in Student Book on *page 5*

Now repeat the activity, getting individual Sts to repeat each question.

c 1 6 Focus on the **Reacting to what someone says** box and go through it with the class.

Tell Sts they are going to hear five conversations, each starting with the questions in **a**, and they must fill in the five blanks for the reactions.

Play the audio once all the way through for Sts just to listen.

Then play the audio again, pausing after each conversation for Sts to complete the expressions and questions.

Get Sts to compare with a partner and then play the audio again as necessary.

Check answers.

See expressions in **bold** in audioscript 1.6

1 6
W = woman, M = man

1
W Do you have a big family?
M Yes actually, I'm one of seven. I have five sisters and a brother.
W **Wow**! That's a huge family.

2
M What don't you like about the place where you live?
W Well, for one thing, I don't like my neighbors very much.
M **Why not**? What's wrong with them?

3
W What sports or games are you good at?
M Well, I'm not really very athletic, but I'm very good at chess.
W **Me too**! We could play a game one day.

4
W Do you think you have a healthy diet?
M Yes, very. In fact, I'm a vegan, so I only eat fruit and vegetables, and grains, and no meat or fish.
W **How interesting**! How long have you been a vegan?

5
M What makes you feel happy?
W Lots of things. Uh...like buying new shoes.
M **Oh, really**? I can't think of anything worse!

d 1 7 Tell Sts that this time they are just going to hear the responses and they must repeat them. Encourage them to use a wide voice range and to get the right rhythm.

Play the audio, pausing after each response for Sts to listen and repeat.

1 7
1 Wow! That's a huge family.
2 Why not? What's wrong with them?
3 Me too! We could play a game one day.
4 How interesting! How long have you been a vegan?
5 Oh, really? I can't think of anything worse!

Now repeat the activity, eliciting responses from individual Sts.

e Put Sts in pairs and get them to ask and answer the questions in **a**. Encourage them to use friendly intonation and to react to their partner's answers.

Have some of the pairs practice in front of the class.

4 READING & VOCABULARY

a Focus on the photo and ask the class the questions.

b Give Sts time to read the article to find the answer to the question. You may want to point out the **Glossary** before Sts start reading.

Check the answer and elicit Sts' own answers.

Extra support

- Before Sts read the article, check it for words and phrases that your Sts might not know and be ready to help with these.

Yes, it is a real question asked at interviews.
Sts' own answers

Extra idea

- It can be difficult to know how long to give when you set a time limit for reading since some Sts are slower readers than others. It is important for Sts to realize that slower readers are not bad readers; in fact, they often retain what they have read better than fast readers. We suggest that you talk about this with your Sts and ask if they are fast or slow readers when they read in their L1. Then set a time limit to suit the mid-pace readers. Tell the fast readers if they have finished already, to go back to the beginning, and encourage very slow readers to try to speed up a little.

c Focus on the **Guessing the meaning of new words and phrases** box and go through it with the class. Many of the texts in *American English File 4* have glossaries, but obviously there will sometimes be other words whose meaning Sts can't guess and will want to check with a dictionary. These days, many Sts will have online dictionaries on their phone. While these can be very useful, it's worth pointing out to Sts that there are circumstances, e.g., in exams, when they need to try to guess the meaning of words and that if they always rely on their phones, they won't develop this skill.

Now tell Sts to read the article again, trying to guess what the highlighted words or phrases mean.

In pairs, they compare guesses.

d Now get Sts to match the highlighted words and phrases with definitions 1–10.

e 1 8))) Play the audio for Sts to listen and check.

Check answers by writing the words on the board and asking Sts which syllable to underline.

See underlining in audioscript 1.8

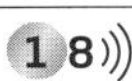

1 demanding	6 rather than
2 flustered	7 crush
3 bizarre	8 recruitment agency
4 think on their feet	9 job seekers
5 approach	10 flapping

Find out how many of the words Sts guessed correctly and help with any other vocabulary questions.

f Focus on questions 1–3 and give Sts, in pairs, a minute or two to answer them. Encourage them to try to use their own words rather than just quoting directly from the article.

Check answers.

1 Extreme interviews are interviews in which candidates have to answer strange, unexpected questions.
2 IT companies / companies in Silicon Valley (in California)
3 Because they give the interview candidate a chance to show who they really are.

g Focus on the task, making sure Sts understand all the lexis in the questions. You could put Sts in pairs, small groups, or do this as an open-class activity.

Extra challenge

- In their pairs or groups, get Sts to answer the questions in the circles. Then get some feedback.

5 LISTENING

a Focus on the questions and elicit answers from the class. If your Sts are too young to have had a job interview, you could ask if they have had any other kind of interview or you could go directly to **b**. If you have a class of older adults, all of whom are likely to have had some kind of job interview, you could put Sts in pairs and then get some class feedback.

b 1 9))) Focus on the task and the chart. Give Sts time to look at the five fill-in-the-blank questions and elicit / teach the meaning of *reincarnated*.

Play story 1 all the way through and then pause the audio. Get Sts to complete the question. Play again as necessary.

Check answers.

Now repeat the process for the four other stories.

Extra support

- Before playing the audio, go through the audioscript and decide if you need to preteach / check any lexis to help Sts when they listen.

1 Do you still **practice philosophy**?
2 What would make you **kick** a **dog**?
3 **How tall** are you? How much **do** you **weigh**?
4 **What animal** would you like to be reincarnated as?
5 Are you planning to **have children**?

1 9)))
(audioscript in Student Book on *page 120*)

1 I was being interviewed for a job with an advertising agency and the interviewer kept checking information on my résumé and then asking me about it, and he saw that I'd studied philosophy in college, and he said, "Oh, I see that you studied philosophy in college. Do you still practice philosophy?" So I said, "Well, I still think a lot." Anyway, he obviously liked the answer because I got the job.

2 At my job interview to become an editor with a publishing company, there were three people asking questions: two managers and a woman from human resources. All the questions had been pretty normal, they were about my studies and experience, and then suddenly the woman from human resources asked me, "What would make you kick a dog?" I was totally flustered, but I managed to answer—I said, "I'd only kick it if the dog had bad grammar and couldn't punctuate properly." I thought it was a clever answer and, in fact, I got the job!

3 When I was applying for a teaching job in Korea, they were doing the interviews by phone because I was in the US. And because of the time difference they were all very early in the morning, which is not my best time. Anyway, the director of studies of this particular school asked me, "How tall are you?" and, "How much do you weigh?" I answered his questions, but after the interview, when I thought about it, I decided that I didn't want to work in a school that would judge me by my height or my weight. So later, when they offered me the job, I turned it down.

4 I was being interviewed for a job and the interviewer asked me, "What animal would you like to be reincarnated as?" So I said a cat because it was the first thing I thought of and because cats have a good life – well at least in the US they do. And then the interviewer immediately looked a little embarrassed and said that he had been told to ask me that question to see how I would react, but that he thought it was a stupid question. In the end I didn't get the job, so maybe the interviewer wasn't very fond of cats...

5 I went for a job interview at a lawyer's office. There were two of us waiting to be interviewed – me and a man about the same age as me – and he was nice, so we were chatting before we went in, and we agreed to have a coffee afterwards. Well, I went in first, and they asked me the usual kinds of questions about my previous job. They had all my personal information on my résumé and so they knew I was married and suddenly they asked me, "Are you planning to have children?" I said, "Not in the immediate future, but maybe one day." Afterward, when I was having coffee with the other candidate, I asked him if he'd been asked the same question, and he said no, even though he was married, too. In fact, we both got offered jobs, but I still think it was a very sexist question to ask.

c Now tell Sts they will hear the audio again and this time they must take notes on how the people answered the questions and what happened in the end.

Play the audio, pausing after each speaker to give Sts time to write. Play again as necessary.

You could get Sts to compare with a partner before checking answers.

Extra support

- Check the answers to the first question (*How did they answer?*), then play the audio again and check the answers to the final question.

1 He answered "I still think a lot."
He got the job.
2 She answered "I'd only kick it if the dog had bad grammar and couldn't punctuate properly."
She got the job.
3 We don't know.
He was offered the job, but didn't accept it.
4 He answered "a cat."
He didn't get the job.
5 She answered "Not in the immediate future, but maybe one day."
She got the job.

Extra support

- If there's time, you could play the audio again while Sts read the audioscript on *page 120*, so they can see what they understood / didn't understand. Translate / explain any new words or phrases.

d Do this as an open-class question and elicit opinions.

6 SPEAKING

a Put Sts in pairs, **A** and **B**, preferably face to face. Tell them to go to **Communication *Extreme interviews*, A** on *page 104*, **B** on *page 108*.

Go through the instructions and make sure Sts know what they have to do. Make sure, too, that Sts understand the questions they're going to ask. You may need to explain, e.g., *aspect* and *deserted* in **A**'s questions, and *lead role* and *financial limitations* in **B**'s questions.

Tell the **A**s to start by asking his / her partner the eight interview questions.

Monitor and help Sts, correcting any errors with question formation.

When they have finished, the **A**s should tell their partner if they got the job and why, or why not if they didn't succeed.

Then they switch roles.

Get feedback to find out if there were any particularly interesting answers. Have Sts raise their hands to find out how many got the jobs.

Extra support

- You could write any new and useful words and phrases from **Communication** on the board for Sts to copy.

Tell Sts to go back to the main lesson **1A**.

b Focus on the task. You may want to elicit a few possible questions from the class so that Sts know what they have to do.

Monitor and correct any mistakes in question formation.

Extra support

- Get Sts to write their questions in pairs. Then divide the class in half (with one student from each pair in each group) for the activity.

c If possible, get Sts to stand up and move around the class asking as many other Sts as possible their three questions.

Help with any vocabulary questions that come up.

d Do this as an open-class question and elicit opinions.

G auxiliary verbs; *the...the...* + comparatives
V compound adjectives, modifiers
P intonation and sentence rhythm

1B Do you believe in it?

Lesson plan

In this lesson, Sts review the use of auxiliary (and modal) verbs in tag question and *So do I* | *Neither do I*, and learn to use them for emphasis (*I do like coffee!*) and in reply questions (**A** *I enjoyed the movie.* **B** *Did you?*).

The first half of the lesson starts with a jigsaw reading based on true stories about the paranormal. Sts then listen to a third story involving fortune-telling in Turkey. Then in Speaking, they exchange stories about the paranormal. After the grammar focus on auxiliary verbs, Sts work on intonation and sentence rhythm in questions and sentences using auxiliaries. Finally, the first half of the lesson ends with the song, *Unbelievable*.

In the second half of the lesson, Sts listen to a graphologist and find out how to interpret personality from signatures. They then learn, in Mini Grammar, how to use the structure *the…the…* + comparatives, e.g., *the sooner the better*. This is followed by Vocabulary, where Sts expand their vocabulary of compound adjectives to describe personality, and use modifiers and compound adjectives to talk about people they know.

STUDY LINK
- **Workbook** 1B
- **Online Practice**
- **iChecker**

Extra photocopiable activities

- **Grammar** auxiliary verbs *page 152*
- **Mini Grammar** *the...the...* + comparatives *page 173*
- **Communicative** The island *page 189* (instructions *page 179*)
- **Song** *Unbelievable page 229* (instructions *page 226*)

Optional lead-in – the quote

- Write the quote at the top of *page 8* on the board (books closed) and the name of the person who said it, or get Sts to open their books and read it.
- Get Sts to say what they think the quote means and whether they agree with Chase's view about people believing in the paranormal.

1 READING & LISTENING

a Focus on the title, *Do you believe in it?*, and ask Sts what they think *it* is to elicit the word *paranormal*. Explain / elicit its meaning.

Now tell Sts they are going to read two true stories involving paranormal happenings. Focus on the beginnings of the stories and give Sts time to read them.

Elicit ideas to the question.

You could ask Sts to raise their hands to find out what proportion of the class believes in the paranormal and what proportion is skeptical (i.e., find it difficult to believe).

b Put Sts in pairs, **A** and **B**, preferably face to face. Tell them to go to **Communication *Hard to believe?***, **A** on *page 104*, **B** on *page 109*.

Focus on **a** and tell Sts as they read they must guess the meaning of the highlighted words and fill in the blanks in their **Glossary**. Set a time limit.

Extra support

- Before the **A**s tell their partner about their story, quickly elicit the words from their **Glossary**.

Noises in the Night:
1 curtains 3 dragging 5 row
2 estate agent 4 carried on

Tell the **A**s to cover their stories and to use the questions to help them retell the story to their partner. They can also look at the **Glossary** for help if they want to.

Extra support

- Before Sts switch roles, quickly elicit the words from the **Glossary** for *The Strange Object on the Hill*.

The Strange Object on the Hill:
1 dome 3 hallucinating 5 binoculars
2 gliding 4 vividly 6 breeze

Now tell the **B**s to retell their story. The **A**s must listen and ask questions to find out as much information as possible.

When they have finished, find out what Sts think of both stories. What do they think the noises and the strange object were?

Extra idea

- As you elicit the words for the glossaries, write them on the board. When Sts have finished retelling their stories, make sure they all copy the words for the story they didn't read and learn the meaning and pronunciation. If there's time, Sts could read the other story now.

Extra support

- You could write any new and useful words and phrases from the stories and **Communication** on the board for Sts to copy.

Tell Sts to go back to the main lesson **1B**.

c Tell Sts they are going to read the beginning of another true story about the paranormal. Focus on the title and ask Sts what you call a person who "reads" coffee cups to elicit *clairvoyants* /klɛrˈvɔɪəns/ and *fortune-tellers* /ˈfɔrtʃən ˈtɛlərs/. Model and drill their pronunciation.

When Sts have finished reading the story, ask them the questions as an open-class activity.

Extra support

- Read the story out loud to the class before asking the questions and eliciting opinions.

d 1 10 Tell Sts that they are going to listen to the rest of the story and emphasize that this is a true story.

Give Sts some time to read the nine questions.

Play the audio once all the way through for Sts just to listen and get the gist of the story.

Play the audio again, pausing at intervals to give Sts time to answer the questions. Play again if necessary.

Check answers.

Extra support

- Before playing the audio, go through the audioscript and decide if you need to preteach / check any lexis to help Sts when they listen.

1 Lots of money and a blond lady. Yes, they were accurate.
2 someone in Chris's family who was very sick
3 Chris wasn't worried, but Adam wasn't very pleased, as he didn't want Fatos to spoil the evening.
4 her sister
5 He went sightseeing in Istanbul.
6 Carla, Chris's girlfriend, called because Chris wasn't answering his phone.
7 Chris's aunt, who lived with his mother, had died.
8 She wasn't surprised.
9 Adam isn't as skeptical about fortune-telling as he used to be.

1 10

(audioscript in Student Book on *page 120*)

Fatos began to look very carefully at the coffee grounds in Chris's cup and to tell him what she could see. I remember that the first thing she said was that she could see "sacks of money" – and this was very accurate because Chris had worked in Saudi Arabia for several years and had earned a lot of money there. She also said that she could see "a blond lady." Well, Carla, Chris's girlfriend at the time, *was* blond, so that was spot on, too. But then Fatos suddenly looked very serious and she said, "I can see somebody in your family who is sick, very sick, at this moment."

I remember thinking, "Oh, no! Don't ruin a nice evening!" But Chris is a very laid-back kind of person and he didn't seem to be too worried by what she'd said. He just said, "Well, as far as I know the people in my family are OK." Chris is an only child and his mother lived with her sister. They were both in their seventies.

Fatos said one or two more things and then we asked the waiter for the check and said our goodbyes. It was a slightly weird end to what *had* been a very enjoyable evening. I can remember feeling relieved that I had said "no" when Fatos asked me if she could read my coffee cup.

Chris and I got a taxi back to our hotel. The next day Chris had a free morning because it was my turn to do the teacher training session in the hotel, so he went out early to go sightseeing in Istanbul. Around nine o'clock I got a call on my cell phone. It was Chris's girlfriend, Carla, calling. She told me that she needed to talk to Chris immediately, but that he wasn't answering his cell phone. I could tell by her voice that she had some very bad news for him, and I immediately thought of what Fatos had said the night before and I felt a shiver run down my spine.

I asked Carla what had happened and she told me that Chris's aunt had died suddenly in the night. So, was it just a spooky coincidence or did Fatos really see what she said she saw in the coffee cup? I spoke to her before I left Istanbul and I told her that Chris's aunt had died the night that we had dinner. She wasn't at all surprised and she just said, "Yes, I saw in the cup that someone in his family was near death, but I didn't want to frighten him, so I just said that the person was very sick." All I can say is that I always used to be very skeptical about fortune-telling, but now, well, I am not so sure.

e 1 11 Focus on the task and give Sts time to read the five fill-in-the-blank extracts from the audio.

Play the audio, pausing after each extract to give Sts time to write. Play again as necessary.

You could get Sts to compare with a partner before checking answers.

See words in **bold** in audioscript 1.11

1 11

1 Well, Carla, Chris's girlfriend at the time, was blond, so that was **spot on**, too.
2 But Chris is a very **laid-back** kind of person and he didn't seem to be too worried by what she'd said.
3 It was a slightly **weird** end to what *had* been a very enjoyable evening.
4 So, was it just a **spooky coincidence**?
5 I always used to be very **skeptical** about fortune-telling...

Now in pairs or as a class discuss what the words mean.

Check answers.

(to be) **spot on** = (to be) exactly right
laid-back = relaxed / easy-going
weird = strange
spooky coincidence = strange and frightening fact of two things happening at the same time by chance, in a surprising way
skeptical /'skɛptɪkl/ = not convinced that something is true or that something will happen

Extra support

- If there's time, you could play the audio again while Sts read the audioscript on *page 120*, so they can see what they understood / didn't understand. Translate / explain any new words or phrases.

2 SPEAKING

Tell Sts they will now tell each other how they feel about the paranormal and then share any experiences they have had or stories they have heard related to the paranormal.

Focus on the **Reacting to a story about something strange** box and go through it with the class.

Now focus on the task and remind Sts that all three stories are true. Check they realize *spookiest* is the superlative of *spooky*. In the **Have you (or anybody you know)...?** section, make sure Sts understand all the lexis, especially *a UFO* and *faith healer*.

Give Sts a few minutes to think about a story they want to tell.

Put Sts in small groups of four or five and get them first to say how they feel about the paranormal and why, what explanation they can think of for each story, and then to tell their stories. As Sts listen they should try to react to each other's stories.

Monitor and help if necessary while Sts are talking.

Help with any vocabulary questions that come up.

Get some feedback from the class. You could also tell the class how you feel about the paranormal and relate any stories you have heard.

3 GRAMMAR auxiliary verbs

a Focus on the task and give Sts time to fill in the blanks with the correct auxiliary verbs. 1, 2, and 4 should be review, but Sts may not be familiar with the emphatic use of the auxiliary in number 3.

Get them to compare with a partner.

b 1 12 Now play the audio for Sts to listen and check.

Check answers.

1 did 2 do 3 did 4 have 5 have

1 12

1 A I heard a noise in the middle of the night.
B You did? What kind of noise?
2 A You don't believe in ghosts, do you?
B No, I don't.
3 A I don't believe you really saw a UFO.
B I did see one! It couldn't have been anything else.
4 A I've never been to a fortune-teller.
B Neither have I.
C I have. It was really interesting!

Now put Sts in pairs and get them to match auxiliaries 1–5 in **a** with A–E.

Check answers.

A 3 B 5 C 2 D 1 E 4

c 1 13 Tell Sts to go to **Grammar Bank 1B** on *page 133*. Focus on the example sentences and play the audio for Sts to listen to the sentence rhythm. You could also get Sts to repeat the sentences to practice getting the rhythm right. Then go through the rules with the class.

Additional grammar notes

auxiliary verbs

- Auxiliary verbs (*are, is, do, did, will*, etc.) and modal verbs (*can, must*, etc.) have a variety of uses in English and a good command of these will help Sts become more proficient speakers. Sts will be familiar with the basic uses, e.g., in question formation and short answers.

rule 2: to say that someone / something is the same

- Highlight that *neither* can be pronounced /ˈniðər/ or /ˈnaɪðər/.

rule 3: to say that someone / something is different

- Highlight that in these kind of responses you must stress the pronoun as well as the auxiliary, e.g., **A** *I loved the movie.* **B** *Really? I didn't.*

rule 4: reply questions

- Highlight that these have a rising intonation (the voice goes up).

rule 5: using auxiliaries to show emphasis

- This will probably be new for many Sts who may find it strange to see an auxiliary verb used in a positive sentence. This use of auxiliaries is common when we contradict or deny what someone has said or when we want to give extra emphasis, e.g.,
A *Are you a vegetarian?* **B** *No, I do eat meat, but I prefer fish.*
A *You can't swim, can you?* **B** *I can swim, but not very well.*
- Highlight that Sts must stress the auxiliary verb in these sentences.

rule 6: tag questions

- These probably won't be new to most Sts, but they are not easy to use with fluency because they require quick manipulation of auxiliaries. In many languages, this kind of question is covered by the simpler "*…, no?*." You may want to demonstrate the two different types and their intonation to Sts.

Focus on the exercises and get Sts to do them individually or in pairs.

Check answers, getting Sts to read the full sentences. You could get two strong Sts to read the conversation in **b**.

a
1 hasn't 6 Is
2 isn't 7 didn't
3 did 8 is
4 would 9 won't
5 does 10 doesn't

b
2 isn't 7 do
3 don't 8 didn't
4 have 9 did
5 don't 10 am
6 do

Tell Sts to go back to the main lesson **1B**.

Extra support

- If you think Sts need more practice, you may want to give them the Grammar photocopiable activity at this point or leave it for later as consolidation or review.

4 PRONUNCIATION

intonation and sentence rhythm

Pronunciation notes

- **Reply questions:** The auxiliary is stressed and the intonation rises as in an affirmative question, e.g., **A** *I'm a vegetarian.* **B** *Are you?*
The important thing is to encourage Sts to use a friendly, interested intonation.
- To say that someone / something is different, both the subject and the auxiliary are stressed, e.g., **A** *I've never been to a fortune-teller.* **B** *I have.*
- ***So (do) I / Neither (do) I:*** In these responses the auxiliary is usually unstressed with the strong stress falling on the other two words, e.g., **A** *I believe in ghosts.* **B** *So do I.*

- **Tag questions:** Here equal stress falls on both the auxiliary and the subject. The intonation native speakers give to a tag question depends on whether we are asking a real question or not. If we genuinely don't know the answer, we tend to use the rising intonation of a question, e.g., *You haven't seen my car keys, have you?* (= I don't know if you have seen my car keys). However, if we are not asking a real question, but are just making conversation or asking for confirmation of something we already know to be true, our intonation falls and the tag question sounds like a statement, not a question, e.g., *It's a beautiful day, isn't it?* (= I know you will agree with me).
- **Using auxiliaries to show emphasis:** In these sentences the auxiliary is stressed strongly.
- As there are several issues of stress, rhythm, and intonation with auxiliary verbs, the pronunciation practice has been broken into two parts. In **a–d**, Sts practice reply questions and *So / Neither do I.* They then (in **e–g**) practice tag questions and auxiliaries for emphasis.

a **1 14**)) Focus on the task and the two dialogues.

Play the audio once all the way through for Sts to listen.

1 14))
See dialogues in Student Book on *page 9*

b Give Sts a few minutes, in pairs, to practice the dialogues, switching roles when they get to the end. Monitor and help them with their rhythm and intonation.

You could get some pairs to practice in front of the class.

Extra support

- Play the audio again, pausing after each line, and get Sts to listen and repeat, copying the rhythm and intonation.

c Focus on the task and give Sts time to complete the eight sentences about themselves. Make sure Sts understand what *a verb phrase* is in sentence 2.

d Focus on the task, making sure Sts are clear that they should first respond with a reply question and then say if they are the same (*Neither am I.*) or different (*I am.*).

Demonstrate the activity first by completing the first two sentences for yourself and getting Sts to respond. Then put them in pairs, **A** and **B**, and get them to respond to each other.

Extra support

- If you think your Sts are going to find the responses difficult, elicit what the alternatives are for the sentences and write them on the board, e.g.,

AREN'T YOU?	NEITHER AM I. / I AM.
ARE YOU?	SO AM I. / I'M NOT.
DO YOU?	SO DO I. / I DON'T.
DON'T YOU?	NEITHER DO I. / I DO.
HAVEN'T YOU?	NEITHER HAVE I. / I HAVE.
WOULD YOU?	NEITHER WOULD I. / I WOULD.
WERE YOU?	SO WAS I. / I WASN'T.
DIDN'T YOU?	NEITHER DID I. / I DID.

e **1 15**)) Focus on the task. Play the audio once all the way through.

Get Sts to compare with a partner and then check answers.

See underlining in audioscript 1.15

1 15))
A You don't like horror movies, do you?
B I <u>do</u> like them. It's just that sometimes they're too scary!

f Give Sts a few minutes, in pairs, to practice the dialogue in **e**, switching roles when they get to the end. Monitor and help them with their intonation.

Get some pairs to practice in front of the class.

Extra support

- Play the audio again, pausing after each sentence, and get Sts to listen and repeat, copying the rhythm and intonation. Then repeat the activity, eliciting responses from individual Sts. Finally, put Sts in pairs and get them to practice the dialogue.

g Put Sts in pairs, **A** and **B**, preferably face to face. Tell them to go to **Communication *You're psychic, aren't you?***, **A** on *page 105*, **B** on *page 109*.

Focus on the title and the instructions for **a**. Elicit / explain that the word *psychic* is both an adjective and a noun. Elicit / explain its meaning, and then model and drill its pronunciation /ˈsaɪkɪk/.

Go through the instructions and make sure Sts know what they have to do. Elicit that when they check their guesses they should be using rising intonation on the tag questions unless they are 100% sure of the information.

Get feedback to find out who was the best psychic in each pair.

Tell Sts to go back to the main lesson **1B**.

5 1 16)) SONG *Unbelievable* ♫

This song was originally made famous by the British band EMF in 1990. For copyright reasons, this is a cover version. If you want to do this song in class, use the photocopiable activity on *page 229*.

1 16))
Unbelievable

Oh!
What the...?
What the...was that?

You burden me with your questions
You'd have me tell no lies
You're always asking what it's all about
Don't listen to my replies
You say to me I don't talk enough
But when I do I'm a fool
These times I've spent, I've realized
I'm gonna shoot through
And leave you

Chorus
The things you say
Your purple prose just gives you away
The things you say
You're unbelievable

Oh!
What the...?
What the...was that?

You burden me with your problems
By telling me more about mine
I'm always so concerned
With the way you say
You always have to stop
Just think first
Being one is more than I'd ever known
But this time, I realize
I'm gonna shoot through
And leave you

Chorus

Oh!
What the...?
What the...?
What the...?
What the...was that?

Seemingly lastless
Don't mean you can ask us
Pushing down the relative
Bringing out your higher self
Think of the fine times
Pushing down the better few
Instead of bringing out
Just what the world
And everything you're asked to
Brace yourself with the grace of ease
I know this world ain't what it seems

What the...was that?
It's unbelievable.

You burden me with your questions
You'd have me tell no lies.
You're always asking what it's all about,
Don't listen to my replies.
You say to me I don't talk enough,
But when I do I'm a fool.
These times I've spent, I've realized,
I'm gonna shoot through
And leave you.

The things, you say
Your purple prose just gives you away
The things, you say
You're so unbelievable.

Chorus

6 LISTENING & SPEAKING

a Tell Sts to imagine they have just written a formal letter, e.g., applying for a job, and get them to write on a piece of paper *I look forward to hearing from you* and then their normal formal signature underneath.

Now get them to exchange pieces of paper. Tell them to put their partner's piece of paper somewhere safe as they will be using it later in the lesson.

b Focus on the signatures in the book and get Sts to answer the question as a class. Elicit also anything Sts know about any of these people's personalities.

Leo Tolstoy (1828–1910) was a Russian writer.
Barack Obama (1961–) was elected the 44th President of the United States on November 4, 2008.
Paris Hilton (1981–) is an American heiress, socialite, and TV personality.
Usain Bolt (1986–) is a Jamaican sprinter and arguably the fastest man in the world.
Charles Schulz (1922–2000) was an American cartoonist.
Charles Dickens (1812–1870) was an English writer and social critic.
Elijah Wood (1981–) is an American actor.
Tom Hanks (1956–) is an American actor, producer, writer, and director.
Paul McCartney (1942–) is an English musician, singer, and songwriter.
Sean Connery (1930–) is a Scottish actor and producer.

c Focus on the task and elicit / explain the meaning of *graphology*. Model and drill its pronunciation /græ'fɒlədʒi/.

Get Sts to read the book extract (or read it out loud to the class).

Ask the question *Do you believe that our signature might say something about our personality?* to the whole class.

d **1 17**)) **1 18**)) **1 19**)) **1 20**)) Tell Sts they are going to listen to a graphologist talking about how to interpret someone's personality from their signature. They will need to take notes as they listen.

Focus on the **Taking notes** box and go through it with the class.

Now tell Sts they are going to listen to the first part, *What's in your signature?* Make sure Sts know what *an initial* is.

Play audio 1.17 once all the way through for Sts to listen. Then give Sts time to see if they can complete some of the notes.

Then play the audio again, pausing if necessary, for Sts to complete the notes. Play again as necessary.

You could get Sts to compare with a partner before checking answers.

Extra support

- Before playing the audio, go through the audioscript and decide if you need to preteach / check any lexis to help Sts when they listen.

Your last name = your public self
You use only initials either for your first name or your last name = you are more secretive and protective about that part of your personality (i.e., private or public).
There is a space between your name and last name = the bigger the space, the more you want to keep the two parts of your personality separate.

1 17))
(audioscript in Student Book on *page 120*)

What's in your signature?
Our signature is very much part of the way in which we present ourselves to the world, so it can definitely give us some clues about the kind of person we are and how we feel about ourselves.

As you know, a person's signature usually consists of a first name and a last name, or an initial and a last name. Your first name represents your private self – how you are with your family – and your last name represents your public self – the way you are at work or school and in your social life.
If you use only initials either for your first name or your last name in your signature, this means that you are more secretive and protective about either your private or public self.

Now look at the space between your name and last name. Are the two names very close together, or is there a reasonable space between them? The more space there is between your name and your last name, the more you wish to keep these two parts of your personality separate.

Now give Sts time to look at the information under *The size of your signature.*

Play audio 1.18 once all the way through for Sts to listen. Then give Sts time to see if they can complete some of the notes.

Then play it again, pausing if necessary, for Sts to complete the notes. Play again as necessary.

Check answers.

Your first name is bigger than your last name = your private self is more important.
Your last name is bigger than your first name = your public self is more important.
Your whole signature is big = you are probably quite self-confident.
You sign in capital letters = you may be big-headed or even arrogant.
Your signature is small = you may be insecure and have low self-esteem.

1 18
(audioscript in Student Book on *page 120*)
The size of your signature
Now let's look at the size of your signature. If your first name is bigger and more prominent in your signature, this usually means that your "private" self is more important to you than your "public" self. If your last name is bigger and more prominent, this probably means that your "public" self is more important to you.

If your whole signature is very big compared with the rest of your writing, this usually means that you are a self-confident person. Some people actually sign in capital letters, which suggests that they may be big-headed or even arrogant rather than just self-confident. On the other hand, people who sign their name with a very small signature tend to be insecure and have low self-esteem.

Now give Sts time to look at the information under *The legibility of your signature*. Check the meaning of *legibility*, and model and drill its pronunciation /lɛdʒə'bɪləti/.

Play audio 1.19 once all the way through for Sts to listen. Then give Sts time to see if they can complete some of the notes.

Then play it again, pausing if necessary, for Sts to complete the notes. Play again as necessary.

Check answers.

Your signature is legible = you have clear ideas and objectives.
Your signature is illegible = you don't think clearly. You may be disorganized and indecisive. You may also be quite secretive.
The more illegible your signature is the less assertive you are.

1 19
(audioscript in Student Book on *page 120*)
The legibility of your signature
Another important factor is how legible your signature is – in other words, how easy it is to read. A legible signature tends to mean that you're a person with clear ideas and objectives. On the other hand, if your signature is difficult to read, this may imply that you are somebody who doesn't think very clearly and that you may be disorganized or indecisive. It can also mean that you are secretive.

Generally speaking, the more illegible your signature is, the less assertive you probably are as a person.

Finally, give Sts time to look at the information under *The angle of your signature.*

Play audio 1.20 once all the way through for Sts to listen. Then give Sts time to see if they can complete some of the notes.

Then play it again, pausing if necessary, for Sts to complete the notes. Play again as necessary.

Check answers.

A rising signature = you work hard to overcome problems. You are determined, optimistic, and ambitious.
A descending signature = you get depressed when you have problems. You are not very self-confident.
A horizontal signature = you are well-balanced, emotionally stable, and generally satisfied with life.
The angle of a signature may change depending on how you are feeling.

1 20
(audioscript in Student Book on *page 120*)
The angle of your signature
Finally, I want to say something about the angle of your signature, that's to say whether your signature is horizontal, or goes up or goes down on the page.

A rising signature, one that goes up, means that you are the kind of person who, when you're faced with problems, will work hard to overcome them. You're a determined person and probably optimistic and ambitious. A descending signature, that is one that goes down, suggests that you're the kind of person who gets disheartened or depressed when you're faced with problems, maybe because you're not very self-confident. A horizontal signature, one that goes straight across the page, usually indicates a person who is well-balanced and emotionally stable, and someone who is generally satisfied with the way their life is going.

But it's worth bearing in mind that the angle of our signature may change at different times of our lives, depending on how we're feeling.

Extra support

- If there's time, you could play the audio again while Sts read the audioscripts on *page 120*, so they can see what they understood / didn't understand. Translate / explain any new words or phrases.

e In pairs, Sts look at the signatures of the famous people and interpret them according to what they heard on the audio. Do their interpretations match what they previously thought about these famous people?

Get some feedback on each signature.

f Now get Sts to look at the pieces of paper they exchanged at the beginning of the lesson with their partner's signature. Tell them to check their partner's signature against the information they heard.

Now get them to explain to each other what their signatures mean.

Get some feedback to see if Sts agree with the interpretation of their signature.

Extra idea

- Before Sts do **f**, you could sign your name on the board and get Sts to tell you what they can find out about you from it, according to what they heard.

g Do this in pairs, small groups, or as an open-class activity.

Get feedback.

7 MINI GRAMMAR *the...the...* + comparatives

a This regular feature focuses on extra, smaller grammar points that come out of a reading or listening. Go through the examples and then the rules.

Highlight that:

– you shouldn't separate *the more*, etc. from the adjective / adverb it goes with, e.g., *The more interesting the book is, the more slowly I read.* NOT ~~*The more the book is interesting...*~~

– occasionally we just use the two comparatives, especially when one of them is *better*, e.g., *the sooner the better* or *the bigger the better*.

Elicit sentence 1 from the whole class (The more you study, the more you learn.) and write the answer on the board.

Get Sts to do the other three.

Check answers.

1 The more you study, the more you learn.
2 The sooner we leave, the earlier we'll get there.
3 The more time you have, the more slowly you do things.
4 The more in shape you are, the better you feel.

b Focus on the task and give Sts time to complete each sentence.

Monitor and help Sts, correcting any errors with the comparatives.

Get Sts to compare with a partner and then elicit some ideas.

Extra idea

- Ask Sts if there are any common expressions in their language with this structure (like *the sooner the better*) and get them to figure out how to say them in English.

Extra support

- If you think Sts need more practice, you may want to give them the Mini Grammar photocopiable activity now or leave it for later as consolidation or review.

8 VOCABULARY compound adjectives

a Tell Sts to look at the three extracts from the listening on graphology. Give them time to figure out what the missing words might be.

Extra challenge

- Elicit some ideas before playing the audio.

b 1.21 Play the audio for Sts to listen and check.

Check answers.

See words in **bold** in audioscript 1.21

1.21

1 Some people actually sign in capital letters, which suggests that they may be big-**headed** or even arrogant.
2 A descending signature suggests that you are the kind of person who gets disheartened or depressed when you are faced with problems, maybe because you are not very self-**confident**.
3 A horizontal signature usually indicates a person who is well-**balanced** and emotionally stable.

Now elicit whether the three compound adjectives in **a** have a positive or negative meaning.

big-headed is negative, but *self-confident* and *well-balanced* are positive characteristics.

Finally, focus on the **Compound adjectives** box and go through it with the class.

c Put Sts in pairs and get them to look at each compound adjective and then decide what it means and whether it describes a positive or negative characteristic.

Check answers.

Positive: good-tempered, open-minded, easygoing, laid-back
Negative: bad-tempered, narrow-minded, absentminded, tight-fisted, two-faced, strong-willed, self-centered

You may want to point out to Sts that *open-minded* and *narrow-minded* are opposites. *Laid-back* and *easygoing* are very similar in meaning: *laid-back* (informal) = calm and relaxed about everything; *easygoing* = relaxed and happy to accept things without worrying or getting angry.

Extra challenge

- Elicit a sentence to describe each of the adjectives, e.g., *A person who is bad-tempered always...*, etc.

d 1.22 Play the audio for Sts to listen and repeat.

1.22
See compound adjectives in Student Book on *page 11*

Now repeat the activity, eliciting responses from individual Sts.

e Focus on the **Modifiers** box and go through it with the class.

Highlight that *pretty* is more informal than *very*, and that *rather* is only used with negative adjectives, e.g., *rather self-centered*.

f Focus on the task and example, showing that Sts need to explain why they have chosen a particular character for someone they know.

Then give Sts a few minutes to think of people with the characteristics listed in ***Do you know somebody who is...?***

Put Sts in pairs and get them to tell each other about the people they have chosen.

Monitor and help if necessary.

Get some feedback from a few pairs.

Extra support

- You could choose one or two characteristics and tell the class about two people you know.

1 Talking about...interviews

Lesson plan

This is the first in a series of five Colloquial English lessons where Sts practice listening to completely unscripted authentic spoken English. Each of these lessons picks up on one of the topics of the preceding File, and consists of a filmed interview with a person who has some expertise related to the topic, and then some short street interviews where members of the public give their opinions on an aspect of the same topic. These lessons give Sts the opportunity to practice listening to the kind of English they will hear if they go to an English-speaking country. The level of challenge in these listening exercises is higher than in the listening exercises in the A–B lessons, something which should be pointed out to Sts. Encourage them to feel pleased with themselves if they can get the "gist" of these interviews, rather than a detailed understanding.
We suggest that after doing the task, teachers let Sts listen while reading the audioscripts. This will let them see what they did or didn't understand, and help to develop their awareness of features of spoken English, e.g., running words together, leaving out pronouns, etc. After listening to the interview, Sts focus on a feature of spoken English which was used by the interviewee (in this lesson, formal words and expressions). After the street interviews, the focus is on colloquial expressions used by the speakers.

In the first part of this lesson, the person interviewed is Jeff Neil, a career coach and the founder of a company called New Career Breakthrough in New York City.

In the second part, people are asked about their experience of job interviews – when did they last have one, how did they prepare, and whether or not they got the job.

The lesson ends with a speaking activity based on the topic of the lesson.

These lessons can be used with *Class DVD*, *iTools*, or *Class Audio* (audio only).

STUDY LINK
- **Workbook** Talking about...interviews
- **Online Practice**
- **iChecker**

Testing Program CD-ROM
- **File 1 Quick Test**
- **File 1 Test**

Optional lead-in (books closed)

- Ask Sts to brainstorm their top three tips for a friend who has a job interview the next day.
- Elicit ideas and write them on the board.

1 VIDEO THE INTERVIEW Part 1

a Books open. Focus on the photo and the biographical information about Jeff Neil. Either read it out loud or give Sts time to read it. Do the question as an open-class activity and elicit / explain that the HR department in a company helps with employing and training people.

b **1 23**))) Focus on the task and give Sts time to read the sentences.

Play the DVD or audio (**Part 1**) once all the way through for Sts to check the things Jeff said.

You could get Sts to compare what they have checked with a partner. Then play again as necessary.

Check answers.

Sts should have checked: 1, 4, and 6

1 23)))
(audioscript in Student Book on *pages 120–121*)
I = interviewer, J = Jeff Neil

Part 1

J My name is Jeff Neil. I'm a career coach, and I help people discover the right career for them and actually go get that job.
I How important is the résumé when you're applying for a job?
J The résumé is really important because it represents you. It's often the first presentation of your skills and abilities to an employer before they actually have a chance to talk with you.
I What are some mistakes that people make with their résumés?
J So some of the biggest mistakes that, that I've seen that people make on their resume is they include everything. Right, as an employer, I don't care what you did 20 years ago or 30 years ago. You may have been a star at something that you did 25 years ago, but as an employer I'm thinking, this has no relevancies to me. You've changed over 25 years. The world has changed over 25 years. So people include far too much information on their resumes. My recommendation is that they only go back about 15 years.
I Are there any other mistakes?
J Another completely, another completely unforgivable mistake is grammatical errors, bad punctuation, and spelling errors. When I see a résumé that has, you know, more than one error, it's done. Right? We live in a world where résumé are expected to be perfect. So word processing has spell check on it. There's just no reason to have something misspelled.
I How important is a candidate's social media presence?
J Yeah, in today's world, almost all hiring managers and HR staff will look for you online before they interview you. So your online profile can actually either help you get an interview, or it can stop you from getting an interview. So for your social media, you want to be really careful, particularly when you're looking for a job. You want to be really careful about what pictures you're showing and what conversations you're posting, um, is public information. You also want to do a Google search on your own name.
I Assuming a candidate gets an interview, how do you help them to prepare for it?

J So the way I help candidates prepare for interviews is I, I have them take the job advertisement. Right, they can get the job advertisement if it's posted online, or a job description from the HR office. And to go through it and simply circle what are the skills and abilities that are required to do that kind of job? And to take an 8 and a half sheet of paper and make 3 columns, and in the first column, list the key skills and abilities that are required to do that position. And then in the second column, list where they've used those skills and abilities in different roles in their career. And then in the third column, to actually create stories that demonstrate how they've used those skills in those different companies.

c Now listen again and go through the **Glossary** with the class.

Focus on the three boxes that the Sts checked. Give Sts time to take notes on Jeff's advice in those areas.

Play the DVD or audio again all the way through.

You could get Sts to compare notes with a partner.

Extra support

- You could pause the DVD or audio after each interview question has been answered and, in pairs, get Sts to compare orally what they have understood.

VIDEO Part 2

a 1 24 Focus on the task and play the DVD or audio (**Part 2**) once all the way through for Sts to decide if the tips are true or false. Have Sts correct the false ones.

Extra support

- Give Sts time in pairs to discuss the tips and to correct the ones they've marked false.

Check the answers.

1 T
2 T
3 F You should arrive at least 5 minutes early.
4 F Make sure your phone and electronic devices are turned off.
5 T

1 24
(audioscript in Student Book on *page 121*)

Part 2

I What tips can you give a candidate for the day itself? For example, how should people dress for an interview?

J It's important to dress appropriately for an interview, because if you're underdressed for an interview it shows a lack of respect. Right? Companies, an employer's going to look at that and say, this isn't, this person's not taking this interview seriously. So I encourage my clients to actually overdress a little bit for an interview. Now, how can you determine the best way to dress for an interview? You might actually get on a company's LinkedIn page and look at their LinkedIn photos, because that'll give you a sense of that company's style. Are they all dressed in suits and they're really formal? Are they more relaxed? Another way, uh, outside of a big city is that you can often stake out the front door, you know, a couple days ahead of time and see how employees are actually going into that office. How are they dressed?

I Obviously you shouldn't be late, but how early should you get there?

J So you want to show up at an interview about 5 minutes early. If you get there earlier than that, just grab a cup of coffee in a nearby, uh, restaurant or shop. And then when you walk into the interview you don't want to have your headphones on. You want to make sure your cell phone is turned off. You don't want to have any interruptions.

I Do you have any other tips before the interview starts?

J As soon as you walk into the building for a job interview, you've already begun the interview. The way that you greet people, the way that you greet the receptionist at the front desk, and security if there is security, all those people are part of the interview process. Because if you don't handle it in the right way, they may tell the person that you're interviewing with how you approached them. And your chances of getting the job can actually be eliminated. So it's important that you treat everyone that you meet in the building as part of the interview process.

b Go through the **Glossary** with the class. Now lead a class discussion and elicit whether Sts think the tips are good advice.

Play the DVD or audio again all the way through. Play again as necessary.

Extra support

- You could pause the DVD or audio at appropriate places and, in pairs, get Sts to compare orally what they have understood.

VIDEO Part 3

a 1 25 Focus on the task and play the DVD or audio (**Part 3**) once all the way through for Sts to fill in the blanks.

Check answers.

1 money / salary
2 Body / tone
3 personality

1 25
(audioscript in Student Book on *page 121*)

Part 3

I Is it OK for a candidate to talk about money or salary during an interview?

J It is OK for a candidate to talk about money and salary during an interview. But the real question is *when* should they talk about money and salary. And the answer is *late*. One of the biggest mistakes that job candidates make is they focus too much on their own needs. Right? So work life balance is important. The number of hours I'm going to work, the amount of vacation I'm going to get, the pay, and the benefits, they're all very important. But we have to understand that the employer is giving us money. What's most important is I want to communicate that I can deliver enough value for this position that you offer me the job. Once an employer believes that I'm the right candidate, and then they offer me a position – that's the right time to start talking about money and benefits. However, I wouldn't raise the topic. I would let the employer raise it first.

I Do you have any other tips for candidates during the interview?

J Body image and body language is really, really important in an interview. I can remember interviewing someone – they were slouched back and they were down and their energy was really, really low and it just communicated to me, this person doesn't really want this job. They didn't feel motivated. And I can remember talking with candidates where they're leaning forward and their, their voice is stronger. They're making a lot of eye contact directly with me.

I can tell that they're really listening to what I'm saying. They're hearing what I'm saying, and that they want to learn about this job to help me understand their value. So body language and eye contact are really, really important. The tone of voice is also really, really important, because when we're unsure or less confident we tend to, you know, not only slouch, but our voice goes down. And that's not communicating the confidence that you, that you're confident in your skills and abilities.

I And just to finish, did you ever ask extreme questions during interviews when you worked in HR?

J As a director of HR, sometimes I would ask extreme questions, such as, if you could be any kind of tree in the world, what kind of tree would you want to be? Because I want to see what it reveals about someone's personality.

I What would a good answer be?

J So one good answer could be, I'd like to be an oak tree, because it's strong and it's steady. Another good answer could be, I'd like to be an apple tree, because it's beautiful when it's blooming and it gives fruit to people that they would enjoy. Another answer could be, I'd like to be a cactus, because cactuses don't need a lot of support and they're very, very persistent. They can survive.

Extra idea

- In pairs or as a class, ask Sts to say how they would answer the two questions. You could also tell Sts your own answers. Ask Sts to raise their hands if they think the "extreme question" is helpful to find the right candidate for the job.

b Focus on the task and give Sts time to read the sentences and answer questions 1–6.

Play the DVD or audio again all the way through for Sts to do the task. Play again as necessary.

Check answers.

Extra support

- You could pause the DVD or audio at the relevant places and, in pairs, get Sts to compare what they have understood before answering the questions.

1 One of the biggest mistakes is for candidates to focus too much on their own needs.
2 The most important thing is to communicate that you can deliver value to the employer for the job they are offering.
3 They are communicating they didn't want the job; they weren't motivated.
4 The strength and tone of voice can communicate confidence in your skills and abilities.
5 If you could be a tree, what would it be?
6 Jeff suggests an oak tree because it is strong and steady, an apple tree because it's beautiful and provides fruit, and a cactus because it doesn't need a lot of support and it is persistent.

Extra support

- If there's time, you could play the DVD or audio again while Sts read the audioscripts on *pages 120–121*, so they can see what they understood / didn't understand. Translate / explain any new words or phrases.

2 LOOKING AT LANGUAGE

a 1 26 This exercise focuses on common expressions with the verbs *make* and *do*, which are often difficult for Sts if their L1 uses one verb.

Focus on the **Make or do** box and go through it with the class.

Now focus on the task and give Sts time to read extracts 1–6.

Play the DVD or audio, pausing after each extract to give Sts time to fill in the blanks. Play again as necessary.

Check answers.

1 make
2 did
3 do
4 make
5 make
6 making

Extra challenge

- Ask Sts if they can remember any of the highlighted words or phrases before they listen to the extracts.

b Focus on sentences 1–7 and have Sts complete the task individually. Have Sts compare answers with a partner before checking answers as a class.

2 make
3 do
4 do
5 made
6 doing
7 make

1 26

1 ...some of the biggest mistakes that, that I've seen that people make on their résumé is they include everything.
2 ...as an employer, I don't care what you did 20 years ago or 30 years ago.
3 You also want to do a Google search on your own name.
4 ... and to take an 8 and a half sheet of paper and make 3 columns...
5 You want to make sure your cell phone is turned off.
6 They're making a lot of eye contact directly with me.

3 VIDEO ON THE STREET

a 1 27 Focus on the photos of the people and the question.

Play the DVD or audio once all the way through for Sts to do the task.

Check answers.

Three people got the job (Jo, Ivan, and Yasuko).

1 27

(audioscript in Student Book on *page 121*)
I = interviewer, Je = Jeanine, Jo = Jo, Iv = Ivan, Y = Yasuko, Jst = Joost

Jeanine
I When did you last have an interview for a job?
Je The last time I had an interview for a job was in 2011.
I How did you prepare for the interview?
Je I took a lot of Rescue Remedy to help the nerves and I, I just practiced every question that they could ask me in my head.
I Did the interview go well?
Je No, it didn't. I didn't get the job.

Jo
I When did you last have an interview for a job?
Jo Uh, about two months ago.
I How did you prepare for the interview?
Jo Well, I looked at the job description and thought about my experience, um, and then tried to match my experience to the various different points on the job interview.
I Did the interview go well?
Jo It did.
I How do you know it went well?
Jo Because they offered me the job.

Ivan
I When did you last have an interview for a job?
Iv I last had an interview for a job a few weeks ago, um, that's the last time I had an interview for a job.
I How did you prepare for the interview?
Iv To prepare for the job interview I read about the company and learned about what they did and to see if I liked the work that they did.
I How do you know it went well?
Iv I think it went well because they followed up with an email, um, to talk about, um, further opportunities at that company.

Yasuko
I When did you last have an interview for a job?
Y Um, the last interview that I had was for my current company that I work for and that was about two years ago.
I How did you prepare for the interview?
Y I prepared for the interview by, um, res... doing a little research on the company, the kind of products that they make, um, the, their philosophy, the history and the background of the company.
I Did the interview go well?
Y I think that the interview went well because it was actually a long interview. I had a lot of good conversation with the managers there, and I also got a few more interviews afterwards, and eventually got the job, so the, the interviews went well.

Joost
I When did you last have an interview for a job?
Jst About three months ago.
I How did you prepare for the interview?
Jst I read about the company and I knew what the job contents was, and I knew everything that I had to know for the interview. I was well-prepared to answer their questions.
I Did the interview go well?
Jst It went well. In the end they said I was too young, so they didn't hire me, but, yeah, they would have if I was older, they said.

b Focus on the task and give Sts time to read the questions.

Play the DVD or audio once all the way through, pausing after each speaker to give Sts time to do the task. Play again as necessary.

Check answers.

Joost didn't get the job because of his age.
Ivan had his interview the most recently.
Jo prepared for the interview by assessing how suitable she was for the job.
Jeanine took some medicine to help make her feel less nervous.
Yasuko tried to find out what the company believed in.

c 1 28 This exercises focuses on some colloquial expressions which were used by the speakers. Focus on the phrases and give Sts time to read them.

Play the DVD or audio, pausing after the first phrase and playing it again as necessary. Elicit the missing word and then the meaning of the whole phrase. Repeat for the other four phrases.

See words in **bold** in audioscript 1.28

1 28

1 I just practiced every question that they could ask me in my **head**.
2 ...and then tried to **match** my experience to the various different points on the job interview...
3 I think it went well because they **followed** up with an email.
4 ...their philosophy, the history, and the **background** of the company.
5 In the end they said I was too young, so they didn't **hire** me.

Extra support

- Tell Sts to go to *page 121* and to look at the audioscript for **ON THE STREET**. Play the DVD or audio again and tell Sts to read and listen at the same time.

Help with any vocabulary questions and get feedback from Sts on what parts they found hard to understand and why, e.g., speed of speech, pronunciation, etc.

4 SPEAKING

Put Sts in pairs and get them to ask and answer the questions, giving as much information as possible.

Monitor and help with vocabulary. Help with any general language problems at the end of the activity.

Get some feedback.

G present perfect simple and continuous
V illnesses and injuries
P /ʃ/, /dʒ/, /tʃ/, and /k/; word stress

2A Call the doctor?

Lesson plan

In this lesson, Sts review and extend their knowledge of the present perfect simple and continuous. These verb forms can be problematic for many Sts because of L1 interference. The lesson topic is illness and injury.

The first half of the lesson starts with a quiz on first aid – the Sts' own knowledge is tested and discussed. Sts then expand their vocabulary of medical words to describe symptoms, illnesses, and treatment. The pronunciation focus is on consonant and vowel sounds, and word stress. This is followed by a grammar focus on the present simple and continuous, which is then further practiced in the **Writing Bank** where Sts write an informal email explaining to a friend why they haven't been well and saying what they have been doing recently.

In the second half of the lesson, Sts read an article from *The Sunday Times* on cyberchondriacs, and focus on topic sentences and medical vocabulary. Then they listen to a radio interview with a doctor talking about cyberchondria, and finally, Sts give their own opinion on the topic. The lesson finishes with the song, *Just Like a Pill*.

STUDY LINK
- **Workbook** 2A
- **Online Practice**
- **iChecker**

Extra photocopiable activities

- **Grammar** present perfect simple and continuous *page 153*
- **Communicative** Doctor, doctor *page 190* (instructions *page 180*)
- **Vocabulary** Illnesses and injuries *page 213* (instructions *page 210*)
- **Song** *Just Like a Pill* *page 230* (instructions *page 226*)

Optional lead-in – the quote

- Write the quote at the top of *page 14* on the board (books closed) and the name of the person who said it, or get Sts to open their books and read it.
- You could tell Sts that Walter Matthau was born in 1920 and died in 2000. He is best known for his role in *The Odd Couple*, which also starred Jack Lemmon.
- Ask Sts what they think of the quote and what it refers to (the healthcare system in the US).

1 VOCABULARY illnesses and injuries

a Focus on the quiz *Help save lives!* and elicit what *first aid* is. Put Sts in pairs and give them time to read all six questions in the quiz and to decide what the highlighted words mean.

Check answers by explaining / translating / miming, or using the illustrations.

choke (v) = to be unable to breathe because the passage to your lungs is blocked
lean (v) = to bend or move from a vertical position
burn (n) = an injury or a mark caused by fire, heat, or acid
bleed (v) = to lose blood, especially from a wound or an injury
press (v) = to push something closely and firmly against something
wound /wund/ (n) = a general word for an injury on the body, especially when there is a cut or hole
treat (v) = to give medical care or attention to a person, an illness, an injury, etc.
pinch (v) = to hold something tightly between the thumb and finger
collapse (v) = to fall down (and usually become unconscious), especially because you are very ill / sick
bandage (n) = a strip of cloth used for tying around a part of the body that has been hurt in order to protect or support it

b Tell Sts to look at all six questions again with their partner and to choose the best answer, a, b, or c. You might want to preteach / check some lexis, e.g., *prevent*, etc.

Then get feedback to see which answers Sts chose, but don't tell them yet if they are right or wrong.

c Put Sts in pairs, **A** and **B**, and tell them to go to **Communication** ***First aid quiz***, **A** on *page 105*, **B** on *page 109* to each check the answers to half the quiz.

When they have finished reading, ask them to close their books or to cover the answers and look at the illustrations, and tell their partner what the correct answer is for each one.

Get feedback to see how many Sts got the right answers.

Extra support

- You could write any new and useful words and phrases from the quiz and **Communication** on the board for Sts to copy.

Tell Sts to go back to the main lesson **2A**.

d Tell Sts to go to **Vocabulary Bank** ***Illnesses and injuries*** on *page 152*.

Focus on **1 Minor illnesses and conditions** and check that Sts know the meaning of *minor*. Get Sts to do **a** individually or in pairs.

1 29 Now do **b**. Play the audio for Sts to check answers. Play the audio again, pausing for Sts to repeat. Practice any words your Sts find difficult to pronounce.

1 29

Illnesses and injuries

Minor illnesses and conditions

a

9 a cough
6 a headache
1 a rash
4 a temperature
2 sunburn
8 She's sick. / She's vomiting.
10 She's sneezing.
3 Her ankle is swollen.
7 Her back hurts. / Her back aches.
5 Her finger is bleeding.

You might also want to point out that *cough* is both a noun and a verb.

Highlight that *ache*, *hurt*, and *pain* can all be used to describe the same thing, e.g., *I have a pain in my back. / My back hurts. / My back aches.* There is a slight difference between *ache* and *hurt*: *ache* = a continuous, dull pain; *hurts* = often stronger (especially sudden) pain, e.g., *Ouch! That hurts! Ache* is used both as a noun and a verb, whereas *hurt* is usually used as a verb, and *pain* is usually used as a noun.

Now get Sts to do **c** individually or in pairs.

1 30 Now do **d**. Play the audio for Sts to check answers. Practice any words your Sts find difficult to pronounce.

1 30

Minor illnesses and conditions

c

1 **B** He has a sore throat. It hurts when he talks or swallows food.
2 **D** He has diarrhea. He's been to the bathroom five times this morning.
3 **E** He feels sick. He feels like he's going to vomit.
4 **C** He's fainted. It's so hot in the room that he's lost consciousness.
5 **H** He has a blister on his foot. He's been walking in uncomfortable shoes.
6 **F** He has a cold. He's sneezing a lot and he has a cough.
7 **A** He has the flu. He has a temperature and he aches all over.
8 **G** He feels dizzy. He feels that everything is spinning around.
9 **I** He's cut himself. He's bleeding.

Some of the words may be similar in Sts' L1, e.g., *diarrhea*, but the pronunciation is likely to be different.

Highlight that *be sick* = *vomit*, but *feel sick* = want to vomit. *Ill* is also sometimes used as a synonym for *sick*, especially in British English. Also highlight the meaning of *swallow*.

Focus on **2 Injuries and more serious conditions** and get Sts to do **a** individually or in pairs.

1 31 Now do **b**. Play the audio for Sts to check answers. Play the audio again, pausing for Sts to repeat. Practice any words your Sts find difficult to pronounce.

1 31

Injuries and more serious conditions

1 **C** He's unconscious. He's breathing, but his eyes are closed and he can't hear or feel anything.
2 **G** He's had an allergic reaction. He was stung by a wasp and now he has a rash and has difficulty breathing.
3 **B** He's twisted his ankle. / He's sprained his ankle. He fell badly and now it's swollen.
4 **D** He has high blood pressure. It's 180 over 140.
5 **E** He has food poisoning. He ate some chicken that wasn't fully cooked.
6 **F** He's choking. He was eating a steak and a piece got stuck in his throat.
7 **A** He's burned himself. He spilled some boiling water on himself.

Focus on the **Common treatments for...** box and go through it with the class. You could model and drill the pronunciation of *sprained*, *allergic*, and *antihistamine* /æntɪˈhɪstəmin/.

Now focus on **3 Phrasal verbs connected with illness** and get Sts to do **a** individually or in pairs.

1 32 Now do **b**. Play the audio for Sts to check answers. Make sure Sts know the meaning of the new words / phrases and practice any words your Sts find difficult to pronounce.

1 32

Phrasal verbs connected with illness

1 *pass out* means faint
2 *lie down* means put your body in a horizontal position
3 *throw up* means vomit, be sick
4 *get over* means get better, recover from something
5 *come around* means become conscious again

Now focus on the title of the **Vocabulary Bank** and explain / elicit the difference between *illness* and *disease*:

illness (n) = the general term for the state of being unwell, e.g., *My uncle has a serious illness.*

disease (n) = is used for infectious illnesses, e.g., malaria, and for illnesses affecting the organs, e.g., *She has heart disease*, and illnesses which have a person's name, e.g., *Parkinson's disease.*

Also ask Sts if they can remember a word that is similar in meaning to *an injury* and elicit *a wound*, which they saw in the quiz (*a wound* = an injury, usually where there is a hole in the skin, e.g., *a bullet wound. Put the bandage over the wound*).

Testing yourself

For **Minor illnesses and conditions** exercise **a**, Sts can cover the words / sentences and look at the pictures, and for **c** they can cover sentences 1–9, look at A–I, and try to remember 1–9. In **Injuries and more serious conditions**, they can do the same with A–G, and in **Phrasal verbs connected with illness**, they can cover 1–5 and try to remember the meaning of the phrasal verbs.

Testing a partner

Alternatively, Sts can take turns testing each other. **B** closes the book and **A** defines or explains a word for **B** to try and remember, e.g., *What's does the phrasal verb "to pass out" mean?* After a few minutes, Sts can switch roles.

In a monolingual class, Sts could also test each other by saying the word in their L1 for their partner to say in English.

Tell Sts to go back to the main lesson **2A**.

Extra support

- If you think Sts need more practice, you may want to give them the Vocabulary photocopiable activity at this point or leave it for later as consolidation or review.

2 PRONUNCIATION & SPEAKING

/ʃ/, /dʒ/, /tʃ/, and /k/; word stress

Pronunciation notes

English sounds

- Sts who have used previous levels of *American English File* should recognize the sound pictures and be fairly confident with phonetic symbols. If your Sts are new to the series, you will need to explain to them that the sound pictures show the phonetic symbols and give a clear example of a word with the target sound to help them remember the pronunciation of the symbol. There is one for each of the 45 sounds of American English. Sts will see the chart and more example words when they go to the **Sound Bank** in **c**.

Word stress

- Remind Sts that if they aren't sure where the main stress is in a word, to first try it out with the stress in different places and see which "sounds best," and if they are still unsure, to check with a dictionary.

a Focus on the four sound pictures and elicit the words and consonant sounds (*shower* /ʃ/; *jazz* /dʒ/; *chess* /tʃ/; *key* /k/).

Then give Sts time to put the words in the correct columns. You might want to remind them that this kind of exercise is easier if they say the words out loud to themselves.

Get Sts to compare with a partner.

b 1 33)) Play the audio for Sts to listen and check.

Check answers.

1 33))

shower /ʃ/	pressure, rash, unconscious
jazz /dʒ/	allergy, bandage
chess /tʃ/	choking, temperature
key /k/	ache, ankle, stomach

Now play it again, pausing after each group of words for Sts to listen and repeat.

Then repeat the activity, eliciting responses from individual Sts.

Finally, get Sts, in pairs, to practice saying the words.

c Now tell Sts to go to the **Sound Bank** on *page 167*. Explain that here and on *page 166* they can find all the sounds of American English and their phonetic symbols and also the typical spellings for these sounds plus some more irregular ones.

Focus on the four sounds that Sts have just been working on and the typical spellings. Highlight that they have to be careful with *ch* because although it is usually pronounced /tʃ/, it can also be /k/ as in *ache* or occasionally /ʃ/ as in *machine*.

d Focus on the task and give Sts a few moments to look at all the words. Get them to focus on the phonetics to see if the words are pronounced the same in English as in their L1.

e 1 34)) Play the audio for Sts to listen to how all the words are pronounced. You could also pause the audio before each word and get Sts to tell you how they think the word is pronounced, and then play the word. Check Sts know what all the words mean.

1 34))

antibiotics	operation	X-ray
symptom	aspirin	cholesterol
medicine	specialist	injection
emergency	acetaminophen	CAT scan

Elicit / point out that *antibiotics* is usually in the plural, *medicine* is usually uncountable, *a specialist* is a doctor who is an expert in a particular area, and the word *painkiller*, which they saw in the **Vocabulary Bank**, is a generic word for aspirin and acetaminophen, etc.

Play the audio again and this time get Sts to underline the stressed syllable.

Check answers by writing the words on the board and underlining the stressed syllable.

See underlining in audioscript 1.34

Finally, play the audio again, pausing after each word for Sts to repeat.

f Focus on the questions and make sure Sts understand all the lexis.

Put Sts in pairs and get them to ask and answer the questions, giving as much information as possible.

Get some feedback and help with any general vocabulary questions that come up.

3 GRAMMAR

present perfect simple and continuous

a 1 35)) Focus on the task. Either tell Sts to close their books and write the questions on the board, or get them to focus on the two questions and cover the rest of the page.

Play the audio once all the way through.

Check answers.

His symptoms are headaches, a cough, and a temperature.

The doctor suggests he should wait a few days to see how his symptoms develop.

1 35))

D = doctor, P = patient

D Good morning, Mr. Blaine. What's the problem?
P I haven't been feeling well for a few days. I keep getting headaches, and I've been coughing a lot, too. And I have a temperature.
D Have you been taking anything for the headaches?
P Yes, acetaminophen. But it doesn't really help. I read on the Internet that headaches can be the first symptom of a brain tumor.
D How many tablets have you taken so far today?
P I took two this morning.
D And have you taken your temperature this morning?
P Yes. I've taken it five or six times. It's high.
D Let me see... Well, your temperature seems to be perfectly normal now.
P I think I need a blood test. I haven't had one for two months.
D Well, Mr. Blaine, you know I think we should wait for a few days and see how your symptoms...develop. Can you send the next patient in please, nurse?

b Focus on the task and then play the audio again for Sts to listen and fill in the blanks. Play again if necessary.

Extra challenge

- Give Sts a few minutes to look at the blanks in the conversation and to guess what the missing verbs might be.

Get Sts to compare with a partner and then check answers.

1 haven't been feeling	4 have you taken
2 've been coughing	5 've taken
3 Have you been taking	6 haven't had

c 1 36 Focus on the task and then play the audio.

Check the answer.

They think he is a hypochondriac.

1 36

D = doctor, N = nurse

N Your next patient is Mrs. Williams. Here are her notes.
D How many times has Mr. Blaine been to the health center this week?
N Um, four times, I think... Yes, I know, he's a complete...

d Focus on the task and give Sts time to circle or check the verb forms in 1 and 2.

Get Sts to compare with a partner and then check answers.

1 ✓ 2 taken

e 1 37 1 38 1 39 Tell Sts to go to **Grammar Bank 2A** on *page 134*. Focus on the example sentences and play the audio for Sts to listen to the sentence rhythm. You could also get Sts to repeat the sentences to practice getting the rhythm right. Then go through the rules with the class.

Additional grammar notes

present perfect simple and continuous

- Sts at this level should already have a reasonable grasp of the uses referenced here for the two tenses.
- Highlight that the present perfect continuous emphasizes both the continuity and / or temporary nature of an action, e.g., *I've been waiting for you for two hours!* (= more common than *I've waited...*).

for* and *since

- Sts should be very familiar with how these words are used (*for* = period of time, *since* = point of time), but you may want to highlight that *for* is omitted with *all day* / *morning* / *night*, etc., e.g., *I've been working all morning* NOT ... ~~*for all morning*~~.

Focus on the exercises and get Sts to do them individually or in pairs.

Check answers, getting Sts to read the full sentences.

a

1 ✓	5 met
2 called	6 been raining
3 been running	7 already had
4 seen	8 ✓

b
1 've known
2 Have you been working out...?
3 hasn't done
4 've moved
5 haven't had
6 've been walking
7 Have...been reading
8 've cut

Tell Sts to go back to the main lesson **2A**.

Extra support

- If you think Sts need more practice, you may want to give them the Grammar photocopiable activity at this point or leave it for later as consolidation or review.

f This is an oral grammar practice activity. Focus on the task and questions. Point out that in question 6 they should choose between *school* or *work* as appropriate.

Check that Sts know what verb forms to use, and encourage them not to write down the questions, but just use the prompts.

Extra support

- Give Sts time to think what the questions are. Then demonstrate the activity by eliciting the questions from Sts and answering them yourself. If necessary, you could write the questions on the board.

1 Do you often get colds? How many colds have you had in the last three months?
2 Are you taking any vitamins or supplements right now? How long have you been taking them?
3 Do you drink much water? How many glasses have you drunk today?
4 Do you play any sports? What (do you play)? How long have you been playing them (playing tennis, going to a gym, etc.)?
5 Do you eat a lot of fruit and vegetables? How many servings have you had today?
6 Do you walk to school (or work)? How far have you walked today?
7 How many hours do you sleep a night? Have you been sleeping well recently?
8 Are you allergic to anything? Have you ever had a serious allergic reaction?

Give Sts time to ask and answer the questions in pairs. Monitor and correct any mistakes with the present perfect.

Get some feedback.

4 WRITING an informal email

This is the first time Sts are sent to the **Writing Bank** at the back of the Student Book. In this section, Sts will find model texts with exercises and language notes, and then a writing task. We suggest that you go through the model and do the exercise(s) in class, but assign the actual writing (the last activity) for homework.

Tell Sts to go to **Writing *An informal email*** on *page 113*.

a Focus on the task. Put Sts in pairs and tell them to look at each mistake highlighted in Anna's email. First, they need to decide what kind of mistake it is, and then they must correct it.

Check answers.

1 haven't (punctuation)
2 temperature (spelling)
3 ~~since~~ for (grammar)
4 Luckily (spelling)
5 Anything exciting? (punctuation)
6 ~~are~~ is (grammar)
7 software company (punctuation)
8 they're (grammar / spelling)
9 May (punctuation)
10 recommend (spelling)
11 sightseeing (spelling)
12 you'll be able to show (grammar)

b Focus on the **Beginning an informal email** box and go through it with the class.

Then focus on the task. Tell Sts to read Anna's email again and to find the three sentences.

Check answers.

I haven't written or called. = I haven't been in touch.

I've been reading and replying to my emails. = I've been catching up on my emails.

Have you being doing anything exciting? = What have you been doing? Anything exciting?

c Tell Sts they are going to write an informal email to Anna to answer her questions. First, they need to complete some expressions in the **Useful language: an informal email** box. Get Sts to do this individually or in pairs.

If Sts worked alone, get them to compare with a partner.

Check answers.

1 for	6 hear	11 Give
2 to	7 luck	12 care
3 not	8 feel / are / get	13 Best
4 hope	9 for	14 PS
5 to	10 forward	

d Go over the plan with the class.

Extra support

- Go over the plan, focusing on each point at a time. Give Sts time to read Anna's email again and check the answers.

1 How are you? What have you been doing? Anything exciting? How is your family? Could you recommend a hotel? Do you think you'll be able to show me around?
2 brother's new job, the conference
3 Sts' own answers

e Tell Sts to answer Anna's questions and to use expressions from the **Useful language** box when they write the email.

You may want to get Sts to do the writing in class or you could assign it as homework. If you do it in class, set a time limit for Sts to write their description, e.g., 15–20 minutes.

f Sts should check their work for mistakes before turning it in.

Tell Sts to go back to the main lesson **2A**.

5 READING & VOCABULARY

a Do this as an open-class activity and elicit ideas. Model and drill *hypochondriac* /haɪpə'kɑndriæk/ and *cyberchondriac* /'saɪbər'kɑndriæk/. You could remind Sts of Mr. Blaine, the patient, in **Grammar**, and tell them he is a good example of a hypochondriac. Don't confirm yet what a cyberchondriac is as Sts find this out in the article.

b Tell Sts to quickly read the article to check their answer to **a**.

Check the answer.

A cyberchondriac is someone who spends hours on the Internet trying to diagnose their symptoms and then imagines that they have a serious condition.

Now focus on the **Topic sentences** box and go through it with the class.

Set a time limit for Sts to read the article again and this time to complete the paragraphs with the topic sentences A–E. Point out that there is a **Glossary** to help them.

Check answers.

1 B 2 E 3 D 4 C 5 A

c Sts now focus on some more medical words and phrases that appear in the article. Put Sts in pairs and get them to look at the highlighted words and phrases, and guess what they mean.

When they have finished, they should match the highlighted words and phrases with definitions 1–11.

d 1 40 Play the audio for Sts to listen and check.

Check answers.

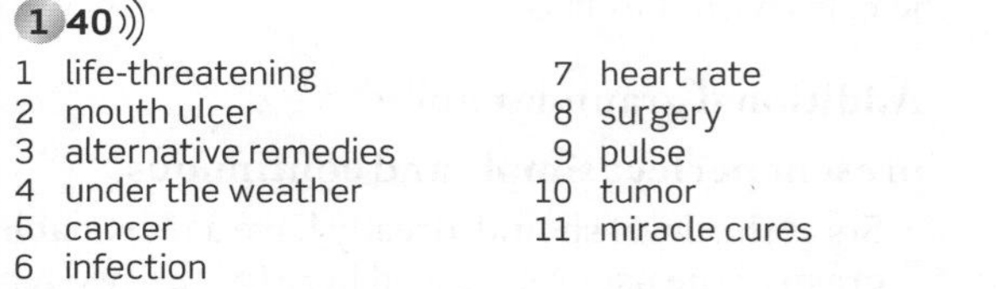
1 40
1 life-threatening
2 mouth ulcer
3 alternative remedies
4 under the weather
5 cancer
6 infection
7 heart rate
8 surgery
9 pulse
10 tumor
11 miracle cures

Help with any other new vocabulary and encourage Sts to write down any useful new lexis from the article.

e Give Sts time to read the four questions and their options.

Now get Sts to read the article again and to answer the questions.

Get Sts to compare with a partner and then check answers.

1 c 2 b 3 a 4 c

! Don't ask Sts yet if they or anyone they know is a cyberchondriac as they will be asked this after the following listening, where a doctor discusses cyberchondria.

6 LISTENING & SPEAKING

a 1 41 Tell Sts they are going to listen to a radio interview with a doctor talking about cyberchondria. They must listen for her general opinion of people using health websites.

Play the audio all the way through for Sts to get the gist.

Check the answer.

Extra support

- Before playing the audio, go through the listening script and decide if you need to preteach / check any lexis to help Sts when they listen.

In general, she thinks it is OK to look up symptoms on health websites, but only if they give reliable information.

1 41

(audioscript in Student Book on *page 121*)
I = interviewer, D = Dr. Roberta

I So, Dr. Roberta, do you meet a lot of cyberchondriacs in your work?
D All the time, I'm afraid. It's very common these days for people to look up their symptoms on health websites on the Internet and to diagnose themselves with weird or exotic illnesses. For example, the other day I had a patient who came in because his back was very red and itchy. He had been looking on Internet medical sites and was absolutely convinced that he had an extremely rare skin condition – he even knew the medical name, *Nodular Panniculitis*. But, in fact, when I examined him and talked to him, it turned out that he had spent the weekend working in his yard in the sun and his back was sunburned.
I So you would prefer your patients *not* to check their symptoms on the Internet?
D No, don't get me wrong, I'm not anti-health websites, I just want people to use them sensibly. The problem is that diagnosis of a condition or an illness doesn't just depend on one specific symptom that you can type into Google. It depends on all kinds of other things like a patient's appearance, their blood pressure, their heart rate, and so on.
I Of course.
D And diagnosis also depends on where you live. For example, if you live in a US city and you haven't traveled overseas, it's very unlikely that you have malaria even if you have some of the symptoms.
I What other problems are there when people use health websites?
D Well, you have to check carefully what kind of site it is that you are looking at. Some websites look as if they have been created by health professionals, but in fact they've been set up by commercial companies that are trying to sell you something. Also, some healthcare sites recommend expensive treatments or medicine that is not available in all parts of the world.
I Are there any websites that you would recommend?
D Oh, yes. Absolutely. For example, people with chronic diseases like asthma can get a lot of help and information from online support groups. These websites have forums where you can talk to other people who have the same condition and illness and you can usually get information about the latest research and new treatments. And there are often online support groups for people who have unusual illnesses, too.
I Finally, do you have any tips for all those cyberchondriacs out there?
D Yes, I have three. First, only look online *after* you've been to the doctor. If you're not feeling well, make a list of the symptoms you have that are worrying you, and go and see your doctor with this list. Then when your doctor has told you what he or she thinks, you could take a look online. Second, make sure you're looking at a reliable and professional medical website. And finally, remember that common symptoms usually have common causes – so if you have diarrhea, for example, it's much more likely to be food poisoning than the Ebola virus.
I Dr. Roberta, thank you very much.

b Give Sts time to look at the three questions and three tips in 4.

Now play the audio again, pausing as necessary to give Sts time to answer the questions.

Get Sts to answer 1–4 with a partner. Play the audio again if necessary.

Check answers.

1 An extremely rare skin disease. He was sunburned.
2 the patient's appearance, their blood pressure, their heart rate, and where they live
3 websites with online support groups, forums
4 i Only look online after you've seen the doctor.
 ii Make sure that the website you are using is a reliable and professional medical website.
 iii Remember that common symptoms usually have common causes.

Extra support

- If there's time, you could play the audio again while Sts read the audioscript on *page 121*, so they can see what they understood / didn't understand. Translate / explain any new words or phrases.

c Put Sts in pairs or small groups and get them to discuss the questions, giving as much information as possible.

Get some feedback. You could tell Sts what you think.

7 1 42 SONG *Just Like a Pill* ♫

This song was originally made famous by American singer Pink in 2002. For copyright reasons, this is a cover version. If you want to do this song in class, use the photocopiable activity on *page 230*.

1 42

Just Like a Pill

I'm lying here on the floor where you left me
I think I took too much
I'm crying here, what have you done?
I thought it would be fun

I can't stay on your life support, there's a shortage in the switch
I can't stay on your morphine, 'cos it's making me itch
I said I tried to call the nurse again but she's
being a little witch,
I think I'll get outta here, where I can...

Chorus
Run just as fast as I can
To the middle of nowhere
To the middle of my frustrated fears
And I swear you're just like a pill
Instead of making me better, you keep making me ill
You keep making me ill

I haven't moved from the spot where you left me
This must be a bad trip
All of the other pills, they were different
Maybe I should get some help

I can't stay on your life support, there's a shortage in the switch,
I can't stay on your morphine, 'cos it's making me itch
I said I tried to call the nurse again but she's being a little witch,
I think I'll get outta here, where I can...

Chorus (x2)

I can't stay on your life support, there's a shortage in the switch,
I can't stay on your morphine, 'cos it's making me itch
I said I tried to call the nurse again but she's being a little witch,
I think I'll get outta here, where I can...

Chorus

G using adjectives as nouns, adjective order
V clothes and fashion
P vowel sounds

2B Older and wiser?

Lesson plan

In this lesson, Sts extend their knowledge of how to use adjectives. They learn to use nationality adjectives as nouns when they talk about the people from a particular country (e.g., *the British, the French*) or a particular group of people (e.g., *the rich, the unemployed*), and they also focus on adjective order when two or more are used to describe a noun.

The lesson begins with a speaking activity on adjectives commonly used to describe teenagers and elderly people. Sts then read an article from *The Times* about two journalists who disguised themselves as people more than twice their age to discover what it was like to be old. The first half of the lesson ends with the grammar focus on adjectives and a speaking activity.

The second half starts with a listening task on whether men and women should dress their age. The lexical focus in the lesson is on clothes and fashion, and Pronunciation looks at short and long vowel sounds and diphthongs. In Speaking, Sts work in groups, giving their opinion on clothes and fashion. Finally, the lesson ends with a writing task, where Sts write two ads selling items of clothing.

STUDY LINK

- **Workbook** 2B
- **Online practice**
- **iChecker**

Extra photocopiable activities

- **Grammar** adjectives *page 154*
- **Communicative** Spot the difference *page 191* (instructions *page 180*)
- **Vocabulary** Clothes and fashion *page 214* (instructions *page 210*)

Optional lead-in – the quote

- Write the quote at the top of *page 18* on the board (books closed) and the name of the person who said it, or get Sts to open their books and read it.
- You could tell Sts that Abigail Van Buren was born Pauline Esther Phillips in 1918 and died in 2013. She was famous for her "Dear Abby" advice column in the newspaper in the 1950s and also a radio program with the same name.
- Get Sts to discuss what they think it means. Do they agree with the quote?

1 SPEAKING

a Focus on the ***old* or *elderly*?** box and go through it with the class.

Make sure Sts know the meaning of all the adjectives, and get them to decide in pairs if each adjective is most often used to describe a teenager or an elderly person (although it may not be their own opinion). Sts may want to put some adjectives in both categories. You might quickly want to check the age range of a teenager (between 13 and 19). Then Sts should decide if the adjectives are mainly positive or negative.

When Sts have finished, write their answers on the board.

The majority of the adjectives in both groups are negative.

b Focus on the task and make sure Sts know the meaning of *stereotypes* and *to conform*.

Now put Sts in pairs or small groups and get them to discuss the three questions, giving as much information as possible.

Monitor and help while Sts are talking.

Get some feedback and help with any general vocabulary problems that come up.

2 READING

a Focus attention on the photos and elicit ideas from the class. Don't tell them if they are right or not.

b Explain to the class that the article they are going to read is about a real TV documentary. Tell them to read the first paragraph of *Trading Ages* to find out the answer to **a**.

Check the answer. You could also elicit / explain the meaning of the title, *Trading Ages* (= exchanging ages).

Karoline Bell and Nick Sydney have been made to look old, so that they could experience life as an old person for one month.

Now put Sts in pairs and get them to look at the highlighted words and phrases and to guess their meaning. Remind them that they are all related to the body.

Check answers, either explaining in English, translating into Sts' L1, or getting Sts to check in their dictionaries.

Help with any other new vocabulary and encourage Sts to write down any useful new lexis from the article.

c Focus on the task and questions 1–3.

In pairs, Sts discuss the questions.

Elicit some ideas.

d Set a time limit for Sts to read the rest of the article and to check their answers to the questions in **c**.

Get Sts to compare with their partner and then check answers.

1 People didn't notice them or were rude to them.
2 They learned that old people are just like young people, but with older bodies and with more experience of life.
3 They understood old people better and it made them think about getting old themselves.

e Focus on the task and questions 1–9.

Now give Sts time to read the article again (make sure they read the whole article again, i.e., from the first paragraph to the end) and answer the questions with the initials or **B** for *both*.

Check answers.

1 B	4 N	7 K
2 B	5 K	8 N
3 K	6 K	9 K

f Tell Sts to look at the highlighted verb phrases and to try to guess what they mean. Then they should match them with their meaning.

Check answers, either explaining in English, translating into Sts' L1, or getting Sts to check in their dictionaries. Explain / elicit that the infinitive of *been* in *been through* is *go through* = experience.

be prepared	5
behave toward you	1
experienced	3
loses control of his / her feelings	2
solve a problem or do a task	4

Help with any other new vocabulary and encourage Sts to write down any useful new lexis from the article.

Now get Sts to cover the text and look at the definitions and try to remember the phrases.

g Do this as an open-class activity.

3 GRAMMAR using adjectives as nouns, adjective order

a Focus on the sentences and give Sts time to check or cross each option.

In pairs, they should discuss why they think some options are wrong.

Check answers, eliciting why the ✗ ones are wrong. In 1, b is wrong because you can't use a definite article when you are talking about a group of people in general. In 2, only c is right because opinion adjectives, e.g., *tall*, go before descriptive adjectives and color, e.g., *blond* comes before origin, e.g., *Swedish*.

1 a ✓	b ✗	c ✓
2 a ✗	b ✗	c ✓

b 1 43)) 1 44)) Tell Sts to go to **Grammar Bank 2B** on *page 135*. Focus on the example sentences and play the audio for Sts to listen to the sentence rhythm. You could also get Sts to repeat the sentences to practice getting the rhythm right. Then go through the rules with the class.

Additional grammar notes

adjectives as nouns
rule 1: nationalities

- Sts should already have a good grasp of nationality adjectives in English, especially for the countries in their part of the world.
- You may want to elicit more examples of nouns used to describe people from a particular country, e.g., Greece – the Greeks, Scotland – the Scots, Spain – the Spaniards, Mexico – the Mexicans, Thailand – the Thais, etc.

adjective order

- It's important to point out that in practice people rarely use more than two adjectives (occasionally three) together, so Sts should not be put off by the chart showing adjective order. Encourage Sts to use their instinct as to what sounds right rather than try to memorize the chart, and to remember that opinion adjectives always come first. Learning common combinations will also help them to remember the rule, e.g., *long fair hair, a big old house*, etc.

Focus on the exercises and get Sts to do them individually or in pairs.

Check answers, getting Sts to read the full sentences.

a

1 the Dutch	6 the Swiss
2 the sick	7 the homeless
3 the blind	8 the unemployed
4 the Chinese	9 the dead
5 the injured	10 the deaf

b
1 an attractive young man
2 dirty old shoes
3 a beautiful black velvet jacket
4 a short heavy American woman
5 a long sandy beach
6 a charming old log cabin
7 a stylish Italian leather bag
8 huge dark eyes
9 a friendly old black dog
10 a striped cotton T-shirt

Tell Sts to go back to the main lesson **2B**.

Extra support

- If you think Sts need more practice, you may want to give them the Grammar photocopiable activity at this point or leave it for later as consolidation or review.

c This is an oral grammar practice exercise. Focus on the six statements and make sure Sts understand the lexis, e.g., *retirement home, to value, wisdom*, etc.

Put Sts in pairs or small groups and tell them to discuss each statement, saying whether they agree or disagree, and why.

Get some feedback from the class.

4 LISTENING

a Focus on the photos and elicit some opinions.

Adele, English singer-songwriter and musician, was born in 1988.
Jane Fonda, American actress, political activist, former fashion model, and fitness instructor, was born in 1937.
Joseph Gordon-Levitt, American actor, director, and producer, was born in 1981.
Mick Jagger, English musician, singer (lead singer of the Rolling Stones), songwriter, was born in 1943.

b 1 45 Focus on the task and make sure Sts understand the topic of the radio program.

Then get Sts to look at the question and the two sentences with blanks. You could point out that each person gives their fashion rule at the end of their turn.

Extra challenge

- Get Sts to predict what the rules might be before they listen.

Play the audio once all the way through. Play the audio again as necessary.

Check answers.

Extra support

- Before playing the audio, go through the audioscript and decide if you need to preteach / check any lexis to help Sts when they listen.

They don't agree.
Liza: Wear whatever you think **suits you** and makes you **feel good**.
Adrian: Dress for **the age you are**, not for **the age you wish you were**.

1 45
(audioscript in Student Book on *pages 121–122*)
P = presenter, L = Liza, A = Adrian

P Welcome to today's program in our series on age. The topic is clothes and the question is, do people these days dress their age, and should they? Our guests are both fashion journalists with well-known magazines. Hello, Liza and Adrian.
L & A Hello. Hi!
P Let's start with you, Liza.
L Well, the first thing I'd like to say to all the young people out there is next time you give your grandma a warm cardigan and some slippers for her birthday, don't be surprised if she asks for the receipt, because she'll probably want to go out and exchange them for something more exciting.
P So you think these days women in their 60s and 70s dress much younger than they used to?
L Oh, absolutely. Think of women like Sophia Loren, Catherine Deneuve, Helen Mirren, and Jane Fonda. Jane Fonda is in her late seventies and last month she was on a talk show wearing a leather miniskirt – she looked fabulous! But, of course, it isn't just famous women who are dressing younger; some recent research says that nine out of ten women say that they try to dress younger than their age.
P Do you think that's true?
L Well, it depends on your age of course. A lot of teenage girls try to dress older than they are, maybe to get into parties. But I would say that from 30 onward most women try to dress younger than they are.
P And do you think there's anything wrong with that?
L Actually, I think it's not a question of dressing older or younger, it's a question of wearing what suits you. And if you looked good in jeans when you were 15, if you keep your figure, you'll probably look good in them when you're 80. There are a few things that can look a little ridiculous on older women, like, let's see...very short shorts, but not many.
P So your fashion rule would be...?
L Wear whatever you think suits you and makes you feel good.
P Adrian, what about men? Do you think they also try to look younger than their age?
A Well, interestingly, in the research Liza mentioned, only 12 percent of the men who were questioned said they had ever thought about dressing to look younger. But actually, I think a lot of them weren't telling the truth. Look at all those middle-aged men you see wearing jeans that are too tight and incredibly bright T-shirts.
P You don't approve?
A No, I don't. Personally, I think that men should take their age into account when they're buying clothes.
P Do you think that some men actually dress older than their age?
A Yes, definitely, some do. Some men in their twenties look as if they were 20 years older by wearing blazers and khakis, or wearing suits and ties when they don't have to. They've maybe started their careers and they want their bosses to take them more seriously. And a lot of men in their thirties realize that they can't dress like a teenager any more, but they go to the opposite extreme and they start buying the kind of clothes that their fathers wear.
P So what would your fashion rule be for men?
A Dress for the age you are, not for the age you wish you were.
P Liza and Adrian, thank you very much.

c Focus on the task and make sure Sts understand all the lexis.

Then play the audio again, pausing as necessary to give Sts time to take notes. Play the audio again if necessary.

You could get Sts to compare with a partner before checking answers.

Liza
a warm cardigan and slippers: If you give your grandma a warm cardigan and some slippers for her birthday, she will probably want to exchange them for something more exciting.
a leather miniskirt: Jane Fonda, who is in her late 70s, wore one and looked great.
teenagers: They try to dress older than they are (maybe to get into parties).
women who are 30+: Most try to dress younger than they are.
very short shorts: Older women can look a bit ridiculous in very short shorts.

Adrian
men in their 20s who wear blazers and khakis or suits: They've maybe started their careers and they want their bosses to take them more seriously.
men in their 30s: They realize that they can't dress like a teenager any more, but they go to the opposite extreme and buy clothes that their fathers wear.

Extra support

- If there's time, you could play the audio again while Sts read the audioscript on *pages 121–122*, so they can see what they understood / didn't understand. Translate / explain any new words or phrases.

d Do this in pairs, small groups, or as an open-class activity.

5 VOCABULARY clothes and fashion

a Focus on the instructions and then give Sts two minutes individually or in pairs to complete the task.

Elicit answers.

Possible answers
on your hands and arms: gloves, rings, a watch, bracelets
around your neck: a scarf, a tie, a necklace, a pendant
on your feet: shoes, boots, socks, sneakers, ankle bracelets
on your head: a hat, a cap, a (head)scarf

b Tell Sts to go to **Vocabulary Bank** ***Clothes and fashion*** on *page 153*.

Focus on **1 Describing clothes** and get Sts to do **a** individually or in pairs.

1 46 Now do **b**. Play the audio for Sts to check answers. Play the audio again, pausing for Sts to repeat. Practice any words your Sts find difficult to pronounce.

1 46
Clothes and fashion
Describing clothes

Fit	**Pattern**
2 loose	9 patterned
1 tight	11 plaid
Style	7 plain
6 hooded	10 dotted
4 long sleeved	8 striped
3 sleeveless	
5 V-neck	

Get Sts to do **c** individually or in pairs.

1 47 Now do **d**. Play the audio for Sts to check answers. Play the audio again, pausing for Sts to repeat. Practice any words your Sts find difficult to pronounce.

1 47
Materials
4 a cotton undershirt
9 a denim vest
5 a fur collar
3 a lace top
1 a linen suit
7 a Lycra swimsuit
8 a silk scarf
6 a velvet bow tie
2 a wool cardigan
11 leather sandals
10 suede boots

Look at **2 Adjectives to describe the way people dress**, focus on the ***trendy, stylish,*** **and** ***fashionable*** box and go through it with the class.

Get Sts to do **a** individually or in pairs.

1 48 Now do **b**. Play the audio for Sts to check answers. Practice words your Sts find difficult to pronounce.

1 48
Adjectives to describe the way people dress
1 Long skirts are really **fashionable** now.
2 She's very **trendy**. She always wears the latest fashions.
3 The Italians have a reputation for being very **stylish** – they wear fashionable and attractive clothes.
4 He looks really **scruffy**. His clothes are old and dirty.
5 Jane looked very **neat** in her new suit. She wanted to make a good impression.
6 That tie's a little **old-fashioned**! Is it your dad's?

Look at **3 Verb phrases**, focus on the ***wear*** **and** ***dress*** box and go through it with the class. Elicit / point out that *wear* always needs an object (e.g., *I'm going to wear a jacket tonight*) and *dress* never has an object, but is usually used with an adverb, e.g., *well, badly*, etc. (e.g., *She dresses well*).

Get Sts to do **a** individually or in pairs.

1 49 Now do **b**. Play the audio for Sts to check answers. Practice any words your Sts find difficult to pronounce.

1 49
Verb phrases
1 **C** I'm going to dress up tonight.
2 **A** Please hang up your coat.
3 **F** These jeans don't fit me.
4 **H** That skirt really suits you.
5 **G** Your bag matches your shoes.
6 **B** I need to get changed.
7 **E** Hurry up and get undressed.
8 **I** Get up and get dressed.
9 **D** That tie doesn't really go with your shirt.

Make sure Sts are aware of the difference in meaning between *match, suit, fit*, and *get changed / dressed / undressed*. Highlight that the phrasal verb *dress up* means *to wear nice, usually fancier, clothes*. Elicit / point out that *dress up, match, fit*, and *suit* are regular verbs and that *hang up* is irregular (past *hung up*).

Testing yourself

For **Describing clothes a** and **c**, Sts can cover the words, look at the pictures, and try to remember the words. For **Adjectives to describe the way people dress**, they can cover the sentences and try to remember the meaning of the adjectives. In **Verb phrases**, they can cover the verb phrases and remember them by looking at definitions A–I.

Testing a partner

See **Testing a partner** *page 29*.

Tell Sts to go back to the main lesson **2B**.

Extra support

- If you think Sts need more practice, you may want to give them the Vocabulary photocopiable activity at this point or leave it for later as consolidation or review.

c This exercise recycles the vocabulary Sts have just learned. Put Sts in pairs and set a time limit to complete the quiz.

Check answers.

1 get dressed ≠ get undressed
short-sleeved ≠ long-sleeved
neat ≠ scruffy
tight ≠ loose
trendy ≠ old-fashioned
2 bicycle shorts: Lycra; jeans: denim; shoes: leather; a sweater: cotton; a tie: silk; tights: wool
3 a It doesn't **fit** me.
b It doesn't **suit** me.
c It **matches** my pants.
4 a when shopping
b to go to a party
c when you get undressed, wash clothes
d when you get back from school / work, get dirty

You could ask Sts to raise their hands to show who got the most right answers.

6 PRONUNCIATION vowel sounds

Pronunciation notes

- Sts can improve their pronunciation by making an effort to distinguish between long and short sounds, and diphthongs (a combination of two vowel sounds, e.g., the sound in *hair* /hɛr/). When Upper-intermediate Sts come across new words they will often instinctively pronounce them correctly, especially if there is a regular sound–spelling relationship. If they are unsure, they should use their dictionaries to check.

a Focus on the **Vowel sounds** box and go through it with the class.

1 50))) Focus on the task and give Sts a few minutes, in pairs, to complete it.

Then play the audio for Sts to listen and check.

Check answers.

1 50)))

boot /u/	suit, loose
bull /ʊ/	hooded, wool
tree /i/	sleeveless, jeans
fish /ɪ/	linen, slippers
egg /ɛ/	checked, leather
cat /ae/	sandals, patterned
clock /a/	cotton, dotted
saw /ɔ/	awful, long

Extra support

- You could play the audio again for Sts to repeat the words.

b Now tell Sts to go to the **Sound Bank** on *page 166*.

Focus on the six sounds that Sts have just been working on and the typical spellings.

c Get Sts to practice saying the phrases to each other in pairs, before choosing individual Sts to say them.

7 SPEAKING

Focus on the questions and go through them, making sure Sts understand all the lexis.

Put Sts in small groups and set a time limit. You could assign one student to ask the questions and organize the discussion.

Monitor and help with vocabulary that Sts need.

Get feedback from the whole class and help with any general vocabulary problems that come up.

8 WRITING

a Focus on the instructions and example. Ask Sts if they have ever bought or sold anything on eBay.

Give Sts time to write their two descriptions – about 25 words in each should be enough. Go around helping with vocabulary.

When everyone is ready, get them to write their name on their ads.

b Focus on the task and explain / elicit the meaning of the verb *bid*.

Either get Sts to move around the class exchanging ads or if possible, put the ads on the class walls and get Sts to move around, reading them. If they find an item of clothing they would like to bid for, they should make a note of it.

Stop the activity when you think most of the Sts have read all the ads.

Get feedback to find out who would like to bid for something.

1&2 Review and Check

There are two pages of review and consolidation after every two Files. The first page reviews the grammar, vocabulary, and pronunciation of the two Files. These exercises can be done individually or in pairs, in class or at home, depending on the needs of your Sts and the class time available. The second page presents Sts with a series of skills-based challenges. First, there is a reading text, which is of a slightly higher level than those in the File, but which reviews grammar and vocabulary Sts have already learned.

Then Sts can watch or listen to a short documentary movie related to one of the topics of the Files and do a short comprehension task. You can find them on the *Class DVD, iTools,* and *Class Audio* (audio only). The aim of this is to give Sts enjoyable and motivating extra listening practice.

We suggest that you use some or all of these activities according to the needs of your class.

Testing Program CD-ROM

- **File 2 Quick Test**
- **File 2 Test**

GRAMMAR

a 1 about 3 does 5 been
2 did 4 have

b 1 a 3 b 5 b 7 a 9 a
2 b 4 c 6 b 8 c 10 c

VOCABULARY

a 1 tempered 3 fisted 5 fashioned
2 laid 4 confident

b 1 bleed 3 bandage 5 rash
2 swollen 4 toothache

c 1 feel 3 fainted 5 getting changed
2 sprained 4 fit

d 1 plain (The others are a pattern.)
2 neat (The others are a type of material.)
3 collar (The others are adjectives.)
4 Lycra (The others are items of clothing.)
5 scruffy (The others are positive adjectives.)

e 1 over 3 throw 5 hang
2 down 4 up

PRONUNCIATION

a 1 ache 3 striped 5 cough
2 suede 4 jeans

b 1 incredibly 3 antibiotics 5 fashionable
2 big-headed 4 swimsuit

CAN YOU UNDERSTAND THIS TEXT?

a Shamans go into a trance and then try to find solutions for people's problems.

b 1 b 2 c 3 b 4 a

c Give Sts time to choose their five words or phrases. Ask volunteers to read their words to the class.

VIDEO CAN YOU UNDERSTAND THIS MOVIE?

1 51

1 T 3 T 5 T 7 F 9 T
2 F 4 F 6 F 8 T 10 F

1 51 Available as MP3 on CD1

A Short Film on the History of Surgery

Hi! I'm in Southwark in London. This area used to be the site of one of London's oldest hospitals – St Thomas'. St Thomas' was here for almost 700 years and had one of the country's first ever operating theaters.

Have you ever had an operation? If you have, it was probably in an operating theater like this. These modern theaters are clean, spacious, and bright. As you can see they are full of hi-tech equipment and they are designed to make surgery as clean and as safe as possible. They usually have an adjustable metal operating table in the center of the room. Above the table, there are several large, fluorescent lights which allow surgeons to see everything. At the head of the table, there's an anaesthetic machine and around the room there are various monitors, measuring heart rate, blood pressure, and blood oxygen levels.

But what about old operating theaters? What were they like? Well, that's why I've come here. You see, St Thomas' old operating theater used to be in the attic of this church. The hospital was moved from here in the 1860s. But when a historian decided to investigate the church's old attic, he found a large abandoned room containing some old-fashioned surgical equipment.

Today this room is part of The Old Operating Theatre Museum. The museum has been teaching visitors about the history of surgery for over 50 years. The first question many people ask when they come here is, why is it called an operating theater? Well, the answer is simple. As you can see, medical students used to stand here and watch the surgery, like an audience watching a play in a theater. During operations the room was always cramped and crowded, and the bigger and bloodier the operation, the bigger the audience! Imagine how frightening it must have been for the poor patient. And they were usually quite poor. The rich had their operations at home, but the poor would tolerate the audience in order to receive surgery they would never be able to afford otherwise.

The patient would lie on this uncomfortable wooden bench while the surgeon worked. There was no anaesthetic, so patients were awake throughout the procedure, unless, of course, they fainted. The surgeons were quick – they could amputate a leg in less than a minute – but they had very little understanding of hygiene. There were no antiseptics and surgeons always wore the same coats, which were usually covered with blood from previous operations. They often used dirty instruments, which were kept on this old, wooden table, and they rarely washed their hands.

Below the operating table there was a wooden box filled with sawdust, or wood shavings. This collected the blood from each operation. But often there was too much blood, so in the end, they built a false floor. The blood could be washed away and collected in the space between the new floor and the original floor.
In such unhygienic conditions, it isn't surprising that patients often died during surgery. After the patient's death, their bones and organs were kept for further study.

All of these practices seem primitive to us today. But without these techniques, we might never have developed the cleaner, safer procedures we have today. That's something we can all be grateful for!

G narrative tenses, past perfect continuous; *so / such...that*
V air travel
P regular and irregular past forms, sentence rhythm

3A The truth about air travel

Lesson plan

In this lesson, Sts review the three narrative tenses they already know (simple past, past continuous, and past perfect) and learn a new one, the past perfect continuous. The topic is air travel.

In the first half of the lesson, Sts listen to some in-flight announcements and Vocabulary focuses on words related to air travel. Sts then read an extract from a best-selling book called *Air Babylon*, which claims to give the inside story about what really happens at airports and on flights. They also learn, in Mini Grammar, how to use *so / such...that*. Finally, they do a speaking activity on aspects of air travel.

In the second half, Sts listen to an interview with a pilot and an air traffic controller, who answer some of the questions air travelers ask themselves when they board a plane. This is followed by grammar on narrative tenses and the pronunciation of tricky irregular past verb forms. In the speaking activity, Sts read and retell a couple of real stories about flying and then tell each other an anecdote. The final activity is the song, *The Airplane Song*.

STUDY LINK
- Workbook 3A
- Online Practice
- iChecker

Extra photocopiable activities

- **Grammar** narrative tenses *page 155*
- **Mini Grammar** *so / such...that* *page 174*
- **Communicative** Talk about it *page 192* (instructions *page 181*)
- **Vocabulary** Air travel *page 215* (instructions *page 210*)
- **Song** *The Airplane Song* *page 231* (instructions *page 226*)

Optional lead-in – the quote

- Write the quote at the top of *page 24* on the board (books closed) and the name of the person who said it, or get Sts to open their books and read it.
- You could tell Sts that Billy Bob Thornton (1955–) was married to Angelina Jolie from 2000 to 2003.
- Ask Sts whether any of them identify with his quote.

1 LISTENING & VOCABULARY air travel

a 2 2))) Focus on the pictures and elicit what Sts think is happening in each one.

Focus on the instructions.

Then play the audio, pausing after each announcement.

Check answers, eliciting from Sts in their own words what information or instructions the passengers are being given in each picture.

A 4 B 2 C 3 D 1

2 2)))
(audioscript in Student Book on *page 122*)

1 Ladies and gentlemen, welcome on board this flight to Hong Kong. Please place all carry-on luggage in the overhead compartments or underneath the seat in front of you. We ask that you please fasten your seat belts and, for safety reasons, we advise you to keep them fastened throughout the flight.
2 We also ask that you make sure your seat backs and tray tables are in their full upright and locked positions for takeoff. Please turn off all personal electronic devices, including laptops and cell phones. We remind you that smoking is prohibited for the duration of the flight.
3 Ladies and gentlemen, we ask for your attention for the following safety instructions. Please read the safety information card located in the seat pocket in front of you. There are six emergency exits on this aircraft, all marked with exit signs. Take a minute to locate the exit closest to you. Note that the nearest exit may be behind you.
4 The safety information card is in the seat pocket in front of you. Please read it. It shows you the equipment carried on this aircraft for your safety. Your life jacket is located under your seat. In the unlikely event of a water landing, place the life jacket over your head, fasten the straps at the front, and pull them tight. Do not inflate the jacket inside the aircraft. As you leave the aircraft, pull down on the red tabs to inflate the vest. If necessary, the life jacket can be inflated by blowing through these tubes.

b Give Sts time to look at 1–7.

Play the audio again, pausing after each announcement for Sts to write the word or phrase they hear. Play again as necessary.

Check answers.

1 carry-on luggage	5 emergency exits
2 overhead compartments	6 life jacket
3 fasten /'fæsn/	7 to inflate
4 electronic devices	

Extra support

- If there's time, you could play the audio again while Sts read the audioscript on *page 122*, so they can see what they understood / didn't understand. Translate / explain any new words or phrases.

c Tell Sts to go to **Vocabulary Bank *Air travel*** on *page 154*.

Focus on **1 At the airport** and get Sts to do **a** individually or in pairs.

2 3))) Now do **b**. Play the audio for Sts to check answers. Play the audio again, pausing for Sts to repeat. Practice any words your Sts find difficult to pronounce.

2 3)))
Air travel
At the airport

1 **A** airport terminal	6 **B** departures board
2 **D** baggage drop off	7 **G** gate
3 **I** baggage claim	8 **H** runway
4 **C** check-in desk	9 **E** security
5 **J** customs	10 **F** VIP lounge

Highlight the difference between *luggage* and *baggage*:

– *luggage* (uncountable) = bags and (suit)cases you take with you when you travel. You can't use it in the plural NOT ~~*I have a lot of luggages*~~.

– *baggage* (uncountable) is a more formal word used by airlines and at airports, e.g., it is used in the expression *excess baggage* and in the sign *baggage claim*. In conversation, we would usually use *luggage*.

Focus on **2 On board** and get Sts to do **a** individually or in pairs.

2 4))) Now do **b**. Play the audio for Sts to check answers. Practice any words your Sts find difficult to pronounce.

2 turbulence
3 cabin crew
4 seat belts
5 direct flights
6 connecting flight
7 long-haul flights
8 jet lag

2 4)))

On board

I often fly to Chile on business. I always choose an aisle seat, so that I can get up and walk around more easily.
Sometimes there is turbulence when the plane flies over the Andes, which I don't enjoy, and the cabin crew tells the passengers to put their seat belts on.
There aren't many direct flights to Chile from Paris, so I usually have to get a connecting flight in Atlanta.
Whenever I take long-haul flights, I always suffer from jet lag because of the time difference, and I feel tired for several days.

Highlight that:

– *aisle* (seat) = the seat next to the passage way between seats on a plane

– *turbulence* = sudden and sometimes violent movement of air

– *jet lag* = tiredness caused by long distance flight, especially when there is a big time difference between where you depart from and your destination

Focus on **3 *Travel, trip,* or *journey?*** and get Sts to do **a** individually or in pairs.

2 5))) Now do **b**. Play the audio for Sts to check answers. Practice any words your Sts find difficult to pronounce.

2 5)))

Travel, trip,* or *journey?

1 We're going on a five-day trip to the mountains.
2 **A** How long was your **journey** across China?
B It was about two months long, and it was amazing.
3 Do you have to **travel** much for your job?
4 Have a good **trip**. See you when you get back.

Now do **c** as an open-class activity.

Travel is usually used as a verb. However, it can be used as an uncountable noun.
The noun ***trip*** means to go somewhere and come back, including the time you stay there.
Journey is also usually used as a noun. It means the time when you travel from one place to another, but does not include the time you stay there.

Focus on **4 Phrasal verbs related to air travel** and get Sts to do **a** individually or in pairs.

2 6))) Now do **b**. Play the audio for Sts to check answers. Practice any words your Sts find difficult to pronounce.

2 6)))

Phrasal verbs related to air travel

1 My husband dropped me off at the airport two hours before the flight.
2 I **checked in** online the day before I was going to fly.
3 As soon as I **got on** the plane, I sat down in the first empty seat.
4 The plane **took off** late because of the bad weather.
5 I **filled out** the immigration form for the US, which the cabin crew gave me shortly before landing.
6 When I **got off** the plane, I felt exhausted after the long flight.
7 When I **picked up** my luggage at baggage claim, I bumped into an old friend who had been on the same flight!

Highlight that *drop someone off* = take someone somewhere by car and stop briefly to let them get out, and that *pick up* (your luggage) = go and get. Remind Sts that you can also pick up a person, e.g., *I'll pick you up at the airport.*

Testing yourself

For **At the airport**, Sts can cover definitions A–J, look at words 1–10, and try to remember their meaning.
For **On board**, they can cover the text and try to remember the meaning of the words in the list.
For ***Travel, trip,* or *journey?***, they can cover the sentences and remember what the words mean.
For **Phrasal verbs related to air travel**, they can cover the sentences and try to remember the meaning of the phrasal verbs in the list.

Testing a partner

See **Testing a partner** *page 29*.

Tell Sts to go back to the main lesson **3A**.

Extra support

- If you think Sts need more practice, you may want to give them the Vocabulary photocopiable activity at this point or leave it for later as consolidation or review.

2 READING

a Focus on the task. Read the back cover out loud and ask Sts why they think the identities of the airline staff "must remain secret" (because if their bosses found out they might lose their jobs). Emphasize that this book really exists.

Give Sts a few minutes in pairs to discuss the questions.

Get feedback, but don't tell them yet if they are right or not.

Extra support

- Ask the questions to the whole class and elicit ideas.

b Set a time limit for Sts to read the extract and check the answers to the questions in **a**.

Get feedback by reading the questions out loud again one by one and eliciting answers.

Yes, it is. In 1996 when a plane landed in the Indian Ocean some passengers inflated their life jackets when they were in the plane and then they couldn't get out.
So that customs officers can look at you from behind the glass and watch your reactions as you walk past.
Because a bird has crashed into the plane and been burned in the engine.
Because some people who don't really need a wheelchair ask for one.

c Focus on the task and give Sts time to read 1–8.

Sts then read the extract again and underline the part of the text with the information regarding 1–8.

Check answers.

1 F (Line 1: Most airline passengers think it is laughable that a small yellow life jacket with a whistle will make any difference...)
2 T (Line 6: Despite instructions...not to pre-inflate their life jackets inside the plane, several passengers did. They were unable to escape the rising water inside the plane.)
3 T (Line 22: The large two-way mirror in Customs, (behind which customs officers sit and watch...)
4 T (Line 26: ...you relax and smile. That's when a customs officer suddenly appears and asks you to open your suit case...)
5 F (Line 33: Smaller birds are less of a problem.)
6 T (Line 36: ...there is often such a strong smell of roast bird...they are often surprised when they're given a choice of fish or beef...)
7 T (Line 42: Not only is there always a shortage of them...)
8 T (Line 51: One flight attendant...gets so annoyed when this happens...she shouts...)

Extra support

- At this point, you could go through the four paragraphs with the class, highlighting useful expressions and eliciting / explaining the meaning of new words and phrases.

Encourage Sts to write down new lexis from the article.

d Do these questions as an open-class activity.

3 MINI GRAMMAR *so / such...that*

a Go through the two examples and then the rules. Highlight that *that* is optional after *so / such*.

You may want to point out that we often use *so / such* simply for emphasis (i.e., without expressing a consequence), e.g., *That steak was so good. We had such a nice day!*

b Elicit sentence 1 from the whole class and write the answer on the board.

Then get Sts to do the rest of the exercise.

Check answers.

1 so	5 such
2 such a	6 so many
3 so	7 so much
4 so	8 such

Extra support

- If you think Sts need more practice, you may want to give them the Mini Grammar photocopiable activity now or leave it for later as consolidation or review.

4 SPEAKING

Focus on the questionnaire.

! Find out if anyone in the class has never flown; if so, pair them with someone who has.

Monitor and help while Sts ask and answer the questions. Sts could either both answer each question as they go through the questionnaire, or they take turns talking about their travel experiences. If time is limited, ask Sts to only choose five questions to answer.

Get some feedback and help with any general vocabulary problems that come up.

5 LISTENING

a Focus on the task and make sure Sts understand who the two speakers are.

Then give Sts time to discuss the eight questions in pairs.

Elicit some ideas, but <u>don't</u> tell Sts if they are right or not.

b 2 7))) Play the audio once all the way through for Sts to listen and see how many questions in **a** they answered correctly.

You could get Sts to compare with their partner before checking answers by eliciting brief responses at this stage.

Ask Sts how many they guessed correctly.

1 when the wind changes direction suddenly
2 no
3 Takeoff is slightly more dangerous.
4 yes, some are
5 confidence
6 not as stressful as people think
7 because it's the official language of air traffic control
8 not many female pilots, but plenty of women air traffic controllers

2 7)))
(audioscript in Student Book on *page 122*)
I = interviewer, R = Richard, B = Brynn

I With me in the studio today I have Richard, who's a pilot, and Brynn, who's an air traffic controller, and they are going to answer some of the most frequently asked questions about flying and air travel. Hello to both of you.
R & B Hello.
I OK, we're going to start with you, Richard. The first question is what weather conditions are the most dangerous when flying a plane?
R Probably the most dangerous weather conditions are when the wind changes direction very suddenly. Uh...this tends to happen during thunderstorms and hurricanes, and it's especially dangerous during takeoff and landing. But it's pretty unusual – I've been flying for 37 years now and I've only experienced this three or four times.
I What about turbulence? Is that dangerous?
R It can be very bumpy and very uncomfortable, but it isn't dangerous. Even strong turbulence won't damage the plane. Pilots always try to avoid turbulence, but it can sometimes occur without any warning, which is why we always advise passengers to wear their seat belt all the time during the flight.

I Which is more dangerous, takeoff or landing?
R Both takeoff and landing can be dangerous. They're the most dangerous moments of a flight. Pilots talk about the "critical eight minutes" – the three minutes after takeoff and the five minutes before landing. Most accidents happen in this period. But I would say that takeoff is probably slightly more dangerous than landing. There is a critical moment just before takeoff when the plane is accelerating, but it hasn't yet reached the speed to be able to fly. If the pilot has a problem with the plane at this point, he or she has very little time – maybe only a second – to abort the takeoff.
I Are some airports more dangerous than others?
R Yes, some are, particularly airports with high mountains around them, and airports in countries with older or more basic navigation equipment. For some difficult airports like, let's say Kathmandu, they only allow very experienced pilots to land there. And for some of these airports, pilots have to practice on a simulator first before they are given permission to land a plane there.
I Thanks, Richard. Over to you, Brynn...What personal qualities do you think you need to be an air traffic controller?
B Um, I think confidence is number one. You need to be a self-confident person; you have to be sure of yourself and of the decisions you're making.
I Most people imagine that being an air traffic controller is very stressful. Do you agree?
B Actually, on a daily basis, the job isn't as stressful as people think. Obviously it's true that stressful situations do arise, but when you're very busy, you just don't have time to get stressed.
I Why is it important for pilots and controllers to have good, clear English?
B English is the official language of air traffic control. We communicate with pilots using very specific phrases, like *runway, wind, cleared for takeoff, turbulence, traffic ahead, to your left, to your right,* things like that, and it's true that you could just learn these specific phrases. But then in an emergency, you don't know what language you might need; it's much less predictable, which is why it's vital for pilots and air traffic controllers to speak really good, clear English.
R If I could just interrupt here. In fact, there have been several air crashes that happened because the air traffic controller misunderstood something that the pilot had said in English, or vice versa, because their pronunciation wasn't clear enough.
B Yes, that's right.
I Finally, people tend to think that most pilots and air traffic controllers are men. Would you say that was true?
B Not in air traffic control – there are lots of women. It may not be 50/50, but there are plenty of us.
R It's true about pilots, though. I mean there are some women pilots, but it's still pretty much a male-dominated job, I'd say.
I Why do you think that is?
R People say it's because men have a better sense of direction.
B Very funny.
I Richard, Brynn, thank you very much.

c Play the audio again for Sts to listen for more detail, pausing as necessary to give Sts time to write their notes. Play the audio again as necessary.

You could get Sts to compare with a partner before checking answers.

Extra support

- Before playing the audio, go through the audioscript and decide if you need to preteach / check any lexis to help Sts when they listen.

1 sudden changes of wind directions, especially during thunderstorms and hurricanes – but it's very unusual
2 Most turbulence isn't dangerous, just bumpy and uncomfortable. It won't damage the plane. Pilots try to avoid it, but it can happen without warning, so keep your seat belt on.
3 Both are dangerous (the critical eight minutes – three minutes after takeoff and five before landing), but takeoff is a little more dangerous, especially if there is a problem just before the plane goes into the air. The pilot may only have one second to abort takeoff.
4 Yes, especially ones with mountains or in countries with older, more basic equipment. Only very experienced pilots are allowed to land at these airports and sometimes have to practice on a simulator first.
5 An air traffic controller needs to be a self-confident person – sure of him or herself and of their decisions.
6 In general, it isn't as stressful as people think. There are stressful moments, but you are too busy to feel stressed.
7 Because it's the official language of air traffic control, e.g., *cleared for takeoff.* Pilots and air traffic controllers need to understand each other, especially in an emergency, so they need good, clear English. There have been accidents because of misunderstandings caused by incorrect pronunciation.
8 There are a lot of female air traffic controllers although it isn't 50–50. There are some female pilots, but most pilots are men.

Extra support

- If there's time, you could play the audio again while Sts read the audioscript on *page 122*, so they can see what they understood / didn't understand. Translate / explain any new words or phrases.

d Do this as an open-class activity.

6 GRAMMAR narrative tenses, past perfect continuous

a Focus on the newspaper article and tell Sts that this is a true story from a British newspaper. Now focus on the task and make sure Sts know the meaning of *incident*.

Set a time limit for Sts to read the story and answer the question. Tell them not to worry about 1–9 in the story.

Check the answer.

An emergency announcement saying the plane had to make an emergency landing on water was played by mistake.

b Get Sts to read the article again and this time they should circle the right form of the verbs in 1–9.

Check answers.

1 took off
2 came out
3 broke out
4 was screaming
5 had been played
6 were trying
7 had happened
8 was
9 said

c In pairs, Sts look at the two sentences and discuss the difference between the highlighted verbs.

Check answers.

1 had flown (The pilot flew this route many times *before* this particular flight.)
2 had been flying (The flight started three hours before the announcement was made.)

d 2 8))) 2 9))) Tell Sts to go to **Grammar Bank 3A** on *page 136*. Focus on the example sentences and play the audio for Sts to listen to the sentence rhythm. You could also get Sts to repeat the sentences to practice getting the rhythm right. Then go through the rules with the class.

Additional grammar notes

rules 1–3: narrative tenses

- This should all be review for Sts at this level.

rule 4: past perfect continuous

- This will probably be new for most Sts. It has the same form as the present perfect continuous except that *had* is used instead of *have* / *has*.

past perfect simple or continuous?

- As with the present perfect simple and continuous, you often have to use one or the other. However, again, there are some instances where either can be used, but with a difference in meaning.
- In the examples given in the box, highlight that *she'd been reading a book* = she may have just finished or still be reading the book. *She'd read the book* = she has definitely finished the book.

Focus on the exercises and get Sts to do them individually or in pairs.

Check answers, getting Sts to read the full sentences.

a
1 were checking in
2 had won
3 had been looking forward to
4 had forgotten
5 had arrived
6 ran
7 went
8 was filling in
9 hurried
10 got

b
1 'd / had been waiting
2 had stolen
3 'd / had been raining
4 'd / had left, 'd / had had to
5 'd / had changed
6 'd / had been sitting; hadn't put on
7 had been arguing
8 'd / had fallen
9 'd / had never seen
10 had you been walking

Tell Sts to go back to the main lesson **3A**.

Extra support

- If you think Sts need more practice, you may want to give them the Grammar photocopiable activity at this point or leave it for later as consolidation or review.

e Focus on the task and get Sts to work either in pairs or groups of three. Set a time limit and remind Sts that they have to try to use the four different narrative tenses in the endings.

Get feedback and accept all correct meaningful sentences.

Some possible ways to complete the sentences

1
...was speeding.
...wasn't wearing a seat belt.
...had gone through a red traffic light.
...had been using his cell phone.

2
...it was very hot.
...I was feeling stressed.
...I had drunk too much coffee after dinner.
...I had been watching a scary movie.

7 PRONUNCIATION irregular past forms, sentence rhythm

Pronunciation notes

- This exercise focuses on commonly mispronounced irregular past verb forms. Sometimes Sts at this level still have some ingrained pronunciation problems with some of the trickier irregular past and past participle forms, e.g., the *-ought* / *-aught* endings.
- There is also a focus on sentence rhythm with narrative tenses and Sts get the opportunity to practice reading a short paragraph.

a Focus on the picture words and elicit the eight sounds.

Then focus on the simple past verb in column C and elicit that it has the same vowel sound. Do the same with the verb in column H.

Now get Sts to look at all the verbs in the list, think of the simple past form for each one, and write it in the correct column.

Extra support

- Check the answers to **a** before doing **b** by getting Sts to spell the verbs to you. Or get Sts to do **a** and **b** in pairs.

b Now tell Sts to look at all the verbs in **a** again and decide which have a past participle form which is *not* the same as the simple past form. They must then write the past participles in the chart as well. You could do the first one with them (*become*, which should go in column H).

Get Sts to compare answers.

c **2 10** Now play the audio for Sts to listen and check.

Check spelling by writing the verbs on the board in a chart.

2 10

boot /uː/	flew, threw
fish /ɪ/	hid
saw /ɔ/	caught, fought, thought
bird /ər/	heard, hurt
phone /oʊ/	drove, rode, told, wrote
up /ʌ/	cut
egg /ɛ/	fell, held, kept, left, read, said, slept
train /eɪ/	became, lay

Remind Sts that:

– verbs ending in *-aught* are pronounced exactly the same as ones which end in *-ought*, e.g., *caught*, *fought*, *thought*.

– the *ea* in *read* is irregular and pronounced /ɛ/.

Play the audio again, pausing after each group of words, and get Sts to listen and repeat.

Extra idea

- At this point, or perhaps at the end of the lesson, you may want to review other common irregular verbs. Refer Sts to the **Irregular verbs** list on *page 165* and explain that this is their reference list. Get Sts to go through the list quickly in pairs, checking that they know what the verbs mean. Encourage them to highlight verbs they didn't know or whose past forms they had forgotten. Test the class or get Sts to test each other. You could use audio 5.46 to drill the pronunciation of the irregular verbs.

N.B. The audio for the Irregular verbs list is available as MP3 on CD1 of the class audio CDs.

d 2 11 Tell Sts they are going to practice sentence rhythm now. Tell them to listen to the extract and notice that the larger words are stressed and the others aren't. Remind Sts that the stressed words are the longer "content" ones (e.g., verbs and nouns) – the ones that convey important information.

Play the audio once all the way through for Sts just to listen.

2 11
See extract in Student Book on *page 27*

e Put Sts in pairs and get them to practice reading the extract, concentrating on getting a good rhythm.

Get some Sts to read a sentence each to the class.

8 SPEAKING

a Put Sts into pairs, **A** and **B**, and tell them to go to **Communication *Flight stories***, **A** on *page 105*, **B** on *page 110*.

Tell Sts they are each going to read a true story about a flight. Go through the instructions and make sure Sts know what they have to do.

Give Sts time to read and retell their stories.

Then do **d** and find out the two details the stories have in common.

They both happened in the US and nobody died.

Extra support

- You could write any new and useful words and phrases from **Communication** on the board for Sts to copy.

Tell Sts to go back to the main lesson **3A**.

b Look at the task and go through the instructions with the class.

Then focus on the **Telling an anecdote** box and go through it with the class.

Tell Sts to look at the topics and to choose one. If they have a real story, they can tell it as it happened. If not, they should make up the details. Later, their partner will have to decide if he / she thinks the story was true or not.

Give Sts plenty of time to plan their stories and go around checking whether they need any help with vocabulary.

Extra support

- Tell one of the stories yourself first and elicit responses and questions from the class. Then ask Sts if they think the story is true or made up.

c Put Sts in pairs, **A** and **B**. Sts **A** start by telling his / her story and **B** should show interest and ask for more information.

Monitor and help, correcting any misuse of narrative tenses and encouraging the listener to listen actively.

Extra support

- Tell Sts to look back at *page 5* to remind them of ways of reacting to what someone says.

When **A** has finished telling his / her story, **B** must guess whether or not it is true.

Sts then switch roles.

Get some Sts to tell their stories to the class. Help with any general vocabulary problems that come up.

9 2 12 SONG *The Airplane Song* ♫

This song was originally made famous by the English band Scouting for Girls in 2007. For copyright reasons, this is a cover version. If you want to do this song in class, use the photocopiable activity on *page 231*.

2 12
The Airplane Song

She's a strawberry milkshake
She's as sweet as a peach
But she's ice cold
She never told me she was leaving
She left on a Friday
I went out for the day
And she left for the year
She never told me she was leaving

Chorus
So get yourself on my aeroplane, 'cos it's been far too long since you went away
Get yourself on my aeroplane, 'cos it's been far too long since you went away
She's so extraordinary
She left last January
And that's the reason I miss you so

She's a messy creation
She hit the road, but the road hit back
Nobody told me you're an island
I will wait for a lifetime
I've been counting the days since you left one-way
Nobody reaches her island

Chorus

So give me a chance
I want you to know
I won't love you and leave you
And then let you go

I need to sort myself out
Can somebody show me the way?

And nobody knows the way (x3)
And nobody knows there's a way

Nobody knows

You gotta give me a chance
And say you'll come home
I won't love you and leave you
And then let you go
Your always hard on yourself

But nobody knows there's a way
And nobody knows the way (x3)
And nobody knows there's a way

Nobody knows the right way

Get yourself on the aeroplane, 'cos it's been far too long since you went away (x6)
She's so extraordinary
She left last January
And that's the reason I miss you so

G the position of adverbs and adverbial phrases
V adverbs and adverbial phrases
P word stress and intonation

3B Incredibly short stories

Lesson plan

The topic of this lesson is stories and reading.

The lesson starts with a grammar focus on adverbs and adverbial phrases, and their position in sentences, which is presented through four 50-word stories with a twist. This is followed by a vocabulary focus on certain pairs of adverbs which are often confused, and in Pronunciation the focus is on word stress and emphatic intonation on certain adverbs. Sts then write their own 50-word stories, and go to the **Writing Bank** to prepare for writing longer stories.

In the second half of the lesson, Sts begin by talking about their reading habits, or about why they don't read for pleasure. They then read and listen to an American short story by O. Henry. The ending of the story is on the audio, in order to create more suspense.

STUDY LINK
- **Workbook** 3B
- **Online Practice**
- **iChecker**

Extra photocopiable activities

- **Grammar** adverbs and adverbial phrases *page 156*
- **Communicative** Tell the story *page 193* (instructions *page 181*)
- **Vocabulary** Adverbs and adverbial phrases *page 216* (instructions *page 210*)

Optional lead-in – the quote

- Write the quote at the top of *page 28* on the board (books closed) and the name of the person who said it, or get Sts to open their books and read it.
- You could elicit / tell Sts that Orson Welles (1915–1985) is most famous for his movie *Citizen Kane* (1941), which he directed and starred in.
- Ask Sts what they think Welles was trying to say.

1 GRAMMAR

the position of adverbs and adverbial phrases

a Focus on the title of the lesson and on the name of the website. Explain that the stories submitted to the website have to tell a story in exactly 50 words.

Now focus on the task and make sure Sts understand the four titles.

Set a time limit for Sts to read the stories and tell them to use the pictures and the **Glossary** to help them.

Check answers.

A In the cards	C Generation gap
B Good intentions	D The story of my life

Get Sts to say what they think each story is about. Do story 1 with the whole class. Elicit the story from Sts by asking, e.g., *Who are the characters?* (a woman, a man, and a fortune-teller), *What did the fortune-teller warn the woman about?* (that she'd have no future with the man) *How long had it been since the woman had first met the man?* (five years) *Why did the woman feel happy?* (because she was finally going to meet him in New York.)

Then get Sts to explain the other three stories in pairs.

Get feedback, encouraging Sts to use their own words to explain each story. Find out which story they most / least enjoyed.

b Focus on the instructions and go through the four categories of adverbs. Make sure Sts understand the categories by focusing on the examples.

Get Sts to write the adverbs in the chart individually or in pairs.

If Sts worked alone, get them to compare with a partner and then check answers.

Time	*immediately, five minutes later, last year*
Manner	*frantic, normally*
Degree	*unbelievably extremely, slightly*
Comment	*unfortunately*

c Explain that one of the problems with adverbs is where to put them in a sentence and elicit / explain that there are three possible positions: at the beginning or end of the phrase / sentence, or in the middle (usually before the main verb). Tell Sts that although the rules may seem a bit complicated, they will probably have a good instinct for where adverbs should go, and to try to see which position sounds best.

In pairs, Sts put the adverbs in the sentences.

Check answers.

1 He speaks Chinese and Spanish **fluently**.
2 I **hardly ever** use public transportation.
3 I thought I'd lost my phone, but **fortunately** it was in my bag.
4 It's **extremely** important that you arrive on time.
5 As soon as I know, I'll tell you **right away**.

d 2 13 Tell Sts to go to **Grammar Bank 3B** on *page 137*. Focus on the example sentences and play the audio for Sts to listen to the sentence rhythm. You could also get Sts to repeat the sentences to practice getting the rhythm right. Then go through the rules with the class.

Additional grammar notes

the position of adverbs

- This is an area of grammar where practice and Sts' own instinct as to what sounds right will probably be more useful in the long run than memorizing rules. A useful tip to tell Sts is that with adverbs that don't end in *-ly* (e.g., *even, just*, etc.), if in doubt, to put them in mid-position, e.g., before the main verb.

rule 1: adverbs of manner

- In spoken English, adverbs of manner usually go after the verb or verb phrase, e.g., *He opened the door quietly*. However, in written English, e.g., a novel, they are sometimes used before the verb for dramatic effect, e.g., *He quietly opened the door and came in. Jane quickly explained why she was leaving.*
- You could give Sts some more examples of adverbs of manner in passive sentences: *Their house is beautifully designed. It's a well-written story.*

Focus on the exercises and get Sts to do them individually or in pairs.

Check answers, getting Sts to read the full sentences.

a
1 very much ✗ She liked the present very much.
2 very ✗ Mark came home very late last night.
3 after a few minutes ✓
4 badly ✗ A young man was badly injured and was taken to hospital.
5 extremely ✓
6 a little bit ✗ She's a little bit lazy about doing her homework.
7 almost ✗, fortunately ✓ I almost forgot your birthday...
8 luckily ✗, just after ✓ Luckily, we had taken an umbrella...
9 always, healthily, often ✓
10 apparently ✗ Apparently, Jack has been fired.

b
1 Their house was badly damaged in the fire last week.
2 Ben is often at his friend's house in the evening.
3 My father usually takes a nap in the afternoon.
4 Julia left early and she didn't even say goodbye.
5 Martin always talks incredibly fast.
6 Apparently, his brother nearly died in a skiing accident.
7 We're probably going to the movies tonight.
8 I rarely send emails nowadays.
9 I've just bought a really beautiful new coat.
10 Eventually, Karen realized that she was never going to learn to drive.

Tell Sts to go back to the main lesson **3B**.

Extra support

- If you think Sts need more practice, you may want to give them the Grammar photocopiable activity at this point or leave it for later as consolidation or review.

e 2 14 This is an oral grammar practice activity. Focus on the instructions and tell Sts the sound effects will tell them what is happening in each situation and they then need to complete each sentence using the adverb in bold. Demonstrate by playing the audio and pausing after 1.

Now continue, pausing the audio each time for Sts to write the sentences. Play each sound effect again if necessary.

Check answers.

Possible answers
1 ...had just gone.
2 ...suddenly the electricity went off / there was a power outage / when the lights suddenly went out, etc.
3 ...luckily he found it in his pocket.
4 ...they hardly know / knew each other.
5 ...it was raining (so) hard, etc.
6 ...he spoke / was speaking incredibly fast / quickly.

2 14

1 *sound effects*
2 *sound effects*
3 **Woman** Can I see your boarding pass?
Man Oh no, I lost it. Where is it? Where is it?
Woman I'm afraid you can't fly if you don't have your boarding pass.
Man Oh, here it is. Thank goodness, it was in my pocket.
4 **Woman** Tom, this is Andrea – but, of course, you two know each, don't you?
Tom Actually, we've only met once, so not really. Hi, Andrea.
Andrea Hello.
5 **Man** I can't see a thing. I think we'd better stop for a little bit.
6 **Juan** Excuse me. Please could you tell me how to get to the train station?
Taxi driver Sure, dude. Right down Main Street, left at the light, straight through the underpass, then it's right in front of you.
Juan *Pardon?*

2 VOCABULARY

adverbs and adverbial phrases

a Focus on the task and give Sts time to read the story.

Check the answer.

It is about a teacher who had to stay up late preparing an exam.

b Put Sts in pairs and get them to discuss the difference between the highlighted adverbs.

Check answers.

a *hard* = needing a lot of effort, *hardly* = almost not
b *near* = close, *nearly* = almost

c Tell Sts to go to **Vocabulary Bank *Adverbs and adverbial phrases*** on *page 155*.

Focus on **1 Confusing adverbs and adverbial phrases** and get Sts to do **a** individually or in pairs. Remind Sts to write in the column on the right side, not in the sentences.

2 15 Now do **b**. Play the audio for Sts to check answers. Practice any words your Sts find difficult to pronounce.

2 15

Adverbs and adverbial phrases

Confusing adverbs and adverbial phrases

1 He trains very **hard** – at least three hours a day.
It's incredibly foggy. I can **hardly** see anything.
2 I hate it when people arrive **late** for meetings.
I haven't heard from Mike **lately**. He must be very busy.
3 **At the end** of a movie I always stay and watch the credits roll.
I didn't want to go, but **in the end** they persuaded me.
4 I love most kinds of music, but **especially** jazz.
My wedding dress was **specially** made for me by a dressmaker.
5 She looks younger than me, but **actually** she's two years older.
Right now they're renting a house, but they're hoping to buy one soon.
6 I've **nearly** finished with my book. I'm on the last chapter.
Excuse me, is there a bank **near** here?
7 Have you found a job **yet**?
He's 35, but he **still** lives with his parents.
8 Have you **ever** been to the US?
I've been all over the US – I've **even** been to Alaska!

Highlight that:

– *actually* does not mean "now" or "at the present moment" (it's a false friend for some nationalities). It means "in fact" and is used to emphasize a fact or comment, or to say that something is really true.

– *especially* = above all (you can't use *specially* here) and *specially* is only used with a participle, e.g., *It's a specially designed umbrella* (NOT ~~*especially designed*~~).

– *at the end* = when something has finished, e.g., at the end of the class / movie etc. *In the end* = eventually, after a period of time or series of events or difficulties, e.g., *It took me two years, but in the end I passed my driving test.*

– *yet* goes at the end of a phrase and *still* in the mid position, e.g., *He hasn't found a job yet. He still hasn't found a job* (*still* = more emphatic).

Focus on **2 Comment adverbs** and get Sts to do **a** individually or in pairs.

2 16 Now do **b**. Play the audio for Sts to check answers. Play the audio again, pausing for Sts to repeat. Practice any words your Sts find difficult to pronounce.

2 16

Comment adverbs

1 ideally	4 obviously	7 anyway
2 in fact	5 gradually	8 eventually
3 basically	6 apparently	

Testing yourself

For **Confusing adverbs and adverbial phrases**, Sts can cover the column on the right, look at sentences 1–8, and see if they can remember the missing adverbs or adverbial phrases. For **Comment adverbs**, they can cover the definitions and try to remember the meaning of the bold adverbs.

Testing a partner

See **Testing a partner** *page 29*.

Tell Sts to go back to the main lesson **3B**.

Extra support

- If you think Sts need more practice, you may want to give them the Vocabulary photocopiable activity at this point or leave it for later as consolidation or review.

3 PRONUNCIATION word stress and intonation

Pronunciation notes

- Comment adverbs and adverbs of degree are often given extra stress and intonation in a sentence to add emphasis to their meaning, e.g., *It's* ***incredibly*** *easy* (extra emphasis and intonation on *incredibly*).

a **2 17** Focus on the adverbs and give Sts time to underline the stressed syllable.

Extra support

- Put Sts in pairs and get them to say each adverb out loud, so they can figure out which syllables are stressed.

Play the audio for Sts to listen and check.

Check answers by writing the adverbs on the board and underlining the stressed syllable.

See underlining in audioscript 2.17

2 17

actually, almost, apparently, basically, definitely, even, eventually, fortunately, gradually, ideally, incredibly, luckily, obviously, unfortunately

Extra support

- Play the audio again, pausing after each adverb for Sts to listen and repeat.

b **2 18** Play the audio once all the way through for Sts just to listen.

2 18

See sentences in the Student Book on *page 29*

Now play the audio again, pausing after each sentence for Sts to listen and repeat.

Then repeat the activity, eliciting responses from individual Sts.

4 WRITING

a If there is time, do this activity in class. If not, assign it for homework. Focus on the instructions.

Then put Sts in pairs and get them to choose two titles.

b Get Sts to think of their plots together.

Encourage them to write the first draft individually and tell them not to count the words yet.

c Now give Sts time to edit their stories together to get the right number of words. Remind them that they have to include at least two adverbs and that contracted forms (*I'm*, *don't*, etc.) count as one word.

Monitor and help as they write, suggesting ways they could cut down or expand their stories.

d When Sts have finished, get them to exchange stories with two other pairs.

Get some feedback.

Extra idea

- You could put corrected stories on the wall of your classroom or on your class website for other Sts to read.

e This second writing stage focuses on using the narrative tenses practiced in **Lesson A** and also on using adjectives and adverbs to make a story more vivid. Tell Sts to go to **Writing *A short story*** on *page 114*.

Focus on **a** and give Sts time to read the story and answer the two questions. Tell them not to worry about the blanks.

> He wrote an email which had a negative comment about his boss's wife in it and he accidentally sent it to his boss.
>
> He was fired.

Extra idea

- Ask Sts a few more questions about the story, e.g., *What company did he work for? Why didn't he like his boss's wife?*, etc.

Now focus on **b**. Remind Sts to think about both the meaning and the position of the blank when they are choosing which word to complete it with.

Check answers.

2 very	5 frequently	8 quick
3 well	6 new	9 immediately
4 aggressive	7 fond	10 An hour later

Focus on the instructions in **c**. Remind Sts that in a story they can either use reported speech or direct speech, e.g., dialogue, but that if they use dialogue, they must punctuate it properly.

Give Sts time to write out the sentence with the correct punctuation. Remind them to look at the dialogue in the story to help them.

Check answers either by getting a student to write the text with punctuation on the board or writing it yourself.

> "I want to talk to you about an email you sent," Mr. Simpson said coldly.

Highlight that quotation marks go outside other punctuation, e.g., periods and commas.

Look at **d**. Focus on the **Useful language: time expressions** box and give Sts time to complete the time expressions.

Check answers.

> 1 **At** that moment
> 2 As soon **as**
> 3 Ten minutes **later**
> 4 **One** morning in September
> 5 just **in** time

Focus on **e** and go through the instructions. Put Sts in pairs and give them time to choose which story to write and to discuss what the plot is going to be.

Focus on **f** and go through points 1–3 with the class. When looking at 1, make sure Sts do not think they have to write another story that is exactly 50 words.

Focus on **g**. If Sts wrote a 50-word story in class, it would probably be best to assign this longer one for homework.

In **h**, Sts should check their work for mistakes before turning it in.

Tell Sts to go back to the main lesson **3B**.

5 SPEAKING

a Put Sts in pairs and focus on the *Reading habits* questionnaire. Show Sts how, after the first section of questions, the questions are then divided into two groups depending on whether they answer *Yes* or *No* to the question *Do you read books for pleasure?* The last section (*Reading and listening*) is for all Sts to answer.

Make sure Sts understand all the text types, e.g., *comics*, *classics*, *manuals*, etc.

Put Sts in pairs and get them to interview each other. Monitor and encourage the student asking the questions to ask for more information when possible.

Sts then switch roles.

b In their pairs, Sts discuss how similar their reading habits are.

Help with any vocabulary problems that come up.

Get some feedback, and find out how many Sts in the class read for pleasure.

Extra idea

- You could ask the questions about reading in English to the class as a whole, e.g., *Do you ever read a novel, a paper, a comic, etc. in English? Do you read anything specifically to improve your English? Do you ever watch movies or TV in English with English subtitles? Do you ever read books and listen to them on audio at the same time, e.g., Graded Readers?* If Sts answer *yes*, ask them how useful they find it, etc.

6 READING & LISTENING

a **2 19** Tell Sts they are going to read and listen to a story in parts and then answer a few questions. You could tell them that the short story is by a famous US writer, O. Henry (1862–1910). The O. Henry Award is an important prize given each year for outstanding short stories.

Give Sts time to read questions 1–4 and also get them to look at the **Glossary**.

Now play **Part 1** on the audio while Sts read and listen at the same time.

Get Sts to discuss the questions with a partner.

Check answers and help with any vocabulary problems that come up.

> 1 She saved it by asking the grocer, the vegetable man, and the butcher to reduce the prices of the food she bought.
> 2 the shabby couch and the broken doorbell
> 3 to show how depressed Della is feeling
> 4 She doesn't have enough money to buy her husband a nice Christmas present.

> **2 19**
> See **Part 1** in Student Book on *page 30*

You could ask a few more comprehension questions, e.g., *What is Della's husband's name? How does Della feel about her husband?*

b 2 20 Focus on the **Glossary** and go through it with the class.

Give Sts time to read questions 1–6.

Play **Part 2** on the audio for Sts to listen.

Then give Sts time to see if they can answer some of the questions.

Play the audio again, pausing from time to time to give Sts time to answer the questions.

Get Sts to compare with a partner and then check answers.

1 his watch and her hair
2 to sell her hair to get money to buy Jim a Christmas present
3 sad at the thought of losing her hair, but then happy at the thought of the present she's going to buy Jim
4 twenty dollars
5 a chain for Jim's watch
6 because it's simple and elegant, quiet and valuable

2 20

(audioscript in Student Book on *page 122*)

Part 2

Della looked at herself in the mirror. She pulled down her hair and let it fall to its full length.

Now, there were two possessions that Jim and Della were very proud of. One was Jim's gold watch that had been his father's and his grandfather's. The other was Della's hair. It reached below her knee and made itself almost like a garment for her.

As she looked in the mirror she had an idea. She did her hair up again nervously and quickly. She hesitated for a minute and stood still while a tear or two fell on the worn red carpet.

But then she put on her old brown jacket; she put on her old brown hat. With a brilliant sparkle in her eyes, she danced out the door and down the stairs to the street.

Where she stopped the sign read: "Mme. Sofronie. Hair Goods of All Kinds." Della ran up one flight of stairs and then stopped, panting.

"Will you buy my hair?" asked Della.

"I buy hair," said Madame. "Take your hat off and let's take a look at it."

Down came the brown hair.

"Twenty dollars," said Madame, lifting the hair with her hand.

"Give it to me quick," said Della.

The next two hours sped by quickly. She hurried through the stores looking for Jim's present.

She found it at last. It surely had been made for Jim and no one else. There was no other like it in any of the stores, and she had turned them all inside out. It was a platinum chain, simple and elegant in design, As soon as she saw it she knew that it must be Jim's. It was like him. Quietness and value – the description applied to both Jim and the chain. She paid twenty-one dollars for the chain, and she hurried home with 87 cents.

You could ask a few more comprehension questions, e.g., *What was Della doing "nervously" and "quickly"? Why? Why did Della say, "Give it to me quick"?*

c 2 21 Tell Sts they are now going to read and listen to **Part 3**.

Give Sts time to read questions 1–5.

Play **Part 3** while Sts read and listen at the same time.

Get Sts to discuss the questions with a partner.

Check answers to 1–3 and elicit ideas for 4 and 5. Help with any other vocabulary problems that come up.

1 to try to make her short hair look better
2 that Jim won't find her beautiful any more
3 He doesn't show any emotion.

2 21

See **Part 3** in Student Book on *page 31*

You could ask a few more comprehension questions, e.g., *What question did Jim ask twice, using different words? Why does Jim look around the room "curiously"?*

d 2 22 Tell Sts that they are now going to hear the end of the story. Focus on the task.

Now play the audio once all the way through.

Get Sts to discuss what they understood and then play the audio again as necessary.

Now focus on the final two questions and elicit opinions.

Check answers.

They each gave up something important to buy the other a gift. They bought each other gifts that they could no longer use.

2 22

Part 4

Jim drew a package from his overcoat pocket and threw it upon the table.

"Don't make any mistake, Dell," he said, "about me. I don't think there's anything that could make me like my girl any less. But if you'll unwrap that package, you may see why I was upset at first."

Della tore at the string and paper. And then a scream of ecstatic joy; and then, alas! a quick change to hysterical tears and crying.

For there lay the set of combs that Della had really wanted. Beautiful combs, just the color to wear in her beautiful vanished hair. They were expensive combs, she knew, and her heart had longed for them without the least hope that she would ever own them. And now, they were hers, but the hair that the beautiful combs should have adorned was gone.

But she hugged them to her chest, and, at length, she was able to look up with dim eyes and a smile and say: "My hair grows so fast, Jim!"

And then Della jumped up. Jim had not yet seen his beautiful present. She held it out to him, "Isn't it dandy, Jim? I hunted all over town to find it. You'll have to look at the time a hundred times a day now. Give me your watch. I want to see how it looks on it."

Instead of obeying, Jim sat down on the couch and put his hands under the back of his head and smiled.

"Dell," he said, "let's put our Christmas presents away and keep `em a while. They're too nice to use right now. I sold the watch to get the money to buy your combs. And now, suppose you put the chops on."

Extra support

- If you photocopy audioscript 2.22 from here, Sts could read and listen to the whole story.

Extra support

- You could write any new and useful words / phrases from the text and audio on the board for Sts to copy.

2&3 Talking about books

Lesson plan

In the first part of this lesson, the person interviewed is Marion Pomeranc, a children's book author and the manager of a non-profit in New York City called Learning Leaders that encourages children to read.

In the second part of the lesson, people in the street are asked about children's books.

STUDY LINK

- **Workbook** Talking about...children's books
- **Online Practice**
- **iChecker**

Testing Program CD-ROM

- **File 3 Quick Test**
- **File 3 Test**

Optional lead-in (books closed)

- Write some characters from famous British and American children's books you think your Sts might have read and see if, in pairs, they can name the book:

1 CHRISTOPHER ROBIN
2 CAPTAIN HOOK
3 HERMIONE
4 LYRA AND WILL
5 PETER, SUSAN, EDMUND, AND LUCY
6 LAURA INGALLS

1 *Winnie-the-Pooh* by AA Milne
2 *Peter Pan* by J.M. Barrie
3 The Harry Potter series by JK Rowling
4 *His Dark Materials* trilogy by Philip Pullman
5 *The Lion, the Witch and the Wardrobe* by C.S. Lewis
6 *Little House on the Prairie* by Laura Ingalls Wilder

1 THE INTERVIEW Part 1

a Books open. Focus on the biographical information about Marion Pomeranc. Either read it out loud or give Sts time to read it.

Do the question as an open-class activity.

b 2 23 Play the DVD or audio (**Part 1**) once all the way through for Sts to do the task.

Check answers.

She mentions the four books because they are all important to her, either as a book she read as a child or a book she read with her own child.

2 23

(audioscript in Student Book on *page 122–123*)
I = interviewer, M = Marion Pomeranc

Part 1

M My name is Marion Pomeranc. I'm the manager of Literary Programs and a nonprofit in New York City called Learning Leaders, and I have also written three children's books.
I What was your favorite book when you were a child?
M My favorite book was *If I Ran the Circus* by Dr. Seuss. Um, it was the first book in my home that was for children. And it was just so exciting to have it, to hold it, to read it. And I still have it.
I What was it that you liked about Dr. Seuss?
M What I love about Dr. Seuss is his use of language. The words, the made-up words, the way the words flow together and sound. It just brought me to a different place. And, uh, loved that.
I Who read to you when you were a child, your mom or dad or both?
M My parents didn't speak English when I was growing up. They were, they were English learners as I was growing up. And I kind of helped them with language. And I think I introduced books to the home, really. Um, they became readers down the road.
I You have a son, right? Did you read to him?
M I have one son. And as a child, books were very important to me. And I think became important to him because of that. We read together every night. We read books like *Stella Luna* and *Corduroy* when he was young. And, and continued to read together, mostly fiction.
I How has writing for children changed over time, maybe in the last 50 years?
M I think books have changed in that authors are more cognizant of writing about real children and real issues. I grew up with stories like Nancy Drew, who lived in this fictional America where everyone was, everyone was white. And everyone had a Mommy and a Daddy. And, and, um, now they write about more honest and, uh, true stories of, of what children's lives are really like.
I And that's a good thing?
M And that's a great thing.

c Focus on the task and go through the **Glossary** with the Sts. Give Sts time to read sentences 1–5. Highlight that they have to correct the ones that are false.

Play the DVD or audio again all the way through.

Play again as necessary. You could get Sts to compare with a partner before checking answers.

Extra support

- You could pause the DVD or audio at the relevant places and, in pairs, get Sts to compare orally what they have understood before marking the sentences true or false.

1 F (She loved it for the use of language.)
2 T
3 T
4 F (Only Marion read to her son; her husband isn't much of a reader.)
5 F (Marion loves that children's books now deal with real-life situations.)

Part 2

a 2 24))) Focus on the task and play the DVD or audio (**Part 2**) once all the way through for Sts to listen and answer the questions.

You could get Sts to compare with a partner before checking answers.

In order to get teenagers to read more, it's important to give them more control over what they read. For small children, it's important to start them reading when they are very young and to have books in the home – and talk about them – from a very early age.

2 24)))

(audioscript in Student Book on *page 123*)

Part 2

I Do you have any thoughts about getting teenagers to read more?

M I do. I think teenagers would read if they were given more control over what they can read. If the choices were their own, and they weren't told what they had to read. If they were told they were allowed to put a book down and start something else. Um, and you can read anything. You can read the ads on the subway. You can read a magazine article. You can read the side of a cereal box. I mean that's all reading.

I Are there good authors or books in pop culture now whose material has encouraged teenagers to read?

M I think that these series books that are really popular these days have helped teenagers want to read. Like the *Twilight* series. The *Harry Potter series*. Kids like to go back, they like to become familiar with a, with a character in the story. And, and I think those books have been successful because of that.

I Going back to kids, what is the key to getting a very young person to start reading?

M I think to get a child to start reading, the key is really to starting when they're young. Have books around your home. Have a library card. Um, share the books that you read with them. Talk about the books the, at, at, at dinner. Know what they're reading, and talk about their books. Take a trip to a publishing house. And, and see what goes into making a book. Meet an author, if you can do that. Go to, go to a bookstore and have someone, hear someone who's written a book talk about a book. I think you have to just get the excitement of books across. If you're excited about books you'll get, they'll get excited about books.

I What kind of books do you think young people enjoy reading?

M The kind of books that children like to read are books maybe with a little s-, subversion in them. Books where maybe the adults are a little goofy, and the kids solve the problems. Children want to relate. They want to feel they have a little bit of power. I think young children feel that way, middle-schoolers feel that way. And I think if you'd look carefully at books that kids really like, it's the one where, where youth dominates. And, uh, kind of rules the world a little bit.

b Focus on the sentences and the **Glossary**. Now give Sts time, in pairs, to see if they can remember any of the answers and check the boxes before they listen again.

Play the DVD or audio again all the way through.

Play again as necessary.

You could get Sts to compare with a partner before checking answers.

Extra support

- You could pause the DVD or audio at appropriate places and, in pairs, get Sts to compare orally what they have understood.

Checked boxes for *Teenagers*: 1, 4, and 5
Checked boxes for *Children*: 1, 2, and 4

Part 3

a 2 25))) Focus on the task and give Sts time to read the question.

Play the DVD or audio (**Part 3**) once all the way through for Sts to do the task.

Discuss the answer as a whole-class activity.

Marion is positive about technology and the future of books.

2 25)))

(audioscript in Student Book on *page 123*)

Part 3

I Do you prefer paper books or e-books, and why?

M So I now prefer to read books on an e-reader, on my Kindle. I, I have tons of books in my house. And I haven't bought a book in 3 years. I only read on my Kindle. And, and love it. Because it's, to me it's more intimate than a book. I've chosen the type of print. And so it's just me and the word. And, and the fact that I can carry 100 books with me at all times is a thrill.

I Do you think e-readers are helpful for kids or teens who want to get into reading?

M I think it would be wonderful for every child to have an e-reader. We're, we're a technological society. And we're used to pushing buttons, and getting things instantly. And I think it might be really helpful for children to, to have their own e-readers and, and start their own collection of books that way. And you can see every book you've read. And you can go back to it in 2 seconds. So why not?

I Do you think social media has decreased or increased people's literacy?

M So I, I think social media has had a positive effect on children. I think they're exposed to many, many more things. They can go online and get information on just about anything. I, I'm not afraid of the changes that any kind of social media brings to kids. They have to read, they have to write. Maybe they'll read a few less books. But maybe they'll write some amazing things about their adventures online. I, I think it's great.

I Do you think, despite all the technology, books will survive?

M Yes. I think there's a great future for books. I think they'll be around for a long time. I think we all like to have our moments with a book. So sure.

I Do you still read for pleasure, and if so, how much?

M I read daily. I read on the subway. I read before I go to sleep. I read to relax. I'm usually reading 3 or 4 books at a time. Whatever pleases me, I go to. I'm always reading.

b Focus on the task and give Sts time to read sentences 1–4.

Play the DVD or audio again all the way through.

Play again as necessary.

You could get Sts to compare with their partner before checking answers.

Extra support

- You could pause the DVD or audio at appropriate places and, in pairs, get Sts to compare orally what they have understood.

1 She can choose the type and it makes it more intimate. She can carry 100 books with her at all times.
2 She thinks it would be great for children to have an e-reader because they can get a book instantly and start their own collections of books.
3 Social media is positive for children because it exposes them to many things; gets them reading and writing about all kinds of topics.
4 Marion reads all the time, for pleasure, to relax, before she goes to sleep. She is often reading 3-4 books at once.

Extra support

- If there's time, you could play the DVD or audio again while Sts read the audioscripts on *pages 122–123*, so they can see what they understood / didn't understand. Translate / explain any new words or phrases.

2 LOOKING AT LANGUAGE

2 26 This exercise focuses on a common feature of speech – giving yourself time to think. Focus on the **Ways of giving yourself time to think** box and go through it with the class. You could ask Sts if they do the same in their own language and in a monolingual class, if you know the Sts' L1, you could elicit examples of this.

Focus on the task and give Sts time to read extracts 1–5.

Play the DVD or audio, pausing after each extract to give Sts time to write.

You could get Sts to compare with their partner before checking answers.

Extra challenge

- Ask Sts if they can remember any of the missing words or phrases before they listen to the extracts.

1 What I love	2 The words	3 I mean
4 kind of	5 So I	

Extra support

- You could get Sts to read completed sentences 1–5 out loud to give them practice using the ways of giving yourself time to think.

2 26

1 I: What was it that you liked about Dr Seuss?
M: What I love about Dr Seuss is his use of language...
2 The words, the made-up words, the way the words flow together and sound.
3 You can read the side of a cereal box. I mean, that's all reading.
4 And I think if you'd look carefully at books that kids really like, it's the one where, where youth dominates. And kind of rules the world a little bit.
5 I: Do you think social media has decreased or increased people's literacy?
M: So I, I think social media has had a positive effect on children.

3 VIDEO ON THE STREET

a 2 27 Focus on the task and find out if any Sts have read any of the books either in English or in their own language.

Play the DVD or audio once all the way through.

Check answers.

Coraline R
Where the Wild Things Are J
The Lion, The Witch, and The Wardrobe S
The *Trixie Beldon* book series J

2 27

(audioscript in Student Book on *page 123*)
I = interviewer, J = Jill, S = Sean, R = Rachel

JILL
I What was your favorite book when you were a child?
J Um...I think my favorite book when I was a child probably is *Where the Wild Things Are.*
I Why did you like it so much?
J I think I liked it because of the fantasy aspects and it was just a creative book. And I think a lot kids like it for that reason.
I Did you see the movie?
J No, I did not see the movie, unfortunately. I should, so...
I Was there a character in a children's book that you identified with?
J Well, I used to read a book series called *Trixie Belden.* Trixie Belden was sort of a teenage or young teen mystery person. And she was very curious and very...liked to solve mysteries. And I always fashioned that, you know, I would too, as well, so...

Sean
I What was your favorite book when you were a child?
S Probably *The Lion, The Witch, and The Wardrobe.*
I Why did you like it so much?
S Um, I remember we had a teacher at school who read it aloud to us, and um, when I was probably six or seven, when I was too young to read it myself, um, and I remember getting the book and then sitting down by myself and reading it. I think it was the first time I realized how much you could get out of a book, I think.
I Was there a character in a children's book that you identified with?
S I can't think of any specific characters. I think I was quite a scruffy child. I always had dirty knees and torn clothes and things like that, so whenever there was a boy who got into lots of trouble, I usually thought that was a little bit like me, but I can't think of one particular one.

Rachel
I What was your favorite book when you were a child?
R I think that...I think *Coraline* by Neil Gaimen was my favorite.
I Why did you like it so much?
R I liked the writing style. A lot of books just sort of have a wall of text that's hard to absorb, but I thought it was easier to read.
I Was there a character in a children's book that you identified with?
R I identified with Coraline because I tend to be curious about stuff. And also because in a lot of those sorts of books that I like, unfortunately, the protagonists are usually male.

b Focus on the task and give Sts time to go through the six questions, making sure Sts understand *imaginative situations* in the sixth question.

Play the DVD or audio again all the way through, pausing after each speaker to give Sts time to do the task. Play again as necessary.

Check answers.

Rachel liked *Coraline* because there wasn't a "wall of text," and that made it easier to read.
Sean heard a teacher at school read *The Lion, The Witch, and The Wardrobe* before he read it.
Jill identified with a character in a book series called *Trixie Belden.*
Sean identified with children in books who were always getting into trouble.
Rachel identified with the character of Coraline because she was a girl protagonist.
Jill liked *Where the Wild Things* Are because of the fantasy aspects and the creativity of the book.

c 2 28 This exercises focuses on some colloquial expressions which were used by the speakers. Focus on the phrases and give Sts time to read them.

Play the DVD or audio, pausing after each sentence to give Sts time to write the missing words. Play the audio again as necessary.

Check answers, eliciting the missing word and then the meaning of the whole phrase.

See words in **bold** in audioscript 2.28

2 28

1 Trixie Belden was sort of a teenage or **young teen** mystery person.
2 I remember we had a teacher at school who read it **aloud** to us...
3 I realized how much you could get **out** of a book, I think.
4 ...so whenever there was a boy who got into lots of **trouble**...
5 I identified with Coraline because I tend to be curious about **stuff**.

Extra support

- Tell Sts to go to *page 123* and to look at the audioscript for **ON THE STREET**. Play the DVD or audio again and tell Sts to read and listen at the same time.

Help with any vocabulary problems and get feedback from Sts on what parts they found hard to understand and why, e.g., speed of speech, pronunciation, etc.

4 SPEAKING

Put Sts in pairs and get them to ask and answer the questions, giving as much information as possible.

Monitor and help with vocabulary. Help with any general language problems at the end of the activity.

Get some feedback.

G future perfect and future continuous
V the environment, the weather
P vowel sounds

4A Eco-guilt

Lesson plan

The topic of this lesson is the environment.

The first half of the lesson begins with a quiz to see how eco-guilty Sts are (e.g., feeling guilty when you leave the tap running because you know it wastes water). The grammar focus is on two tenses which will be new for most Sts: the future perfect and future continuous.

In the second half of the lesson, Sts expand their weather vocabulary by reading an article and going to a **Vocabulary Bank**. The pronunciation focus is on combinations of vowels which can be pronounced in different ways, e.g., *ea* and *oo*. After listening to three people talking about their experiences of extreme weather in the US, Sts talk about their own experiences. The lesson ends with the song, *Heatwave*.

STUDY LINK
- **Workbook** 4A
- **Online Practice**
- **iChecker**

Extra photocopiable activities
- **Grammar** future perfect and continuous *page 157*
- **Communicative** In 20 years *page 194* (instructions *page 181*)
- **Vocabulary** Weather *page 217* (instructions *page 211*)
- **Song** *Heatwave page 232* (instructions *page 227*)

Optional lead-in – the quote
- Write the quote at the top of *page 34* on the board (books closed) and the name of the person who said it, or get Sts to open their books and read it.
- Ask Sts what they think Eddison was saying in the quotation and whether they agree with him.

1 READING & SPEAKING

a Focus on the title, *Eco-guilt*, and elicit what Sts think it means. Don't tell them yet if they are right or not.

b Now give Sts time to read the introduction to the article to check their answer in **a**.

Get Sts to compare with a partner and then check the answer.

> Eco-guilt is what people feel when they do something that they know they shouldn't do because it is bad for the environment.

Now get Sts to do the questionnaire, checking the sentences that are true for them, and adding up their score as they go along.

c Put Sts in pairs. Get them to compare their answers and the meaning of their scores.

Get some feedback from the class. Have Sts raise their hands to find out how many belong to each group.

Help with any general vocabulary problems that come up, and encourage Sts to write down any new lexis from the questionnaire.

2 GRAMMAR

future perfect and future continuous

a Focus on the photo and ask Sts what they can see (wind turbines, an electric car, solar panels, a snow cannon to create artificial snow, etc.). Elicit / explain that the red things on the roof are wind cowls, which provide ventilation into homes while minimizing heat loss.

Now focus on the instructions. Tell Sts to read the predictions and put each one into categories 1–3.

Get them to compare their ideas with a partner.

Elicit some opinions from the class.

b Now get Sts to read the predictions again, choose their two predictions, and compare with a partner.

Then ask the question to the whole class and get feedback.

c Focus on the instructions. In pairs, Sts should look at the highlighted verbs in the predictions and decide whether they refer to an action or situation that will be finished or still in progress in the future.

Check answers.

> a *will have installed, will have been banned, will have disappeared, will have risen, will have closed, will have disappeared*
> b *will be recycling, will be driving, will be running out, will be getting, will be having*

Elicit / explain the basic difference between the future perfect and the future continuous:

– the future perfect + time expression = an action will be finished (at the latest) by that time

– the future continuous + time expression = an action will be in progress at that future time

Highlight that *by* + time expression = that time at the latest

d 2 29))) 2 30))) Tell Sts to go to **Grammar Bank 4A** on *page 138*. Focus on the example sentences and play the audio for Sts to listen to the sentence rhythm. You could also get Sts to repeat the sentences to practice getting the rhythm right. Then go through the rules with the class.

Additional grammar notes

- Although Sts will probably have seen these two tenses passively in reading, they are probably not yet part of their active knowledge.
- If Sts have the same or similar tense in their L1, it will be worth drawing comparisons. If not, then you will need to make sure the concept is clear. Both tenses are projections in the speaker's mind into the future.
- If we use **the future perfect** instead of the simple future, we are **emphasizing the certain completion of the action**. However, the difference between the two tenses is often quite small.
- The future continuous, though often used for an action in progress at a future time, is also very commonly used as an alternative to *going to* or the present continuous to ask about future plans or arrangements, e.g., *Will you be going out this evening?*

Focus on the exercises and get Sts to do them individually or in pairs.

Check answers, getting Sts to read the full sentences. You could get two strong Sts to read the dialogue in **b** out loud.

a
1 'll / will be flying
2 'll / will have saved
3 'll / will be driving
4 'll / will be having
5 'll / will have paid
6 'll / will have finished
7 'll / will have written
8 'll / will be working out
9 'll / will have downloaded

b
1 won't be lying
2 'll / will be working
3 will have disappeared
4 will have doubled
5 will have moved
6 will have grown
7 will have run out
8 will have invented
9 'll / will be flying

Tell Sts to go back to the main lesson **4A**.

Extra support

- If you think Sts need more practice, you may want to give them the Grammar photocopiable activity at this point or leave it for later as consolidation or review.

e This is an oral practice activity. Focus on the ***definitely, probably,* and *likely* / *unlikely*** box and go through it with the class. Point out that the opposite of *likely* is *unlikely*, which is often used instead of *not likely*, e.g., *He's unlikely to come now.* / *He isn't likely to come now.* However, we don't use *improbably*. Instead we say *probably not*, e.g., *He probably won't come now.*

Now focus on the first prediction, ask the class what they think, and elicit ideas.

Get Sts to continue in pairs.

Monitor and help Sts, correcting any mistakes with future forms.

Get some feedback.

Extra idea

- You could elicit some more personalized oral practice with the futures by asking individual Sts: *What will you be doing a) in two hours? b) this time tomorrow? When do you think you will have finished all of your classes?*, etc.

3 READING & VOCABULARY the weather

a Focus on the cartoon and ask the two questions to the class.

b Focus on the task and questions.

Give Sts time to read the article and answer the questions. You might want to point out the **Glossary** to the Sts.

Get them to compare with a partner and then check answers.

The Santa Ana winds blow in Los Angeles, California.
The Santa Ana winds can make people feel nervous or angry.

c Focus on the task and give Sts time to read sentences 1–6.

Get Sts to read the article again, mark each sentence T (true) or F (false), and underline the part of the article that gave them the answer.

Get Sts to compare with a partner and then check answers.

1 F (Line 15: ..."We've noticed an increase in anger and irritability after prolonged exposure.")
2 T (Line 17: "In addition, thyroid hormones are particularly susceptible to changes in temperature.")
3 T (Line 22: "...March 2008, we'd had over 16 feet of snow," says Catherine Viel, with the Québec City Police. "During that month, we had several incidents...")
4 F (Line 27: ...from 1950 to 1995, rates of serious assaults were higher during hotter years, according to research...)
5 T (Line 33: They predicted at least 115,000 additional serious and fatal assaults a year in the United States due to global warming.)
6 F (Line 36: "...springtime, sunny days and warm weather seem to boost mood and have a broadening effect on cognition, basically opening the mind to new ideas...")

d Focus on the highlighted words and phrases related to the weather. Get Sts, in pairs, to guess their meaning. Tell them to read the whole sentence as the context will help them guess.

Check answers, either explaining in English, translating into Sts' L1, or getting Sts to check in their dictionaries.

Help with any other new vocabulary and encourage Sts to write down any useful new lexis from the article.

e Tell Sts to go to **Vocabulary Bank *Weather*** on *page 156*.

Focus on **1 What's the weather like?** and point out that the phrases in the top row refer to not very cold / hot / rainy / windy weather, and the phrases in the bottom row refer to very cold / hot / rainy / windy weather.

Get Sts to do **a** and **b** individually or in pairs.

2 31 Now do **c**. Play the audio for Sts to check answers to **a** and **b**. Play the audio again, pausing for Sts to repeat. Practice any words your Sts find difficult to pronounce.

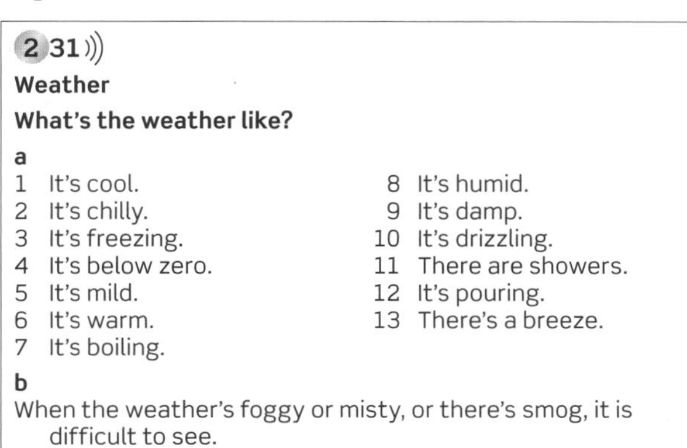
2 31

Weather

What's the weather like?

a

1 It's cool.	8 It's humid.
2 It's chilly.	9 It's damp.
3 It's freezing.	10 It's drizzling.
4 It's below zero.	11 There are showers.
5 It's mild.	12 It's pouring.
6 It's warm.	13 There's a breeze.
7 It's boiling.	

b

When the weather's foggy or misty, or there's smog, it is difficult to see.

Mist isn't usually very thick, and it often occurs in the mountains or near the ocean.

Fog is thicker and can be found in towns and in the country.

Smog is caused by pollution and usually occurs in big cities.

Highlight that with the weather it's important to be sure whether the word you are using is an adjective or a noun:

– compare: ***It's*** *windy* (adj) with ***There's a*** *strong wind* (n).

– the difference between *chilly* and *cool* is a question of how pleasant / unpleasant it is; 50° may be cool for one person and chilly for another. This may also vary depending on the part of the world where Sts are.

Focus on **2 Extreme weather** and get Sts to do **a** individually or in pairs.

2 32 Now do **b**. Play the audio for Sts to check answers. Play the audio again, pausing for Sts to repeat. Practice any words your Sts find difficult to pronounce.

2 32

Extreme weather

1 heat wave	6 blizzard
2 drought	7 flood
3 hail	8 hurricane
4 lightning	9 monsoon
5 thunder	

Focus on **3 Adjectives to describe weather** and get Sts to do **a** individually or in pairs.

2 33 Now do **b**. Play the audio for Sts to check answers. Play the audio again, pausing for Sts to repeat. Practice any words your Sts find difficult to pronounce.

2 heavy	6 bright
3 thick	7 changeable
4 icy	8 sunny
5 clear	9 settled

2 33

Adjectives to describe weather

In the western part of New York it will be very cold, with strong winds and heavy rain. There will also be thick fog in the hills and valleys, though it should clear by midday. Driving will be dangerous because the roads will be icy. However, the Hudson Valley and the tri-state area will have clear skies and it will be bright and sunny, though the temperature will still be low. Over the next few days the weather will be changeable, with some showers, but occasional sunny periods. It should become more settled over the weekend.

Point out that:

– despite having similar meanings, certain adjectives are only used with certain nouns, e.g., you can say *strong winds*, but not *strong rain* (you have to say *heavy rain*), and we say *bright sunshine* (not *strong sunshine*).

– *settled* is the opposite of *changeable*.

Testing yourself

For all the sections, tell Sts to look at the words in the lists and try to remember what kind of weather they are associated with.

Testing a partner

See **Testing a partner** *page 29*.

Tell Sts to go back to the main lesson **4A**.

Extra support

- If you think Sts need more practice, you may want to give them the Vocabulary photocopiable activity at this point or leave it for later as consolidation or review.

f Do this as an open-class activity.

4 PRONUNCIATION vowel sounds

Pronunciation notes

- The letters *ow* can be pronounced /aʊ/ or /oʊ/.
- The letters *ea* are usually pronounced /i/ or occasionally /ɛ/, e.g., *head*.
- The letter *i* between consonants is usually /ɪ/, but sometimes /aɪ/.
- The letters *oo* are usually pronounced /u/, but they are occasionally /ʌ/, e.g., in *blood* and *flood*.
- *ought* is usually /ɔt/ – *drought* is an exception.
- The letter *u* between consonants is usually /ʌ/, but can be /yu/, e.g., *music*.
- The letters *or* are usually pronounced /ɔr/, but /ər/ after *w*.

a Focus on the **Spelling and pronunciation** box and go through it with the class.

Then focus on the instructions. Encourage Sts to say the words out loud to help them to identify the one that is different.

b 2 34 Play the audio for Sts to listen and check.

Check answers by eliciting the word that sounds different.

1 showers	3 mild	5 flood	7 humid
2 heat	4 warm	6 drought	8 world

> **2 34**
> See groups of words in Student Book on *page 37*

Play the audio again, pausing after each group of words for Sts to listen and repeat.

Extra support

- You may want to give Sts the rules in the **Pronunciation notes**.

c **2 35** Focus on the task and tell Sts to first listen to the five sentences.

Play the audio once all the way through for Sts just to listen.

Then play it again, pausing after each sentence to give Sts time to write. Play the audio again as necessary.

Check answers by writing the sentences on the board.

> **2 35**
> 1 It'll be below zero tomorrow with some snow showers.
> 2 He was sweating heavily because of the heat.
> 3 It's windy, chilly, and starting to drizzle.
> 4 The river is going to flood soon.
> 5 Summer days are usually sunny and humid.

Give Sts a few minutes to practice saying the sentences.

d Focus on the questions, making sure Sts know the meaning of *mood* in the third bullet. They saw *moody* in **File 2B**.

Put Sts in pairs and get them to interview each other.

Get some feedback from various pairs. You could do the last question as a class. Help with any general vocabulary or pronunciation problems that come up.

5 LISTENING & SPEAKING

a **2 36** Focus on the photo and the task, and give Sts time to read the questions. The photo illustrates one of the stories.

Play the audio once all the way through for Sts to listen and then give them time to complete the task.

Check answers.

Extra support

- Before playing the audio, go through the audioscript and decide if you need to preteach / check any lexis to help Sts when they listen.

Speaker 1 was both relieved and scared by the weather.
Speaker 3 got stressed because of the weather.
Speaker 2 really enjoyed themselves in spite of the weather.

> **2 36**
> (audioscript in Student Book on *page 123*)
>
> **1** It was just at the end of the summer in 2013, yeah, and I was a college student at the University of Colorado in Boulder. It had been really dry that summer – hardly any rain at all, and it was incredibly hot. Then toward the end of September, the rain came, and it rained almost an entire week. At first, everyone was so relieved because the rain brought cooler temperatures and made the grass green. But then, it just kept raining and raining. Streams and creeks started flooding and roared out of the mountains, and it was really scary. The stream that goes through my college campus flooded several dorm buildings, and kids had to find safe places to stay. Some rooms had three to four feet of water in them!
> I was OK because I lived on a high floor in my dorm. Even though there was a lot of damage to the campus and to a lot of the towns surrounding Boulder, there was a bright side. Kids on the athletic teams served lunch to flood victims in the community. Other students donated their clothes, shoes, and books to kids who had lost their belongings in flooded dorm rooms. So...uh...even though the flooding was extremely severe, it really made me realize that we have a supportive college community here.
>
> **2** This was in the summer of 2003 and there was a pretty intense heat wave in New York City. I remember it really well because I'd just started working as an office assistant in a civil engineering firm – and I'd only been at my new job for a few weeks. Around 4 o'clock in the afternoon on August 14th, the electricity went out all across New York City. The massive blackout – caused in part by everyone using their air-conditioners—affected seven states in the eastern US along with parts of Canada. My boss told me to go home, so I did. First, I had to walk down 17 flights of stairs because the elevators didn't work. Then I had to walk nearly four miles from Manhattan to Brooklyn in the heat because the subways didn't work. Thank goodness I could walk over the Brooklyn Bridge to get back to Brooklyn! When I finally got home around eight in the evening, I was absolutely surprised and happy to see all my apartment building neighbors outside cooking on grills and getting to know one another. It was too hot to stay inside, so I enjoyed the evening sitting outside on the sidewalk with my neighbors. It's been over ten years since that blackout, and I have very fond memories of that day, but I don't really want to go through that experience again anytime soon!
>
> **3** On October 29, 2011, I was visiting friends in upstate New York when it started snowing. It's pretty unusual for snow to fall in New York during late October, but I was safe with my friends, so I didn't mind. The next day it was time for me to drive home. It had only snowed about three inches in Albany and the roads there were completely clear, so I thought my two-hour trip home would be uneventful.
> However, as I started driving south, I noticed the snow was getting deeper. Trees were bent over and many had fallen. Driving was rather stressful because the roads were slippery and dangerous.
> When I finally got home – almost five hours later – there was nearly two feet of snow on the ground and I couldn't drive up my driveway, which only added to my stress. I parked on the street and trudged up to my house, only to discover there was no electricity. I ended up booking a room in a local hotel for a week until work crews reconnected the electrical wires.
> That storm caused billions of dollars of damage across the northeast. Over three million people were without electricity, some for up to three weeks, and cities across the northeast reported record snowfall totals.
> In addition, many communities had to cancel or postpone Halloween celebrations. It wasn't safe for the children to walk in the snow. Luckily for me, no trees had fallen on my house during the storm, but I was mad that it took me several days to shovel my driveway.

b Focus on the task and the questions in the chart. You could get Sts to copy the chart in their notebooks, so they have enough space to take notes.

Now play the audio again for Sts to complete the task.

Pause the audio after each speaker to give Sts time to write. Play again as necessary.

You could get Sts to compare with a partner before checking answers.

Speaker 1
1 in the summer of 2013
2 University of Colorado in Boulder
3 a rainstorm/flood
4 There was a lot of damage to the campus and to a lot of the towns surrounding Boulder.

Speaker 2
1 in the summer of 2003
2 in New York City
3 a heatwave
4 There was a massive blackout, affecting seven states in the eastern US along with parts of Canada.

Speaker 3
1 October 29, 2011
2 Albany, NY
3 a snowstorm
4 That storm caused billions of dollars of damage across the northeast. Over three million people were without electricity.

Extra support

- If there's time, you could play the audio again while Sts read the audioscript on *page 123*, so they can see what they understood / didn't understand. Translate / explain any new words or phrases.

c Focus on the **Modifiers with strong adjectives** box and go through it with the class. Remind Sts that *really* can be used with both everyday adjectives, e.g., *It's really cold*, and strong adjectives, e.g., *It's really freezing*. Remind Sts too that we usually say these adjectives with extra stress and intonation.

Get Sts to focus on the situations and the three questions. Tell them to think about which situation they will talk about.

Put Sts in small groups of three and tell them to use the three questions to help them tell their story. One student starts by saying *I'm going to tell you about a time when…* (you could write this on the board as a prompt).

Monitor and correct any misuse of modifiers.

Help with any vocabulary problems that come up.

When Sts have finished, get feedback by eliciting one experience for each type of weather.

Extra support

- Demonstrate first by telling Sts about an experience of your own.

6 2.37 SONG *Heatwave* ♫

This song was originally made famous by American group Martha and the Vandellas in 1963. For copyright reasons, this is a cover version. If you want to do this song in class, use the photocopiable activity on *page 232*.

2.37

Heatwave

Whenever I'm with him
Something inside
Starts to burning
And I'm filled with desire
Could it be a devil in me?
Or is this the way love's supposed to be?

Chorus
It's like a heatwave
Burning in my heart
I can't keep from crying
It's tearing me apart

Whenever he calls my name
So softly and plain
Right then, right there, I feel that burning flame
Has high blood pressure got a hold on me?
Is this the way love's supposed to be?

Chorus
Sometimes I stare in space,
Tears all over my face
I can't explain it, don't understand it
I ain't never felt like this before
Now this funny feeling has me amazed
Don't know what to do, my head's in a haze
It's like a heatwave.

Yeah yeah
Yeah yeah
Ha ohhh yeah

Yeah yeah
Yeah yeah
ohhh yeah

I feel it, burning, right here in my heart,
Don't you know it's like a heatwave

Yeah yeah
Yeah yeah
ohhh

Yeah, don't you know it's like a heatwave?
Burning right here in my heart.

G zero and first conditionals, future time clauses
V expressions with *take*
P sentence stress and rhythm

4B Are you a risk taker?

Lesson plan

In this lesson, Sts expand their knowledge of future time clauses and real conditionals, and see the variety of tenses that can be used apart from the simple present and simple future. The topic is risk.

In the first half, Sts listen to six people answering the question *Are you a risk taker?* and they then interview each other to find out if they too are risk takers. This is followed by the grammar focus on conditionals, and in Pronunciation, Sts have more practice with sentence rhythm with conditionals.

In the second half of the lesson, Sts read an article from *The Sunday Times* about therapy classes for drivers who are addicted to speeding. This is followed by a listening on the risks of driving. The vocabulary focus is on common collocations with *take* (e.g., *take a risk*, *take seriously*), and finally Sts go to the **Writing Bank** to focus on "For and against" essays.

STUDY LINK
- **Workbook** 4B
- **Online Practice**
- **iChecker**

Extra photocopiable activities

- **Grammar** conditionals and future time clauses *page 158*
- **Communicative** Finish the sentences *page 195* (instructions *page 182*)

Optional lead-in – the quote

- Write the quote at the top of *page 38* on the board (books closed) and the name of the person who said it, or get Sts to open their books and read it.
- You might want to tell Sts that Mark Zuckerberg was born in 1984 in New York State and co-founded Facebook in 2004.
- Ask Sts whether they agree with his quote.

1 LISTENING & SPEAKING

a Focus on the photo and ask Sts if the photo makes them nervous. You might want to tell Sts that this is part of a photo by a South Korean artist, Ahn Jun, who has produced a series of photos of herself sitting on ledges on top of various buildings.

Now focus on the task. Go through the questions and elicit / explain the phrase *the edge of a precipice*. Model and drill the pronunciation of *precipice* /ˈprɛsəpəs/.

Give Sts a few minutes to discuss the questions with a partner.

Get some feedback.

b 2 38))) Focus on the task and the question.

Play the audio once all the way through for Sts to listen and do the task.

Check the answer.

Extra support

- Before playing the audio, go through the audioscript and decide if you need to preteach / check any lexis to help Sts when they listen.

Three people see themselves as risk takers (two women and one man).

2 38)))

(audioscript in Student Book on *pages 123–124*)

1 **Woman**
Yes, I think I am, or anyway more than I used to be. I think my attitude to risk has changed as I've gotten older. For example, I'm more open to risking a change in appearance because I think I'm less self-conscious now. I often change hairstyles and color, but when I was younger I had the same hairstyle for years and years. I also think I would take more risks traveling now because I'm more self-confident, so I'm pretty sure I could cope with any problems.

2 **Man**
Yes, I'm definitely a risk taker. I take risks to do things that I enjoy, like skiing, or riding a bike in New York City, which is pretty dangerous. In fact, I think the element of risk probably makes them even more enjoyable. The only time I wouldn't take a risk would be if I couldn't see that I was going to get any pleasure from it – I wouldn't do something risky just for the sake of it.

3 **Woman**
I'm the kind of person who likes to know exactly what I'm doing and when I'm doing it, so there's not much room for risk in my life. For me, risk means not being completely in control, and that can make me feel really nervous. For example, if I'm meeting a friend for dinner, I always make sure we have a table booked somewhere nice. I wouldn't risk just turning up and hoping that there was a table. And I never buy clothes online because I don't want to run the risk of them being the wrong size and having to send them back.

4 **Woman**
I'm definitely not a risk taker. I might like to think that I am because it seems exciting, but I'm not. I live in a suburb of Boston and I'd never walk home on my own in the evening when it's dark because that just seems like an unnecessary risk to take. And I'd never get into a taxi on my own at night. But on the other hand, I would love to do something like bungee jumping or paragliding, which other people would probably think is risky.

5 **Man**
I don't see myself as a risk taker. I've done a lot of mountain climbing, and everyone assumes because of this that I'm attracted to risk, but it isn't really true. In fact, when you're climbing high mountains you're always trying to minimize the risk. The biggest risk I've ever taken in my life was a professional one – after 20 years in the same job, I left and set up my own company – and that's given me a lot more sleepless nights than climbing in the Andes or the Himalayas.

6 **Woman**
I am happy to take risks. I love driving fast. In fact, I bought myself a sports car when I had some money and I got quite a few speeding tickets – though probably not as many as I deserved! I also take risks with money, like lending to people who probably won't pay me back, or spending all I have on something a little bit unnecessary. Last year I went on a balloon ride and I was amazed that so many people said, "Ooh, I wouldn't do that." I loved it and I'd happily do it again – it was fantastic!

c Tell Sts they will listen to the audio again and this time they must answer the six questions. Give them time to read the questions.

Play the audio again, pausing after each speaker. Then play again as necessary.

Check answers.

Speaker 2 says some activities are enjoyable because they are a little bit risky.
Speaker 1 thinks that her attitude to risk is different from what it was before.
Speaker 3 thinks that taking risks means losing control.
Speaker 6 had to pay some money because of her risky behavior.
Speaker 4 worries about her personal safety.
Speaker 5 does something that most people think of as very risky, but which he says is not.

d Focus on the task and the questions *What examples of risks do the speakers say they would take, or have taken? What things wouldn't they do?*.

Extra support

- Write the questions on the board in columns and get Sts to copy it:

  RISKS:
  WOULD TAKE/HAVE TAKEN? WOULDN'T DO?
  SPEAKER 1
  SPEAKER 2, etc.

Play the audio again, pausing after each speaker. Then play again as necessary.

Check answers.

Speaker 1 would risk changing her appearance, e.g., her hairstyle, and she'd take risks when traveling.
Speaker 2 takes risks doing things he enjoys, e.g., skiing or riding his bike. He wouldn't take a risk if he didn't get any pleasure out of it.
Speaker 3 wouldn't risk going to a restaurant without having booked in advance. She would never risk buying clothes online.
Speaker 4 wouldn't risk walking home or get a taxi alone at night. She would risk bungee jumping or paragliding.
Speaker 5 goes mountain climbing, but he doesn't think it is risky. His biggest risk was leaving a job after 20 years and setting up his own company.
Speaker 6 drives fast, takes risks with money, and went on a balloon ride.

Put Sts in pairs and get them to discuss if they identify with any of the speakers, explaining their answer.

Get feedback.

Extra support

- Do this last question as an open-class activity.

Extra support

- If there's time, you could play the audio again while Sts read the audioscript on *pages 123–124*, so they can see what they understood / didn't understand. Translate / explain any new words or phrases.

e Focus on the task and instructions, making sure Sts understand what they have to do.

Put Sts in pairs, **A** and **B**, and get them to interview each other.

Monitor and help while Sts are talking.

f When Sts have finished, get them to look at all the circles they have written an "R" in and decide in which areas of life their partner is a risk taker.

Sts share their results and discuss whether or not they agree with the conclusions.

Finally, they should decide which of them is the bigger risk taker.

Get some feedback and help with any general vocabulary problems that come up.

2 GRAMMAR conditionals and future time clauses

a Focus on the sentence halves and give Sts time to match them.

Check answers.

1 B	3 C	5 F	7 H
2 D	4 G	6 E	8 A

b Give Sts time, in pairs, to answer the questions.

Check answers.

a) in the *if- / when*-clause: any present tense, e.g., simple present, present continuous, or present perfect
b) in the main clause: any future form, e.g., *will*, *going to*, present continuous (with future meaning), future perfect, future continuous, or an imperative

Extra support

- Do **b** and **c** as an open-class activity.

c Focus on the task and sentences.

Check the answer.

b) They refer to things that always happen.

d 2 39))) 2 40))) 2 41))) Tell Sts to go to **Grammar Bank 4B** on *page 139*. Focus on the example sentences and play the audio for Sts to listen to the sentence rhythm. You could also get Sts to repeat the sentences to practice getting the rhythm right. Then go through the rules with the class.

Additional grammar notes
zero and first conditionals, future time clauses

zero conditional

- This kind of conditional has not previously been focused on. Emphasize here that a zero conditional is used to generalize or give facts, e.g., *If you heat water, it boils.*
  Although zero conditionals are usually based on present tenses, they can also be used in the past, e.g., *If people didn't have money, they didn't eat.*

first conditional

- Up to now, Sts have probably been given a simplified version of the first conditional (e.g., that we always use *if* + simple present, future). In this lesson, they learn that a wider variety of tenses is possible (including the two new tenses they have just studied in **4A** – the future perfect and continuous).
- Remind Sts that although a present tense is used after *if*, the meaning here is future.

future time clauses

- Perhaps the most important point to emphasize is that a future tense can never be used after *if* or after *when, as soon as, until, unless, before, after, in case*.
- Typical mistakes are:
  – *I'll be ready as soon as ~~I'll have had a shower~~.*
  I'll have dinner as soon as ~~I'll get home~~.
  – *We'll probably be watching the game when ~~you'll arrive~~.*

in case

- This expression may be new to Sts. Be careful that they do not confuse it with *in case of* which is sometimes seen in notices, e.g., *In case of fire, break glass.*
- You may want to point out that *in case* can also be used in the past tense, e.g., *I took a jacket in case it got cold later.* Also point out that unlike the other expressions, *in case* cannot be used at the beginning of a sentence.

Focus on the exercises and get Sts to do them individually or in pairs.

Check answers, getting Sts to read the full sentences.

a

1	're not feeling	6	won't get
2	'll have sold	7	aren't wearing
3	have	8	'll catch
4	'll have scored	9	always gets
5	'll be bathing	10	won't go

b

1	before	6	If
2	in case	7	in case
3	unless	8	until
4	when	9	After
5	as soon as	10	unless

Tell Sts to go back to the main lesson **4B**.

Extra support

- If you think Sts need more practice, you may want to give them the Grammar photocopiable activity at this point or leave it for later as consolidation or review.

e Focus on the sentence stems and get Sts to complete them in pairs. Elicit ideas for sentence 1 from the whole class to demonstrate the activity.

Get feedback. You could write the phrases on the board and get the class to vote for the best tips.

Possible answers

1 ...they can swim. / ...there is an adult watching them.
2 ...it's a hot day. / ...you are going to be away for a long time.
3 ...someone has an accident. / ...someone cuts themself.
4 ...they are at least 12 years old. / ...they are old enough.
5 ...you finish. / you have finished using them.
6 ...a child or baby tries to eat or drink them.
7 ...they show you identification. / ...you are sure who they are.
8 ...don't throw water on it. / ...cover it with a towel.

3 PRONUNCIATION sentence rhythm

a 2.42 Tell Sts that the six sentences that they are going to hear are the missing parts of the two dialogues.

First, play the audio all the way through for Sts just to listen.

Now play the audio again, pausing after each sentence to give Sts time to write. Play again as necessary.

Check answers by writing the sentences on the board.

See audioscript 2.42

2.42

Dialogue 1
1 I'll tell you as soon as I know my plans.
2 If six of us go, it won't be too expensive.
3 We'll have to book soon if we want to get something nice.

Dialogue 2
4 I'll be waiting by the ticket office when you get there.
5 What will you do if I'm late?
6 Well, give me my ticket in case I get there at the last minute.

b 2.43 Focus on the task and play the audio again for Sts to underline the stressed words in the sentences they wrote in **a**.

Check answers by underlining the stressed words in the sentences on the board.

See underlining in audioscript 2.43

2.43

A If we rent a house in the mountains, will you come skiing with us?
B I'll tell you as soon as I know my plans. How much do you think it'll cost?
A If six of us go, it won't be too expensive.
B Well, I'll have to check my dates first.
A OK, but we'll have to book soon if we want to get something nice.
****
A How will I find you at the theater?
B I'll be waiting by the ticket office when you get there.
A What will you do if I'm late? I don't finish work until 7:00.
B I'll wait for you until 7:20 and then I'll go to my seat.
A Well, give me my ticket in case I get there at the last minute.

c Give Sts time to practice saying the dialogues in pairs.

4 READING

a Do these questions as an open-class activity. If you have done either of these things, tell the class about it.

b Focus on the article. Elicit ideas on the meaning of the title and elicit / explain what *a speedaholic* is. Ask Sts if they know where *-aholic* comes from (*alcoholic*).

In self-help groups where people have addiction problems, people usually introduce themselves at the first meeting by saying, e.g., *I'm (James)...I'm an addict*. This is because it is considered very important that people actually admit to others that they have an addiction.

Now set a time limit for Sts to read the article and answer questions 1–3. Point out the **Glossary** and tell Sts not to worry about the blanks in the article.

Check answers for 1 and 2. Elicit opinions for 3.

1 They can attend a speedaholics course or get points on their license.
2 They learn that speeding is a huge risk, which may cause their death.

c Now get Sts to read the article again carefully and to fill in the blanks 1–5 with A–E.

Get Sts to compare with a partner and then check answers.

1 C 2 D 3 A 4 E 5 B

d Put Sts in pairs and get them to discuss what the highlighted phrases mean.

Check answers, either explaining in English, translating into Sts' L1, or getting Sts to check in their dictionaries.

Help with any other new vocabulary and encourage Sts to write down any useful new lexis from the article.

e Do this as an open-class activity and tell Sts what you think.

5 LISTENING

a Focus on the task and instructions.

Give Sts time to look at sentences 1–8 and choose which they think is the right option.

Now put Sts in pairs and get them to discuss their choices.

Elicit some opinions, but don't tell Sts if they are right or not.

b **2 44**))) Play the audio once all the way through for Sts to listen and check their answers to **a**.

Check answers.

Extra support

- Before playing the audio, go through the audioscript and decide if you need to preteach / check any lexis to help Sts when they listen. You might also want to tell Sts that a mile equals 1.6 kilometers and a yard is nearly the same as a meter.

1 a	3 b	5 c	7 a
2 a	4 b	6 c	8 c

2 44)))
(audioscript in Student Book on *page 124*)
H = Host, S = Sandra

H For most of us, the riskiest thing we ever do is to get into a car and drive. And because this is something that we do almost every day of our lives, we need to take the risks involved in driving very seriously. Sandra, you're an expert on road safety. How dangerous is driving compared to other ways of getting around?
S Driving gets a lot of bad publicity. Statistics show that, mile for mile, it's riskier to be a pedestrian or a jogger than to drive a car or ride a motorcycle.
H But car accidents *do* happen. What's the main reason?
S Many fatal accidents occur because someone has broken the law. The most frequent cause of fatal accidents in the US is distracted driving – when a driver focuses his attention on a cell phone or to eat something, and the second most frequent is driving too fast. And the third major cause of fatal accidents is drunk driving.
H Tell us about some of the other factors that can increase our chances of having an accident.
S Well, the time of day we're on the road is a very significant factor. Generally speaking, driving at night, for example, is four times as dangerous as during the day. This is mainly because visibility is so much worse when it's dark. By day, a driver's visibility is roughly 500 yards, but at night, driving with headlights, it can be as little as 120 yards.
H Are there any times of day or night that are particularly risky?
S Research shows that you're most likely to have an accident between five and seven p.m. during the week, that's to say, during the evening rush hour, and especially in the winter when it's dark. And the day of the week when you're most likely to have an accident is Saturday. In the US, more accidents happen on a Saturday than on any other day.
H Why do you think that is?
S It's probably because the weekend is when the highest number of people are driving. Therefore, the more people driving on the roads increases the chances of having an accident.
H Which brings us to *where* accidents happen.
S Just over fifty percent of accidents happen within five miles of where we live. Statistically the most common kind of accident is crashing into a parked car near our home. Research shows that drivers concentrate less well when they're driving on familiar roads. Fortunately, most of these accidents are not fatal.
H So what about fatal accidents? Where do these tend to happen?
S As far as fatal accidents are concerned, the riskiest kind of road to drive on is a rural road. More fatal car crashes in the US happen on country roads than on city streets. In fact, 4,000 more car accidents happen on a country road than on an urban road.
H And why is that?
S Drivers often think that it's OK to break the speed limit on these roads because there's less traffic and consequently they take more risks.
H And the safest kind of road to drive on?
S A freeway is by far the safest kind of road.
H People – usually men – say that women have more accidents than men. Is that true?
S Well, it *is* true that, mile for mile, women have more minor accidents than men, but a man is twice as likely to be killed in a car accident as a woman.
H So men really are more dangerous drivers then?
S Women, by nature, are usually much more careful and cautious drivers than men. In general, men take far more unnecessary risks when they're driving than women.
H The age of a driver must be an important factor, too?
S Yes, in fact it's probably *the* most important factor. A driver aged between 17 and 24 has double the risk of having an accident than an older driver. The reasons for this are obvious. This is the age when drivers have very limited experience with driving, but it's also when they're most likely to drive too fast and take unnecessary risks, particularly if there are other young people in the car.
H Which is why a lot of people would like to see the age limit for having a driver's license raised to 21?
S I think it would be a very good idea.
H Well, that's all we have time for. Thank you very much for coming into the studio today, Sandra. And to all you drivers out there who are listening...drive safely!

c Play the audio again, pausing after each paragraph (see audioscript), and give Sts time to take notes. Play again as necessary.

You could get Sts to compare with a partner before eliciting as much of the information as possible.

1 Being a pedestrian or a jogger is more dangerous than being a driver.
2 Most fatal accidents happen because people break the law. The most frequent cause is distracted driving.
3 By day, a driver can see about 500 yards ahead, but at night, it is much worse – maybe as little as 120 yards.
4 Statistics show that more accidents in the US happen on a Saturday. It's probably because the weekend is when the highest number of people are driving. Therefore, the more people driving on the roads increases the chances of having an accident.
5 Just over fifty percent of accidents happen within five miles from where we live. The most common kind of accident is crashing into a parked car near our home. Drivers concentrate less well when they are driving on roads they know.
6 Four thousand more car accidents happened on a country road than on an urban road. Drivers think it is safer to break the speed limit on these roads because they are quieter.
7 Men take too many unnecessary risks when they're driving. Women are generally much more careful drivers.
8 This is the age when drivers have very little experience with driving and it's also the age when they are most likely to drive too fast and take unnecessary risks.

Extra support

- If there's time, you could play the audio again while Sts read the audioscript on *page 124*, so they can see what they understood / didn't understand. Translate / explain any new words or phrases.

d Put Sts in pairs or small groups to discuss the five questions. Monitor and help with vocabulary.

Get feedback.

Extra support

- Do these as open-class questions.

6 VOCABULARY expressions with *take*

a Focus on the task and either get Sts to do it in pairs or do it as an open-class activity.

If Sts worked in pairs, check answers.

take out insurance = to pay for a service (here to be insured when you're on vacation)
taking risks = to do something dangerous even though you know that something bad could happen as a result
take (something) very seriously = to think that something is important and needs your attention
Take out is a phrasal verb.

b Focus on the task and get Sts to match the expressions and phrasal verbs 1–9 with meanings A–I.

Get Sts to compare with a partner and then check answers.

1 A	4 D	7 G
2 H	5 F	8 E
3 C	6 I	9 B

c Focus on the **Giving examples** box and go through it with the class.

Now look at questions 1–8 and quickly go through them, making sure Sts understand any new vocabulary, e.g., *a demonstration*.

Focus on the first question and elicit the missing phrasal verb (*take after*).

Then get Sts to fill in the blanks in the other questions.

Check answers.

1 after	5 part in
2 care of	6 up
3 your time	7 place
4 advantage of	8 into account

Get Sts to choose a few questions to ask you.

Now put them in pairs and give them time to interview each other. First, **A** interviews **B** with all the questions, and then they switch roles.

Get some feedback.

7 WRITING *For and against*

Tell Sts to go to **Writing *For and against*** on *page 115*.

a Focus on the task. Give Sts time to read the blog and answer the question. Tell them not to worry about the blanks.

Elicit opinions.

b Tell Sts to read the blog again and to fill in the blanks 1–10 with the linking expressions from the list. Point out that two of the expressions are interchangeable – can be switched around.

Get Sts to compare with a partner and then check answers.

2 For example
3 Another advantage
4 Furthermore / In addition
5 On the other hand
6 Although
7 for example
8 Because of
9 Furthermore / In addition
10 To sum up

c Focus on the **Useful language: linking expressions** box and get Sts to complete the chart with the linking expressions from **b**.

Check answers.

To list advantages / disadvantages: Another advantage
To add more points to the same topic: Furthermore / In addition
To introduce an example: For example
To make contrasting points: On the other hand / although
To give a reason: Because of
To introduce the conclusion: To sum up

d Focus on the task and give Sts time to choose which topic they want to write about in their blog.

e Focus on the task and go through points 1–3 with the class.

f Focus on the instructions, making sure Sts know what *colloquial expressions* means.

Then either get Sts to write their blog in class (set a time limit of, e.g., 20 minutes) or get them to write it at home for homework.

g Sts should check their work for mistakes before turning it in.

3&4 Review and Check

For instructions on how to use these pages see *page 39*.

Testing Program CD-ROM

- **File 4 Quick Test**
- **File 4 Test**

GRAMMAR

a 1 a 2 c 3 a 4 b 5 a 6 c 7 c 8 b 9 c 10 b

b 1 'll / will be lying
2 will...have started
3 has landed / lands
4 drink
5 finish / 've finished

VOCABULARY

a 1 gate 2 baggage claim 3 aisle 4 turbulence 5 jet lag

b 1 lately 2 even 3 hard 4 luggage 5 especially

c 1 blew 2 dropped 3 poured 4 got 5 took

d 1 blizzard (The others relate to wind.)
2 chilly (The others relate to hot temperatures.)
3 damp (The others are nouns.)
4 bright (The others relate to cold temperatures.)
5 drought (The others relate to storms.)

e 1 out 2 off 3 up 4 after 5 place

PRONUNCIATION

a 1 hardly 2 clear 3 lounge 4 humid 5 aisle

b 1 eventually 2 gradually 3 especially 4 passenger 5 hurricane

CAN YOU UNDERSTAND THIS TEXT?

a No. There are a dozen professionals and a handful of people who have ever tried it.

b 1 D 2 E 3 A 4 F 5 C

c Get Sts to compare their five words with a partner and practice pronouncing each word.

VIDEO CAN YOU UNDERSTAND THIS MOVIE?

2 45

1 11, CBS
2 sleeting
3 snowstorm
4 tough
5 meet / connect with, complain
6 72
7 7 day
8 30 day
9 computer, apps
10 32

2 45 Available as MP3 on CD1

A short movie on the weatherman
H = Host, M = Mr. G

H New York is known for sometimes having extreme weather, so where do New Yorker's go for the most up-to-date weather forecasts? They watch their favorite TV weatherman: Mr. G.
M Hi, I'm Mr. G. I'm the meteorologist at Channel 11 here in New York, WPIX-TV. And also CBS Radio in New York. So I'm in charge of telling a story, building a drama of cold temperatures, wind chill factors, snow on the ground for 35 days.
M (B-roll) For the 19th time this season, flakes are in the air!
M It's been snow to sleet. It's been sleet to snow. It's been snow to sleet to rain. It's been raining on Long Island, sleeting in the city, snowing in the suburbs. I want to build up this story to announce what people don't want to hear, another possible snowstorm.
M (B-roll) Polar Vortex is back! More on this later on.
M Does a cold winter mean a warm summer? No, it's folklore.
H So how do New Yorkers handle all this bad weather news?
M Certain kind of weather affects people. I mean, it's been a winter where snow has been on the ground a long time that affects people. I think people have been indoors a lot. But New Yorkers are a tough group. I think people want to connect. And weather's a great way to connect. Whether you're single and you want to meet somebody, talk about the weather. When you want to complain, talk about the weather.
H And even though the weather may not be getting any better, the technology we use to predict it is.
M When I first started in the business, it was 72-hour forecasts. As the science progressed now everybody sees a 7-day forecast. Well, what you're going to see in 2 years is a 10-day forecast. And when my daughter grows up, it will be a 30-day forecast.
H So what makes for a great TV weatherman?
M Connecting is a big part of the job. The people know the weather. They get it on the computer, they get it on the app. 32% of the audience between 10 and 11 o'clock in New York City watches the news. Which means to me that they still want to get it from somebody they trust. So they watch Mr. G for a reason. I still haven't found out that reason. But I know I work hard to tell a good story every night.

G unreal conditionals
V feelings
P word stress in 3- or 4-syllable adjectives

5A The survivors' club

Lesson plan

The topic of this lesson is survival.

In the first section, Sts talk about how they think they would react in an emergency situation and they read an extract from a book called *The Survivors Club*, by Ben Sherwood, about people's reactions to disasters. The vocabulary focus is on feelings, e.g., *devastated*, *stunned*, etc., and Pronunciation looks at word stress in 3- or 4-syllable adjectives.

The second section of the lesson is based on the true story, later made into a documentary for Discovery TV, about three young backpackers and their guide who got lost in the Amazon jungle. Sts read and listen to the story. The grammar focus is on unreal conditionals, e.g., second and third conditionals. Sts should have seen both these structures before, but will still need practice in using them, especially third conditionals. Finally, Sts go to the **Writing Bank** and focus on writing an article.

STUDY LINK
- **Workbook** 5A
- **Online Practice**
- **iChecker**

Extra photocopiable activities

- **Grammar** unreal conditionals *page 159*
- **Communicative** What would you do? *page 196* (instructions *page 182*)
- **Vocabulary** Feelings *page 218* (instructions *page 211*)

Optional lead-in – the quote

- Write the quote at the top of *page 44* on the board (books closed) and the name of the person who said it, or get Sts to open their books and read it.
- You could point out / elicit that George Orwell (born Eric Arthur Blair 1903–1950) wrote two of the most famous novels of the 20th century, *Animal Farm* and *1984*.
- Ask Sts what they think Orwell was saying in the quotation and whether they agree with him.

1 SPEAKING & READING

a Focus on the questionnaire, making sure Sts understand all the situations, e.g., *become hysterical*, *confront the intruder*, etc.

Put Sts in pairs and give them time to read and discuss answers to each question.

Get some feedback, but <u>don't</u> tell them yet what the right answer / best thing to do is.

b Set a time limit for Sts to read the article and answer questions 1–3.

Check answers.

1 The key to survival is to slow down and divide the challenges into small tasks, one goal at a time, one decision at a time.
2 When faced with an emergency, 80% of people freeze, 10% lose control, and 10% keep calm.
3 The other important factor is knowing the right thing to do in a crisis.

c Get Sts to look at the highlighted words and phrases, and to try and figure out what they mean. Remind them to read the whole sentence or paragraph.

Then get them to match the highlighted words and phrases to definitions 2–8.

Check answers, and model and drill pronunciation.

2 stunned	5 rational	8 manageable tasks
3 challenge	6 overcome	
4 bewildered	7 keep calm	

Help with any other new vocabulary and encourage Sts to write down any useful new lexis from the article.

d Focus on the task and then put Sts in small groups of three, **A**, **B**, and **C**. Tell them to go to **Communication *It's an emergency!*, A** on *page 106*, **B** on *page 110*, **C** on *page 112*.

Monitor and help while Sts are reading their survival tips. Then give them time to underline what they think is the most important information.

When they are ready, each student should tell the other two people in their group what they should and shouldn't do in that particular situation. Encourage Sts to do this in their own words, without looking at the text.

Get feedback for each emergency situation.

Extra support
- You could write any new and useful words and phrases from the quiz and **Communication** on the board for Sts to copy.

Tell Sts to go back to the main lesson **5A**.

e Finally, get Sts to look back at their answers to questions 2–4 in **a** to see if they chose the right answers.

Check answers.

2 c 3 a 4 c

Have Sts raise their hands to find out how many chose the right answers.

2 VOCABULARY feelings

a Focus on the task and give Sts time to choose the three adjectives in **1c** that describe how people are feeling.

Check answers.

overwhelmed, stunned, bewildered

b Tell Sts to go to **Vocabulary Bank** ***Feelings*** on *page 157*.

Focus on **1 Adjectives** and get Sts to do **a** individually or in pairs.

3 2)) Now do **b**. Play the audio for Sts to check answers. Practice any words your Sts find difficult to pronounce. Make sure Sts are clear about the meaning of the new words. *Nervous* may be a false friend for your Sts, depending on their L1. In English, it means anxious, worried, or frightened about something that is going to happen in the future, e.g., a job interview, an exam, etc.

3 2))

Feelings

Adjectives

1 **J**	I'm very offended.	6 **H**	I'm really nervous.
2 **F**	I feel a little homesick.	7 **C**	I'm very grateful.
3 **E**	I'm a little disappointed.	8 **A**	I'm shocked.
4 **G**	I'm very lonely.	9 **D**	I'm so relieved.
5 **I**	I'm incredibly proud.	10 **B**	I feel a little guilty.

Focus on the ***fed up*** **and** ***upset*** box and go through it with the class. Point out that *fed up* is always followed by *with*, e.g., *I am fed up with this awful weather.* Model and drill pronunciation.

Focus on **2 Strong adjectives** and get Sts to do **a** individually or in pairs.

3 3)) Now do **b**. Play the audio for Sts to check answers. Practice any words your Sts find difficult to pronounce.

3 3))

Strong adjectives

1 stunned	4 thrilled	7 overwhelmed
2 devastated	5 astonished	8 bewildered
3 delighted	6 desperate	9 horrified

Focus on the **Modifiers with strong adjectives** box and go through it with the class.

Look at **3 Informal or slang words and expressions** and get Sts to do **a** and **b** individually or in pairs.

3 4)) Now do **c**. Play the audio for Sts to check answers. Practice any words your Sts find difficult to pronounce.

3 4))

Informal or slang words and expressions

1 **B** I was scared stiff when I heard the bedroom door opening.
2 **A** You look a little down. What's the problem?
3 **D** I'm absolutely worn out. I want to relax and put my feet up.
4 **F** When I saw her, I couldn't believe my eyes. She looked ten years younger!
5 **E** I'm sick and tired of hearing you complain about your job.
6 **C** He finally passed his driver's test. He's jumping for joy!

Testing yourself

For **Adjectives**, Sts can cover 1–10, look at situations A–J, and try to remember the adjectives. For **Strong adjectives**, they can cover the definitions, look at the strong adjectives in the list, and try to remember what each one means.

For **Informal or slang words and expressions**, Sts can cover feelings A–F and try to remember what 1–6 mean.

Testing a partner

See **Testing a partner** *page 29*.

Tell Sts to go back to the main lesson **5A**.

Extra support

- If you think Sts need more practice, you may want to give them the Vocabulary photocopiable activity at this point or leave it for later as consolidation or review.

3 PRONUNCIATION

word stress in 3- or 4-syllable adjectives

Pronunciation notes

- There are not many clear rules to give Sts regarding the pronunciation of three- and four-syllable adjectives, and the stress may fall on the first, second, or third syllable. It is worth reminding Sts that prefixes and suffixes are not stressed, e.g., *dishonest*, *ungrateful*, *dangerous*, etc.
- It is also worth reminding Sts that the unstressed /ə/ sound often occurs after or before the stressed syllable in multi-syllabic words and may even occur twice, e.g., *desperate* /ˈdɛspərət/.

a Focus on the task and give Sts time to underline the stressed syllable in each bold adjective. Remind Sts that this kind of exercise is easier if they say the adjectives out loud to themselves.

Extra support

- Get Sts to do this activity in pairs.

b 3 5)) Play the audio for Sts to listen and check.

Check answers by writing the adjectives on the board and underlining the stressed syllables.

1 desperate	6 delighted
2 offended	7 devastated
3 disappointed	8 horrified
4 bewildered	9 overwhelmed
5 astonished	

3 5))

See dialogues in Student Book on *page 45*

Extra challenge

- You could ask Sts to tell you in which words the schwa sound /ə/ occurs and which syllable: *desperate*, *offended*, *disappointed*, *bewildered*, *astonished*, *devastated*, *overwhelmed*.

Now put Sts in pairs and get them to practice the dialogues, paying attention to intonation and stress in the adjectives. Make sure they switch roles.

Get a different pair to read each dialogue to the class.

c Focus on the task and give Sts time to think.

Put Sts in pairs and get them to tell each other their situations for the two adjectives they have chosen. Get them to give as many details as possible.

Get some feedback.

4 READING & LISTENING

a Put Sts in pairs and get them to answer the two questions.

Get some feedback.

Extra support

- Do this as an open-class activity. Elicit ideas and write them on the board.

b Focus on the beginning of the story and the photos. Stress that this is a true story, which happened some years ago. Set a time limit for Sts to read the beginning of the story and answer the questions.

Get Sts to compare with a partner and then check answers to 1–3, and elicit from Sts their own ideas for 4 and 5.

1 to go into the rainforest for seven days and visit an undiscovered Indian village, then raft (= travel on a small boat usually made of wood) back down the river After seven days they still hadn't found the village and there were tensions in the group, so they decided to turn around and go back to Apolo, their starting point.
2 a Karl (the guide) didn't seem to know where the village was.
  b Marcus was complaining about everything, especially his feet.
3 Because Kevin still wanted to raft, as they had originally planned, but didn't want Marcus to come. He persuaded Yossi to join him.

Now check whether there is any vocabulary Sts couldn't guess and elicit / explain the meaning. Encourage Sts to write down any new lexis.

Extra support

- If you want to check that Sts have really understood the first part, you could ask them the following comprehension questions before moving on to the listening:
  What did Karl promise the three friends? What promise did they make to each other? How do you think the three friends felt before going into the jungle? What decision did Kevin make?, etc.

c 3 6))) 3 7))) 3 8))) 3 9))) 3 10))) 3 11))) Now focus on the instructions and photos. Get Sts to look at the photos first and use them to preteach *footprint* and *jaguar.*

3 6))) Play the audio for Sts to listen to the first part. Play it again and then get Sts to answer the questions orally in pairs.

Check answers and elicit opinions in answer to the questions in green. Make sure Sts use the right verb form "*I would rather have been in X's situation…*".

Extra support

- Before playing the audio, go through the audioscripts and decide if you need to preteach / check any lexis to help Sts when they listen, e.g., *rapids, hiking boot, log*, etc.

1 They went faster and faster, and then hit a rock. Kevin swam to land, but Yossi was swept away.
2 He swam to the river bank and found their backpack with a lot of important and useful things in it, e.g., the map.

3 6)))

(audioscript in Student Book on *page 124*)

Yossi and Kevin soon realized that going by river was a big mistake. The river got faster and faster, and soon they were in rapids. The raft was swept down the river at an incredible speed until it hit a rock. Both men were thrown into the water. Kevin was a strong swimmer and he managed to swim to land, but Yossi was swept away by the rapids.
But Yossi didn't drown. He was carried several miles downriver by the rapids, but he eventually managed to swim to the river bank. He was totally exhausted. By an incredible piece of luck, he found their backpack floating in the river. The backpack contained a little food, insect repellent, a lighter, and most important of all…the map. But the two friends were now separated by a canyon and three or four miles of jungle.

You may want to ask a few more questions before moving on to the next part to make sure Sts got all the details (e.g., *Can you remember what was in the backpack?*).

3 7))) Repeat the process for part 2.

3 Kevin – desperate, responsible for what had happened to Yossi. Yossi – very optimistic, sure he would find Kevin.
4 Yossi woke up and found a jaguar looking at him, but he managed to scare it away (by setting fire to insect repellent with a cigarette lighter).

3 7)))

(audioscript in Student Book on *page 124*)

Kevin was feeling desperate. He didn't know if Yossi was alive or dead, but he started walking downriver to look for him. He felt responsible for what had happened to his friend because he had persuaded him to go with him on the river.
Yossi, however, was feeling very optimistic. He was sure that Kevin would look for him, so he started walking upriver calling his friend's name. But nobody answered.
At night Yossi tried to sleep, but he felt terrified. The jungle was full of noises. Suddenly, he woke up because he heard a branch breaking. He turned on his flash light. There was a jaguar staring at him… Yossi was trembling with fear. But then he remembered something that he had once seen in a movie. He used the cigarette lighter to set fire to the insect repellent spray…and he managed to scare the jaguar away.

3 8))) Repeat the process for part 3.

5 Because he was exhausted and starving. Then he found a footprint which he thought was Kevin's, but eventually he realized it was his own. He had been walking around in a circle.

3 8)))

(audioscript in Student Book on *page 124*)

After five days alone, Yossi was exhausted and starving. Suddenly, as he was walking, he saw a footprint on the trail – it was a hiking boot. It had to be Kevin's footprint! He followed the trail until he discovered another footprint and then another. But suddenly he realized that the footprints weren't Kevin's footprints. They were his own. He had been walking around in a circle. At that moment Yossi realized that he would never find Kevin. In fact, he felt sure that Kevin must be dead. He felt totally depressed and at the point of giving up.

3 9))) Repeat the process for part 4.

6 He had been looking for Yossi.
7 He decided to save himself.
8 He had floated down the river on a log and had been rescued by two Bolivian hunters, who hunted in that part of the rainforest once a year.

3 9

(audioscript in Student Book on *page 124*)

But Kevin wasn't dead. He was still looking for Yossi. But after nearly a week, he was also weak and exhausted from lack of food and lack of sleep. He decided that it was time to forget Yossi and try to save himself. He had just enough strength left to hold onto a log and let himself float down the river.
Kevin was incredibly lucky – he was rescued by two Bolivian hunters, who were traveling downriver in a canoe. The men only hunted in that part of the rainforest once a year, so if they had passed by a short time earlier or later, they wouldn't have seen Kevin. They took him back to the town of San José, where he spent two days recovering.

3 10 Repeat the process for part 5.

9 He asked the Bolivian army to look for Yossi.
10 Because the plane had to fly too high and the forest was too dense. They couldn't see anything.
11 He paid a local man to take him in his boat to look for Yossi.

3 10

(audioscript in Student Book on *page 124*)

As soon as Kevin felt well enough, he went to a Bolivian army base and asked them to look for Yossi. The army officer he spoke to was sure that Yossi must be dead, but in the end Kevin persuaded them to take him up in a plane and fly over the part of the rainforest where Yossi might be. But the plane had to fly too high over the rainforest and the forest was too dense. They couldn't see anything at all. It was a hopeless search. Kevin felt terribly guilty. He was convinced that it was all his fault that Yossi was going to die in the jungle. Kevin's last hope was to pay a local man with a boat to take him up the river to look for his friend.

3 11 Repeat the process for part 6. Encourage Sts to use *must have*, *might have*, etc. when they speculate about what happened to Marcus and Karl.

12 For nearly three weeks. He was starving, exhausted, and slowly losing his mind.
13 He thought it was a bee, but in fact it was the engine of the boat Kevin was in.

3 11

(audioscript in Student Book on *page 124*)

By now, Yossi had been on his own in the jungle for nearly three weeks. He hadn't eaten for days. He was starving, exhausted, and slowly losing his mind. It was evening. He lay down by the side of the river ready for another night alone in the jungle. Suddenly, he heard the sound of a bee buzzing in his ear. He thought a bee had got inside his mosquito net. But when he opened his eyes, he saw that the buzzing noise wasn't a bee... It was a boat. Yossi was too weak to shout, but Kevin had already seen him. It was a one-in-a-million chance that Kevin would find his friend, but he did – Yossi was saved.
When Yossi had recovered, he and Kevin flew to the city of La Paz and they went directly to the hotel where they had agreed to meet Marcus and Karl.
But Marcus and Karl were not at the hotel. The two men had never arrived back in the town of Apolo. The Bolivian army organized a search of the rainforest, but Marcus and Karl were never seen again.

Extra support

- If there's time, you could play all the audio again while Sts read the audioscripts on *page 124*, so they can see what they understood / didn't understand. Translate / explain any new words or phrases.

d Do this as an open-class activity.

You might like to tell Sts that Yossi Ghinsberg now works giving talks at conferences about motivation based on his experience. He has also devoted a lot of time and raised money to help protect the rainforest where he got lost. He lives in the Australian rainforest. Kevin Gale works as a manager of a gym. The documentary made about their experience is based on Yossi's book *Jungle* and can be seen on the Discovery Channel as part of the series called *I shouldn't be alive*.

5 GRAMMAR unreal conditionals

a Focus on the task and tell Sts to fill in the blanks.

Get Sts to compare with a partner and then check answers.

1 were, got lost
2 'd / would call, wouldn't confront
3 had been
4 would have died

b Either get Sts to do this individually or do it as an open-class activity. Before they start, make sure they know the meaning of *hypothetical*.

If Sts worked alone, check answers.

3 and 4 refer to a hypothetical situation in the past.
1 and 2 refer to a hypothetical situation in the present or future.

c **3 12** **3 13** **3 14** Tell Sts to go to **Grammar Bank 5A** on *page 140*. Focus on the example sentences and play the audio for Sts to listen to the sentence rhythm. You could also get Sts to repeat the sentences to practice getting the rhythm right. Then go through the rules with the class.

Additional grammar notes

unreal conditionals

- Sts will have studied both the second and third conditionals separately, but here they are contrasted. Sts should be fairly confident with the concept of both, although they will probably still have problems using them orally with fluency, especially the third conditional.
- Sts also widen their knowledge of the second and third conditionals by seeing how other forms can be used in either clause.

second or third conditional?

- The point to emphasize here is that the second conditional refers to a hypothetical situation in **the present or future**, which can sometimes be changed and sometimes not, e.g., *If she were taller, she could get a job as a model* (situation can't be changed). *If you studied more, you would pass the exam* (situation could be changed).
- The third conditional refers to hypothetical situations in the past, **which didn't happen**, e.g., *If we had known you were in the hospital, we would have visited you* (we didn't know, so we didn't visit you).

Mixed conditionals

- Sometimes the second and third conditionals are mixed. We suggest that you draw Sts' attention to this for passive recognition, but this is not practiced in the exercises.

Focus on the exercises and get Sts to do them individually or in pairs.

Check answers, getting Sts to read the full sentences.

a
1 wouldn't have made
2 wouldn't lend
3 'd / would ask
4 wouldn't have had
5 were / was
6 'd / had looked (or had been looking)
7 would enjoy
8 changed
9 'd / had been able
10 'd / had asked

b
1 If Luke hadn't missed the train, he wouldn't have been late for the interview.
2 Maxie would have bought the top if she'd had / she had had some money.
3 If it hadn't started snowing, we'd have reached / we would have reached the top.
4 If Rebecca didn't drink so much coffee, she wouldn't sleep (so) badly.
5 I'd drive/ I would drive to work if there weren't / wasn't so much traffic.
6 If Matt treated his girlfriend better, she'd stay / she would stay with him.
7 You'd feel / You would feel a lot healthier if you did some exercise.
8 The taxi driver wouldn't have found the street if he hadn't had GPS.
9 If Jim had bought the right size, I wouldn't have had to exchange the sweater.
10 If you got up earlier, you wouldn't waste half the morning.

Tell Sts to go back to the main lesson **5A**.

Extra support

- If you think Sts need more practice, you may want to give them the Grammar photocopiable activity at this point or leave it for later as consolidation or review.

d Focus on the task and give Sts time to complete the four stems.

Get some feedback.

Possible endings
1 + ...I would have a better social life.
– ...I wouldn't need a car.
2 + ...I had turned off "roaming" when I was traveling.
– ...I hadn't spoken to my sister in the UK for an hour.

e Put Sts in pairs, **A** and **B**, and tell them to go to **Communication *Guess the conditionals*, A** on *page 106*, **B** on *page 111*.

Demonstrate the activity by writing in large letters on a piece of paper the following sentence:

If I'd known it was your birthday, I would have bought you a present.

Don't show the sentence to your Sts.

Then write on the board:

If I'd known it was your birthday, I ____________ ____________. (+)

Tell Sts that you have this sentence completed on a piece of paper and they have to try to guess what it is.

Elicit possible completions with a positive (+) verb phrase (e.g., *would have called you* | *would have sent you a card*). Say "*Try again*" if they say something different, until someone says the phrase *I would have bought you a present*, and say "*That's right.*"

Now go through the instructions. Emphasize that Sts should write their ideas next to the sentence, but not in the blank, and only fill in the blank when their partner says "*That's right.*"

Sts continue in pairs. Monitor and help.

Tell Sts to go back to the main lesson **5A**.

6 WRITING an article

Tell Sts to go to **Writing *An article*** on *page 116*.

a Focus on the task and three pictures.

Elicit ideas from the class or get Sts to discuss the question in pairs.

If Sts worked in pairs, elicit ideas, but don't tell them if they are right or not.

Now give Sts time to read the article to check.

Check answers.

The parents should have kept the knives in drawers that children can't reach. They shouldn't have put a bed under a window. They shouldn't have put cleaning liquids where children can reach it.

b Focus on the task and make sure Sts understand what they have to do. Point out that the first one has been done for them.

Get Sts to compare with a partner and then check answers.

New paragraph after "...the child falls out."
New paragraph after "...leave them in a locked cabinet."
New paragraph after "...liquids are in high cabinets."

c Focus on the task and give Sts time, in pairs, to choose which topic they want to write about in their article.

d Focus on the task and go through points 1 and 2 with the class.

Give Sts time, in pairs, to brainstorm possible tips and an introductory sentence.

e Focus on the **Useful language: giving advice** box and go through it with the class.

Then either get Sts to write their article in class (set a time limit of, e.g., 20 minutes) or get them to write it at home for homework.

f Sts should check their work for mistakes before turning it in.

G structures after *wish*
V expressing feelings with verbs or *-ed* / *-ing* adjectives
P sentence rhythm and intonation

5B It drives me crazy!

Lesson plan

The topics in this lesson are things that annoy us in our daily lives (e.g., a sister borrowing clothes without asking) and regrets we have about the present and the past. They provide the context for Sts to learn to use *I wish....* To make it easier for Sts to assimilate the grammar, it has been split into two separate presentations and so there are two visits to the **Grammar Bank** in this lesson. This is a tricky grammar point, so do not expect your Sts to assimilate how it is used immediately.

The first section of the lesson starts with the grammar focus on the construction *I wish...* to express annoyance (*I wish my sister wouldn't borrow my clothes*). This is followed by a vocabulary and speaking focus on different ways of expressing feelings, with a verb or with an *-ed* or *-ing* adjective, e.g., *It annoys me* | *I'm annoyed* | *It's annoying.*

In the second section of the lesson, Sts read about some people's regrets and then guess what most people's top five regrets are. Then there is a grammar focus on ways to express present and past regrets (*I wish I were taller, I wish I hadn't said that*). The pronunciation focus is on sentence rhythm. In the listening activity, Sts listen to people talking about things they regret, before talking about their own regrets. Finally, Sts listen to the song, *Same Mistake*.

STUDY LINK
- **Workbook** 5B
- **Online Practice**
- **iChecker**

Extra photocopiable activities

- **Grammar** structures after *wish* *page 160*
- **Communicative** Wishes *pages 197–198* (instructions *page 182*)
- **Song** *Same Mistake* *page 233* (instructions *page 227*)

Optional lead-in – the quote

- Write the quote at the top of *page 48* on the board (books closed) and the name of the person who said it, or get Sts to open their books and read it.
- Ask Sts what his quote means and if they agree with it.

1 GRAMMAR *wish + would*

a Focus on the task and make sure Sts know what *a Twitter thread* is, *to tweet*, and *annoy*.

Give Sts time to read all the tweets and check the ones that annoy them.

b Focus on the **Useful language** box and go through it with the class. Model and drill the intonation in the three phrases that express annoyance.

Get Sts to choose their top three and then to compare with a partner using the expressions in **Useful language**.

Get some feedback and tell the class your top three, too. You could find out which is the top annoying habit for the whole class.

c 3 15))) Tell Sts to go to **Grammar Bank 5B** on *page 141*. Focus on the example sentences and play the audio for Sts to listen to the sentence rhythm. You could also get Sts to repeat the sentences to practice getting the rhythm right. Then go through the rules with the class.

Additional grammar notes

wish + would* | *wouldn't

- In the first person, *I wish...* is often used as an exclamation. The contracted form of *would* (*'d*) is often used after *wish*.
- Highlight the fact that we only use this structure to talk about things we would like other people (or things) to do or not to do. We don't use this structure with *I*, e.g., NOT *I wish I ~~would have~~ more money*. Tell Sts they will learn how to express this idea later in the lesson.

Focus on exercise **a** only and get Sts to do it individually or in pairs.

Check answers, getting Sts to read the full sentences.

a
1 I wish salespeople would be more polite.
2 I wish you wouldn't turn the heat up all the time.
3 I wish my sister would clean our room.
4 I wish the neighbor's dog wouldn't bark at night.
5 I wish it would stop raining.
6 I wish Jane wouldn't talk about her boyfriend so much.
7 I wish my dad wouldn't sing in front of my friends.
8 I wish you wouldn't drive so fast!
9 I wish my husband would do the dishes.
10 I wish the bus would come.

Tell Sts to go back to the main lesson **5B**.

d Focus on the task. Tell Sts individually to think of three more things which annoy them in their daily life, e.g., at home, in school / work, on the street, driving, on public transportation, etc. and to write a tweet similar to the ones in **a** for each one.

Help with any vocabulary Sts may need.

e Now put Sts in pairs or small groups to compare their tweets. Do they have any similar tweets?

Get feedback from the whole class and write some of the best ones on the board. You could tell Sts some of your own personal "pet hates."

2 VOCABULARY & SPEAKING expressing feelings with verbs or *-ed* / *-ing* adjectives

In the previous lesson, Sts learned adjectives for describing how people feel (*shocked*, *disappointed*, etc.). In this lesson, other ways of talking about feelings are covered, e.g., using *It* structures with verbs like *annoy* (*It really annoys me when…*).

a Focus on the **Ways of talking about feelings** box and go through it with the class.

Extra support

- Give Sts another example as follows:

  verb: ***to bore***; adjectives: ***bored*** | ***boring***, *e.g., This program* ***bores*** *me.* | *This program is* ***boring***. = *I'm* ***bored*** *with watching this program.*

Then focus on the instructions, making sure Sts know the meaning of all the verbs in bold. Do the first one with the class as an example.

Give Sts time to do the task either individually or in pairs.

b 3.16 Play the audio for Sts to listen and check.

Check answers. Model and drill any adjectives your Sts might find difficult to pronounce. You could use the audio to do this.

See words in **bold** in audioscript 3.16

3.16

1 It really **infuriates** me when people drive close behind me.
2 I get very **frustrated** when something goes wrong with my Internet connection and I don't know how to fix it.
3 It's so **embarrassing** when I can't remember someone's name, but they can remember mine.
4 I used to love shopping during a big sale, but now I find it **exhausting**. After an hour I just want to go home.
5 I'm often **disappointed** with my birthday presents. My expectations are obviously too high!
6 It **amazes** me that some people still don't buy things like books and music online.
7 I find speaking in public absolutely **terrifying**. I hate doing it.
8 I've often been **inspired** by reading about how some successful people have overcome difficulties.
9 I never find instructions for electronic devices helpful, in fact, usually they just **confuse** me.
10 When I travel I'm always **thrilled** if I manage to communicate something in a foreign language.

Put Sts in pairs and get them to look at each sentence and say whether or not it is true for them. They should give examples or reasons whenever possible.

Get some feedback.

c Focus on the **Feelings adjectives that have an *-ed* form, but not an *-ing* form** box and go through it with the class.

Now look at the example (number 1) together and elicit the meaning (feeling admiration). Model and drill pronunciation of the two adjectives and elicit which syllable is stressed.

Give Sts time to fill in the blanks.

Check answers and elicit which syllable is stressed. Model and drill the pronunciation of the adjectives.

2 stressful 3 scary 4 delightful 5 offensive

Extra challenge

- You could call out the sentences in **c** in random order, saying *blank* instead of the adjective / verb and get the class to call out the missing word, e.g.,

T *I'm very stressed by my new job. My job is very BLANK.*
Sts *stressful*

d Focus on the task, which activates orally some of the adjectives in **a** and **c**.

Give Sts a couple of minutes to think about which three of the subjects they can talk about.

Now put them in pairs and tell them to take turns talking. The first student can start by saying *I'm going to tell you about….*

Monitor and help.

Help with any vocabulary problems that come up.

e Find out if any pairs felt exactly the same way about certain things.

You could tell Sts some of your own experiences / feelings, too.

3 READING & SPEAKING

a Focus on the task. Look at 1–5 together and make sure Sts understand them.

Now put Sts in pairs and get them to discuss with their partner whether they think the sentences are true or not.

Elicit some opinions, but don't tell Sts if they are right or not.

b Give Sts time to read the first part of the article once all the way through to check their answers to **a**. Before they start, point out that there is a **Glossary**.

Get Sts to compare with a partner and then check answers. Ask Sts to tell you which part of the text gave them the answer.

1 T (Line 3: …on average, we spend 44 minutes a week thinking about things we could or should have done differently.)
2 T (Line 4: Our main areas of regret are our love lives…)
3 F (Line 7: On average, most people have two main regrets in life.)
4 F (Line 8: 17%…laid the blame at someone else's door.)
5 T (Line 9: But two thirds…thought their regrets had led them to act more positively and that they had learned from their mistakes.)

c Tell Sts to cover the article and to think of other ways of saying the percentages.

Check answers.

1 three quarters
2 two thirds
3 a quarter

Encourage Sts to write down any new lexis from the article.

Extra idea

- Get Sts to see if they can remember what the three percentages refer to:
  1. the percentage of people who said it was impossible to live without regrets
  2. the percentage of people who said they thought their regrets had led them to act more positively and that they had learned from their mistakes
  3. the percentage of people who said their regrets had made them into the person they are today

d Focus on the list of top regrets and make sure Sts understand them all. Emphasize that they are not in order, so the Sts must guess what the top five are.

Now give Sts time to read the list of regrets.

Put Sts in pairs and get them to decide which they think are the top five regrets (in order).

Elicit some ideas, but <u>don't</u> tell Sts if they are right or not.

Finally, focus on the ***regret doing* or *regret having done?*** box and go through it with the class.

e **3 17** Tell Sts they are going to hear the regrets in reverse order. Play the audio for Sts to listen and check.

Check answers and find out if any Sts chose all five correctly.

> **3 17**
> The top five regrets were, in reverse order, number five "Having started smoking," number four "Not having saved enough money," number three "Not having exercised more or eaten more healthily," number two "Not keeping in touch with friends," and the number one regret was "Not having traveled more and seen more of the world."

Do the last question as an open-class activity.

4 GRAMMAR *wish* + simple past or past perfect

a Focus on the task and give Sts time to read the four comments.

Get Sts to compare with a partner and then elicit some ideas.

Point out the idiom "cry over spilled milk" in the third comment (*It's no use crying over spilled milk.*) and elicit its meaning (to waste time worrying about something that has happened that you cannot do anything about).

b Focus on the task and give Sts time to do it.

Check answers.

1. I wish I'd traveled more when I had the time. (past perfect)
2. There's nothing that I wish was different about my life. (simple past)
3. I wish I'd stayed in college. (past perfect)
4. I wish I'd married my ex. (past perfect)
5. I really wish I hadn't wasted all that money on cigarettes. (past perfect)
6. I wish there was a song called *Je regrette tout*. (simple past)

Now ask Sts the two questions and elicit answers.

Sentences 1, 3, 4, and 5 are the past perfect and refer to the past.
Sentences 2 and 6 are the simple past and refer to the present.

c **3 18** Tell Sts to go to **Grammar Bank 5B** on *page 141*. Focus on the example sentences and play the audio for Sts to listen to the sentence rhythm. You could also get Sts to repeat the sentences to practice getting the rhythm right. Then go through the rules with the class.

Additional grammar notes
***wish* + past simple or past perfect**

- **rule 1:** In the first person *I wish…* is often used as an exclamation.
- **rule 2:** Remind Sts that both *would* and *had* can be contracted to *'d*, so they will need to focus on the main verb to see what the structure is. Compare:
  *I wish he'**d come**.* (= *would come* – you want him to come)
  *I wish he'**d come**!* (= *had come* – you're sorry that he didn't come)
- The information about *If only* in the box on the right applies to all uses of *wish*. *If only* is a stronger and more dramatic way of expressing a wish, e.g., *If only it would stop raining!* We usually use an exclamation mark after *If only…!*

Focus on exercise **b** and get Sts to do it individually or in pairs.

Check answers, getting Sts to read the full sentences.

b

1	had	7	didn't get
2	didn't live	8	could
3	'd / had started	9	hadn't packed
4	had	10	had gone / were going
5	'd / had bought	11	weren't / wasn't
6	'd / had been	12	'd / had learned

Tell Sts to go back to the main lesson **5B**.

Extra support

- If you think Sts need more practice, you may want to give them the Grammar photocopiable activity at this point or leave it for later as consolidation or review.

Extra challenge

- Tell Sts they are going to write their own response to the article. They need to write at least two sentences, one referring to the past using *I wish* + the past perfect and one using *I wish* + simple past for the present. Tell them to write between 50 and 75 words.
- Get Sts to exchange pieces of paper, so they can read each other's regrets.
- Get feedback. You could find out if any Sts had the same regrets or if they found any regrets surprising.

5 PRONUNCIATION

sentence rhythm and intonation

a 3 19 Focus on the task and play the audio once all the way through for Sts just to listen.

Then play it again, pausing after each sentence to give Sts time to write.

Finally, play the audio once more for Sts to check their sentences.

Check answers by writing the sentences on the board.

3 19
1 I wish I hadn't eaten two pieces of cake.
2 I wish I'd gone to college.
3 I wish it wasn't my turn to cook tonight.
4 I wish I knew where we were.
5 I wish we didn't have to go to your parents for dinner.
6 I wish I'd bought those shoes I saw on sale.

Extra support

- Play the audio for Sts to listen and repeat the sentences, trying to copy the rhythm.

b Focus on the task and give Sts time to match the six *I wish* sentences they wrote in **a** to A–F. Do the first one with the class as an example.

c 3 20 Play the audio for Sts to listen and check.

Check answers.

1 D 2 C 3 F 4 B 5 A 6 E

3 20
1 **A** I wish I hadn't eaten two pieces of cake.
B Well, it's not my fault. You have no self-control!
2 **A** I wish I'd gone to college.
B Well, it isn't too late. You're only 22.
3 **A** I wish it wasn't my turn to cook tonight.
B Sorry, but it is. And I'm getting hungry.
4 **A** I wish I knew where we were.
B Well, don't ask me! I've never been here before.
5 **A** I wish we didn't have to go to your parents for dinner.
B Do you want me to call and make an excuse?
6 **A** I wish I'd bought those shoes I saw on sale.
B Why don't you go back to the store and see if they still have them?

Now put Sts in pairs and get them to practice the six two-lined dialogues. Encourage Sts to concentrate on getting the rhythm right by stressing the longer "content" words, especially in the *I wish*… sentences.

Get some pairs to practice in front of the class.

6 LISTENING & SPEAKING

a 3 21 Focus on the task and go through regrets A–F, making sure Sts understand them.

Tell Sts just to listen the first time and try to get the gist of what they hear without writing anything. Remind them that there is one sentence they don't need to use.

Play the audio once all the way through for Sts just to listen.

Then play it again, pausing after each speaker to give Sts time to choose their answer. Play the audio again as necessary.

You could get Sts to compare with a partner before checking answers.

Extra support

- Before playing the audio, go through the audioscript and decide if you need to preteach / check any lexis to help Sts when they listen.

Speaker 1	E	**Speaker 3**	B	**Speaker 5**	A
Speaker 2	F	**Speaker 4**	C		

3 21
(audioscript in Student Book on *pages 124–125*)

1 **Man**
The only thing I really regret is, is not having had the courage to talk to a girl I met at a party last summer. I really liked her – she was very attractive – but I just wasn't brave enough to start a conversation. I wish I'd tried. I'm absolutely positive we would have gotten along well. Now it's too late – she's engaged to another guy!

2 **Woman**
At the risk of sounding really negative, the one thing I really regret in my life is getting married. My sister said to me in the car on the way to the registry office, "Someone has to say to you that you really don't have to do this, you know" and, um, I ignored her because I thought, "What do you know? You're still single." But, in fact, the next day when I woke up I realized it was a terrible mistake, and I spent the next 15 years trying to get out of it. So...and I would never do it again. So that's probably my biggest regret.

3 **Woman**
Um, I really wish I'd been able to know my grandmother better. She died when I was 12, and since then I've discovered that she must have been a really fascinating person, and there are so many things I would love to have been able to talk to her about. She was Polish, but she was in Russia, in St. Petersburg, during the Russian Revolution and she knew all kinds of interesting people at the time – painters, writers, people like that. I was only a child, so I never asked her much about her own life. Now, I'm discovering all about her through reading her old letters and papers, but I wish she'd lived longer so that I could have talked to her about those times face-to-face.

4 **Man**
When I was 15 I had a weekend job, um, in a supermarket — stocking shelves and that kind of thing. My friend also worked there, and he persuaded me one day to help him steal a carton of cigarettes – 200 cigarettes – from the stockroom. It was a crazy idea and totally out of character for me to do something like that. I'd always been very honest until then. Anyway, the store manager found where we'd hidden the cigarettes and he called the police. So when we came to work that evening the police were waiting for us. Although we got off with just a warning – we were only kids – the police came to my house and talked to my mom. I felt so awful. But in the long run it was probably a good thing because it meant that I never, ever thought about stealing something again.

5 **Woman**
When I was 16 I got the chance to change schools and go to a better school to do my last two years. My parents were really eager for me to change schools because they thought I'd probably get better scores on the college aptitude test, and have a better chance of going to college. But I was totally against the idea because I didn't want to leave all my friends behind, and I didn't know anyone at the other school. So in the end, I managed to convince them and I stayed at my old school. I did OK on the test, but not super well. Um, now I regret not listening to my parents because I think it would have been better for my future career, but at the time I just couldn't see it.

b Focus on the task and give Sts time to read 1–5.

Play the audio again, pausing after each speaker to give Sts time to do the task.

Play each part again if necessary and then check answers.

1 *"I really liked her."* – He was attracted to the girl.
"Now it's too late." – It's too late because the girl who he was too afraid to talk to is now engaged to be married.
2 *"Someone has to say to you that you really don't have to do this."* – This is what her sister said on the way to her wedding.
"I spent the next 15 years trying to get out of it." – This is how long it took her to get divorced.
3 *the Russian Revolution* – Her (Polish) grandmother was in Russia during the revolution and met many interesting people (painters, writers). Her granddaughter wishes she could have talked to her about this time.
old letters – By reading her old letters the granddaughter is finding out about her life.
4 *"It was a crazy idea and totally out of character"* – The man was usually very honest.
"in the long run it was probably a good thing" – He realizes now that in the end it probably had a positive effect on his life because he never stole anything again.
5 *"My parents were really eager for me to change schools"* – Her parents wanted her to go to a better school.
"but I was totally against the idea" – At the time she didn't want to change schools.

Extra support

- If there's time, you could play the audio again while Sts read the audioscript on *pages 124–125*, so they can see what they understood / didn't understand. Translate / explain any new words or phrases.

c Focus on the task and give Sts time to think about two regrets for each situation.

Now put Sts in small groups of three or four and get them to compare regrets. Encourage Sts to ask each other for more information.

Help with any vocabulary problems that come up.

Get some feedback from the class about some of their regrets. You could tell Sts about some of your regrets, too.

7 3 22 SONG *Same Mistake* ♫

This song was originally made famous by the British singer James Blunt in 2007. For copyright reasons, this is a cover version. If you want to do this song in class, use the photocopiable activity on *page* 233.

3 22

Same Mistake

Saw the world turning in my sheets
And once again I cannot sleep
Walk out the door and up the street
Look at the stars beneath my feet
Remember rights that I did wrong
So here I go

Chorus
I'm not calling for a second chance
I'm screaming at the top of my voice
Give me reason, but don't give me choice
'Cos I'll just make the same mistake again

And maybe someday we will meet
And maybe talk and not just speak
Don't buy the promises
'Cos there are no promises I keep
And my reflection troubles me
So here I go

I'm not calling for a second chance
I'm screaming at the top of my voice
Give me reason, but don't give me choice
Because I'll just make the same mistake
I'm not calling for a second chance
I'm screaming at the top of my voice
Give me reason, but don't give me choice
'Cos I'll just make the same mistake again

Saw the world turning in my sheets
And once again I cannot sleep
Walk out the door and up the street
Look at the stars
Look at the stars fall down
And wonder where
Did I go wrong?

4&5 Talking about waste

Lesson plan

In the first part of this lesson, the person interviewed is Candida Brady, a British journalist and filmmaker.

In the second part of the lesson, people on the street are asked about recycling.

STUDY LINK

- **Workbook** Talking about waste
- **Online Practice**
- **iChecker**

Testing Program CD-ROM

- **File 5 Quick Test**
- **File 5 Test**
- **Files 1–5 Progress Test**

Optional lead-in (books closed)

- Write the name JEREMY IRONS on the board and ask Sts if they know him and what nationality he is (he is a British actor), and if they have seen him in any films (e.g., *The Borgias*, *Margin Call*, *The Man in the Iron Mask*, *Lolita*, *Casanova*, *The Kingdom of Heaven*, *Eragon*, *Beautiful Creatures*, etc.)

1 VIDEO THE INTERVIEW Part 1

a Books open. Focus on the biographical information about Candida Brady. Either read it out loud or give Sts time to read it.

Focus on the question and do it as an open-class activity.

b 3 23 Focus on the task and give Sts time to read sentences 1–6. Remind Sts that they do not need to correct the false ones at this stage.

Go through the **Glossary** with the class.

Play the DVD or audio (**Part 1**) once all the way through for Sts to do the task.

You could get Sts to compare with a partner before checking answers.

Extra support

- You could pause the DVD or audio at the relevant places and, in pairs, get Sts to compare orally what they have understood before marking the sentences true or false.

1 T 2 F 3 T 4 F 5 T 6 F

3 23

(audioscript in Student Book on *page 125*)
I = interviewer, C = Candida Brady

Part 1

I What were you hoping to do by making the film *Trashed*?
C Well, I think, um, the role of the film, um, for me was to raise awareness, um, on the topic and get it into the press so that people could start having a, a meaningful conversation about waste which, um, is not a particularly, um, attractive subject, let's say.
I How many countries did you film in?
C We ended up actually filming in 11 countries, um, but the stories that I've chosen are universal, and obviously, I spoke to, to people in communities, um, in more countries, um, than we actually filmed in, um, but their stories are certainly not isolated, they were repeated around the world, sadly wherever you kind of want to pick actually.
I How did you persuade Jeremy Irons to get involved in the film?
C I had worked with Jeremy some years ago on a, on a different film and I was generally aware that he doesn't like waste either, um, he will, you know, wear his jumpers until they're worn out, he'll keep his cars until they're falling apart, you know, he'll repair everything, so he's always seen, you know, the value in reusing things, it's just something natural to him as well, so he just felt like a natural, um, first approach, and, and so I sent him the treatment and amazingly he loved it.
I And how did you get Vangelis to write the soundtrack?
C Well, Jeremy and Vangelis have been friends for years, so, um, Jeremy sent him the rough cut of the film and Vangelis absolutely loved it. He, he is also a committed environmentalist, so he's always been aware, um, he was aware because he worked with, um Cousteau, sort of various people, you know, he was aware of issues for the seas and so on, um, but generally again he was very shocked, um, by the film and really wanted to get involved, so...
I What research did you do before you started making the film?
C I spent about a year, um, talking to communities, talking to experts, um, you know, obviously reading an awful lot, um, and, um, just ingesting it all because obviously again it's such an enormous topic to take on.

c Focus on the task and play the DVD or audio again all the way through for Sts to correct sentences 2, 4, and 6.

You could get Sts to compare with a partner before checking answers.

2 Jeremy Irons keeps things a long time until they are worn out, e.g., jumpers (sweaters), car. He doesn't like waste.
4 Vangelis is Jeremy's friend.
6 She spent a year talking to people – communities and experts.

VIDEO Part 2

a 3 24 Focus on the task and play the DVD or audio (**Part 2**) once all the way through for Sts to answer the questions.

You could get Sts to compare with a partner before checking answers.

1 trying not to make it too depressing
2 water pollution

3 24))
(audioscript in Student Book on *page 125*)

Part 2

I Rubbish isn't very attractive visually. Was that a problem for you as a filmmaker?

C Uh, yes and no, um, strangely enough. Obviously I had a wonderful, um, DOP, Director of Photography, so, um, he can pretty much make anything look beautiful, I think, but, um, I wanted to choose – as I've, as I've said earlier, um, you know, I'd a lot of research and so, sadly, these things were repeatable and, and in every country around the world – so I wanted to choose, um, beautiful places wherever possible, um, that had been ruined unfortunately by, um manmade rubbish, so, um, the ancient port of Saida in Lebanon, um the fact that, you know, you've got this huge mountain of waste, which was formerly a flat sandy beach.

I Documentaries about how we're destroying the planet can be very depressing, was that also a challenge for you?

C A huge challenge, yes. Um, I would have preferred to make a much more cheerful, um, documentary than, um, I think *Trashed* is. I think it has got hope, um, I think we were very much aware that we wanted to offer solutions at the end of it, but you are, um, the subject is not a cheerful subject. Um, I could have gone further I think with it, but I didn't want to because actually, you know, you could sort of end up feeling that you just want to go and shoot yourself, which is not what I wanted. I wanted to feel, you know, people feel that they can make a difference to this topic.

I In the film you focus on air pollution, land pollution, and water pollution – which do you think is the most worrying?

C Um, if I had to pick one, um, which I would be reluctant to do, uh, it would be water without a doubt. I think that what has happened to all of the oceans and beaches actually as well, um, in the world in the last 30 years is astonishing in the scale and the speed. Um, you know, there are certain places in the world, that you know, that you have to dig down on a beach, um, over a foot, before you'll find sand that doesn't have plastic in it. Unfortunately, what's happened with the way that soft plastic degrades in water is that, um, the pieces become so fragmented that they're the same size as the zooplankton, um, which is obviously in the food chain.

b Focus on the six sentences and the **Glossary**.

Play the DVD or audio again all the way through for Sts to complete the task. Play again as necessary.

You could get Sts to compare with a partner before checking answers.

Extra support

- When you play the DVD or audio the second time, pause after each question has been answered to give Sts time to write the missing words.

1 wonderful	3 cheerful	5 plastic
2 ruined	4 solutions	6 food

VIDEO Part 3

a 3 25)) Focus on the task and **Glossary**.

Give Sts time to read the three questions.

Play the DVD or audio (**Part 3**) once all the way through for Sts to do the task.

You could get Sts to compare with a partner before checking answers.

Extra support

- You could pause the DVD or audio at appropriate places and, in pairs, get Sts to compare answers.

1 She tries not to blame one person.
2 because San Francisco shows that zero waste can be achieved on a big scale
3 no

3 25))
(audioscript in Student Book on *page 125*)

Part 3

I Who do you think is mostly to blame for the problems we have with waste?

C I tried very hard actually not to blame one person or things, um, in the film, actually quite deliberately because I think in a way, um, it lets us off the hook, um, and it also, um, I think we all need to work on the, the problem together because it's too complicated to blame one person or one thing or one act or, um, you know, I think it's, it's multi-faceted, unfortunately.

I Your film finishes on an optimistic note with the example of San Francisco's zero waste policy. Can you tell us a bit about that?

C Well, I, I actually in the film ended up, um, using San Francisco as the example because I wanted to show, er, that zero waste could be achieved on a big scale. When you go and stay in San Francisco in your hotel room, you'll have four different bins and you'll have signs on the wall of what goes into each bin, so it's very, very easy to, to recycle and I think that's a huge part of what we should be doing.

I Has the film changed your own habits regarding waste?

C I don't think the film has particularly changed my own habits dramatically, um, because I've always been thrifty, um, by nature because, um, I was lucky enough to spend a lot of time with my grandparents when I was growing up and the post war, sort of, philosophy of never wasting anything, it just, you know, it was instilled in me. I ride the same bicycle that I've had since I was 15 years old and over the years obviously had it repaired and repaired, but I take tremendous pride in the fact that I've always, um, ridden the same bike and you know I have lovely memories of it, so and with it, so, um I think, I think we need a slight change of mindset to make things cool the longer you have them in a way, than actually this perpetual thing of buying new things for the sake of it.

b Focus on the task and give Sts time, in pairs, to see if they can remember why she mentioned the three things.

Play the DVD or audio all the way through. Play again as necessary.

You could get Sts to compare with a partner before checking answers.

Extra support

- You could pause the DVD or audio at appropriate places and, in pairs, get Sts to compare orally what they have understood.

1 They have four different bins and signs on the wall of what goes into each bin, so it's very easy to recycle.
2 She spent a lot of time with her grandparents when she was growing up. They taught her not to waste anything because they had lived through the war.
3 She still rides the bike she got when she was 15.

Extra support

- If there's time, you could play the audio again while Sts read the audioscripts on *page 125*, so they can see what they understood / didn't understand. Translate / explain any new words or phrases.

2 LOOKING AT LANGUAGE

3 26 This exercise focuses on a common feature of spoken English – the use of comment adverbs. Focus on the **Comment adverbs** box and go through it with the class.

Focus on the task and give Sts time to read extracts 1–7.

Play the DVD or audio, pausing after each extract to give Sts time to write the missing adverbs.

Check answers.

1 actually	5 strangely
2 obviously	6 sadly
3 amazingly	7 Unfortunately
4 generally	

3 26

1 We ended up actually filming in 11 countries...
2 ...but the stories that I've chosen are universal and, obviously, I spoke to, to people in communities, um, in more countries, um, than we actually filmed in...
3 ...and so I sent him the treatment and amazingly he, um, he loved it.
4 ...but generally, again, he was very shocked, um, by the film and really wanted to get involved...
5 ...yes and no, strangely enough. Obviously, I had a wonderful, DOP, Director of Photography, so he can pretty much make anything look beautiful...
6 I did a lot of research and so, sadly, these things were repeatable and, and in every country around the world...
7 Unfortunately, what's happened with the way that soft plastic degrades in water is that, um, the pieces become so fragmented...

3 VIDEO ON THE STREET

a 3 27 Focus on the task.

Play the DVD or audio once all the way through.

Check the answer.

Jo has the most positive attitude.

3 27
(audioscript in Student Book on *page 125*)
I = interviewer, S = Sally, Jo = Jo, J = Jill, P = Pranjal

Sally
I How much recycling do people in your country do?
S I don't think we do enough, I think we could do a little bit more. I'm not wonderful myself, but we try and do a little bit of recycling.
I How responsible are you personally?
S Well, we probably do about, probably about 30% we recycle.
I What do you think the government, or individuals, could do to make people recycle more?
S Well, they could give you all these, um, boxes and bins and things at home to help you recycle. The Germans seem to do it quite well.

Jo
I How much recycling do people in your country do?
Jo I think people are quite good at recycling, I think, um, now that the, the waste companies come and collect recycling from the houses, people haven't really got an excuse not to recycle any more.
I How responsible are you personally?
Jo Uh, I, I recycle as much as I can.
I What do you think the government, or individuals, could do to make people recycle more?
Jo Um, well maybe they could offer a financial incentive for, for recycling, um, or maybe for producing less rubbish that can't be recycled.

Jill
I How much recycling do people in your country do?
J I think that recycling is getting better in this country, I think that we still have a long ways to go. I think it's still done largely in pockets and not necessarily nationwide as much as it could be.
I How responsible are you personally?
J Actually, in the town where I live we have a very strong recycling program and so I participate in, um, filling it up with cans and bottles, newspapers and all kinds of stuff, and they come and get it every other week, so. Easy, too.
I What do you think the government, or individuals, could do to make people recycle more?
J Well, incentives always work. Besides, above and beyond monetary incentives, just incentives to promote, you know, benefits to the environment.

Pranjal
I How much recycling do people in your country do?
P I don't think people in the US recycle enough. I think we should recycle more and I'm even, uh, you know, I'm even guilty of not recycling enough, but I don't think we recycle enough.
I How responsible are you personally?
P Personally, I'm not really that responsible in recycling, I don't really recycle that often, but if I do get the opportunity to recycle, I will.
I What do you think the government, or individuals, could do to make people recycle more?
P Well, I think it's important for individuals to realize that even the smallest difference makes a big difference, and so if everyone could just get in that mindset that the smallest change they can make in their lives makes a big difference. I think that will, in fact, make a big difference.

b Focus on the task and give Sts time to read the questions.

Play the DVD or audio again all the way through, pausing after each speaker to give Sts time to do the task. Play again as necessary.

Check answers.

Jo and Jill think the government should offer money for recycling and producing less garbage.

Pranjal thinks it's up to people themselves to realize that it's worth recycling.

Sally thinks the government should provide more containers for recycling.

Jill thinks the government should do more to show people why recycling is good for the environment.

c 3 28 This exercise focuses on some colloquial expressions which were used by the speakers. Focus on the phrases and give Sts time to read them.

Play the DVD or audio, pausing after the first phrase and playing it again as necessary. Elicit the missing word and then the meaning of the whole phrase. Repeat for the other four phrases.

See words in **bold** in audioscript 3.28

3 28

1 ...well maybe they could offer a **financial** incentive for, for recycling...
2 ...I think we still have a **long way** to go.
3 Besides, above and beyond monetary incentives, just incentives to promote, you know, benefits to the environment.
4 ...filling it up with cans and bottles, newspapers and all **kinds** of **stuff**...
5 ...and so if everyone could just get in that **mindset** that the smallest change they can make in their lives makes a big difference.

Extra support

- Tell Sts to go to *page 125* and to look at the audioscript for **ON THE STREET**. Play the DVD or audio again and tell Sts to read and listen at the same time.

Help with any vocabulary problems and get feedback from Sts on what parts they found hard to understand and why, e.g., speed of speech, pronunciation, etc.

4 SPEAKING

Put Sts in pairs and get them to ask and answer the questions, giving as much information as possible.

Monitor and help with vocabulary. Help with any general language problems at the end of the activity.

Get some feedback.

G gerunds and infinitives
V music
P words that come from other languages

6A Music and emotion

Lesson plan

The topic of this lesson is music and how it affects our emotions.

The first section of the lesson begins with a vocabulary and pronunciation focus on common "borrowed" words related to music, e.g., *cello, choir,* and *ballet,* and on other foreign words that are used in English. This is followed by a speaking activity where Sts talk about their musical tastes and experiences. Sts then read an article from *The Times* about a young American whose deafness was cured and who was suddenly able to listen to music for the first time in his life.

In the second section of the lesson, Sts listen to an interview with a music psychologist, who explains why we listen to music and how music can affect us emotionally. The lesson continues with a grammar focus on the uses of gerunds and infinitives. Sts review the basic rules about when to use a gerund or an infinitive after a verb and then learn about certain verbs (e.g., *remember, try*) which can be followed by either a gerund or infinitive, but with a change in meaning. The lessons finishes with the song, *Sing*.

STUDY LINK
- **Workbook** 6A
- **Online Practice**
- **iChecker**

Extra photocopiable activities

- **Grammar** gerunds and infinitives *page 161*
- **Communicative** Gerund or infinitive? *page 199* (instructions *pages 182–183*)
- **Song** *Sing page 234* (instructions *page 227*)

Optional lead-in – the quote

- Write the quote at the top of *page 54* on the board (books closed) and the name of the person who said it, or get Sts to open their books and read it.
- You could tell Sts that G.K. Chesterton (1874–1936) is probably best known for his series about the priest-detective Father Brown, who appeared in 50 stories.
- Ask Sts if they agree with the quote.

1 VOCABULARY & PRONUNCIATION
music, words from other languages

a **3 29** Tell Sts they are going to hear some musical extracts and they have to match them to the words in the list.

Play the audio once or twice as necessary.

3 29
1 *Bach cello suite number 1*
2 *somebody playing drums*
3 *soprano singing*
4 *somebody playing a bass guitar*
5 *orchestra playing*
6 *jazz player playing saxophone*
7 *somebody playing a flute*
8 *a conductor rehearsing an orchestra*
9 *extract from Beethoven's Ninth Symphony*
10 *somebody playing a keyboard*
11 *somebody playing the violin*

b **3 30** Now play the audio for Sts to listen and check.

Check answers. Elicit and practice the pronunciation of the words, modeling where necessary.

See words in **bold** in audioscript 3.30

3 30
1 *Bach cello suite number 1*: **a cello**
2 *somebody playing drums*: **drums**
3 *soprano singing*: **a soprano**
4 *somebody playing a bass guitar*: **a bass guitar**
5 *orchestra playing*: **an orchestra**
6 *jazz player playing saxophone*: **a saxophone**
7 *somebody playing a flute*: **a flute**
8 *a conductor rehearsing an orchestra*: **a conductor**
9 *extract from Beethoven's Ninth Symphony*: **a choir**
10 *somebody playing a keyboard*: **a keyboard**
11 *somebody playing the violin*: **a violin**

In pairs Sts practice saying the words.

Give Sts, in pairs, a few minutes to think of any other words they know for instruments and musicians.

Elicit answers on the board in two columns headed INSTRUMENTS and MUSICIANS. Get Sts to spell the words and then elicit / drill pronunciation where necessary.

Possible suggestions
instruments: trumpet, triangle, recorder, harp, harmonica, banjo, trombone, clarinet, organ, etc.
musicians: cellist, drummer, bass guitarist, pianist, violinist, keyboard player, saxophonist, rapper, tenor, singer-songwriter, composer, lead singer, band, etc.

Pronunciation notes

- English has borrowed many words from other languages. Some of them have been anglicized, e.g., *boeuf* (French) to *beef*. Others have been unchanged, e.g., *cello*. Where English uses a foreign word, the consonants are often pronounced in a way which is similar to the language of origin, e.g., in *cello* the *c* is pronounced /tʃ/ – similar to the Italian pronunciation. On the other hand, vowels are usually anglicized, e.g., the final *o* in *cello* is pronounced /oʊ/ as in English.
Note: in borrowed French words that include the letters *en*, e.g., *genre*, the vowel is pronounced in a similar way to French, and sounds like the *o* in *on* /ɑn/.

c Focus on the **Foreign words that are used in English** box and go through it with the class.

Now put Sts in pairs and tell them to look at all the words in *Borrowed words related to music*, say them to each other, and underline the stressed syllable.

d 3 31 Play the audio for Sts to listen and check.

Check answers.

See underlining in audioscript 3.31

3 31

cello, concerto, mezzo-soprano

orchestra, choir, chorus, microphone, rhythm, symphony

ballet, encore, genre

Now play the audio again, pausing after each group of words. Elicit how the pink letters are pronounced.

The letter *c* in *cello* and *concerto* is pronounced /tʃ/.
The letters *zz* in *mezzo* are pronounced /ts/.
The letters *ch* in *orchestra, choir,* and *chorus* are pronounced /k/.
The letters *ph* in *microphone* and *symphony* are pronounced /f/.
The letters *rhy* in *rhythm* are pronounced /rɪ/.
The letters *et* in *ballet* are pronounced /eɪ/.
The letters *en* in *encore* are pronounced /ɑŋ/.
The letter *g* in *genre* is prononuced /ʒ/ and the letters *en* are pronounced /ɑn/.

Play the audio again, pausing after each group of words, and get Sts to repeat them.

Then repeat the activity, eliciting responses from individual Sts.

e Focus on the task and point out that these words are not related to music. You might want to highlight that Sts have seen a lot of these words in previous lessons.

Put Sts in pairs, get them to say the words to each other and then guess their origin.

Say each word in turn and ask Sts which language they come from and their meaning. Model and drill pronunciation as necessary.

f 3 32 Now play the audio for Sts to find out which language the words come from.

Check answers.

3 32

From Italian	barista, cappuccino, graffiti, macchiato, paparazzi, villa
From Greek	architecture, hypochondriac, philosophy, photograph, psychic, psychologist
From French	bouquet, chauffeur, chef, chic, croissant, fiancé

Play the audio again, pausing after each group of words for Sts to repeat.

Then repeat the activity, eliciting responses from individual Sts.

Finally, give Sts time to practice saying them.

2 SPEAKING

Focus on the questionnaire and give Sts time to read through it. Remind them that in the last question *live* is an adjective and is pronounced /laɪv/.

Put Sts in pairs and tell them to take turns telling each other their answers to the questions (rather than do this as an interview).

Montior and help if necessary.

Help with any vocabulary problems that come up.

Finally, get some quick feedback from the class on some of the questions, e.g., find out how many Sts can, e.g., read music, play an instrument, what the best live concert was that they have seen, etc.

Extra idea

- Tell Sts your own answers to some of the questions in the questionnaire, particularly if you have a strong interest in music or play an instrument, etc.

3 READING

a Focus on the task and then give Sts time to think of their answers.

Either put Sts in pairs and get them to share their answers or do this as an open-class activity. If you have a particular piece of music you remember hearing and liking as a child, tell Sts.

b Focus on the title, *What music would you play to an alien?*, and make sure Sts know the meaning of *an alien*.

Set a time limit for Sts to read the article once to find out why the writer chose this title.

Extra support

- Before Sts read the article, check it for words and phrases that your Sts might not know and be ready to help with these (but not the words in **c**).

Check the answer.

Before getting his new hearing aid, Austin Chapman had never heard music. He went on the Internet and asked for suggestions of what to listen to. Someone on the site reddit.com wrote that introducing Austin to music is like introducing music to an alien since we imagine that aliens would never have heard any music either.

c Now set a time limit for Sts to re-read the first paragraph of the article and to find the words / phrases for definitions 1–5.

Get Sts to compare with a partner and then check answers.

1 profoundly (line 1)
2 make a fool of themselves (line 2)
3 moved to tears (line 4)
4 with no great expectations (line 7)
5 a cacophony (line 9)

d Focus on the question and do it as an open-class activity.

whir = a low continuous sound, for example, the sound made by the regular movement of a machine or the wings of a bird
hum = a low continuous sound, for example, the sound made by a machine, such as a refrigerator
clacking = if two hard objects clack, they make a short loud sound when they hit each other

Help with any other new vocabulary and encourage Sts to write down any useful new lexis from the article.

e Now get Sts to read the whole article again and to find why 1–9 are mentioned.

Then, in pairs, Sts use their own words to explain what they read about 1–9.

Check answers.

1 The *Lacrimosa* is the first piece of music Austin listened to. It made him cry.
2 After *Lacrimosa* his friends played all these bands and singers.
3 Someone on the reddit.com website told Austin to start with classical music and then move on to music from the fifties.
4 Austin decided to listen to music from each decade and he started with Guillaume de Machaut's *Agnus Dei*.
5 Austin doesn't like country music because he thinks it is too depressing.
6 This is his favorite piece for the time being.
7 These are two pieces of music he also likes.
8 He hasn't listened to them yet.
9 This is still his favorite sound. It makes him feel peaceful.

f Put Sts in pairs and get them to discuss the questions.

Get some feedback, particularly about the music they would recommend.

4 LISTENING & SPEAKING

a 3 33))) Focus on the task.

Play the extracts one by one and elicit some opinions to the first question. Then have Sts raise their hands to find out how many would like to continue listening or not. If Sts say *yes*, you could elicit what kind of music it is.

3 33)))
Extracts:
1 *classical music* (*Lacrimosa*, from Mozart's *Requiem*)
2 *drum and bass*
3 *a waltz* (*The Blue Danube*, by Johann Strauss II)
4 *contemporary classical music*
5 *traditional jazz*
6 *Indian sitar music*
7 *country music*
8 *rap*
9 *New Age*

Extra support

- Before playing the music extracts, elicit from Sts how music can make you feel, e.g., *happy*, *sad*, *sleepy*, *angry*, etc. Write all the adjectives they suggest on the board. Then play each piece of music one at a time.

b 3 34))) Tell Sts that they are going to listen to a music psychologist talking about why we listen to music. Focus on the task and tell Sts that the first time they listen they should try to complete sentences 1–3 with a phrase. The second time they should try to listen for at least one example.

Play the audio twice and give Sts time to write their notes.

You could get Sts to compare with a partner before checking answers.

Extra support

- Before playing the audio, go through the audioscript and decide if you need to preteach / check any lexis to help Sts when they listen.

1 to make us **remember important moments in the past**, e.g., when we met someone for the first time
2 to help us to **change activities**, e.g., we play a certain kind of music to prepare us to go out in the evening (another kind to relax us when we get home from work).
3 to intensify **the emotion that we are feeling**, e.g., if we are sad, we play sad music to make us even sadder (if we are feeling angry, we play angry music to make us angrier; we play romantic music to make a romantic dinner more romantic).

3 34)))
(audioscript in Student Book on *page 125*)
I think it's very interesting that human beings are the only animals that listen to music for pleasure. A lot of research has been done to find out why we listen to music, and there seems to be three main reasons. Firstly, we listen to music to make us remember important moments in the past, for example, when we met someone for the first time. Think of Humphrey Bogart in the film *Casablanca* saying "Darling, they're playing our song." When we hear a certain piece of music, we remember hearing it for the first time in some very special circumstances. Obviously, this music varies from person to person.
Secondly, we listen to music to help us to change activities. If we want to go from one activity to another, we often use music to help us make the change. For example, we might play a certain kind of music to prepare us to go out in the evening, or we might play another kind of music to relax us when we get home from work. That's mainly why people listen to music in cars, and they often listen to one kind of music when they're going to work and another kind when they're coming home. The same is true of people on buses and trains with their iPods.
The third reason why we listen to music is to intensify the emotion that we're feeling. For example, if we're feeling sad, sometimes we want to get even sadder, so we play sad music. Or we're feeling angry and we want to intensify the anger, then we play angry music. Or when we're planning a romantic dinner, we set the table, we light candles, and then we think, "What music would make this even more romantic?"

c 3 35))) Focus on the task and give Sts time to look at the incomplete notes. Make sure they understand *to exploit* on the last line.

Play the audio twice and give Sts time to complete their notes by pausing between each section.

You could get Sts to compare with a partner before checking answers.

Extra support

- Before playing the audio, go through the audioscript and decide if you need to preteach / check any lexis to help Sts when they listen.

Three important human emotions
2 sadness
3 anger
How we feel affects the way we speak, e.g.,
2 sad – speak more slowly / lower
3 angry – raise voice / shout
Music copies this, e.g.,
2 slow music with falling pitches makes us feel sad
3 loud music with irregular rhythms makes us feel angry
Examples (pieces of music):
1 happy, e.g., Beethoven's *Seventh Symphony*
2 angry, e.g., *Mars* from *The Planets* by Holst
3 sad, e.g., Albinoni's *Adagio for strings*.
This is especially exploited in movie soundtracks, e.g., the shower scene in *Psycho* (nothing is happening, but the music makes it terrifying).

3 35

(audioscript in Student Book on *page 125*)

Let's take three important human emotions: happiness, sadness, and anger. When people are happy, they speak faster and their voice is higher. When they are sad, they speak more slowly and their voice is lower, and when people are angry, they raise their voices or shout. Babies can tell whether their mother is happy or not simply by the sound of her voice, not by her words. What music does is it copies this, and it produces the same emotions. So faster, higher-pitched music will sound happy. Slow music with lots of falling pitches will sound sad. Loud music with irregular rhythms will sound angry.
It doesn't matter how good or bad the music is, if it has these characteristics, it will make you experience this emotion.
Let me give you some examples. For happy, for example, the first movement of Beethoven's *Seventh Symphony*. For angry, say *Mars*, from *The Planets* by Holst. And for sad, something like Albinoni's *Adagio for Strings*.
Of course the people who exploit this most are the people who write film soundtracks. They can take a scene that visually has no emotion and they can make the scene either scary or calm or happy just by the music they write to go with it. Think of the music in the shower scene in Hitchcock's movie *Psycho*. All you can see is a woman having a shower, but the music makes it absolutely terrifying.

Extra support

- If there's time, you could play the audio again while Sts read the audioscripts on *page 125*, so they can see what they understood / didn't understand. Translate / explain any new words or phrases.

d Focus on the questions and then set a time limit for Sts to go through them in pairs and compare answers and choices of music. When answering question 3, encourage Sts to be as specific as possible in their answers, e.g., by specifying not just the kind of music they would play, but also the name of the artist or song / piece of music.

Monitor and help while Sts do the task.

Help with any general vocabulary problems that come up.

Get some feedback from individual Sts.

5 GRAMMAR gerunds and infinitives

a Focus on the task and extracts 1–3 and give Sts a couple of minutes to put the verbs into the gerund or infinitive.

Get them to compare with a partner.

b **3 36** Now play the audio for Sts to listen and check.

Check answers.

1 remember 2 hearing 3 to go, to make

3 36
1 Firstly, we listen to music to make us remember important moments in the past.
2 When we hear a certain piece of music, we remember hearing it for the first time...
3 If we want to go from one activity to another, we often use music to help us make the change.

c This exercise introduces a new grammar point that certain verbs can use either the gerund or infinitive, but with a change in meaning.

Focus on the task and give Sts time to try and figure out the difference between the two sentences.

Check answers.

1 is about the past. 2 is about the future.

d **3 37** **3 38** Tell Sts to go to **Grammar Bank 6A** on *page 142*. Focus on the example sentences and play the audio for Sts to listen to the sentence rhythm. You could also get Sts to repeat the sentences to practice getting the rhythm right. Then go through the rules with the class. Make sure they understand the meaning of all the listed verbs and phrases, e.g., *can't stand* = hate, *happen to* = do something by chance.

Additional grammar notes

- Previously, Sts have seen the basic rules governing the use of gerunds and infinitives (with and without *to*) after certain verbs. Here they review and expand their knowledge of verbs that can take the gerund and those that take the infinitive with or without *to* – something that even the most advanced Sts make mistakes with. They then learn to use verbs that can take either form, but with a change in meaning.

verbs followed by the gerund and verbs followed by the infinitive

- **rules 1–3:** A full list of the most common verbs that take the gerund or infinitive is included in the **Appendix *Verb patterns: verbs followed by the gerund or infinitive*** on *page 164*. After reminding students of the three verb patterns (Rules 1–3), take a few minutes to go through the **Appendix** and make sure Sts know the meaning of the verbs. You could ask Sts to review the three groups as self-study and test them on the material.
- **rule 3: *make*** and ***let*** Highlight that the verb form following these verbs depends on whether the sentence is active or passive.

verbs that can be followed by either gerund or infinitive with *to*

- **rule 2:** This grammar rule will be new to most Sts. In Sts' L1, some of these concepts may be covered by using two different verbs, so if you know your Sts' L1, you can use it to make the meaning clear.
- With *need to do* / *needs doing*, highlight that *needs doing* is an alternative to a passive construction, e.g., *The house needs painting* / *to be painted*.

Focus on the exercises and get Sts to do them individually or in pairs.

Check answers, getting Sts to read the full sentences.

a

1 taking	6 clean
2 to drive	7 to call
3 do	8 coming
4 waiting	9 to eat out / eating out
5 to carry	10 working

b

1 seeing	5 to turn
2 to call	6 painting
3 taking	7 to send
4 locking	8 learning / to learn

Tell Sts to go back to the main lesson **6A**.

Extra support

- If you think Sts need more practice, you may want to give them the Grammar photocopiable activity at this point or leave it for later as consolidation or review.

e Put Sts in pairs for this oral grammar practice activity and focus on the task. Give Sts time to think and plan what they are going to say before getting them to speak.

Monitor and help Sts, correcting any errors with gerunds and infinitives.

Get some feedback.

6 3 39))) **SONG** *Sing* ♫

This song was originally made famous by the American rock band My Chemical Romance in 2010. For copyright reasons, this is a cover version. If you want to do this song in class, use the photocopiable activity on *page 234*.

3 39)))

Sing

Sing it out
Boy, you've got to see what tomorrow brings
Sing it out
Girl, you've got to be what tomorrow needs
For every time that they want to count you out
Use your voice every single time you open up your mouth

Chorus
Sing it for the boys
Sing it for the girls
Every time that you lose it sing it for the world
Sing it from the heart
Sing it till you're nuts
Sing it out for the ones that'll hate your guts
Sing it for the deaf
Sing it for the blind
Sing about everyone that you left behind
Sing it for the world
Sing it for the world

Sing it out
Boy, they're gonna sell what tomorrow means
Sing it out
Girl, before they kill what tomorrow brings
You've got to make a choice
If the music drowns you out
And raise your voice
Every single time they try and shut your mouth

Chorus

Cleaned up, corporation progress
Dying in the process
Children that can talk about it
Living on the railways
People moving sideways
Sell it till your last days
Buy yourself the motivation
Generation Nothing
Nothing but a dead scene
Product of a white dream
I am not the singer that you wanted
But a dancer
I refuse to answer
Talk about the past
And rooting for the ones who want to get away

Keep running!

Chorus

We've got to see what tomorrow brings
Sing it for the world
Sing it for the world
Girl, you've got to be what tomorrow needs
Sing it for the world
Sing it for the world

6B Sleeping Beauty

Lesson plan

The context of this lesson is several different angles on sleep.

In the beginning of the first section of the lesson, Sts listen to three people who all have some kind of sleep problem and they then talk about their own experiences. Sentences taken from the listening provide the context for the grammar presentation, which reviews the use of *used to* to talk about repeated past actions, and introduces *be used to* and *get used to* (doing something) to talk about actions or activities which have become, or are becoming, familiar. The Pronunciation focus is on sentence stress and linking. Sts then read an article about how video games help people control their dreams, followed by two more articles that they read separately, and tell each other about, on some other unusual aspects of sleep.

In the second section of the lesson, Sts listen to a radio program in which they hear about an ex-chef who cooks while sleepwalking. They also hear an expert talking about sleepwalking. The lesson ends with a vocabulary focus on sleep (e.g., *oversleep, jet lagged*) and a speaking activity to recycle the new lexis.

STUDY LINK
- **Workbook** 6B
- **Online Practice**
- **iChecker**

Extra photocopiable activities

- **Grammar** *used to, be used to, get used to page 162*
- **Communicative** *usually, used to, get used to page 200* (instructions *page 183*)

Optional lead-in – the quote

- Write the quote at the top of *page 58* on the board (books closed) and the name of the person who said it, or get Sts to open their books and read it.
- You could tell Sts that Anthony Burgess (1917–1993) is best known for his novel *A Clockwork Orange*.
- Ask Sts what they think the quote means and if they agree with it.

1 LISTENING & SPEAKING

a Do this in pairs or as an open-class activity.

b 3 40))) 3 41))) 3 42))) Focus on the task. Tell Sts they will hear each speaker at least twice. For each person, they should write down what the speaker's problems are and what has caused the problem.

Play audio 3.40 for Sts to listen and do the task for the first speaker.

You could get Sts to compare with a partner and then play the audio again for Sts to check and complete their answers.

Then repeat for the other two speakers (audio 3.41 and 3.42).

Check answers.

Extra support

- Before playing the audio, go through the audioscripts and decide if you need to preteach / check any lexis to help Sts when they listen, e.g., *blinds*, etc.

Speaker 1: He is from a rural area and moved to the city three years ago. He has problems getting to sleep and wakes up when he is asleep because his bedroom isn't dark enough. He prefers to sleep in complete darkness with closed blinds (which he always used to do where he grew up), but his wife doesn't. Their room has thin curtains that don't keep out all the light. His wife would feel claustrophobic with heavier curtains.

Speaker 2: He is a police officer and has to work different shifts (one-week nights, the next-week days). When he works at night, he feels tired, but then he can't get to sleep when he gets home because it's too noisy and everybody else is getting up. Just when his body gets used to working nights, it's time to change to working during the day.

Speaker 3: She travels to New York very often for work and suffers from jet lag because of the time difference. When she arrives it's evening for her, but it's one o'clock local time, so when it is her bedtime, she still has to work and go out for dinner. When she finally gets to bed, she wakes up in the night because her body clock is still on UK time. So she feels tired the next day. By the time she gets used to New York time, it's time to go home, but flying home (west to east) is worse – she arrives home in the morning UK time, but it is night for her body.

3 40)))
(audioscript in Student Book on *page 126*)
I = interviewer, S = speaker

1
I Why do you have problems sleeping?
S Well, I'm from a pretty rural area, but I moved to the city a few years ago when I got married. I've been living in the city for three years now. I have a lot of problems getting to sleep at night because our bedroom just isn't dark enough. I can't get used to sleeping in a bedroom where there's light coming in from the streetlights outside. Where I grew up, I always used to sleep in complete darkness because my bedroom window had blinds and when I went to bed I used to close the blinds completely. But here in the city, our bedroom window just has curtains and curtains don't block out the light very well. It takes me a long time to get to sleep at night, and I always wake up more often than I used to.
I So why don't you just get heavier curtains?
S Because my wife doesn't like sleeping in a completely dark room. She says that she feels claustrophobic if the room is too dark.
I Hmm, yes, a lot of people do feel like that.

3 41
(audioscript in Student Book on *page 126*)

2

I Why do you have problems sleeping?
S Well, I'm a police officer and so I have to work different shifts, which means I work at night every other week, so I start work at 10 o'clock at night and end at six in the morning the following day. The main problem is that my body's used to sleeping at night, not during the day. So it's hard to get used to being awake all night and trying to work and concentrate when your body is just telling you to go to bed.
I But isn't it something you get used to?
S Actually no, because I work during the day for one week and then the next week I work at night, which means that just when my body has gotten used to being awake at night, then I go back to working in the day. And then, of course, I can't get to sleep at night because my body thinks it's going to have to work all night. The other problem is that when I get home after working a night shift, everyone else is just starting to wake up, so that means that it can be really noisy. The neighbors turn the radio on, and bang doors, and shout to wake their children up. So even though I'm really tired, it's just very hard to get to sleep.
I How many hours do you usually sleep?
S Before I became a police officer, I used to sleep about eight or nine hours a night, but I think now I probably don't sleep more than six hours.

3 42
(audioscript in Student Book on *page 126*)

3

I Why do you have problems sleeping?
S I have a lot of problems sleeping because of jet lag. I have to travel a lot in my job and I take a lot of long-haul flights. I fly to New York quite often, and I arrive maybe at six in the evening my time, but when it's only one o'clock in the afternoon in New York. So at five in the afternoon local time, I'll be feeling tired and ready for bed because it's my bedtime, but I can't go to sleep because I'm probably still working or having dinner with my American colleagues. Then when I do finally get to bed at say midnight local time, I find that I wake up in the middle of the night because my body thinks that it's morning because it's still working on UK time.
I And can you get back to sleep when you wake up?
S No, that's the problem, I can't get back to sleep. And then the next day when I have meetings I feel really sleepy. It's very hard to stay awake all day. And just when I'm finally used to being on New York time, then it's time to fly home. And flying west to east is even worse.
I Oh, why's that?
S Because when I get off the plane it's early morning in the UK. But for me, on New York time, it's the middle of the night. It takes me four or five days to recover from one of these trips.
I Gosh, that must be really difficult for you.

Extra support

- If there's time, you could play the audio again while Sts read the audioscripts on *page 126*, so they can see what they understood / didn't understand. Translate / explain any new words or phrases.

c Focus on the three questions and make sure Sts understand them.

Put Sts in pairs and get them to interview each other, giving as much information as possible.

Monitor and help while Sts do the task.

Help with any general vocabulary problems that come up.

Get some feedback.

2 GRAMMAR *used to, be used to, get used to*

a Focus on the task and the sentences that contrast the meaning of *used to*, *be used to*, and *get used to*.

Give Sts time to match the highlighted phrases to meanings 1–3 and to answer the question.

Check answers.

I always used to sleep	1
It's hard to get used to being	3
I'm finally used to being on New York time	2

a) After *used to* the verb that follows is in the infinitive without *to*.
b) After *be / get used to* the verb that follows is in the *-ing* form (because *to* is a preposition here, not an infinitive).

b **3 43** **3 44** Tell Sts to go to **Grammar Bank 6B** on *page 143*. Focus on the example sentences and play the audio for Sts to listen to the sentence rhythm. You could also get Sts to repeat the sentences to practice getting the rhythm right. Then go through the rules with the class.

Additional grammar notes

used to / didn't use to + infinitive

- At this level, Sts should be confident about using *used to* (*do something*) although they may still make mistakes like using *I use to…* instead of *I usually…* to describe a present habit. This can cause misunderstanding as a listener may understand *I used to…* (e.g., a past habit).

be used to / get used to + gerund

- These structures are introduced for the first time. Their similarity in form to *used to* means that they sometimes get mixed up in Sts' minds. A very common mistake is to use these structures with the infinitive instead of the gerund (e.g., *I'm used to ~~wake up~~ early*).
- Point out to Sts that *to* here is a preposition, and can also be followed by a noun (e.g., *I'm used to living in London now; I'm used to the weather here now*).
- The meaning of *be used to doing something* may not be immediately obvious to Sts. A formal equivalent would be *be accustomed to doing something*.
- You may also want to point out that the difference between *be used to* and *get used to* is like the difference between *be angry* and *get angry*, and that here *get* = *become*.
- The use of *would* to refer to repeated actions in the past is referenced here, but not practiced in the grammar exercises. You may want to point out that *would* is used, especially in written English, as a variant to *used to*, e.g., *We* ***used to*** *spend all our vacations at the ocean. We* ***would*** *get up early every morning and run to the beach…*

Focus on the exercises and get Sts to do them individually or in pairs.

Check answers, getting Sts to read the full sentences.

a
1 ✗ used to play
2 ✗ couldn't get used to eating
3 ✗ Have you gotten used to living
4 ✓
5 ✓
6 ✗ used to have
7 ✗ I'm used to it
8 ✓
9 ✗ to get used to living
10 ✓

b

1	get used to getting up	6	get used to wearing
2	used to have	7	isn't used to sharing
3	used to rent	8	gotten used to having
4	used to spend	9	didn't use to like
5	is used to working	10	get used to eating

Tell Sts to go back to the main lesson **6B**.

Extra support

- If you think Sts need more practice, you may want to give them the Grammar photocopiable activity at this point or leave it for later as consolidation or review.

3 PRONUNCIATION sentence stress and linking

Pronunciation notes

- Although Sts should be familiar with the stress patterns of English, i.e., stressing the information words, they will still need more practice to be able to speak fluently with the right rhythm. They should also know the rules for linking words when one ends with a consonant and the next one begins with a vowel, as in *get up*, or when a word ends with a consonant sound and the next one begins with the same or a very similar sound, as is the case with *used to* /yustə/.

a 3 45 Focus on the task.

Play the audio once all the way through for Sts just to listen.

3 45
See sentences in Student Book on *page 58*

Now play it again, pausing after each sentence for Sts to repeat. Make sure they pay attention to the rhythm and linking.

Finally, repeat the activity, eliciting responses from individual Sts.

b 3 46 Focus on the task.

Play the audio once all the way through for Sts just to listen.

3 46
1 I'm not used to sleeping on such a hard bed.
2 I'll never get used to living alone.
3 Did you use to sleep a lot when you were a teenager?

Now play the audio again, pausing after each sentence to give Sts time to write. Play again as necessary.

Check answers by writing the sentences on the board.

See sentences in audioscript 3.46

Extra challenge

- Tell Sts to listen again and this time to try and underline the stressed words. Play the audio.
- Elicit the stressed words and underline them on the board:

1 I'm not used to sleeping on such a hard bed.
2 I'll never get used to living alone.
3 Did you use to sleep a lot when you were a teenager?

- Elicit that the stressed words are always the words that carry the information, e.g., nouns and verbs.

c Put Sts in pairs and get them to say the sentences to each other.

Get some individual Sts to say the sentences.

d This exercise recycles the grammar. Put Sts in pairs and get them to discuss 1–3, giving as much information as possible.

Get some feedback.

Extra support

- Demonstrate the activity by answering some of the questions yourself.

4 READING & SPEAKING

a Focus on the instructions and then give Sts time to read the introduction.

Then elicit answers to the three bulleted questions below the introduction. Don't tell Sts if they are right or not, but tell them they will find out the answers later.

b Focus on the task and sentences 1–6, helping with any vocabulary problems (the term "*lucid*" *dream* is explained in the article).

Give Sts time to read *Living your dreams* and answer T or F for each statement. Remind them to underline the part in the article that gave them the answer.

Get Sts to compare with a partner and then check answers.

Extra support

- Before Sts read the article, check it for words and phrases that your Sts might not know and be ready to help with these (but not the ones from **d**).

1 T (Line 6: A lucid dream is one in which we are aware that we are dreaming.)
2 F (Line 7: In a lucid dream, the dreamer is sometimes able to control or influence what is happening to them...)
3 T (Line 12: Gamers spend hours a day in a virtual reality and they are used to controlling their game environments, and this seems to help them to do the same when they are dreaming.)
4 T (Line 17: Some experts believe that we have nightmares to help us practice for life-threatening situations in a safe environment.)
5 F (Line 19: Since video gamers already practice those (life-threatening) situations regularly in games...video gamers may have less need of nightmares.)
6 T (Line 25: When they – a gamer – have a frightening experience in a dream, they don't run away like most of us do, they turn round and fight back.)

c Put Sts in pairs, **A** and **B**, and tell them to go to **Communication *Three things you (probably) didn't know about sleep***, **A** on *page 106*, **B** on *page 111* to find out the answers to the other two questions they discussed in **a**.

Give Sts time to read their texts and answer the questions.

When they are ready, they should use their answers to tell each other about what they read.

Extra support

- You could write any new and useful words and phrases from the article and **Communication** on the board for Sts to copy.

Tell Sts to go back to the main lesson **6B**.

d Focus on the Vocabulary quiz and give Sts a time limit to answer it in pairs. 1–3 are from *Sleeping Beauty*, 4–6 are from *How our ancestors used to sleep*, and 7–9 are from *Living your dreams*.

If Sts wrote their answers on a separate piece of paper, get them to exchange with another pair. Check answers.

1 syndrome	6 pray
2 loyal	7 gamer
3 deep	8 lucid
4 century	9 turn around
5 nightfall	

Have Sts raise their hands to show how many pairs got all the answers right.

e Focus on the questions and then put Sts in pairs to discuss them.

Monitor and help if necessary.

Get some feedback from the class and tell them what you think.

5 LISTENING & SPEAKING

a Focus on the title, *The chef who cooks in the middle of the night*, and the illustration, and ask Sts why they think he cooks.

Elicit answers, but <u>don't</u> tell Sts if they are right or not.

b 3 47 Tell Sts they are going to listen to a radio program about sleep with the chef and his wife as guests. Focus on the task and play the audio once all the way through.

Get Sts to compare with a partner and then if necessary, play the audio again.

Check answers.

Extra support

- Before playing the audio, go through the audioscript and decide if you need to preteach / check any lexis to help Sts when they listen.

Robert cooks in the middle of the night because he cooks when sleepwalking.
He cooks all kinds of things, e.g., omelettes, spaghetti bolognese, chips, etc.
It is a problem because he doesn't know he is doing it and it could be dangerous.

3 47
(audioscript in Student Book on *page 126*)
P = **presenter**, **R** = **Robert**, **E** = **Eleanor**

P And finally today the story of a sleepwalker who gets up in the middle of the night and goes to the kitchen and starts...you guessed it, cooking. Robert Wood, who's 55 years old, used to be a chef until he retired last year. We have Robert and his wife, Eleanor, with us in the studio today. Robert, tell us what happens.
R Well, I've been a sleepwalker for about 40 years now. I think it first started when I was about 14 or so. Anyway, these days I get up about four or five times a week and I always end up in the kitchen, and I start cooking something.
P Do you always cook?
R No, not always. I've done other things, too. I remember once I put the TV on at full volume and once I filled the bath with water, although I didn't get in it. But I usually cook.
P Eleanor, do you wake up when this happens?
E Yes, I usually wake up because he's making a noise. I go downstairs and usually I find him in the kitchen. Once he was just laying the table, but other times he's been cooking.
P What kinds of things does he cook?
E All sorts of things. I've caught him cooking omelettes and spaghetti bolognese, and I even caught him frying chips once. That was a bit scary because he could easily have burnt himself or started a fire.
P Do you ever eat the things that Robert cooks?
E No. It always looks lovely, but I must admit I've never tried it – not at three o'clock in the morning. And the trouble is he always leaves the kitchen in a terrible mess. The last time he sleepwalked he spilt milk all over the place.
P So, Robert, you don't know that you're cooking?
R No, I haven't. I really am asleep and afterwards I just have no recollection of having cooked anything.
P You're getting some help to see if you can cure your sleep walking, aren't you?
R Yes, I've been going to a sleep clinic in Edinburgh, where they think they'll be able to help me.
P Well, good luck with that, and thank you both for coming into the studio today. Now we're going to a break, but join us again in a few minutes...

c Focus on the task and give Sts time to read the article and fill in the blanks.

Get Sts to compare with a partner and then play the audio again for them to listen and check.

Check answers.

1 55	5 the bath
2 chef	6 omelettes
3 14	7 chips
4 four or five	8 fire

d Now tell Sts they are going to listen to the second half of the program where an expert on sleepwalking joins the guests. Put Sts in pairs and tell them to decide with their partner if they think sentences 1–10 are true or false.

e 3 48 Tell Sts the first time they listen they just need to mark the sentences true or false. Then they will listen again and they will need to correct the false ones.

Play the audio once all the way through.

Get Sts to compare with their partner and then play the audio again.

Check answers.

Extra support

- Before playing the audio, go through the audioscript and decide if you need to preteach / check any lexis to help Sts when they listen.

1 T
2 F (It **isn't** easy to know if someone is sleepwalking because sleepwalkers usually have their eyes open.)
3 F (About **18%** of the population have a tendency to sleepwalk.)
4 T
5 T
6 F (You **can** wake a sleepwalker up without any problem.)
7 F (Sleepwalkers **can** hurt themselves – if a sleepwalker is walking around the house, they might trip or fall over a chair, or even fall down stairs.)
8 T
9 T
10 F (Sleepwalking **is** an excuse if you commit a crime – a man killed his mother-in-law while sleepwalking. The man was charged with murder, but he was found not guilty.)

Extra support

- Before playing the audio a second time, quickly check which sentences are true and which are false. Do not ask Sts yet to correct the false sentences. Then play the audio again.

3 48

(audioscript in Student Book on *page 126*)
P = presenter, M = Professor Maurice

P We've been talking to Robert, the sleepwalking cook, and his wife, Eleanor. And we're now joined by Professor Maurice from Rochester, New York, who is an expert in sleepwalking.
P Hello. Welcome. Professor Maurice, does this story surprise you?
M No, it doesn't. Not at all. I've treated people who have driven cars, ridden horses, and I had one man who even tried to fly a helicopter while he was asleep.
P Do people usually have their eyes open when they sleepwalk?
M Yes, sleepwalkers do usually have their eyes open. That's why sometimes it's difficult to know if someone is sleepwalking or not.
P How common is sleepwalking?
M More common than you might think. Research shows that about 18% of the population have a tendency to sleepwalk. But it's much more common in children than in teenagers or adults. And curiously, it's more common among boys than girls. Adults who sleepwalk are usually people who used to sleepwalk when they were children. They might do it after a stressful event, for example, after a traffic accident.
P People always say that you should never wake a sleepwalker up when they're walking. Is that true?
M No, it isn't. People used to think that it was dangerous to wake up a sleepwalker. But in fact, this isn't the case. You can wake a sleepwalker up without any problem, although if you do, it is pretty common for the sleepwalker to be confused, so they probably won't know where they are for a few minutes.
P So, if we see someone sleepwalking, should we wake them up?
M Yes, you should remember that another of the myths about sleepwalkers is that they can't injure themselves while they are sleepwalking. But this isn't true. If a sleepwalker is walking around the house, they might trip or fall over a chair, or even fall down stairs. There was a case a while ago of a nine-year-old girl who opened her bedroom window while she was sleepwalking and fell 30 feet to the ground. Luckily, she wasn't seriously injured. So you see, Eleanor, you're right to worry that Robert might burn himself when he's cooking. You need to wake him up and get him back to bed.
P How long does sleepwalking usually last?
M It can be very brief, for example, a few minutes. The most typical cases are people getting up and getting dressed, or people going to the bathroom. But it can occasionally last much longer, maybe half an hour or even more, as in Robert's case.
P And what happens when sleepwalkers wake up? Do they remember the things they did while they were sleepwalking?
M No, as Robert says, a sleepwalker usually doesn't remember anything afterwards.
P So, is a sleepwalker responsible for his or her actions?
M That's a very good question, actually. A few years ago a man from Canada got up in the middle of the night and drove 20 miles from his home to the house where his parents-in-law lived and, for no apparent reason, he killed his mother-in-law. The man was charged with murder, but he was found not guilty because he had been asleep at the time he committed the crime.
P What a sad story. Professor Maurice, thank you very much for joining us today.

Extra support

- If there's time, you could play the audio again while Sts read the audioscripts on *page 126*, so they can see what they understood / didn't understand. Translate / explain any new words or phrases.

f Do this as an open-class question. If you have any experience with sleepwalking or know anyone who does, tell Sts about it.

6 VOCABULARY & SPEAKING sleep

a **Vocabulary race**. Put Sts in pairs. Focus on the task and set a time limit. Sts should already know some of these words / phrases, others have come up earlier in the reading text, and others, e.g., *sleep like a log*, may be completely new. Use the example word (*sleepy*) to demonstrate, and elicit / explain the difference between *sleepy* and *tired*.

b **3 49**)) Play the audio for Sts to listen and check.

Check Sts understand all the words and phrases. If necessary, explain the difference between *a blanket* (a large cover made of wool or cotton) and *a comforter* (a bed covering filled with feathers or synthetic material). You might also want to point out that *jet-lagged* is an adjective and *jet lag* a noun, as seen in **1C**.

Model and drill pronunciation of any words you think might be difficult, e.g. *insomnia* /ɪnˈsɑmniə/.

See words in **bold** in audioscript 3.49

3 49))

1 Most people start feeling **sleepy** around 11:00 at night.
2 They often open their mouth and **yawn**.
3 They go to bed and **set** their **alarm** clock.
4 They get into bed and put their head on the **pillow**.
5 They cover themselves up with a **comforter**, or with **sheets** and **blankets**.
6 Soon they **fall asleep**.
7 Some people make a loud noise when they breathe. In other words, they **snore**.
8 During the night some people have bad dreams, called **nightmares**.
9 If you don't hear your alarm clock, you might **oversleep**.
10 If you drink coffee in the evening, it may **keep you awake**.
11 Some people can't sleep because they suffer from **insomnia**.
12 These people often have to take **sleeping pills**.
13 Some people take a **siesta** or **nap** after lunch.
14 A person who sleeps well "sleeps like a **log**."
15 Someone who is tired after flying to another time zone is **jet-lagged**.
16 Someone who is sleeping very deeply is **fast asleep**.

c Focus on the task and get Sts to cover the words in the right-hand column, and then to try to remember them by reading sentences 1–16 again and saying the missing words from memory.

If there's time, you could quickly elicit the words from the whole class to wrap up the activity.

d Focus on the task and the questions. Give Sts a few minutes to read through them, and check they know the meaning of *recurring dreams*.

Put Sts in pairs, **A** and **B**. **A** asks **B** the blue questions and **B** asks the red ones. If you have plenty of time, you could ask Sts to return the questions with *What about you?*.

Monitor and help while Sts ask and answer the questions.

Help with any vocabulary problems that come up.

Get some feedback from various pairs.

Extra idea

- You could get Sts to ask you some of the questions.

5&6 Review and Check

For instructions on how to use these pages see *page 39*.

Test and Assessment CD-ROM

- **File 6 Quick Test**
- **File 6 Test**

GRAMMAR

a 1 hadn't found
2 didn't work
3 wouldn't have gone
4 wouldn't be
5 used to driving
6 to have
7 to getting up
8 I could speak
9 I'd learned to play
10 you wouldn't leave

b 1 meeting
2 cleaning
3 to get
4 not to be
5 living

VOCABULARY

a 1 proud
2 homesick
3 grateful
4 guilty
5 stunned

b 1 exhausting
2 shocked
3 embarrassed
4 stressful
5 annoys
6 disappointing
7 amazes
8 horrified
9 offensive
10 scary

c 1 a conductor
2 a chorus / a choir
3 a cello
4 a soprano
5 a keyboard

d 1 pillow
2 snore
3 nap
4 nightmare
5 set

PRONUNCIATION

a 1 threaten
2 nap
3 chauffeur
4 architect
5 guilty

b 1 up<u>set</u>
2 <u>de</u>vastated
3 <u>or</u>chestra
4 in<u>som</u>nia
5 <u>sleep</u>walk

CAN YOU UNDERSTAND THIS TEXT?

a his contact lens solution (which he drank) and the training he did for a career in the Armed Services

b 1 a
2 c
3 c
4 b
5 a
6 c
7 c
8 b
9 a
10 b

c Get Sts to compare their five words with a partner and practice pronouncing each word.

VIDEO CAN YOU UNDERSTAND THIS MOVIE?

3 50

1 c 2 b 3 a 4 b 5 c

3 50 Available as MP3 on CD1

A Short Movie on Sleep Research

Did you get enough sleep last night? I didn't. Nor the night before. These days lots of people have trouble getting a good night's sleep. Insomnia – the inability to get to sleep – is now a major issue for many people. In Britain, over half of the adult population often struggle to fall asleep and ten percent of people regularly take sleeping pills.

Even when people do get to sleep, they often sleep badly. Some people even struggle with sleeping disorders. These range from the common to the bizarre. Common sleep disorders include sleepwalking and somniloquy, also known as sleep-talking. Stranger disorders include sleep paralysis, where people wake up unable to move and exploding head syndrome, where people hear a loud noise, like a bomb, just before they sleep.

In order to combat these sleep disorders we need to understand more about sleep's effects. The problem is sleep is still a mystery. I've come to the sleep unit at the Surrey Clinical Research Centre to meet the scientists who are trying to find out more. These scientists all study sleep. Instead of laboratories, they have bedrooms full of high-technology equipment. These machines measure a person's brain activity and body movement during sleep. Scientists use these measurements to analyze people's sleeping patterns. They hope to discover what sleep is for and what happens to us when we don't sleep enough. We already know that sleep deprivation affects the part of the brain that controls our behavior, our personality and our emotions. So, when we don't get enough sleep, all of these things are affected.

But why are we so sleep deprived? Researchers here say that we are sleeping enough hours, but that our sleep patterns are more irregular. The average adult sleeps for about seven and a quarter hours per night. This is almost exactly the same amount of sleep our ancestors used to get over a hundred years ago. The difference is they slept for just over seven hours *every* night, but we don't. Our sleeping patterns have changed to fit modern life. Today, most people lead busy lives and we often sleep less during the week. Sometimes we only sleep for five or six hours because we stay up late to work or spend time with friends. Then, at the weekend, people spend longer in bed and can sleep for ten hours! Perhaps this irregularity in sleeping patterns is something our brains find difficult to get used to. And this, in turn, affects our health and general well-being. That's why sleep clinics like this one are trying to learn more, so we can all sleep a little easier.

G past modals: *must have*, etc.; *would rather*
V verbs often confused
P weak form of *have*

7A Don't argue!

Lesson plan

The topic of this lesson is arguments: what causes them, how to argue, and how men and women argue differently.

The first section of the lesson starts with the grammar presentation where Sts listen to some people arguing, a context in which past modals of deduction can naturally occur. Your Sts will have learned to use present modals of deduction (*must* / *might* / *can't* + infinitive) and *should* (+ infinitive) for advice in *American English File* 3. In this lesson, they learn how to use these same modals to make deductions about the past (e.g., *You must have taken a wrong turn*) and to make criticisms (e.g., *You shouldn't have said that*). The pronunciation focus is on weak forms of *have* in sentences with past modals (e.g., *You should have told me*). Then Sts read an article from *The Times* about how men and women argue in different ways.

In the second section of the lesson, Sts listen to an expert talking about how to argue in a calm and controlled way. Sts then put the advice into action in a speaking activity where they role-play having two arguments. Then there is a Mini Grammar focus on the use of *would rather* and a vocabulary focus on verbs that are sometimes confused, e.g., *argue* and *discuss*. The lesson finishes with the song, *My Girl*.

STUDY LINK
- **Workbook** 7A
- **Online Practice**
- **iChecker**

Extra photocopiable activities

- **Grammar** past modals *page 163*
- **Mini Grammar** *would rather page 175*
- **Communicative** Guess my verb *page 201* (instructions *page 183*)
- **Vocabulary** Verbs often confused *page 219* (instructions *page 211*)
- **Song** *My Girl page 235* (instructions *page 227*)

Optional lead-in – the quote

- Write the quote at the top of *page 64* on the board (books closed) and the name of the person who said it, or get Sts to open their books and read it.
- Make sure Sts know what *an argument* is. Model and drill its pronunciation.
- Ask Sts to tell you what the quote means and if they think it is funny.

1 GRAMMAR past modals: *must have*, etc.

a 4 2))) Focus on the photos and the question. Elicit ideas for each one, but don't tell Sts if they are right or not.

Play the audio once all the way through.

Check answers.

1 The two people share an apartment and they are arguing because the man has drunk and finished the woman's milk.
2 They are arguing about how to get to the woman's cousin's house.

4 2)))
(audioscript in Student Book on *page 126*)
F = female student, M = male student

Conversation 1
F Where's my milk? It's not here.
M I haven't seen it. You must have finished it.
F I definitely didn't finish it. I was keeping some for my cereal this morning. You must have used it.
M Me? I never take anything from the refrigerator that isn't mine. You might have given it to the cat last night and then forgotten about it.
F The cat drinks water not milk, so I couldn't have given it to the cat. Last night there was half a carton of milk in the refrigerator. My milk.
M Well, I don't know what happened to it.
F What are you drinking?
M Just coffee.
F Yes, white coffee. That's where my milk went. Well, you can go to the supermarket and get me some more.
M OK, OK, calm down. I'll go and get you some milk.

Conversation 2 W = woman, M = man
GPS At the traffic circle, take the second exit.
W Why are you taking the third exit? She said the second exit.
M I'm sure it's this one. I remember when we came here last time.
W According to that sign, this is Sunrise Highway.
M Sunrise Highway? Oh, no. We must have gone the wrong way.
W Of course we've gone the wrong way. We should have taken the second exit at the traffic circle. What's the point of having a GPS if you don't do what it says?
M OK. I may have made a mistake. But if you knew the way to your cousin's house, then we wouldn't have to use the GPS.
GPS Turn round as soon as possible...

b 4 3))) Tell Sts that they are now going to hear how *must* / *might* / *can't* and *should* can be used to talk about the past. Focus on the instructions.

Give Sts time to read the extracts. Then play the audio, pausing after each conversation for Sts to complete the sentences. Play the audio again as necessary.

Check answers.

See words in **bold** in audioscript 4.3

4.3

1 You **must have** finished it.
2 You **might have** given it to the cat last night.
3 I **couldn't have** given it to the cat.
4 Oh, no! We **must have** gone the wrong way.
5 We **should have** taken the second exit at the traffic circle.
6 OK, I **may have** made a mistake.

c Focus on the task and give Sts time to do it in pairs.

Check answers and elicit that A = *must have*, B = *might* (or *may*) *have*, C = *can't have*, and D = *should have*.

Conversation 1		
1 A	2 B	3 C
Conversation 2		
4 A	5 D	6 B

Extra support

- You could play audio 4.3 again and get Sts to listen and repeat, copying the rhythm and intonation.

d 4.4 4.5 Tell Sts to go to **Grammar Bank 7A** on *page 144*. Focus on the example sentences and play the audio for Sts to listen to the sentence rhythm. You could also get Sts to repeat the sentences to practice getting the rhythm right. Then go through the rules with the class.

Additional grammar notes

***must* | *might* | *may* | *can't* | *couldn't* + *have* + past participle**

- Sts have previously seen these modal verbs to make deductions about the present, e.g., *John must be sick, She might be French*, and, in the case of *should*, to give advice or to express an opinion (*You should get a new phone. The government should change the law*). Here they learn to use the same modals to make deductions about the past (*You must have made a mistake*) and criticize somebody's actions (*You should have turned left*).
- **rule 1:** Sts may sometimes try to use *mustn't have* (which doesn't exist) instead of *couldn't have*, e.g., *You couldn't have seen me yesterday. I was in bed all day.* NOT *You ~~mustn't have~~*...
- **rule 2:** Remind Sts that *may* and *might* in these sentences are interchangeable (although *might have* must be used in reported speech). Highlight that *could* | *couldn't have*... can also be used.

***should have* + past participle**

- Remind Sts that they can also use *ought to have* here. At this level, they should be able to use both forms with some fluency.

Focus on the exercises and get Sts to do them individually or in pairs.

Check answers, getting Sts to read the full sentences.

a
1 She might have had an argument with her boyfriend.
2 Ben must have read my email.
3 Sam and Ginny couldn't have gotten lost.
4 You couldn't have seen Ellie yesterday.
5 John might not have seen you.
6 Lucy must have bought a new car.
7 Alex couldn't have been very sick.
8 They might not have received the invitation.
9 You must have used too much sugar.
10 It couldn't have been my phone.

b
1 You should have / ought to have written it down.
2 You shouldn't have come by car.
3 You shouldn't have invited her.
4 You shouldn't have bought so many shoes.
5 I should have / ought to have gone to bed earlier last night.
6 You should have / ought to have taken it out of the freezer earlier.
7 You shouldn't have sat in the sun all afternoon...
8 She shouldn't have eaten so much chocolate cake yesterday.

Tell Sts to go back to the main lesson **7A**.

Extra support

- If you think Sts need more practice, you may want to give them the Grammar photocopiable activity at this point or leave it for later as consolidation or review.

2 PRONUNCIATION weak form of *have*

Pronunciation notes

- When *have* is an auxiliary verb, not a main verb, it usually has a weak pronunciation, e.g., *I might have lost it* = /əv/. Sts may sometimes misunderstand this as the weak form of *of*.
- If you want to encourage Sts to use the weak form of *have*, the most important thing for Sts is to stress the modal and the participle strongly and not to stress *have* at all.

a 4.6 Focus on the instructions and the extracts from the conversations in **1b**.

Play the audio, pausing after each sentence for Sts to underline the stressed words.

Check answers and elicit that the modal verbs and the main verbs are stressed, but that *have* is not stressed and is pronounced /əv/.

See underlining in audioscript 4.6

1 You must have finished it.
2 You might have given it to the cat last night.
3 I couldn't have given it to the cat.
4 Oh, no! We must have gone the wrong way.
5 We should have taken the second exit at the traffic circle.
6 OK, I may have made a mistake.

b Focus on the task and example. Highlight that in 2–4 Sts are given the modal verb, but in 5–8 they have to choose an appropriate one.

Give Sts time in pairs to complete **B**'s responses.

Elicit ideas from different pairs. Accept responses that are grammatically correct and make sense in the context.

Some possible answers
2 You must have left it at home.
3 They may have gotten lost.
4 You shouldn't have gone to bed so late.
5 You couldn't have worked very hard. / You should have studied more.
6 One of them might have met someone else. / One of them might have gotten accepted to a school in another city.
7 He might have been sick. / He should have come – it was a really good class.
8 We should have left earlier. / We shouldn't have driven.

Then get Sts to read their dialogues in pairs, practicing stressing the right words.

Finally, check their pronunciation by getting a different pair to read each dialogue.

3 READING & SPEAKING

a Focus on the task and make sure Sts understand the questions. Do this as an open-class activity. You could write the different strategies you elicit from the class on the board.

b Focus on the task and then give Sts time to read the article to find the answers to **a**.

Check answers.

c Focus on the task and give Sts time to read sentences 1–8, making sure they understand all the lexis, e.g., *to be supposed to*, *assertive*, and *upset*.

Now set a time limit for Sts to re-read the article and to mark each sentence true or false and underline where they found the answer.

Get Sts to compare with a partner and then check answers, getting Sts to tell you why the answers are true or false, according to what it says in the article.

1 T (Line 4: ...she blamed her husband.)
2 F (Line 13: The fury can last up to 45 minutes, during which time the husband is expected to keep quiet.)
3 F (Line 20: ...men prefer not to argue at all, wherever possible.)
4 T (Line 28: ...I can only argue convincingly when I have all the evidence to back up my argument ready to use...)
5 T (Line 35: ...the younger men that I see tend to be much more willing to understand their own feelings and talk about them. Older men find it more difficult.)
6 F (Line 40: Crying is a good tactic.)
7 T (Line 45: When I finally come out after half an hour, he's just watching TV as if nothing happened.)
8 F (Line 50: The way you deal with emotion is learned in your family. To understand this, and then make a conscious decision that you will do it differently, requires a lot of maturity.)

d Focus on the highlighted words and phrases related to arguing. Get Sts, in pairs, to guess their meaning. Tell them to read the whole sentence because the context will help them guess.

Check answers, either explaining in English, translating into Sts' L1, or getting Sts to check in their dictionaries.

Help with any other new vocabulary and encourage Sts to write down any useful new lexis from the article.

e Do this as an open-class activity.

4 LISTENING & SPEAKING

a  4 7 Focus on the task and make sure Sts understand it. You might want to check that Sts know the meaning of *mediate* and *postpone*.

Give Sts time to read sentences 1–10.

Play the audio once all the way through.

Check answers.

Extra support
- Before playing the audio, go through the audioscript and decide if you need to preteach / check any lexis to help Sts when they listen.

Sts should have checked 1, 3, 5, 6, 7, and 9.

4 7
(audioscript in Student Book on *pages 126–127*)

In life, we sometimes have disagreements with people. It could be with your partner, with your boss, with your parents, or with a friend. When this happens, the important thing is to try not to let a difference of opinion turn into a heated argument. But, of course, it's easier said than done.

The first thing I would say is that the way you begin the conversation is very important. Imagine you're a student and you share an apartment with another student, who you think isn't helping out with the housework. If you say, "Look, you never help out with the housework. What are we going to do about it?", the discussion will turn into an argument. It's much more constructive to say something like, "I think we'd better take another look at how we divide up the housework. Maybe there's a better way of doing it."

My second piece of advice is simple. If you're the person who's in the wrong, just admit it! This is the easiest and best way to avoid an argument. Just apologize to your roommate, your parents, or your husband, and move on. The other person will have more much respect for you if you do that.

The next tip is don't exaggerate. Try not to say things like, "You always come home late when my mother comes to dinner," when maybe this has only happened once before, or, "You never remember to buy the toothpaste." This will just make the other person get very defensive because what you're saying about them just isn't true.

If you follow these tips, you just might be able to avoid an argument. But if an argument does start, it's important to keep things under control, and there are ways to do this. The most important thing is not to raise your voice. Raising your voice will just make the other person lose their temper, too. If you find yourself raising your voice, stop for a moment and take a deep breath. Say, "I'm sorry I shouted, but this is very important to me," and continue calmly. If you can talk calmly and quietly, you'll find the other person will be more ready to think about what you're saying.

It's also very important to stick to the point. Try to stay on the topic you're talking about. Don't bring up old arguments, or try to bring in other issues. Just concentrate on solving the one problem you're having, and leave the other things for another time. So, for example, if you're arguing about the housework, don't start talking about cell phone bills, too.

And my final tip is that, if necessary, call "Time out," like in a basketball game. If you think that an argument is getting out of control, then you can say to the other person, "Listen, I'd rather talk about this tomorrow when we've both calmed down." You can then continue talking about it the next day when maybe both of you are feeling less tense and angry. That way, there's a better chance that you'll be able to reach an agreement. You'll also probably find that the problem is much easier to solve when you've both had a good night's sleep.

But I want to say one last thing that I think is very important. Some people think that arguing is always bad, but that isn't true. Conflict is a normal part of life, and dealing with conflict is an important part of any relationship, whether it's three people sharing an apartment, a married couple, or just two good friends. If you don't learn to argue constructively, then when a real problem comes along, you won't be prepared to face it together. Think of the smaller arguments as training sessions. Learn how to argue cleanly and fairly. It will help your relationship become stronger and last longer.

b Get Sts to focus on the six sentences they have checked. Play the audio again, pausing after each tip is mentioned to give Sts a minute or two to discuss briefly with a partner what else the psychologist said.

Then elicit all the extra information from Sts.

1 The way you begin the conversation is very important.

Repeat for the next five tips.

3 If you're in the wrong, admit it. This is the easiest and best way to avoid an argument. Apologize and move on. The other person will have more much respect for you.
5 Don't exaggerate. This will just make the other person get very defensive.
6 Do not raise your voice. Raising your voice will just make the other person lose their temper, too. If you find yourself raising your voice, stop and take a deep breath, and continue calmly. If you can talk calmly and quietly, you'll find the other person will be more ready to think about what you are saying.
7 Stick to the point. Try to stay on the topic you're talking about. Don't bring up old arguments, or try to bring in other issues. Just concentrate on solving the one problem you are having and leave the other things for another time.
9 If necessary, call "Time out." You can then continue talking about it the next day when maybe both of you are feeling less tense and angry. That way, there's a better chance that you'll be able to reach an agreement.

Finally, play the last part (from *But I want to say one last thing…*). Pause at this point and ask Sts if they can remember what the last important thing was. Elicit ideas and then play the audio to the end.

Elicit the reasons why the psychologist says that arguing can be a good thing.

If you don't learn to argue constructively, then when a real problem comes along, you won't be prepared to face it together.

Extra support

- If there's time, you could play the audio again while Sts read the audioscript on *pages 126–127*, so they can see what they understood / didn't understand. Translate / explain any new words or phrases.

c 4 8))) Focus on the eight sentences from the listening. Give Sts time, individually or in pairs, to read the sentences and try to guess / remember any of the missing phrases or at least some of the words. Tell them to write their suggestions in pencil at the end of each sentence.

Play the audio, pausing after each sentence to give Sts time to write.

You could get Sts to compare with a partner before checking answers. Make sure Sts understand the meaning of the phrases.

See words in **bold** in audioscript 4.8

4 8)))

1 But, of course it's easier said **than done**.
2 If you're the person who's **in** the **wrong**, just admit it!
3 …it's important to **keep** things **under** control…
4 Raising your voice will just make the other person **lose** their **temper**, too.
5 …stop for a moment and **take** a **deep** breath.
6 It's also very important to **stick to** the point.
7 There's a better chance that you'll be able to **reach** an **agreement**.
8 …**dealing with** conflict is an important part of any relationship…

d Put Sts in pairs and get them to discuss which two tips they think are the most useful and why.

Get some feedback.

e Sit Sts in pairs, **A** and **B**, preferably face to face. Tell them to go to **Communication *Argument!***, **A** on *page 107*, **B** on *page 110*. Where you have a mixed-sex pair, get the male to be **B**. Explain that they are going to "act out" two arguments and they have to read their roles carefully before they start. A male student may have to play a female role and vice versa.

Get Sts to read their role in role-play 1. Then tell the **B**s to start. Monitor to see if Sts are doing any of the things the psychologist said they shouldn't.

Stop the role-play when you think it has gone on long enough. Then tell Sts to read their roles for the second role-play, and then tell **A**s to start. Monitor as before.

! If you have a young class and you think they might not enjoy or be able to do the husband / wife role-play successfully, just get them to do role-play 2.

Tell Sts to go back to the main lesson **7A**.

f Do this as open-class questions. You could also tell Sts about any things you noticed they were doing that, according to the psychologist, they shouldn't have done.

5 MINI GRAMMAR *would rather*

a Focus on the two examples and read the rules with the class.

Give Sts time to rewrite sentences 1–6 with *would rather.*

Check answers.

1 I'd rather go to the movies than to a dance club.
2 I'd rather not go to the party...
3 Would you rather meet on Thursday...?
4 My wife would rather not fly.
5 My husband would rather take a train to Boston...
6 I'd rather come on Sunday...

b Focus on the task and example. Make sure Sts know what an *SUV* is.

Put Sts in pairs and get them to take turns asking and answering each question. Remind them to start with *Would you rather...?* when asking their partner a question and to explain their reasons when answering.

Monitor and help, correcting any errors of the use of *would rather.*

Get some feedback.

Extra support

- If you think Sts need more practice, you may want to give them the Mini Grammar photocopiable activity now or leave it for later as consolidation or review.

6 VOCABULARY verbs often confused

a Focus on the task and give Sts a few minutes to circle the right verb in each extract.

Get Sts to compare with a partner and then check answers.

1 remember (*remind* = make someone remember, e.g., *This song reminds me of last summer.*)
2 avoid (*prevent* = stop someone from doing something)
3 raise (*rise* = to go up, e.g., *the sun rises.*)

b Tell Sts to go to **Vocabulary Bank** ***Verbs often confused*** on *page 158*.

Get Sts to do **a** individually or in pairs. Remind Sts they might need to change the form of the verb and to write their answers in the **verbs** column.

4 9))) Now do **b**. Play the audio for Sts to check answers. Play the audio again, pausing for Sts to repeat. Practice any words your Sts find difficult to pronounce.

4 9)))

Verbs often confused

1 I need to **discuss** the problem with my boss.
2 I often **argue** with my parents about doing housework.
3 I didn't **realize** you were so unhappy.
4 I didn't **notice** that Karen had changed her hair color.
5 Jack always tries to **avoid** arguing with me.
6 My dad can't **prevent** me from seeing my friends.
7 I've spoken to her husband twice and he **seems** very nice.
8 Carol doesn't **look** very well. I think she's working too hard.
9 My parents don't **mind** if I stay out late.
10 It doesn't **matter** if we are five minutes late.
11 Can you **remind** me to call my mom later?
12 **Remember** to turn off the lights before you go.
13 I **expect** that Daniel will forget our anniversary. He always does.
14 We'll have to **wait** half an hour for the next train.
15 I **wish** I were a little taller!
16 I **hope** that you can come on Friday. I haven't seen you for ages.
17 The Dallas Cowboys **won** the game 28–10.
18 The Dallas Cowboys **beat** the New York Jets 28–10.
19 Tom always **refuses** to discuss the problem.
20 Tom always **denies** that he has a problem.
21 The cost of living is going to **rise** again this month.
22 It's hard not to **raise** your voice when you're arguing with someone.
23 Last night I came home and **lay** on the sofa and went to sleep.
24 I **laid** the baby on the bed and changed his diaper.
25 The men had been planning to **rob** the bank.
26 If you leave your bike unlocked, somebody might **steal** it.
27 I think I should **warn** you that Liam doesn't always tell the truth.
28 My teachers are going to **advise** me on what subjects to study next year.

Testing yourself

Sts can cover the **verbs** column, look at the sentences, and see if they can remember the missing verbs.

Testing a partner

See **Testing a partner** *page 29*.

Tell Sts to go back to the main lesson **7A**.

Extra support

- If you think Sts need more practice, you may want to give them the Vocabulary photocopiable activity at this point or leave it for later as consolidation or review.

c Focus on the task and give Sts a few minutes either in pairs or individually to fill in the blanks. Remind Sts that they may need to change the form of the verb.

Check answers.

1 mind, matter
2 remember, remind
3 robbed, stolen
4 advise, warn
5 prevent, avoid

Now put Sts in pairs and get them to ask each other the questions. Encourage them to ask for more information when appropriate.

Help with any general vocabulary problems that come up.

Get feedback from different pairs.

7 4 10 **SONG** *My Girl* ♫

This song was originally made famous by the British band Madness in 1979. For copyright reasons, this is a cover version. If you want to do this song in class, use the photocopiable activity on *page 235*.

4 10

My Girl

My girl's mad at me
I didn't wanna see the film tonight
I found it hard to say
She thought I'd had enough of her
Why can't she see
She's lovely to me?
But I like to stay in
And watch TV on my own
Every now and then

My girl's mad at me
Been on the telephone for an hour
We hardly said a word
I tried and tried but I could not be heard
Why can't I explain?
Why do I feel this pain?
'Cos everything I say
She doesn't understand
She doesn't realize
She takes it all the wrong way

My girl's mad at me
We argued just the other night
I thought we'd got it straight
We talked and talked until it was light
I thought we'd agreed
I thought we'd talked it out
Now when I try to speak
She says that I don't care
She says I'm unaware
And now she says I'm weak

G verbs of the senses
V the body
P silent letters

7B Actors acting

Lesson plan

The general topic of this lesson is body language.

The first section of the lesson is based on a book of photography, where a photographer asked actors to imagine they were a person in a particular situation and then he took their photo. The grammar focus is on verbs of the senses and how they are used grammatically, e.g., *he looks tired, he looks like his father, he looks as if he has seen a ghost*. This is followed by a speaking activity where Sts put the grammar into practice. Sts then listen to an interview with an actor talking about how radio acting is different from other kinds of acting. The first section ends with a Mini Grammar focus on the use of *as*.

In the second section of the lesson, Sts extend their vocabulary related to the body, learning, in addition to new body parts, verbs and verb phrases connected to the body. The pronunciation focus that follows is on silent letters. Then Sts read an article about an FBI agent, who is an expert at analyzing body language and has written a book explaining how certain postures and movements can betray our emotions. Sts then look at some pictures and try to figure out how the people are feeling; after that, they listen to someone analyzing the pictures. The lesson ends with Sts describing two photos to each other and finally writing a description of a photo.

STUDY LINK
- **Workbook** 7B
- **Online Practice**
- **iChecker**

Extra photocopiable activities

- **Grammar** verbs of the senses *page 164*
- **Mini Grammar** *as page 176*
- **Communicative** Spot the difference *page 202* (instructions *page 183*)
- **Vocabulary** The body *page 220* (instructions *page 211*)

Optional lead-in – the quote

- Write the quote at the top of *page 68* on the board (books closed) and the name of the person who said it, or get Sts to open their books and read it.
- Check Sts understand the meaning of the quote.
- Ask Sts if they agree with Rachel Weisz.

1 GRAMMAR verbs of the senses

a Focus on the task. You could tell Sts that Fran Drescher (1957–) is an American movie and television actress, comedian, and producer.

Get Sts to read the introduction, or read it out loud for the class, and then, in pairs, tell them to look at Fran Drescher and choose the best options for 1–3.

Elicit some opinions, but don't tell Sts if they are right or not.

b **4 11** Tell Sts to listen to the audio to see if their answers to **a** are right.

Play the audio once all the way through for Sts to listen. Play again as necessary.

> **4 11**
> (audioscript in Student Book on *page 127*)
> I love this photo, especially the way she's using her hands... and the expression in her eyes and her mouth. Here she is in the role of a young single mother who heard a noise in the kitchen in the middle of the night. You can see the fear in her eyes, that she's worried about her child. I think she suggests all that beautifully...

Then elicit the answers (1a, 2b, 3c) and ask Sts to raise their hands to show how many of them chose correctly. If most of them did, then the actress was clearly playing her role well!

c Focus on the task and do it as an open-class activity.

> *looks* + adjective
> *looks like* + noun
> *looks as if* + subject and verb

d **4 12** Tell Sts to go to **Grammar Bank 7B** on *page 145*. Focus on the example sentences and play the audio for Sts to listen to the sentence rhythm. You could also get Sts to repeat the sentences to practice getting the rhythm right. Then go through the rules with the class.

Additional grammar notes

look* | *feel* | *smell* | *sound* | *taste

- Sts have previously studied *look* + adjective and *look like* + noun. Here Sts learn the other verbs of the senses and also the structure *as if* (e.g., *He looks as if he needs a vacation*).
- **rule 3:** Point out to Sts that we sometimes use *like* instead of *as if* (e.g., *He looks like he needs a vacation*) in conversation. In written English *as if* or *as though* are usually preferred.

Focus on the exercises and get Sts to do them individually or in pairs.

Check answers, getting Sts to read the full sentences.

a

2 G	4 B	6 J	8 E	10 I
3 A	5 K	7 C	9 D	11 H

b

1 look as if	6 feels
2 smells	7 look
3 sounds like	8 feels like
4 taste like	9 tastes
5 sound as if	10 smells as if

Tell Sts to go back to the main lesson **7B**.

Extra support

- If you think Sts need more practice, you may want to give them the Grammar photocopiable activity at this point or leave it for later as consolidation or review.

e **4 13** Focus on the instructions. Tell Sts they are going to hear some sounds that they have to identify. You could do this as a whole-class activity and get Sts to call out answers as you play each sound, or get Sts in pairs to silently write down their answers and check answers at the end.

Point out that Sts may feel they are missing some of the vocabulary they need to describe the sounds accurately (*saw, drill*, etc.). Encourage them to use the words that they know to describe what they think is happening, e.g., *It sounds as if someone is cutting down a tree. It sounds like a dentist*, etc. with each one.

4 13

Sound effects:
1 *soccer crowd shouting after a near miss*
2 *hair being cut*
3 *plane taking off*
4 *someone opening a bag of chips and eating them*
5 *somebody opening a can with a ring pull*
6 *dentist drill*
7 *cell phone vibrating on a table*
8 *the rumble of a subway train about to arrive at a station*
9 *somebody switching on a computer*
10 *hundreds of camera shutters clicking on a red carpet*

f Put Sts in pairs, **A** and **B**, and tell them to go to **Communication *Guess what it is*, A** on *page 107*, **B** on *page 111*.

Go through the instructions, making sure Sts understand they must not say what the picture is, but they must describe it using *look / smell / feel / taste like* or *as if ...*, etc.

When Sts are ready, focus on the instructions in **b–d**.

Get feedback and find out who guessed the most right.

Tell Sts to go back to the main lesson **7B**.

2 SPEAKING & LISTENING

a Focus on the photos and the instructions. Either put Sts in pairs, small groups, or do it as an open-class activity, and elicit ideas.

b Put Sts in pairs and get them to answer questions 1–6.

Elicit some ideas, but don't tell Sts if they are right or not.

c **4 14** Play the audio for Sts to listen and check their ideas in **b**.

Play the audio again as necessary and then elicit the answers.

Extra support

- Before playing the audio, go through the audioscript and decide if you need to preteach / check any lexis to help Sts when they listen.

1 Jason Schwartzman	4 Dan Hedaya
2 Steve Guttenberg	5 Jane Lynch
3 Ellen Burstyn	6 Cheryl Hines

4 14

(audioscript in Student Book on *page 127*)

1 Here is actress Cheryl Hines. If you think she looks furious, that's because she is! She's playing a wife who's opening the door to her husband at one o'clock in the morning. Her husband forgot that she was giving a dinner party, and he went off to play poker with his friends and turned his phone off. She looks as if she's going to tell him to leave and never come back.

2 I love this one. This is Jason Schwartzman and he's playing a five-year-old boy. He's in the process of quietly putting his pet rat into his seven-year-old sister's clothes drawer. He looks pretty confident about what he's doing, and as if he's really looking forward to hearing her scream when she finds it!

3 Here Ellen Burstyn is playing a high school drama teacher. She is in the audience at the Oscar ceremony and one of the winners is an ex-student of hers. Her ex-student actually mentions her name when she makes her winner's speech. You can see how proud she is, and how moved she is to have been mentioned.

4 In this photo I see pure horror and fear. This is the actor Dan Hedaya. He's playing the part of a long-distance truck driver who was tired and closed his eyes for a few moments. He opens them to see that he's – you guessed it – on the wrong side of the road, with cars racing toward him. Do you think he looks as if he's going to react in time? I think probably not.

5 Here the actress Jane Lynch was given the role of a child. She's swallowing a spoonful of medicine that her mom promised would taste good. Of course it didn't, and now her mom is telling her that if it didn't taste awful, it wouldn't work. She looks as if she's about to spit it out! I can remember reacting just like that when I was kid, and my mom saying those exact same words!

6 When you look at this last one of Steve Guttenberg, I think you can immediately see from his expression that he's worried and maybe nervous. He's playing the role of a married man, who's begging his wife to give him one more chance. But I think he looks as if he's done something bad, and is pretty desperate, so I'm not sure if his wife's going to forgive him!

d Focus on the task and make sure Sts understand what they have to listen for.

Play the audio again, pausing after each speaker has finished talking about the photo. Elicit the role the actor was playing and then repeat for the other five photos.

1 She was playing a wife who's opening the door to her husband at one o'clock in the morning. Her husband forgot that she was giving a dinner party, and he went to play poker with his friends and turned his phone off.
2 He was playing a five-year-old boy who is quietly putting his pet rat into his seven-year-old sister's clothes drawer.
3 She was playing the role of a high school drama teacher, who is in the audience at the Oscar ceremony and one of the winners is an ex-student of hers. Her ex-student mentions her name when she makes her winner's speech.
4 He was playing the part of a long-distance truck driver who was tired and closed his eyes for a few moments. He opens them to see that he's on the wrong side of the road, with cars racing towards him.
5 She was playing the role of a child who's swallowing a spoonful of medicine that her mom promised would taste good.
6 He was playing the role of a married man who's begging his wife to give him one more chance.

Extra support

- If there's time, you could play the audio again while Sts read the audioscript on *page 127*, so they can see what they understood / didn't understand. Translate / explain any new words or phrases.

e Focus on the question and elicit some ideas from the class.

f **4 15** Focus on the task. You could write the question on the board and get Sts to close their books.

! The actor speaks quickly in this recording, so you may need to replay the recording several times or replay parts of it.

Play the audio once all the way through.

Check the answer.

Extra support

- Before playing the audio, go through the audioscript and decide if you need to preteach / check any lexis to help Sts when they listen.

The main way in which radio acting is different is that you can't use your body, only your voice.

4 15
(audioscript in Student Book on *page 127*)
I = interviewer, T = Tim Bentinck

I How difficult is it to express feelings when you can't use body language?
T Radio acting is a different style of acting from visual acting because, obviously, you only have your voice to, to use. But you can use your voice and you can use timing to convey everything. When I started off as a radio actor somebody said to me, "You have to be able to raise one eyebrow with your voice," which I loved. Because you haven't got your body, you have to put it into your voice, and so, therefore, the way that a radio actor works isn't totally naturalistic in the way that it would be on the television or on film.
I What techniques do you use to help you to express emotions, feelings?
T Mmm, well, there's a big difference between speaking with a smile and not speaking with a smile. There's a huge difference between being happy and being really sad, and really angry.
I Is it hard for actors who don't have experience in radio to do radio acting?
T Well, people don't realize that it is a different technique. You would get famous people coming in, not realizing that there was a technique to radio acting and thinking that you could do total naturalism, and it isn't totally naturalistic. It's as naturalistic as you can make it sound to lift it off the page, to make it sound as though you're not reading it.

g Focus on the task and give Sts time to read questions 1–4. Make sure Sts understand *to convey* and *eyebrow*.

Play the audio again the whole way through.

Get Sts to compare with a partner and then if necessary, play again.

Check answers.

1 their voice and timing
2 You have to be able to **raise** one eyebrow with your **voice**.
3 He speaks with a smile.
4 They are trying to make it sound like they aren't reading.

Extra support

- If there's time, you could play the audio again while Sts read the audioscript on *page 127*, so they can see what they understood / didn't understand. Translate / explain any new words or phrases.

h Do this as an open-class activity.

3 MINI GRAMMAR *as*

a Focus on the extract from Tim Bentinck's interview and go through the four different uses of *as* with the class. In a monolingual class, you could also contrast how the examples would be expressed in the Sts' own language.

b Focus on the task and give Sts time to match sentences A–G with uses 1–4 in **a**.

Get Sts to compare with a partner and then check answers.

A 2	C 1	E 3	G 1
B 3	D 4	F 4	

Extra support

- If you think Sts need more practice, you may want to give them the Mini Grammar photocopiable activity now or leave it for later as consolidation or review.

4 VOCABULARY the body

a **4 16** Focus on the photo and ask Sts if they know anything about Glenn Close, the movie and stage actress. Ask if any of them have seen her movies and what they thought of them. Elicit / explain that Glenn Close has played diverse roles and starred in a number of hit movies, including *The Big Chill, Fatal Attraction,* and *101 Dalmatians.*

Extra support

- Before you start the exercise, you could review the basic vocabulary of the face. Quickly sketch a face on the board with eyes, nose, ears, head, hair, and mouth, and check that Sts can remember and pronounce these words.

Now focus on the words in the list and get Sts, in pairs or individually, to match them with 1–9 in the photo.

Play the audio for Sts to listen and check.

4 16

6 cheek	4 eyelash	7 lips
8 chin	3 eyelid	9 neck
2 eyebrow	1 forehead	5 wrinkles

Practice any words your Sts find difficult to pronounce, modeling and drilling as necessary. You could use the audio to do this.

b Tell Sts to go to **Vocabulary Bank *The body*** on *page 159*.

Focus on **1 Parts of the body and organs** and get Sts to do **a** individually or in pairs.

4 17 Now do **b**. Play the audio for Sts to check answers. Play the audio again, pausing for Sts to repeat. Practice any words your Sts find difficult to pronounce.

4 17

The body

Parts of the body and organs

3	ankle	9	chest
1	calf (calves)	13	hip
2	heel	11	thigh
6	elbow	10	waist
5	fist	14	brain
8	nails	17	heart
4	palm	16	kidneys
7	wrist	15	liver
12	bottom	18	lungs

Focus on **2 Verbs and verb phrases** and get Sts to do **a** individually or in pairs.

4 18 Now do **b**. Play the audio for Sts to check answers. Play the audio again, pausing for Sts to repeat. Practice any words your Sts find difficult to pronounce.

4 18

Verbs and verb phrases

a

1 bite your **nails**
2 blow your **nose**
3 brush your **hair** / brush your **teeth**
4 comb your **hair**
5 fold your **arms**
6 hold somebody's **hand**
7 touch your **toes**
8 suck your **thumb**
9 shake **hands**
10 shrug your **shoulders**
11 shake your **head**
12 raise your **eyebrows**

Extra idea

- Pause the audio after each line and get Sts to mime the action.

Now focus on **c**. Explain that these verbs are not used with a part of the body as in **a**, but describe the movement of a part of the body, e.g., *wink* (demonstrate it). Then get Sts, individually or in pairs, to do the exercise.

4 19 Now do **d**. Play the audio for Sts to check answers. Play the audio again, pausing for Sts to repeat. Practice any words your Sts find difficult to pronounce.

4 19

Verbs and verb phrases

c

1 **eye**
2 **teeth**
3 **arms**
4 **nails**
5 **hand**
6 **knee**
7 **forehead**
8 **eyes**
9 **mouth** / **arms**
10 **finger**

Testing yourself

For **Parts of the body and organs**, Sts can cover the words, look at the pictures, and try to remember the words. For **Verbs and verbs phrases**, they can cover the parts of the body in the list and try to remember them.

Testing a partner

See **Testing a partner** *page 29*.

Tell Sts to go back to the main lesson **7B**.

Extra support

- If you think Sts need more practice, you may want to give them the Vocabulary photocopiable activity at this point or leave it for later as consolidation or review.

c **4 20** Tell Sts they are going to hear instructions and they have to mime the action. Demonstrate by saying *Shake hands with the person next to you* and check Sts are all doing the right thing.

Play the audio, pausing after each imperative and checking that Sts are doing it correctly.

Extra idea

- You could repeat the activity by reading the instructions out loud yourself in a different order.

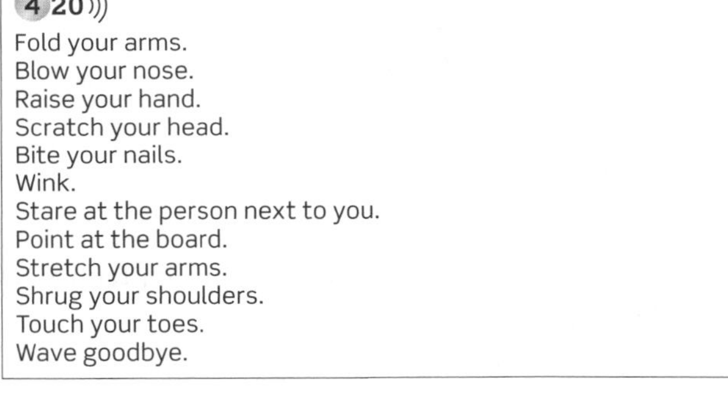

4 20

Fold your arms.
Blow your nose.
Raise your hand.
Scratch your head.
Bite your nails.
Wink.
Stare at the person next to you.
Point at the board.
Stretch your arms.
Shrug your shoulders.
Touch your toes.
Wave goodbye.

5 PRONUNCIATION silent letters

Pronunciation notes

- Many English words have a silent letter (often a consonant) that is not pronounced. Emphasize to your Sts that when they check the pronunciation of a new word in a dictionary, the phonetic transcript will help them to see when a letter (or syllable) is not pronounced.

a Focus on the task. Remind Sts to say the words out loud to help them.

b **4 21** Play the audio for Sts to listen and check.

Check answers by getting Sts to write the words on the board and cross out the silent consonant.

calf wrist palm wrinkles comb kneel thumb

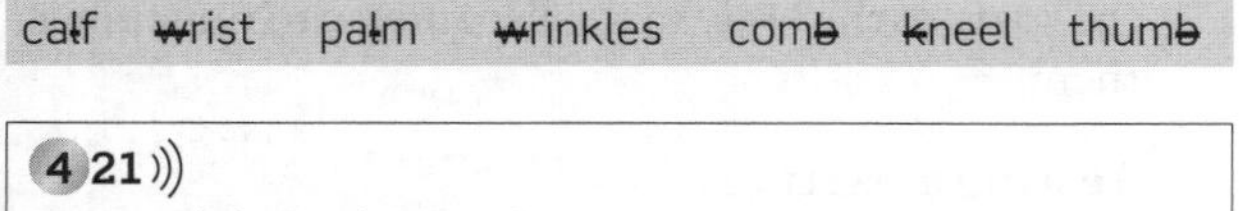

4 21
See words in Student Book on *page 70*

Then ask Sts the two questions.

The *w* in words beginning with *wr* is silent as is the *k* in words beginning with *kn*.
The *b* is silent in words ending in *mb*.

Extra idea

- Elicit more words beginning with *wr* and *kn*, e.g., *wrong, wrap, write, know, knife*, and ending in *mb*, e.g., *bomb, lamb*, etc.

c Focus on the task and give Sts time to do it in pairs. You could do the first two with the class.

d **4 22** Play the audio for Sts to listen and check.

Get Sts to write the words on the board and cross out the silent consonant. You could make sure Sts can remember the meaning of all the words.

aisle	doubt	knock
calm	fasten	muscle
climb	half	whistle
design	honest	whole

4 22
See words in Student Book on *page 70*

Now focus on the phrases and get Sts to practice saying them in pairs.

Get some Sts to say the phrases to the class.

Extra support

- Read each phrase to the class, getting Sts to repeat it after you. Then put Sts in pairs and get them to practice saying them.

6 READING & LISTENING

a Focus on the task and do it as an open-class activity.

Elicit the answer.

The writer called his book *What Every Body is Saying* because it is about body language – the way we use our bodies, not just our voices, to communicate things to other people – not about what everybody (= all people) is saying.

Ask Sts whether they think the information in the subheading is true. Do they believe 80% of our interaction is through body language?

b Focus on questions 1–6 and make sure Sts understand them. You could elicit / explain that *FBI* stands for *The Federal Bureau of Investigation* and is the police department in the US that is controlled by the national government.

Give Sts time to read the article.

Put Sts in pairs and get them to answer the questions. You could get them to do this either orally or in writing.

Check answers. Highlight that an *ice pick* is a tool with a very sharp point for breaking ice with, and a *hammer* is a tool with a heavy, blunt end, used for hitting nails into wood.

1 Because he had an alibi.
2 Because one of the weapons had been used in the murder and only the killer knew which one. The agent wanted to observe the man's reaction when he asked him about each weapon.
3 He closed his eyes when the weapon used in the crime, the ice pick, was mentioned, and he kept them closed until the next question.
4 Because he has caught many criminals. / Because he knows how to "read" people and has caught many criminals.
5 verbal (spoken language) and non-verbal (silent language)
6 Because we haven't learned to recognize them.

c Tell Sts to read the article again and to look for synonyms for the 12 words or phrases.

Check answers.

Paragraph 1
1 credible 2 sincere 3 pressed on
Paragraph 2
1 observed 2 significance 3 witnessed
Paragraph 3
1 credited with 2 decipher 3 enable
Paragraph 4
1 spot 2 achieve 3 combine

Help with any other new vocabulary and encourage Sts to write down any useful new lexis from the article.

d Now tell Sts to look at the photos and, in pairs, to tell their partner how they think the people are feeling.

Elicit some ideas, but don't tell Sts if they are right or not.

e Focus on the task and make sure Sts know the meaning of *gesture*. Model and drill its pronunciation /ˈdʒɛstʃər/.

In their pairs, Sts now try to match each photo to a feeling.

Elicit some ideas, but don't tell Sts if they are right or not.

f 4 23 Focus on the ***-ward*** box and go through it with the class.

Now play the audio for Sts to listen and check their ideas in **e**.

Check answers.

Extra support

- Before playing the audio, go through the audioscript and decide if you need to preteach / check any lexis to help Sts when they listen.

1 nervous	5 insecure
2 in a good mood	6 friendly and interested
3 relaxed	7 stressed
4 dominant	

4 23

(audioscript in Student Book on *page 127*)

1 Touching or stroking their neck is a very typical sign that a person is nervous and is trying to calm themselves down. A woman may also play with a necklace, and a man may tighten his tie.

2 When somebody's standing and they point one of their toes upward, this is a clear sign that the person is in a good mood, often because they are thinking about, or have just heard, something positive. If you see someone standing talking on the phone and they suddenly point one foot up, you can be sure that they have just been told some good news.

3 Crossing their legs, whether they're sitting or standing, is a sign that a person feels relaxed and comfortable. If the person is sitting with their legs crossed and their feet toward another person, that shows that they are interested in this person. However, if someone they don't like appears, you may find that they quickly uncross their legs.

4 This position, standing with your hands on your hips and your elbows pointing out, is a pose used to show dominance. If you watch police officers or soldiers, you'll notice that they often use this pose. Men tend to use it more than women, and it's something we teach women executives to do in meetings, where there are a lot of men present, to show that they are confident and won't be bullied.

5 We all know that thumbs up is a positive sign, meaning we feel good or approve of something. But what about when somebody puts their thumbs downwards, in their pockets? As you might guess, this usually means that their confidence is low and they are feeling unsure of themselves. So try not to do this if you are in a situation where you need to look confident and in control.

6 Putting their head to one side is a powerful sign that a person feels friendly and interested in someone or something. It's an automatic, genuine gesture, unlike a smile, which might be artificial, and so it's a good sign of real interest. It's also very difficult to do naturally around people you don't like.

7 If you look at people in a stressful situation, for example, witnesses who are answering questions in courts, you'll often see that it looks as if their lips have disappeared inwards. In fact, this is one of the most universal signs of stress, as if a person wanted to disappear completely.

Play the audio again and get Sts to listen for more details.

Elicit as much information as possible.

See script 4.23

g Focus on the instructions and then put Sts in pairs, **A** and **B**.

The **A**s start by doing any of the seven gestures for the **B**s to guess the meaning.

Extra idea

- Write the adjectives and phrases in **e** on the board and get the Sts who are guessing the meaning of the gestures to close their books.

Make sure Sts switch roles.

Find out if any Sts guessed all seven gestures correctly.

h Do this as an open-class activity. You could also ask the class if there is a gesture that you do a lot and what they think it means.

7 SPEAKING & WRITING

a Put Sts in pairs, **A** and **B**, and tell them to go to **Communication *Two photos***, **A** on *page 108*, **B** on *page 112*.

Focus on the **Describing a photo** box and tell Sts to use this language when describing their photos.

Then go through the instructions and make sure Sts understand what they have to do.

Monitor and encourage Sts to use the expressions in the box.

Get feedback to find out who did / didn't create an image that their partner then recognized.

Tell Sts to go back to the main lesson **7B**.

b Tell Sts to go to **Writing *Describing a photo*** on *page 117*.

Focus on **a** and give Sts time to look at the photo and read the description. Tell them not to worry about the blanks.

Elicit some opinions.

Now focus on **b**. Remind Sts to think about both the meaning and the position of the blank when they are choosing which word to complete it with.

Check answers.

2 In the center	6 In the background
3 in front of	7 behind
4 To her right	8 across from
5 outside	

Focus on the **Useful language: describing a photo or picture** box and go through it with Sts. You could first ask Sts to cover the box and elicit the phrases they saw in **Communication**.

Focus on **c** and go through the instructions. Put Sts in pairs to discuss what they think the people in the photo are thinking or feeling. Tell them also to discuss how they will divide the information into two paragraphs.

Focus on **d** and either get Sts to write the description in class (set a time limit of, e.g., 20 minutes) or get them to write at home for homework.

In **e**, Sts should check their work for mistakes before turning it in.

COLLOQUIAL ENGLISH

6&7 Talking about acting

Lesson plan

In the first part of this lesson, the person interviewed is Simon Callow, a British actor, stage director, and author.

In the second part of the lesson, people in the street are asked about acting.

STUDY LINK

- **Workbook** Talking about acting
- **Online Practice**
- **iChecker**

Testing Program CD-ROM

- **File 7 Quick Test**
- **File 7 Test**

Optional lead-in (books closed)

- Tell Sts that they are going to listen to an interview with an actor who has worked in theater and in the movies. Write on the board:
  ACTING IN THEATER / ACTING IN THE MOVIES
- Give Sts two or three minutes in pairs to think of some of the differences between these two kinds of acting.
- Get feedback from the class and write their ideas on the board.

1 VIDEO THE INTERVIEW Part 1

a Books open. Focus on the biographical information about Simon Callow. Either read it out loud or give Sts time to read it. You might want to point out that a CBE (Commander of the Order of the British Empire) is an award given by the Queen to someone who has made a distinguished contribution in their area of activity.

Focus on the question and do it as an open-class activity.

b 4 24))) Focus on the task and give Sts time to read sentences 1–5. Remind Sts that they do not need to correct the false ones at this stage.

Go through the **Glossary** with the class.

Play the DVD or audio (**Part 1**) once all the way through. Play again as necessary.

You could get Sts to compare with a partner before checking answers.

Extra support

- You could pause the DVD or audio at the relevant places and, in pairs, get Sts to compare orally what they have understood before marking the sentences true or false.

1 F 2 T 3 T 4 T 5 F

4 24)))
(audioscript in Student Book on *pages 127–128*)
I = interviewer, S = Simon Callow

Part 1

I How did you get into acting?

S I was about 18, it was my first real job, and it was a very unusual job because I was working in the box office of the Old Vic Theatre. And not only did I get to see an awful lot of plays, but I also met the actors and I was able to sneak in to rehearsals, in the theater, quite illegally, and I became fascinated by the work of the theater.

I What in particular fascinated you?

S The thing that fascinated me, as I said, was when I was in rehearsals there was this, the work of the theater, the sort of work it was, so I'd stand at the back of the Old Vic Theatre when the actors were rehearsing, but mostly it consisted of people sitting rather glumly about saying, "I don't know how to do this, I don't know how to do this, I don't know how to make this scene work, I don't understand my character," and the director would try to help them to understand the character or suggest a move here or a move there or maybe they'd try walking in a different way or putting on a different hat, and bit by bit it started to fall into place and I thought what a wonderful job, what a fantastically interesting job to wrestle with these kinds of problems, try to understand the characters, try to find out how best to express them and show them off, so I, I came to acting very much from that point of view.

I The role that first made you famous as a young actor was playing Mozart in the original theater production of *Amadeus*, which later went on to become a film. What was the most challenging thing about playing the part of Mozart?

S What was a challenge was that Mozart was a person who'd actually lived and was indeed one of the greatest artistic geniuses of the whole of Western civilization, and I was a great lover and admirer of Mozart's music, so there was a tremendous, uh, challenge to bridge the character that Peter Shaffer had written. Peter Shaffer knows all about Mozart, he could so that Mozart was, was, uh, uh sort of a smutty, uh, hysterical child really, er, in a lot of the play. My job was to reconcile that with the fact that he wrote *The Marriage of Figaro* and that was tremendously hard.

I Was Mozart one of your most satisfying roles?

S No, I wouldn't say that, that it was the most satisfying, it was the most exciting because its, its fame uh, almost from the moment it was announced, was overwhelmingly greater than anything I had ever done, and to be honest ever have done since. The fact that the play was very, very controversial when it opened proved to be, uh, very, um, um shocking for many people, only increased the excitement around it, and it was, uh, uh astonishing to look out into the auditorium every night and to see Paul Newman or, or, or, or Robert Redford or, or, or Ava Gardner, or Margaret Thatcher sitting out there because everybody had to see that play.

c Before Sts listen again, put them in pairs to discuss why they think 1 and 5 are false.

Play the DVD or audio again all the way through, pausing as necessary.

Check answers.

1 His first job was in the box office of the Old Vic Theatre.
5 It was the most exciting role he has had because it made him famous.

Part 2

a **4 25** Focus on the task and **Glossary**.

Give Sts time to read 1–4, making sure they know the meaning of *crucial* and *utterly* in number 2.

Play the DVD or audio (**Part 2**) once all the way through. Then play again if necessary.

You could get Sts to compare with a partner before checking answers.

1 He loves them both.
2 There's an **audience**.
Every single performance is utterly **different**.
3 The director and editor because they can change the way the scene or the characters appear by the way they edit it (e.g., they can make a sad scene funny or an actor appear to be stupid).
4 No, because when you act, you have the cameras right in front of you.

4 25
(audioscript in Student Book on *pages 127–128*)

Part 2

I Over your career you have acted in the theater, and you have also acted in many films. Which do you prefer?

S They're absolutely different media, they require different things from you as an actor – I love them both. But they are each of them completely different, you bring completely different things to them. Obviously, the crucial difference with the theater is that there's an audience there and that's such an important aspect of it in every way. It's important because you have to reach out to them, make sure that everybody can hear and see what you're doing. The beauty of the theater is that every single performance is utterly different from every other one.

I How do you motivate yourself to play the same character again night after night?

S I think as you get older you realize that, um, you never get it right. I, I mean I've, I've probably about half a dozen times in my 40 years of acting have thought well that was a really good performance, uh, but it can always be better. And so one goes to the theater every day hoping that it will be in some way better. Uh, uh, you know there is always the possibility you might get it right. I mean you never do, you never can.

I So what for you is the main difference with film acting?

S Uh, in movies or, or television film, which is what almost all television is nowadays, um, a lot of those responsibilities are, lie with the director and the editor. And having directed a film myself, I know perfectly well that you can make a sad scene funny, you can make a slow scene fast, uh, uh, in the editing suite, it's, it's an astonishing, uh, power that a director and editor have. Um, uh, you can make a character seem stupid just by editing them a certain way or make them seem brilliant by editing them in a different way. So, in that sense, the actor is rather powerless.

I Anything else?

S The other thing that's very hard about acting on film is that hilariously it's regarded as a sort of naturalistic medium, but in no sense is it that for the actor, because you're, you're, you know, first of all there are some, you know, little metal objects right in front of you, sort of, staring at you as you're doing your love scene or whatever else it might be.

b Focus on the task and give Sts time to read 1–4.

Play the DVD or audio again all the way through.

You could get Sts to compare with a partner before checking answers.

Extra support

- When you play the DVD or audio the second time, pause after each question has been answered and get Sts to compare what they have understood.

1 He is referring to the audience in a theater.
2 He is saying that you can never give the perfect performance as a theater actor.
3 The film actor can't do anything as the editor has all the power.
4 He is referring to the cameras.

Part 3

4 26 Focus on the photos and ask Sts if they know either of the actors.

Now focus on the **Glossary** and the task.

Play the DVD or audio (**Part 3**) once all the way through for Sts to do the task. Play again as necessary.

You could get Sts to compare with a partner before checking answers.

Extra support

- When you play the DVD or audio the second time, pause after each question has been answered and get Sts to compare what they have understood.

1 When they are good, he loves it. When they aren't good, it is painful.
2 He was very lucky to see them. Most people nowadays have forgotten them. They were wonderful on stage.
3 He is the only modern actor who approaches his roles as the great actors used to.
4 He hates wearing it. It's uncomfortable and sticky.
5 He doesn't get stage fright, but he becomes very self-conscious.

4 26
(audioscript in Student Book on *page 128*)

Part 3

I Do you enjoy watching other actors acting?

S I love watching other actors acting. I've been obsessed by acting since I was a child and I'm a great connoisseur of it, and I think I'm quite a good judge of it, and so I adore watching other actors work when it's good, when it's not it's a great pain to me.

I Who were the first great actors you saw?

S As a young man, and a boy, I was extraordinarily lucky to see that fabled generation of actors, of, of Gielgud and Richardson, Olivier, Edith Evans, Peggy Ashcroft, people now, almost all completely forgotten. Uh, uh, uh, even if they made movies, it's unlikely that people of a younger generation know who they are, but, but er, when, when they were alive and kicking, and, er, doing their extraordinary work on stage it, it, it was something quite, quite remarkable, I mean it was, it was the sort of thing that nobody attempts any more.

I Do any modern actors come close to that golden generation?

S In movies, not always but, but sometimes Daniel Day-Lewis does, uh, I think probably approach a role in the way a lot of them might have approached it.

I Is there anything you don't like about acting?

S I don't much like wearing makeup. I sweat a lot, it comes off, it's uncomfortable, it's sticky, and I do everything I can to avoid wearing makeup.

I Do you still get stage fright?

S I don't get stage fright, but I do get self-conscious and I hate that and I wish I didn't, particularly at events like first nights, because I don't know how it's impossible to ignore the fact that there are at least 100 people sitting out there judging you, you know, I think almost all actors feel tremendous longing for the first night to be over, but it has to happen, it's like a sort of operation, it's, you know it's got to happen, it's going to hurt, but you will feel better afterwards.

Extra support

- If there's time, you could play the DVD or audio again while Sts read the audioscripts on *pages 127–128*, so they can see what they understood / didn't understand. Translate / explain any new words or phrases.

2 LOOKING AT LANGUAGE

4 27 This exercise looks at a feature of spoken English that is illustrated by the interviewer – using modifiers to make his language more expressive. Focus on the **Modifiers** box and go through it with the class.

Now focus on the task and give Sts time to read extracts 1–7.

Play the DVD or audio, pausing after each extract to give Sts time to write.

You could get Sts to compare with a partner before checking answers.

1 fantastically
2 hard
3 greater
4 absolutely
5 completely
6 different
7 extraordinarily

4 27

1 ...I thought what a wonderful job, what a fantastically interesting job...
2 My job was to reconcile that with the fact that he wrote *The Marriage of Figaro*, and that was tremendously hard.
3 ...its fame, almost from the moment it was announced, was overwhelmingly greater than anything I had ever done...
4 They're absolutely different media, they require different things from you as an actor...
5 ...you bring completely different things to them.
6 The beauty of the theater is that every single performance is utterly different from every other one.
7 As a young man, and a boy, I was extraordinarily lucky to see that fabled generation of actors, of, of Gielgud and Richardson, Olivier,...

3 VIDEO ON THE STREET

a 4 28 Focus on the task.

Play the DVD or audio once all the way through.

Check answers.

Anne Hathaway: Iv	Meryl Streep: Y
Jennifer Aniston: H	Robert De Niro: S
Christian Bale: Iv	Sandra Bullock: H
Meg Ryan: H	Tom Hanks: H

4 28

(audioscript in Student Book on *page 128*)
I = interviewer, H = Heyleen, S = Sean, Iv = Ivan, Y = Yasuko

Heyleen
I What actors do you enjoy watching?
H Um, well my favorite actors are Meg Ryan. Um...I like Jennifer Aniston. Um all that has to do with *Friends*. And, um, I like Tom Hanks...Sandra Bullock.
I Why do you like them?
H Um...Sandra Bullock, for example, I like her because she's... I mean, she can make different roles, and she kills it. She's really good at it.
I Why do you like Sandra Bullock's performance in *Miss Congeniality*?
H Um, I like it because she first shows a side of her that's not too girly. She's like, um, I don't care...whatever. And then she showed that she could, um, change her character into this girly woman. That was really good.

Sean
I What actors do you particularly enjoy watching?
S I don't really have a favorite actor I don't think, but, um, I always enjoy watching Robert De Niro.
I Why do you like him?
S I think he just has an intensity, and a presence that makes you want to watch him, makes you want to think about why he's doing what he's doing, I think even if it's something quite silly, um, it's still always interesting to watch.
I What performance of his do you particularly enjoy?
S I think my favorite film and my favorite performance of all time is *The Deer Hunter*.

Ivan
I What actors do you particularly enjoy watching?
Iv I particularly like watching Christian Bale, uh, as an actor. And maybe an actress...Anne Hathaway?
I Which of their performances did you particularly enjoy?
Iv I enjoyed Christian Bale as Batman, and also in the movie *The Prestige*.
I Why do you like Anne Hathaway?
Iv I like Anne Hathaway because she's very attractive. And I liked her in *The Dark Knight Rises*.

Yasuko
I What actors do you particularly enjoy watching?
Y An actress that I do like is Meryl Streep. Um, I think she's a very powerful actress. I think she does well in any role that's given to her. Um...I really do admire her. She's very moving. Anything that she does, she moves me.
I Are there any particular films in which you enjoyed her performance?
Y My favorite movie with Meryl Streep is *Julie and Julia*.
I Why did you like her performance?
Y Um...she...I think she did a really good job capturing Julia Child. She sounded like her. She was able to just become her. So, I loved it.

b Focus on the task and give Sts time to go through the questions.

Play the DVD or audio again all the way through, pausing after each speaker to give Sts time to do the task. Play again as necessary.

Check answers.

Yasuko likes the actor she mentions because she can cause strong feelings or emotions with her work.

Heyleen thinks her favorite actor can show different sides of a character well.

Ivan enjoyed watching his favorite actor in several different roles.

Sean says the actor he likes best was also in the movie he likes best.

c 4.29 This exercises focuses on some colloquial expressions that were used by the speakers. Focus on the phrases and give Sts time to read them.

Play the DVD or audio, pausing after the first phrase and playing it again as necessary. Elicit the missing word and then the meaning of the whole phrase. Repeat for the other four phrases.

See words in **bold** in audioscript 4.29

4.29

1 Um, I like it because she first shows a side of her that's not too girly.
2 I think he just has an intensity, and a **presence** that makes you want to watch him.
3 ...my favorite film and my favorite performance of **all time** is *The Deer Hunter.*
4 Anything that she does, she **moves me**.
5 I think she did a really **good job** capturing Julia Child.

Extra support

- Tell Sts to go to *page 128* and to look at the audioscript for **ON THE STREET**. Play the DVD or audio again and tell Sts to read and listen at the same time.

Help with any vocabulary problems and get feedback from Sts on what parts they found hard to understand and why, e.g., speed of speech, pronunciation, etc.

4 SPEAKING

Put Sts in pairs and get them to ask and answer the questions, giving as much information as possible.

Monitor and help with vocabulary. Help with any general language problems at the end of the activity.

Get some feedback.

8A Beat the robbers...and the burglars

Lesson plan

In this lesson, the general topic is crime.

In the first section, there is a reading and listening that gives practical tips on how to avoid being robbed on the street and on how to protect your house from being burglarized. Sts then expand their crime and punishment vocabulary. The pronunciation focus is on the different pronunciations of the letter *u*. The first section ends with Sts talking about crime and punishment in their country and a Mini Grammar focus on *have something done*.

In the second section of the lesson, crime provides a natural context for the review of passive forms and Sts also learn how to use the structure *it is said that... / he is thought to...* They then read an article about the problems caused by the illegal downloading of music. Sts then discuss whether certain activities are illegal or not. The lesson ends with Sts writing a magazine article expressing their opinion on the legality of downloading music or squatters' rights.

STUDY LINK
- **Workbook** 8A
- **Online Practice**
- **iChecker**

Extra photocopiable activities

- **Grammar** the passive *page 165*
- **Mini Grammar** *have something done page 177*
- **Communicative** Good laws? *page 203* (instructions *page 184*)
- **Vocabulary** Crime and punishment *page 221* (instructions *page 212*)

Optional lead-in – the quote

- Write the quote at the top of *page 74* on the board (books closed) and the name of the person who said it, or get Sts to open their books and read it.
- Ask Sts what they think of the quote. Do they think it is funny?

1 READING & LISTENING

a First, focus on the title of the lesson and tell Sts they are going to read about how to avoid being robbed on the street and in their home.

Now focus on the questions. Either get Sts to answer the questions in pairs or do them as an open-class activity. If you have been robbed yourself, you could tell your own anecdote.

b Focus on the text, which is adapted from an article on the CNN website, and the reading task. Go through headings A–F and make sure Sts know the meaning of *smart*, *cab*, *rich*, and *locals*.

Set a time limit for Sts to read the article and match the headings to the paragraphs.

Get Sts to compare with a partner and then check answers.

1 C　2 D　3 F　4 E　5 B　6 A

c Focus on the instructions and then give Sts time to read the article again.

Put Sts in pairs, get them to cover the article, look at A–F, and tell each other from memory what the advice is.

For more practice, get the class to tell you from memory the advice for each of the six headings.

Encourage Sts to write down new lexis from the article.

Finally, focus on the question *What advice would you give someone to avoid being robbed in your town?* and elicit ideas.

d Tell Sts they are going to look at some questions about burglars and how to reduce the chances of one breaking into your house.

Elicit / explain the meaning of the word *burglar* and drill its pronunciation /ˈbərglər/. Highlight the difference between *a robber* (= someone who robs you on the street) and *a burglar* (= someone who breaks into your house and steals things). You could also elicit the verb *to burgle,* and let Sts know that the verb *to rob* is used more frequently, for both home and street crimes. Finally, you might want to check Sts know the meaning of *valuable*s in question 8.

Give Sts time to read each question and predict the answers.

Elicit ideas, but <u>don't</u> tell Sts if they are right or not.

Extra idea

- After focusing on the meaning of *burglar* and *to burgle* or *rob*, you could ask Sts if they or their family have ever been robbed and what the burglars took.

e **4 30**))) Now tell Sts they are going to listen to an interview with an ex-burglar. They must listen and check their ideas to the questions in **d**.

Play the audio once all the way through for Sts to listen and check.

Check answers.

Extra support

- Before playing the audio, go through the audioscript and decide if you need to preteach / check any lexis to help Sts when they listen.

1 twenty minutes
2 laptops or tablets
3 a dog
4 It looks expensive, there are good places to hide around the house, and no one is at home.
5 so they won't get surprised in the house when the owners come home
6 during the day
7 by removing a door or window
8 a child's bedroom

4 30))

(audioscript in Student Book on *page 128*)
H = Host, D = Danny

H So, welcome to the program, Danny. Now you're an ex-burglar yourself, so you can obviously give us the inside story here. Tell me, how long does a burglar usually take to rob a house?
D I'd say that an experienced burglar would never spend more than 20 minutes in a house. Twenty minutes maximum and then out.
H And how much would they probably take in that time?
D Maybe four thousand or five thousand buck's worth of goods. It depends on the house.
H And what are the favorite things for burglars to steal?
D Well, these days they're usually looking for things like laptops and tablets. They're easy to sell, you know, and not so easy for the owner to identify, if the burglar later gets caught.
H What one thing would be likely to stop a burglar from breaking into a house?
D I'd say definitely a dog, especially a noisy one. Burglars don't like dogs because they're unpredictable.
H What kind of things would actually make a burglar choose a particular house to break into?
D Well, it has to look like a house where there'll be things worth taking, so a burglar will usually go for a house that looks expensive, in a good area. And they'll also often choose a house where there are trees or bushes outside that are good places to hide while they're watching the house before they break in – and also where they could hide when they come out of the house. That way there's less chance of neighbors seeing them. And, obviously, they'll usually wait for the house to be empty before they break in.
H So a burglar wouldn't break in if they thought the owners were at home?
D Not usually no, though there are some burglars who actually prefer it if the owners are at home in bed. That way they won't get surprised by them suddenly coming home when they're in the middle of things.
H Oh, not a very nice thought. What's the most common time of day for a burglar to break into your house?
D People always think of burglars as working at night, and of course some do, but the majority of burglaries happen between around ten in the morning and lunchtime. A burglar will watch a house and then wait for the adults to go to work and the kids go to school, and then he can be sure the house is empty.
H What's the easiest way for a burglar to break into a house?
D The easiest way is just taking out a window or a patio door, usually at the back of the house. You can do this really quickly and it doesn't make much noise if you have good equipment, which a serious burglar would usually have.
H And finally, what's the safest room to hide your valuables in? What's the last place a burglar would look?
D There's a typical order burglars use when they search a house. They start with the main bedroom, because that's often where people leave their valuables, and then the living room. Um, after that, probably the dining room if there is one, a home office, and then the kitchen. The last place would probably be a kid's bedroom. You wouldn't usually expect to find anything worth taking there.
H So a child's bedroom is the best place to hide things?
D Well, in theory, though of course if any burglars out there have been listening to this program, they might start looking there first...

f Tell Sts they are going to listen to the interview again and this time they must take notes on the reasons the ex-burglar gives for his answers.

Play the audio, pausing after each of the ex-burglar's answers to give Sts time to write. Play again as necessary.

You could get Sts to compare with a partner before checking answers.

1 Twenty minutes is the maximum length of time a burglar would spend in a house.
2 Laptops and tablets are easy to sell and not so easy for the owner to identify if the burglar gets caught later.
3 a dog because it is noisy and unpredictable
4 An expensive house will have things worth taking.
A house where there are good places to hide, so they can watch the house before they break in and they could hide when they come out. There's also less chance of neighbors seeing them.
Some burglars wait for no one to be at home.
5 (no extra details)
6 You are most likely to be robbed during the day – the majority of burglaries happen between around ten in the morning and lunchtime. A burglar will watch a house and then wait for the adults to go to work and the children to go to school.
7 Burglars are more likely to get into a house by removing a door or window at the back of the house. They can do this quickly and it doesn't make much noise.
8 a child's bedroom because you wouldn't usually expect to find anything worth taking there

Now ask the class what tips they have learned to avoid a home burglary.

Extra support

- If there's time, you could play the audio again while Sts read the audioscript on *page 128*, so they can see what they understood / didn't understand. Translate / explain any new words or phrases.

g Give Sts time to look back at the article in **b** and the information in **d**, and to decide which they think is the most useful tip.

Get some feedback from the class as to which tip they have chosen and why.

2 VOCABULARY crime and punishment

a Focus on the instructions and give Sts time to match the words with the definitions.

Get them to compare with a partner.

b 4 31)) Play the audio for Sts to listen and check.

Elicit the answers and write them on the board.

See audioscript 4.31

Then play the audio again and get Sts to underline the stressed syllable.

Check answers and drill pronunciation. You can use the audio to do this.

See underlining in audioscript 4.31

4 31))

1 burglar	3 shoplifter	5 mugger
2 robber	4 pickpocket	6 thief

Extra support

- Help Sts to remember the words by getting them to close their books and ask *What's a thief? What's a shoplifter?* or *What do you call a person who...?*, etc.

c Tell Sts to go to **Vocabulary Bank *Crime and punishment*** on *page 160*.

Focus on **1 Crimes and criminals** and get Sts to do **a** individually or in pairs.

4 32)) Now do **b**. Play the audio for Sts to check answers. Practice any words your Sts find difficult to pronounce.

> 4 32))
> **Crime and punishment**
> **Crimes and criminals**
> 1 **I** blackmail, blackmailer, blackmail
> 2 **L** bribery, bribe
> 3 **E** burglary, burglar, break in / burgle
> 4 **D** forgery, forger, forge
> 5 **K** fraud, fraudster, commit fraud
> 6 **F** hacking, hacker, hack into
> 7 **C** hijacking, hijacker, hijack
> 8 **A** kidnapping, kidnapper, kidnap
> 9 **O** mugging, mugger, mug
> 10 **B** murder, murderer, murder
> 11 **J** robbery, robber, rob
> 12 **G** smuggling, smuggler, smuggle
> 13 **P** stalking, stalker, stalk
> 14 **M** terrorism, terrorist, use violent actions
> 15 **N** theft, thief, steal
> 16 **H** vandalism, vandal, vandalize

Point out that:

– the words for the criminal and the verb are usually another form of the word for the crime.
The exceptions are *terrorism* where there is no general verb, *fraud* where we use the verb *to commit fraud*, and *theft* where the verb is *steal*.

– all new verbs are regular except for *set* (*set* – *set*), and *steal* and *sell* which Sts should already know.

Now focus on **2 What happens to a criminal** and get Sts to do **a** individually or in pairs.

4 33)) Now do **b**. Play the audio for Sts to check answers. Practice any words your Sts find difficult to pronounce.

> 4 33))
> **What happens to a criminal**
> **The crime**
> 1 Carl and Adam **committed** a crime. They robbed a large supermarket.
> 2 The police **investigated** the crime.
> 3 Carl and Adam were **caught** driving to the airport in a stolen car.
> 4 They were **arrested** and taken to a police station.
> 5 The police **questioned** them for ten hours.
> 6 Finally, they were **charged** with armed robbery.
> **The trial**
> 7 Two months later, Carl and Adam appeared in **court**.
> 8 They were **accused** of armed robbery and car theft.
> 9 **Witnesses** told the court what they had seen or knew.
> 10 The **jury** (of 12 people) looked at and heard all the **evidence**.
> 11 After two days the jury reached their **verdict**.
> 12 Carl was found **guilty**. His fingerprints were on the gun used in the robbery.
> 13 The **judge** decided what Carl's **punishment** should be.
> 14 He **sentenced** him to ten years in prison.
> 15 There was no **proof** that Adam had committed the crime.
> 16 He was **acquitted** and allowed to go free.

Highlight that:

– *charged with something* = formally accused of something.

– *trial* is used for more serious offenses and *court case* for less serious cases.

– *court* can refer to the building or to the institution, e.g., judge and jury. Common expressions with *court* are *to go to court* or *take someone to court*.

– the difference between *evidence* (= things that indicate that someone might be guilty) and *proof* (= things that show that someone is definitely guilty).

Testing yourself

For **Crimes and criminals**, Sts can cover the chart and try to remember the words for the crimes by reading the example cases A–Q. They could then cover the right-hand part of the chart to test themselves on the criminals and verbs. For **What happens to a criminal**, Sts can look at the words in the two lists and try to remember their meaning.

Testing a partner

See **Testing a partner** *page 29*.

Tell Sts to go back to the main lesson **8A**.

Extra support

- If you think Sts need more practice, you may want to give them the Vocabulary photocopiable activity at this point or leave it for later as consolidation or review.

3 PRONUNCIATION & SPEAKING

the letter *u*

Pronunciation notes

- Like all vowels in English, the letter *u* can be pronounced in different ways and crime vocabulary has several examples of the different pronunciations. Highlight to Sts that *ur*, unless followed by an *e*, is usually pronounced /ər/, and they should watch out for the "hidden" /y/ in words like *accuse*, *music*, etc.

a Focus on the task and elicit the sound and picture word for each column: /ʌ/ *up*, /ər/ *bird*, /ɔ/ *saw*, /yu/, and /ʊ/ *tourist*.

Now get Sts, individually or in pairs, to put the words in the correct column. Encourage them to say the words out loud before deciding which column they go into.

b 4 34)) Play the audio for Sts to listen and check.

Check answers and then elicit the answer to the question.

See audioscript 4.34

> 4 34))
> /ʌ/ drugs, judge, mugger, punishment, smuggling
> /ər/ burglar, murderer
> /ɔ/ caught, court, fraud
> /yu/ accuse
> /ʊr/ jury

Now play the audio again, pausing after each group of words for Sts to listen and repeat.

Then repeat the activity, eliciting responses from individual Sts.

c Focus on the sentences and get Sts to read them alternately in pairs.

Extra support

- Read each sentence to the class, getting Sts to repeat it after you. Then put Sts in pairs and get them to practice saying them.

Get some Sts to read the sentences to the class.

d Focus on the task and put Sts in pairs.

Give them time to ask and answer the questions. Encourage them to give as much information as possible.

Monitor and correct pronunciation where necessary.

Finally, get feedback from individual Sts and contribute opinions / experiences of your own if appropriate.

Extra support

- You could do this as an open-class activity, especially with a small class, eliciting answers from different Sts and contributing yourself.

4 MINI GRAMMAR *have something done*

a Focus on the examples and go through the rules. Highlight that *have something done* is used when you get someone else to do something for you, often paying a professional, e.g., *have your car repaired.*

Focus on sentences 1–5 and elicit from the class the answer to the first one.

Then give Sts time to fill in the blanks and check answers.

1 How often do you **have** your hair **cut**?
2 Where did you **have** it **repaired**?
3 Do you usually **have** your passport or ID card **renewed**...?
4 Have you **had** a burglar alarm **installed**...?
5 Have you ever **had** your photo **taken**...?

b Now put Sts in pairs and get them to ask and answer the questions in **a**, giving as many details as possible.

Get some feedback.

Extra support

- If you think Sts need more practice, you may want to give them the Mini Grammar photocopiable activity now or leave it for later as consolidation or review.

5 GRAMMAR the passive (all forms); *it is said that..., he is thought to..., etc.*

a Focus on the story and the two questions. Tell Sts not to worry about the alternative forms 1–9 for the time being.

Give Sts time to read the story and answer the questions.

Check answers.

The story advises the readers to be careful with deals that are too good to be true.
The woman paid $400 for an iPad that was in fact just a piece of wood with some glass stuck to the front.

Extra challenge

- Alternatively, get Sts in pairs to retell the story from memory.

b This exercise reviews different forms of the passive and Sts' ability to choose between the active and passive forms.

Get Sts to read the story again and to circle the right form of the verb.

Get them to compare with a partner and then check answers.

1 learned
2 had
3 was later caught
4 were found
5 had been made
6 had been cut
7 didn't know
8 has been charged
9 is being held

c 4 35))) Tell Sts they are going to listen to another crime story and give them time to read questions 1–6.

Play the audio once all the way through for Sts to listen and answer the questions.

Get Sts to compare with a partner and play the audio again. Play again as necessary.

Check answers.

1 in houses shared by students / (in the area between Broadway and 9th Street) in New York
2 drugs, electronics, and other gadgets
3 He helped himself to food and had a shower.
4 He pretended to know someone there.
5 Two students saw him in the area with a laptop and a backpack that he had just stolen from their house.
6 hiding behind some bushes

4 35)))

(audioscript in Student Book on *page 128*)

And last on our crime news stories from around the world, a burglar who's been fooling even the most intelligent students. The area near Broadway and 9th Street in New York City is where students often head to when they're looking for an apartment to share. This was something well known to Daniel Stewart Cooper, who also knew that students in a shared house often go out and leave the door unlocked, maybe thinking that another roommate is still inside. This situation suited Cooper perfectly, and he is thought to have committed between 50 and 100 burglaries in the area. It is believed that he was mainly interested in finding illegal substances, but that if he found electronics or other gadgets lying around, he took those, too. And he didn't just steal things. Cooper is also said to have made himself at home in the houses, helping himself to food from the refrigerator and even taking a shower. Although he usually tried to make sure that the residents were out, if he did meet people, it's thought that he would pretend to know someone there, and so was able to leave without raising suspicions.
However, on September 5th, Cooper was finally caught after two students saw him in the area with a laptop and a backpack that he had just stolen from their house. Dylan John, one of the victims, told CBS News that Cooper had taken some food, too. Cooper, who ran off as soon as he realized that the students suspected him, was found by the police hiding behind some nearby bushes.

d Focus on the task and give Sts time to read the four extracts from the listening.

Play the audio once all the way through for Sts to listen and fill in the blanks. Play the audio again, pausing after each sentence to give Sts time to write.

Get Sts to compare with a partner and then check answers.

1 ...he is thought **to have committed** between 50 and 100 burglaries in the area.
2 It is believed **that he was** mainly interested in finding drugs...
3 Cooper is also said **to have made** himself at home in the houses.
4 ...It's thought **that he would pretend** to know someone there.

Now ask Sts how the structure changes after *he is thought* and after *it is thought*.

After *he is thought* (*said / believed*), etc. you use *to* + infinitive.
After *it is thought* (*said / believed*), etc. you use *that* + a clause.

You might want to highlight that after *I / you / we / they*, you also use *to* + infinitive.

e 4 36))) 4 37))) Tell Sts to go to **Grammar Bank 8A** on *page 146*. Focus on the example sentences and play the audio for Sts to listen to the sentence rhythm. You could also get Sts to repeat the sentences to practice getting the rhythm right. Then go through the rules with the class.

Additional grammar notes

the passive (all forms)

- Sts at this level should be familiar with all the different forms of the passive, but it is likely that they will be more confident with the present and past forms that they have been using since *American English File* 2 than with the more complex forms (e.g., past continuous, past perfect, gerund, and infinitive).

the use of *by* in passive sentences

- Some Sts may tend to overuse *by* and want to include it every time they use the passive. One of the exercises here tries to correct this tendency.

it is said that..., he is thought to...

- These "advanced" passive structures are included more for recognition than production because they are low frequency in spoken English. However, Sts will certainly come across them if they read news websites or watch TV in English.

Focus on the exercises and get Sts to do them individually or in pairs.

Check answers, getting Sts to read the full sentences.

a
1 The road was closed after the accident.
2 My bag has been stolen.
3 My house is being painted.
4 A meeting will be held / is being held tomorrow...
5 If the burglar hadn't been found in time,...
6 You can be arrested for driving without a license.
7 Miranda thinks she was followed / was being followed last night.
8 I hate being / to be woken up when I'm fast asleep.
9 The local police station is going to be closed.

b
1 It is believed that the burglar is a local man. The burglar is believed to be a local man.
2 It is said that the muggers are very dangerous. The muggers are said to be very dangerous.
3 It is thought that the robber entered through an open window. The robber is thought to have entered through an open window.
4 It is said that the murderer has disappeared. The murderer is said to have disappeared.
5 It is expected that the trial will last three weeks. The trial is expected to last three weeks.

Tell Sts to go back to the main lesson **8A**.

Extra support

- If you think Sts need more practice, you may want to give them the Grammar photocopiable activity at this point or leave it for later as consolidation or review.

f Focus on the newspaper story and get Sts to use the prompts to write the missing phrases.

Get them to compare with a partner and then check answers.

1 is believed to be America's most polite armed robber
2 is said to be an unemployed 65-year-old father
3 is thought to be the same man
4 is reported that Mr. Hess was apprehended

Finally, ask Sts which of the three stories they thought was the most incredible (although they are all true).

6 READING

a Focus on the title of the article, *Crime online*, and elicit from the class what kind of crime(s) they think will be mentioned. Don't tell them if they are right or not.

b Focus on the task and the three summaries, making sure Sts know the meaning of *ultimately* and *harm* in **C**.

Set a time limit for Sts to read the article once and choose the best summary according to the writer's opinion.

Check the answer.

The best summary is C.

c Give Sts time to read questions 1–6, making sure they understand *idol*, *drown*, and *in the long run*.

Get Sts to read the article again.

Put Sts in pairs and get them to discuss the six questions.

Extra idea

- You could get Sts to underline the parts of the text that give them the answers.

Check answers.

1 People think that anything in the online world is free.
2 If people wanted a song on a CD, they wouldn't just take it from the store because it is stealing, but online they feel they can help themselves.
3 The government wanted to punish illegal downloaders with Internet disconnection. A group of artists and musicians opposed this because they said it reduced people's rights.
4 She thinks people who download music illegally should be punished (for example, being banned from using the Internet).
5 Because they love music, but they are watching the music industry suffer.
6 Because the music industry will get smaller and music magazines will close. People who want to work in the music industry will find that the salaries are very low because of money lost through illegal downloading.

d Focus on the highlighted words and phrases related to crime. Get Sts, in pairs, to guess their meaning. Tell them to read the whole sentence because the context will help them guess.

Check answers, either explaining in English, translating into Sts' L1, or getting Sts to check in their dictionaries.

Help with any other new vocabulary and encourage Sts to write down any useful new lexis from the article.

7 SPEAKING

a Focus on the **Useful language: saying what you think (1)** box and go through it with the class. Model and drill the pronunciation of *illegal* /ɪ'ligl/ and *law* /lɔ/.

Now focus on the instructions and go through each activity, eliciting the meaning of any words you think your Sts don't know, e.g., *breed*, *squatting*, *fence*, etc.

Put Sts in groups of three or four. They should choose a note-taker who will write down their decisions. You may want to set a time limit, but extend it if they need more time.

Monitor and encourage Sts to use the structures from the **Useful language** box.

b Get feedback. Start with the first activity and ask each note-taker what their group concluded.

If there's time, do the same with the other activities.

Help with any vocabulary problems that come up.

8 WRITING expressing your opinion

Tell Sts to go to **Writing *Expressing your opinion*** on *page 118*.

a Focus on the task and read the title of the magazine article out loud to the class. Elicit / explain what *community service* means. Then ask Sts if they agree or disagree with the title.

Give Sts time to quickly read the article to find out what the writer's opinion is. Tell them not to worry about the blanks.

Elicit the writer's opinion.

The writer thinks that, in general, community service is the wrong punishment for sports stars who commit a crime.

b Tell Sts to read the article again and this time to fill in the blanks with words or phrases from the list.

Get Sts to compare with a partner and then check answers.

2 In most cases	7 In addition
3 First	8 Finally
4 For instance	9 so
5 whereas	10 In conclusion
6 Second	

c Focus on the task and the two titles.

Give Sts a little time to think about which title they want to write about.

Get Sts to find someone who has chosen the same title.

d Focus on the instructions and go through points 1–3 with the class.

Now give Sts time, in their pairs, to discuss the reasons they are going to write about in the main paragraphs.

e Focus on the **Useful language: ways of giving your opinion** and **Ways of giving examples** box and go through it with the class.

Go through the instructions. Then either get Sts to do the writing in class (set a time limit of, e.g., 20 minutes) or get them to write at home for homework.

f Sts should check their work for mistakes before turning it in.

G reporting verbs
V the media
P word stress

8B Breaking news

Lesson plan

The topic of this lesson is the media.

The first section starts with a questionnaire where Sts talk about the different media they use, e.g., for the news, weather, etc., and which sections of newspapers they read. They then listen to a story from the press and read two more stories that provide a context to review the basic rules of reported speech. A fourth news story introduces reporting verbs, such as *offer, convince, admit, deny*, etc., that are followed by gerund or infinitive constructions. Sts then decide which story is in fact invented. After Sts have been to the **Grammar Bank** and learn more reporting verbs, there is a pronunciation focus on word stress in two-syllable verbs.

In the second section of the lesson, Sts read an extract from the book *24 Hours in Journalism* about what six journalists do between 6:00 and 8:00 in the morning. The vocabulary of the media is developed in the **Vocabulary Bank** and a speaking activity about the media. Sts then listen to an interview with a paparazza and then discuss their opinion of the paparazzi in general. Finally, they listen to the song *News of the World*.

STUDY LINK

- **Workbook** 8B
- **Online Practice**
- **iChecker**

Extra photocopiable activities

- **Grammar** reporting verbs *page 166*
- **Communicative** TV political debate *page 204* (instructions *page 184*)
- **Vocabulary** The media *page 222* (instructions *page 212*)
- **Song** *News of the World* *page 236* (instructions *page 228*)

Optional lead-in – the quote

- Write the quote at the top of *page 78* on the board (books closed) and the name of the person who said it, or get Sts to open their books and read it.
- Ask Sts what they think the quote means and whether they agree with it.

1 SPEAKING & LISTENING

a Focus on the title of the lesson, *Breaking news*, and ask Sts where they have seen this phrase (on TV news programs and websites). Elicit the meaning (it is used when a news channel has an important new story).

Now focus on questions 1–3 and get Sts to discuss them in pairs.

Get some feedback. You could do question 3 as an open-class activity.

b Focus on the task and either put Sts in pairs or do it as an open-class activity. You could ask Sts why the headline is funny (Because it is a play on the expression *Love at first sight*).

If Sts worked in pairs, elicit some ideas, but <u>don't</u> tell Sts if they are right or not.

c 4 38))) Focus on the task.

Play the audio once all the way through for Sts to listen and check their guesses in **b**.

Find out if any Sts had guessed correctly.

Extra support

- Before playing the audio, go through the audioscript and decide if you need to preteach / check any lexis to help Sts when they listen.

The story is about a tiger who ate a tiny video camera keepers had put in a snowman.

4 38)))
(audioscript in Student Book on *page 128*)

And for our last story today, have you ever wondered what it would be like to be eaten by a tiger? Well, now we know, thanks to Soundari, a seven-year-old Siberian tiger, living at Longleat Safari Park. Last week when it snowed, the zookeepers decided to build some snowmen to entertain the tigers, and they hid a tiny video camera inside one of the snowmen to video the tigers' reactions. At first the tigers just sniffed at the snowman, but then one of them, named Soundari, began attacking the snowman and started to eat it and the camera. However, she didn't like the taste of the camera, so after a while she spat it out. Amazingly, the camera hadn't stopped recording and was still working when the zookeepers recovered it. The video that the hidden camera had taken was incredible. For the first time you could feel what it would be like to be attacked by a tiger and see its open mouth coming at you, and see its enormous razor sharp teeth and its rough tongue. In fact, a spokesman for the safari park said that the shots of Soundari's teeth were so clear that it gave them the chance to do a quick health check on her mouth, gums, and teeth!

d Give Sts time to read questions 1–6.

Play the audio again all the way through for Sts to listen and answer the questions.

You could get Sts to compare with a partner before checking answers.

1 Soundari is a seven-year-old Siberian tiger living at Longleat Safari Park.
2 to entertain the tigers
3 a tiny video camera
4 She ate it.
5 because you could feel what it would be like to be attacked by a tiger and see its open mouth, its enormous sharp teeth, and its rough tongue
6 They could see what it would be like to be eaten by a tiger and they were able to give Soundari's mouth, gums, and teeth a quick health check.

Extra support

- If there's time, you could play the audio again while Sts read the audioscript on *page 128*, so they can see what they understood / didn't understand. Translate / explain any new words or phrases.

e Focus on the task and either put Sts in pairs to discuss the two headlines or do it as an open-class activity.

If Sts worked in pairs, elicit some ideas, but don't tell them if they are right or not. Tell Sts they will find out later.

f Put Sts in pairs, **A** and **B**, and tell them to go to **Communication *Strange, but true***, **A** on *page 107*, **B** on *page 112*.

Go through the instructions, making sure Sts understand they must highlight key information to help them retell the story to their partner.

Extra support

- You could put **A**s and **B**s together to do **a** first. Then get them to check they've gotten the key elements of the story before putting them in their pairs, **A** and **B**.

When Sts are ready, focus on the instructions in **b** and **c**.

Get some Sts to tell the stories to the class, making sure they mention the main points.

Extra challenge

- As feedback to the class, get **A**s to retell the story of *Dog calls for help* and **B**s to retell *Lost tourist finds herself*.

Find out if any Sts had made correct guesses in **e**.

Tell Sts to go back to the main lesson **8B**.

Extra support

- You could write any new and useful words and phrases from **Communication** on the board for Sts to copy.

2 GRAMMAR reporting verbs

a Focus attention on the photo of the two chefs and the title. Give Sts time to read the article and answer the questions.

Check answers.

> Two chefs got into a fight about a dish that they both said they had invented.
> The newspaper invited both chefs to prepare the dish at a restaurant. Newspaper staff ate both dishes and voted for Andrew's dish.

Elicit what the dish is (cold chicken with strawberry mayonnaise) and then ask Sts whether they would like to try it.

b Here Sts quickly review the basic rules for reported speech. Focus on the task and then give Sts time to read the article again and match the highlighted phrases with A–F.

Check answers.

> A 6 B 2 C 5 D 3 E 4 F 1

c Do this as an open-class activity, getting Sts to raise their hands to vote for the story they think isn't true.

Finally, tell Sts that the invented story is *Chicken fight*. The others are all true news stories.

d 4 39))) Tell Sts to go to **Grammar Bank 8B** on *page 147*. Focus on the example sentences and play the audio for Sts to listen to the sentence rhythm. You could also get Sts to repeat the sentences to practice getting the rhythm right. Then go through the rules with the class.

Additional grammar notes

- Sts should be familiar with regular reported speech with *say* / *tell* / *ask*, e.g.,
  Direct speech: *"I'm sorry."*
  Reported (or indirect) speech: *He said he was sorry.*
- In this lesson, Sts are introduced to a number of specific reporting verbs that are followed by either the infinitive or gerund. Some of these verbs and the structure following them have already been studied in **6A**.
- Highlight that using these reporting verbs is an alternative and more exact way of reporting what someone says, e.g.,

direct speech	*"I'm sorry I stole your recipe."*
reported speech	*He said he was sorry he had stolen the recipe.*
reporting verb	*He apologized for stealing the recipe.*

- Emphasize the use of the negative infinitive (*not to go*) and the negative gerund (*not going*) after these reporting verbs.
- Some of these verbs can also be used with *that* + clause, e.g., *He admitted that he had stolen the recipe.*

Focus on the exercises and get Sts to do them individually or in pairs.

Check answers, getting Sts to read the full sentences.

a

1 paying	6 not to leave
2 to work	7 trying / having tried
3 not to walk	8 not remembering
4 stealing	9 to come
5 to give up	10 damaging

b

1 suggested going	5 invited me to have
2 accused him of copying	6 reminded Jack to call
3 threatened to call	7 promised never to do
4 refused to go	8 recommended trying

Tell Sts to go back to the main lesson **8B**.

Extra support

- If you think Sts need more practice, you may want to give them the Grammar photocopiable activity at this point or leave it for later as consolidation or review.

3 PRONUNCIATION word stress

Pronunciation notes

- Sts have, by now, built up an instinct for how words in English are pronounced and will know that many English two-syllable nouns are stressed on the first syllable. However, many two-syllable verbs are stressed on the second syllable (e.g., *depend*). In fact, almost all the reporting verbs that Sts learn in this lesson are stressed on the second syllable.
- Highlight the difference between the /s/ sound in *convince, persuade, promise*, and *suggest*, and the /z/ sound in *accuse, advise*, and *refuse*.

a Focus on the task and give Sts time, individually or in pairs, to underline the stressed syllable in each verb and to circle the four exceptions.

b 4 40 Play the audio for Sts to listen and check.

Elicit the four exceptions with the stress on the first syllable.

Students should have circled *offer, order, promise*, and *threaten.*

4 40

accuse, admit, advise, agree, convince, deny, insist, invite, offer, order, persuade, promise, refuse, regret, remind, suggest, threaten

Focus on the **Spelling of two-syllable verbs** box and go through it with the class.

c Focus on the task and give Sts time to complete the sentences with the correct reporting verb.

Get them to compare with a partner.

d 4 41 Play the audio for Sts to listen and check.

Check answers.

See verbs in **bold** in audioscript 4.41

4 41

1. He **offered** to make some coffee.
2. He **refused** to go.
3. He **agreed** to help me.
4. He **promised** to call me.
5. He **reminded** me to lock the door.
6. He **advised** me to buy a new car.
7. He **invited** me to have dinner.
8. He **denied** breaking the window.
9. He **admitted** stealing the money.
10. He **regretted** marrying Susan.
11. He **suggested** going to a dance club.
12. The police **accused** him of stealing the laptop.

e 4 42 Focus on the task and explain that Sts are going to hear the sentences on the left in **c**, but in a different order and that they must respond with the corresponding reported sentence. Focus on the example or demonstrate the activity yourself before you play the audio. Highlight that Sts should use the pronoun *He* each time, except with the verb *accuse* when they should begin "*The police...*"

Now get Sts to either close their books or cover the examples in **c**. Play the audio, pausing after each sentence for Sts to call out the reported sentence.

4 42

1. I didn't break the window! (*pause*) He denied breaking the window.
2. I wish I hadn't married Susan. (*pause*) He regretted marrying Susan.
3. I'll call you. Believe me. (*pause*) He promised to call me.
4. Let's go to a dance club. (*pause*) He suggested going to a dance club.
5. You stole the laptop. (*pause*) The police accused him of stealing the laptop.
6. No, I won't go. (*pause*) He refused to go.
7. OK, I'll help you. (*pause*) He agreed to help me.
8. Remember to lock the door! (*pause*) He reminded me to lock the door.
9. I'll make some coffee. (*pause*) He offered to make some coffee.
10. Would you like to have dinner? (*pause*) He invited me to have dinner.
11. Yes, it was me. I stole the money. (*pause*) He admitted stealing the money.
12. You should buy a new car. (*pause*) He advised me to buy a new car.

Extra challenge

- You could play the audio again and this time get individual Sts to respond.

4 READING & VOCABULARY the media

a Focus on the task and point out the **Glossary** to Sts.

Then read the first paragraph of *24 Hours in Journalism* with the class.

Set a time limit for Sts to read the extract and match each section with a kind of journalist. Tell them not to worry about the blanks at this stage. Sts may not know *advice columnist*, but they should be able to match it to its piece of text by a process of elimination and then figure out its meaning. Highlight that *paparazzo* is the singular form of *paparazzi.*

Get Sts to compare with a partner and then check answers.

1. the online editor of the magazine *Marie Claire*
2. a radio newscaster
3. a war reporter
4. a paparazzo
5. a freelance journalist
6. an advice columnist

b Tell Sts to read the extract again and this time to fill in the blanks with one of the options, a, b, or c.

Get Sts to compare with a partner and then check answers.

1 a	4 a	7 b	10 c
2 c	5 b	8 a	11 a
3 b	6 a	9 b	12 b

Help with any other new vocabulary and encourage Sts to write down any useful new lexis from the article.

c Put Sts in pairs and get them to discuss the questions.

Get some feedback from the class.

d Tell Sts to go to **Vocabulary Bank *The media*** on *page 161*.

Focus on **1 Journalists and people in the media** and get Sts to do **a** individually or in pairs.

4 43))) Now do **b**. Play the audio for Sts to check answers. Play the audio again, pausing for Sts to repeat. Practice any words your Sts find difficult to pronounce.

> 4 43)))
> **The media**
> **Journalists and people in the media**
> 1 critic
> 2 sports commentator
> 3 reporter
> 4 editor
> 5 news anchor
> 6 freelance journalist
> 7 newscaster
> 8 paparazzi
> 9 advice columnist

Focus on **2 Adjectives to describe the media** and get Sts to do **a** individually or in pairs.

4 44))) Now do **b**. Play the audio for Sts to check answers.

Check answers.

> 4 44)))
> **Adjectives to describe the media**
> **1 D** The reporting in the paper was very sensational.
> **2 E** The news on Channel 12 is really biased.
> **3 B** I think *The New York Times* is the most objective of the Sunday papers.
> **4 A** The movie review was very accurate.
> **5 C** I think the report was censored.

Then get Sts to look at the adjectives and try to guess their exact meaning. In a monolingual class, and if you know the L1, elicit the meaning in your Sts' language or get them to check with a dictionary. Practice any words your Sts find difficult to pronounce, modelling and drilling as necessary.

Now look at **3 The language of headlines** and focus on the information box. Go through it with the class.

Get Sts to do **a** individually or in pairs.

4 45))) Now do **b**. Play the audio for Sts to check answers.

Check answers.

> 4 45)))
> **The language of headlines**
> **1 A** Famous actress in restaurant bill spat
> **2 E** Team manager to quit after shocking defeat
> **3 G** Prince to wed 18-year-old TV soap star
> **4 L** President backs senator in latest scandal
> **5 I** Tarantino tabbed to direct new thriller
> **6 B** Thousands of jobs axed by US companies
> **7 K** Stock market hit by oil fears
> **8 C** Police quiz witness in murder trial
> **9 D** Astronaut bids to be first man on Mars
> **10 J** Politicians clash over new car tax proposal
> **11 H** Tennis star vows to avenge defeat
> **12 F** Actor and wife split over affair with cleaner

! Highlight that *wed*, *quiz*, and *vows* would not usually be used in conversation.

Then look at the headlines again and ask Sts to think how they would say them in everyday English. Ask Sts *What kind of words get left out in headlines? What form or tense is used for a) the future b) the passive (all tenses)?* Elicit that articles and auxiliary verbs are often left out, e.g., *A man was run over by a bus* becomes *Man run over by bus*. The future is expressed by an infinitive, e.g., *Michael Jordan to go*, and passives by a past participle, e.g., *Man stabbed on subway*.

Testing yourself

For **Journalists and people in the media**, Sts can cover the words, look at the definitions, and try to remember the words. For **Adjectives to describe the media**, they can cover 1–5, look at sentences A–E, and try to remember the adjectives. For **The language of headlines**, they can cover definitions A–L, read the headlines, and try to remember what the highlighted verbs mean.

Testing a partner

See **Testing a partner** *page 29*.

Tell Sts to go back to the main lesson **8B**.

Extra support

- If you think Sts need more practice, you may want to give them the Vocabulary photocopiable activity at this point or leave it for later as consolidation or review.

5 SPEAKING

The new vocabulary is recycled in this speaking activity. Focus on the **Useful language: saying what you think (2)** box and go through it with the class.

Focus on questions 1–4 and give Sts time to read them and think about how they are going to answer.

Put Sts in small groups of three or four. Now set a time limit for the groups to discuss each question.

Monitor and help if necessary.

Get some feedback and help with any general vocabulary problems that come up.

Extra support

- Answer the questions yourself first to help Sts with ideas.

6 LISTENING

a 4 46))) Focus on the photos and find out if Sts know anything about these celebrities.

Now focus on the task.

Play the audio once all the way through for Sts to listen and take notes. Play the audio again if necessary, pausing after the celebrities are mentioned, and then check answers.

Extra support

- Before playing the audio, go through the audioscript and decide if you need to preteach / check any lexis to help Sts when they listen.

> 1 Brad Pitt doesn't like the paparazzi.
> 2 and 3 Britney Spears and Lindsay Lohan call the paparazzi to tell them where they are going and then get money from the photos taken.
> 4 and 5 Julia Roberts and Kate Bosworth hate being photographed by paparazzi.
> 6 Jennifer Buhl got the most money from a photo she took of Paris Hilton going into jail, carrying a Bible.

4 46

(audioscript in Student Book on *page 129*)
I = interviewer, J = Jennifer Buhl

I Brad Pitt said recently, "They call my kids by their names. They shove cameras in their faces. I really believe there should be a law against it." He was talking, of course, about paparazzi. But are the paparazzi really as bad as Brad Pitt says they are? Today in the studio with us is Jennifer Buhl, who is an actual – is it *paparazzi* or *paparazzo*?
J *Paparazzo* for a man, *paparazza* for a woman. *Paparazzi* is the plural.
I So, Jennifer, are you good, bad, or in between?
J Well, I think I'm a good girl. But some people would probably not like me.
I A lot of people say there's a working relationship between celebrities and paparazzi. Would you say that was true? That celebrities actually tell you where they're going to be.
J Yes, of course. That happens all the time. But I think that's what a lot of the public doesn't realize. You know, people shout at us and insult us when there's a big crowd of us around, let's say, Britney Spears or Lindsay Lohan. I just want to tell them that they called us. After we've sold the photos, we split the money between the stars and us.
I I've often thought that must be true. I mean, nobody just goes to the gym with their hair done and makeup on unless they're actually expecting to be photographed.
J Exactly. But don't get me wrong, it's not like all the celebrities want to be photographed. If a celebrity wants to go out and avoid the paparazzi, it's pretty easy to do. Celebrities that don't like it rarely get photographed; they very rarely get photographed.
I Give me some example of celebrities who genuinely don't want to be photographed. Like, who really hates it?
J Julia Roberts hates it. Kate Bosworth hates it.
I Are photos of them worth more money if they hate it?
J It depends. No, not necessarily. Because they don't get photographed often; then nobody sees them in magazines, and they lose interest in them. Because they become boring.
I What shot have you taken that you got the most money for?
J Probably one of the shots that sold the best, that I didn't expect, didn't even know, was Paris Hilton carrying the Bible right before she went to jail. There were lots of paparazzi there, but I was the only one that got the Bible.
I Do you think we need stricter laws to keep paparazzi away?
J There are already enough laws. We don't need more laws, or anti-paparazzi laws, or anything else. There are places where celebrities can go to where they know they won't be followed, and places where they know they will be.
I For example?
J We don't go into restaurants, we don't go into stores, and, of course, we don't go into people's homes. That's private property. But a beach or a park isn't.
I So you don't think that being followed and photographed by the paparazzi is really stressful for celebrities?
J I think there are only a few people for whom it's really and truly stressful. I'd say that in most cases, the star not only doesn't mind, but has actually told the paparazzi, "This is where I'm going to be this afternoon."
I Fascinating. Thank you very much for coming into the studio. Jennifer Buhl, everybody!

b Tell Sts they are going to listen to the interview again and this time they must check the things in 1–9 that Jennifer says.

Give Sts time to read 1–9.

Play the audio again all the way through for Sts to listen and do the task.

Check answers.

Extra support

- You could get Sts to compare their answers with a partner between the first and second playing of the audio.

Sts should have checked 1, 4, 5, 6, 8, and 9.

Extra support

- If there's time, you could play the audio again while Sts read the audioscript on *page 129*, so they can see what they understood / didn't understand. Translate / explain any new words or phrases.

c Do this as an open-class activity.

7 4 47 SONG *News of the World* ♫

This song was originally made famous by the British band The Jam in 1978. For copyright reasons, this is a cover version. If you want to do this song in class, use the photocopiable activity on *page 236*.

4 47

News of the World

Punk rock
Power pop

I read about the things that happen throughout the world
Don't believe in everything you see or hear
The neighbors talk
Day in day out
About the goings on
They tell us what they want
They don't give an inch

Look at the pictures taken by the cameras
They cannot lie
The truth is in what you see
Not what you read
Little men tapping things out
Points of view
Remember their views
Are not the gospel truth

Don't believe it all
Find out for yourself
Check before you spread
News of the world
News of the world

Never doubt
Never ask
Never moan
Never search
Never find
Never know
News of the world
News of the world

Each morning our key to the world comes through the door
More than often it's just a comic, not much more
Don't take it too serious – not many do
Read between the lines and you'll find the truth

Read all about it
Read all about it
News of the world
News of the world

Read all about it
Read all about it
News of the world
News of the world

7&8 Review and Check

For instructions on how to use these pages see *page 39*.

Testing Program CD-ROM

- **File 8 Quick Test**
- **File 8 Test**

GRAMMAR

1 must have
2 should have told
3 couldn't have gotten
4 rather do
5 as if
6 tastes like
7 as a waiter
8 was being repaired
9 never be found
10 to be
11 is said
12 burglar alarm installed
13 to talk
14 killing her husband
15 apologized for being

VOCABULARY

a 1 remind 2 matter 3 stole 4 raise 5 argue 6 refuses

b 1 calf (The others relate to hands.)
2 hip (The others are organs.)
3 wink (The others are things you do with your hand.)
4 vandal (The others are all kinds of thieves.)
5 smuggler (The others are crimes.)
6 evidence (The others are people.)

c 1 chew 2 scratch 3 stare 4 frown 5 hack 6 blackmail 7 bribe 8 quit

d 1 critic 2 biased 3 censored 4 newscaster 5 accurate

PRONUNCIATION

a 1 frown 2 biased 3 court 4 stare 5 jury

b 1 realize 2 kidney 3 kidnap 4 commentator 5 objective

CAN YOU UNDERSTAND THIS TEXT?

a Generally, hijackers of that time were political extremists or worked alone. But DB Cooper did it for money and he has never been found.

b 1 F 2 T 3 F 4 T 5 T 6 T 7 F 8 T 9 T 10 F

CAN YOU UNDERSTAND THIS MOVIE?

4 48

1 They just have to post an article online.
2 30,000
3 Blackbeard / Edward Teach
4 Journalists would ride their horses to the nearest town that had a printing press.
5 because the roads were very bad
6 the telegraph
7 They were very biased / had no objectivity and they were usually censored.
8 radio and television
9 by (live) Twitter (feeds)
10 because photos were taken on smartphones and uploaded to Twitter within seconds

4 48 Available as MP3 on CD1

A Short Film on the Speed of News

Hi, my name's Matt Wilder. I'm a freelance journalist based in Washington DC. At the moment I'm trying to find a good story. I have a six o'clock deadline, but nothing's going on. I know, I'll see what topics are trending on Twitter.

Today we live in the era of new media. People can access the news at any time, from any place on all kinds of digital devices. The Internet and social media sites such as Twitter and Facebook allow these news consumers to become news producers. If you want to be a journalist, all you have to do is post an article online and it can be read instantly by anyone anywhere in the world.

Journalism has changed a lot during the first days of the newspaper and most of these changes have been driven by technology. There's no better place to discover this than Washington DC – home of the Newseum. There are over 30,000 newspapers here covering over 500 years of news. This is the Boston News-Letter, thought to be the first continuously published newspaper in North America. This edition, from 1718, reports on the sensational killing of Edward Teach – better known as Blackbeard – believed to be one of the most dangerous pirates at the time.

Reporting in the early days of journalism must have been very difficult. Journalists would ride their horses to the nearest town that had a printing press. Their reports were then published in a newspaper, which was often just a single sheet of paper, and distributed on horseback. The roads were bad, so it was very difficult to send news over long distances. By the time most people read these newspapers, the news was often very out of date.

This all changed when the first telegraph line was built in 1844. Suddenly, journalists could send stories quickly. The telegraph is said to have revolutionized news reporting. This new style of journalism came just in time for the American Civil War. For the first time news could be sent at the same time as battles were being fought. War correspondents, and the stories they sent, became very popular. But there were still problems. These war reports were very biased because journalists represented their own side in the war. There was no objectivity and reports were usually censored by the army or the government. So stories were often inaccurate and sometimes completely wrong!

It wasn't until the invention of radio and television that news could be broadcast live. This completely transformed news and created the age of the mass media, where news could be communicated to a huge audience. Throughout the twentieth century, demand for news stories increased and news technology continued to advance. By the end of the century, there were hundreds of cable TV channels, lots of 24-hour news channels, and the Internet had been invented. Suddenly, we were in the Information Age.

This is the HP New Media Gallery. It shows the news as it is today. Visitors to this exhibit are placed right at the center of the digital news revolution. They are instantly connected to the day's news by live Twitter feeds showing the day's trending news stories. They can also check out major news stories which were first reported on social media. These pictures of a plane landing on New York's Hudson River were taken on a smartphone and uploaded to Twitter seconds after the incident had occurred.

Speaking of smartphones...Ah, fantastic! A tweet from The White House. Oh! There's a big announcement in 25 minutes. I'd better go! Bye!

G clauses of contrast and purpose; *whatever, whenever,* etc.
V advertising, business
P changing stress on nouns and verbs

9A Truth and lies

Lesson plan

The topic and lexical area of this lesson is business and advertising.

In the first section, the focus is on honesty (or dishonesty) in advertising. Sts read an article about four famous misleading advertisements and then listen to a radio program about how companies try to trick us through the use of misleading advertisements. This leads to the grammar, which is on clauses of contrast after expressions like *Even though…*, *In spite of…*, etc. and clauses of purpose or reason after expressions like *so that…*, *in order to…*, etc.

The honesty link is continued in the second section of the lesson where Sts read and listen to an extract from the best-selling book *Freakonomics* about a man who set up a business selling bagels in companies and unintentionally designed an interesting test of honesty. This is followed by a Mini Grammar focus on *whatever, wherever,* etc.
In Vocabulary, Sts look at words and phrases related to business, and there is a pronunciation focus on how stress changes in words like *export*, which can be used both as nouns and verbs. Sts then talk about business in their country before finally listening to the song, *The Truth*.

STUDY LINK
- **Workbook** 9A
- **Online Practice**
- **iChecker**

Extra photocopiable activities

- **Grammar** clauses of contrast and purpose *page 167*
- **Mini Grammar** *whatever, whenever,* etc. *page 178*
- **Communicative** Tell me about... *page 205* (instructions *page 184*)
- **Vocabulary** Business *page 223* (instructions *page 212*)
- **Song** *The Truth page 237* (instructions *page 228*)

Optional lead-in – the quote

- Write the quote at the top of *page 84* on the board (books closed) and the name of the person who said it, or get Sts to open their books and read it.
- Ask Sts if they agree with the quote.

1 READING & VOCABULARY

a In pairs, Sts look at the advertisement and discuss questions 1–3. Tell them not to read the article. Before they start you could elicit / explain what *a physician* is.

Elicit answers, but don't tell Sts if they are right or not.

b Now tell Sts to read the first paragraph of the article and check their answers to **a**.

Check answers.

1 the soft drink 7Up
2 from the 1950s
3 They used babies in the ad to convince the public that soda is good for you, i.e., even for babies.

c Sts now read the whole article. Focus on the task and sentences A–F, making sure Sts understand them. Point out to Sts that they might need to write more than one number next to some of the sentences.

When they have finished, get them to compare with a partner and then check answers.

A 3 and 4	C 2	E 2
B 4	D 3	F 3

d Focus on the highlighted words and phrases, and give Sts time to try and figure out what they mean. Remind them to read the whole sentence or paragraph.

Then get Sts to match the highlighted words and phrases with definitions 2–11.

Check answers, and model and drill pronunciation.

2 commercials	7 brands
3 ads	8 sued
4 claiming	9 misleading
5 celebrity endorsers	10 consumers
6 airbrushed	11 an advertising campaign

Give Sts some practice pronouncing the words.

Help with any other new vocabulary and encourage Sts to write down any useful new lexis from the article.

e Do this in pairs, small groups, or as an open-class activity.

2 LISTENING & SPEAKING

a Focus on the task and the photo, and make sure Sts know what *mascara* is.

Put Sts in pairs and give them time to discuss the question.

Elicit some ideas and then tell Sts that the ad was withdrawn after people complained (and L'Oréal admitted) that Penélope Cruz, the actress in the ad, was wearing false eyelashes, rather than simply the mascara she was advertising.

b 5 2))) Focus on the task and make sure Sts know what *a trick* is.

Give Sts time to look at all the items in the list. You might also want to check Sts know what *a slogan* is.

Play the audio once all the way through for Sts to listen and do the task.

Check answers.

Extra support

- Before playing the audio, go through the audioscript and decide if you need to preteach / check any lexis to help Sts when they listen.

Sts should have checked: free gifts, limited supplies of the product, crowds of people, attractive models, doctors and celebrities, and recent studies

5 2))

(audioscript in Student Book on *page 129*)

The first point to bear in mind is that nothing, I repeat, nothing is ever free. How often have you seen ads saying things like, "Get a free MP3 player when you subscribe to our magazine for six months"? There's something about the word *free* that immediately attracts us – I want it! It makes us feel smart, as if we are going to get something for nothing. But, of course, that MP3 player (which, incidentally, will probably break the second time you use it) wasn't free at all. In spite of what the ad said, its price was really included in the magazine subscription. So don't trust any ad that offers something for free.

A second trick that advertisers use is when they tell us, "There are only a few left! Buy now while the stock lasts!" What happens to us when we read or hear these words? Even though we don't really need the products, and maybe don't even like them, we immediately want to be among the lucky few who have them. But – let's be clear about this – companies just don't run out of products. Do you really think the manufacturers couldn't produce a few more if they thought they could sell them? Of course they could.

When it comes to new products we, the consumers, are like sheep and we follow each other. So another way advertisers get us to use something is to tell us, "Everybody's using it." And of course, we think everybody can't be wrong, so the product must be fantastic. So as to make us believe it, they use expressions like, "It's a must-have" or "It's the in thing," and they combine this with a photograph of a large group of people, so that we can't fail to get the message. But don't be fooled. Even if everybody is using it (and they may not be), everybody can be wrong.

Another favorite message is, "You, too, can look like this," accompanied by a photo of a fabulous-looking man or woman. But the problem is, you can't look like this because actually the woman or man in the photo is a model and also because he or she doesn't really look like that either. The photo has been airbrushed in order to make the model look even slimmer, with perfect skin, and even more attractive than they are in real life.

Finally, what most annoys me is, "Trust me, I'm a doctor" or "Trust me, I'm a celebrity." The idea is that if a celebrity is using the product, it must be fantastic, or if a doctor recommends it, it must really work. But be careful. Although the actress is holding the product in the photo, do you really think she colors her hair with it at home? And the doctor in the ad, is he really a doctor or just an actor wearing a white coat? Ads also often mention a particular organization which recommends their product, for example, things like, "Our dog biscuits are recommended by the International Association of Dog Nutritionists" – well, that's probably an organization that the company set up themselves. Or, "A recent independent study found that our toothpaste cleans your teeth better than any other brand." What study was it? Who commissioned the study? It was probably produced for the company itself and paid for by them, too.

c Focus on the task and get Sts to write the six things they checked on a piece of paper as headings for the notes they are going to be taking.

Now play the audio again. You could pause after each trick is mentioned to give Sts time to take notes.

You could get Sts to compare with a partner and then if necessary, play again.

Check answers.

free gifts: consumers are attracted to the word *free*, but nothing is free. The price of the "free gift" is included in the price of the product.
limited supplies of the product: companies don't run out of products. They could easily produce more.
crowds of people: advertisers say "everyone is using it"; this might not be true, plus everyone could have made a bad choice.
attractive models: advertisers say we can look like models, but we can't because we aren't models and also because the photos have been airbrushed.
doctors and celebrities: the celebrity advertising the product might not be using it. The "doctor" advertising a product might not even be a doctor.
recent studies: these might have been done or paid for by the advertising company themselves.

Extra support

- If there's time, you could play the audio again while Sts read the audioscript on *page 129*, so they can see what they understood / didn't understand. Translate / explain any new words or phrases.

d Focus on the task and go through the questions, making sure Sts know the meaning of *logo* and the correct pronunciation of *viral* /ˈvaɪrəl/.

Put Sts in small groups and give them time to discuss 1–5. If they ask you what a viral ad is (in number 3), you can give the example of a video clip advertising a product that is produced by a company, but is then spread like a virus from person to person via the Internet and other social networks.

Monitor and help while Sts are doing the activity.

Help with any vocabulary problems that come up.

Get some feedback.

3 GRAMMAR clauses of contrast and purpose

a Focus on the task and on phrases A–G, which Sts have to insert in the extracts. Although this grammar is being focused on for the first time, Sts should have seen most of the highlighted expressions before and the context will help them to fill in the blanks even if they are unsure of the exact meaning of some of the highlighted phrases.

Get Sts to compare their answers with a partner.

Extra support

- You could do the first one with the class as an example.

b 5 3)) Play the audio for Sts to listen and check.

Check answers.

1 F 2 E 3 D 4 C 5 G 6 B 7 A

5.3

1 In spite of what the ad said, its price was really included in the magazine subscription.
2 Even though we don't really need the products, and maybe don't even like them, we immediately want to be among the lucky few who have them.
3 So as to make us believe it, they use expressions like, "It's a must-have"...
4 ...and they combine this with a photograph of a large group of people, so that we can't fail to get the message.
5 The photo has been airbrushed in order to make the model look even slimmer, with perfect skin, and even more attractive than they are in real life.
6 Although the actress is holding the product in the photo, do you really think she colors her hair with it at home?
7 It was probably produced for the company itself, and paid for by them, too.

Now focus Sts' attention on the seven highlighted phrases and ask them, in pairs, to decide if they express a contrast or a purpose (= the aim or function of something).

Check answers.

A contrast	In spite of..., Even though..., Although...
A purpose	So as to, so that, in order to, for

c 5.4 5.5 Tell Sts to go to **Grammar Bank 9A** on *page 148*. Focus on the example sentences and play the audio for Sts to listen to the sentence rhythm. You could also get Sts to repeat the sentences to practice getting the rhythm right. Then go through the rules with the class.

Additional grammar notes

clauses of contrast

- **rule 1:** Sts should be familiar with the meaning and use of *although*. Here they are introduced to *even though* and *though*.
- **rule 2:** Sts will have seen *in spite of* or *despite*, e.g., in reading texts, but in this lesson, they learn how to use them.

clauses of purpose

- Sts have previously learned to use *to* + infinitive to express purpose. Here they learn other ways of expressing the same idea.
- **rule 1:** *In order to* and *so as to* are more formal than *to*. Make sure Sts don't use *for* + infinitive here. NOT *I went to the bank ~~for~~ to talk to my bank manager.*
- **rule 2:** Stress that *for* + gerund is used to describe the purpose of a thing (often in answer to the question *What's it for?*). *For* can also be used to express the purpose of an action if that purpose is expressed with a noun, e.g., *We went to Venezuela for a vacation*, but not when it is expressed with a verb phrase, e.g., NOT *I come to this school ~~for learning~~ English.*
- **rule 3:** Point out that when there is a new subject in a clause of purpose we <u>must</u> use *so that* (and not *to, in order to, so as to*), e.g., *We bought a big car so that the children would have more space.* NOT *...~~in order to~~ the children have more space.*
- **rule 4:** The main point to stress here is that the most common way of expressing purpose in spoken English (*to* + infinitive) <u>can't</u> be used to express negative purpose; you have to use *so as not to...* or *in order not to...*

Focus on the exercises and get Sts to do them individually or in pairs.

Check answers, getting Sts to read the full sentences.

a
1 despite
2 even
3 to
4 as
5 order
6 spite
7 that
8 although
9 for
10 Despite

b
1 ...we wouldn't arrive late.
2 ...she earns a fortune, she drives a very old car.
3 ...the sad ending. / the ending being sad. / the fact that the ending was sad.
4 ...the weather conditions were terrible.
5 ...not to offend her.
6 ...to explain the new policy.

Tell Sts to go back to the main lesson **9A**.

Extra support

- If you think Sts need more practice, you may want to give them the Grammar photocopiable activity at this point or leave it for later as consolidation or review.

d **Sentence race:** Put Sts in pairs. Focus on the task and make sure Sts know what they have to do and how long they have to do it.

Monitor while pairs are writing their sentences and point out any incorrect sentences you see, but do not correct them.

When the time limit is up, elicit several possible answers for each sentence and write them on the board.

Some possible answers
1 ...small children don't see them.
2 ...the new product didn't sell very well.
3 ...young people still buy them.
4 ...experience life in a big city.
5 ...not being very good at his job.
6 ...it wasn't true.
7 ...get a refund.
8 ...a meeting.

4 READING & LISTENING

a Focus on the instructions. Elicit some ideas from Sts, but don't tell them if they are right or not.

b Give Sts a time limit to read the article to find the answer to **a**.

Check the answer.

> The bagel test showed how honest his customers were – what type of people / companies stole compared to those who didn't. It also looked at whether certain circumstances made people less honest.

Now focus on phrases 1–7, making sure Sts understand all the lexis.

Put Sts in pairs and tell them to discuss what they can remember about items 1–7. If necessary, let them read the article again.

Check answers.

1 He worked in Washington. / He worked for the US Navy. / He held senior-level jobs. / He earned a good salary. / He was the head of the public research group.
2 At the office Christmas party, his colleagues introduced him as "the guy who brings in the bagels" (instead of "the head of the public research group").
3 It started as a way of thanking his employees when they won a contract. Every Friday he brought in bagels and cream cheese.
4 People from other departments wanted bagels, too. Finally, he was bringing in so many bagels that he needed to charge to cover his costs. 95% of people paid.
5 His friends thought he was crazy ("lost his mind"). His wife supported him.
6 Within a few years he was delivering thousands of bagels (8,400) a week to many companies (140).
7 He discovered how honest his customers were and what kind of people and companies stole more or less.

c Focus on the task and give Sts time, in pairs, to predict the answers to questions 1–6.

Get some feedback from the class on what they think the right answers will be and why. Don't tell them if they are right or not.

d 5 6))) Play the audio all the way through for Sts to check their answers to **c**.

Check answers and find out how many Sts had guessed correctly.

Extra support

- Before playing the audio, go through the audioscript and decide if you need to preteach / check any lexis to help Sts when they listen.

1 b (80–90%)
2 Smaller offices were more honest.
3 The cash box has hardly ever been stolen.
4 They cheated more during bad weather.
5 They cheated more before Christmas because many people often feel anxious and stressed before this holiday and don't look forward it.
6 Executives cheated more than lower status employees.

5 6)))

(audioscript in Student Book on *page 129*)

When Paul Feldman started his business, you know, he really thought that at least 95 percent of the people would pay for their bagels. This was presumably because that was the payment rate that he got in his own office. But, in fact, this rate wasn't representative at all. I mean, in his office, most people paid probably just because Feldman worked there himself, and they knew him personally, and probably liked him.

So when Feldman sold his bagels in other offices, he had to accept less. After a while, he considered that a company was "honest" if over 90 percent of the people paid. Between 80 and 90 percent was what he considered to be normal, you know, the average rate. He didn't like it, but he had to accept it. It was only if a company habitually paid less than 80 percent – which luckily not many did – that he would feel he had to do something. First, he would leave a note, sort of giving them a warning, and then, if things didn't improve, he would simply stop selling there. Interestingly, since he started the business, the boxes he leaves to collect the cash have hardly ever been stolen. Obviously, in the mind of an office worker, to steal a bagel isn't a crime, but to steal the money box is.

So, what does the bagel data tell us about the kind of offices that were not honest, the ones that didn't pay? Well, first of all, it shows that smaller offices are more honest than big ones. An office with 20 to 30 employees generally pays three to five percent more than an office with two to three hundred employees. This seems to be because in a smaller community people are more worried about being dishonest – probably because they would feel worse if they were caught.

The bagel data also suggests that your mood, how you feel, affects how honest you are. For example, the weather is a really important factor. When the weather is unusually good, more people pay, but if it's unusually cold or rainy, fewer people pay. And people are also affected by holidays, but in different ways – it depends which holiday. Before Christmas and Thanksgiving, people are less honest, but just before the 4th of July and Labor Day, they are more honest. This seems to be because holidays like the 4th of July are just a day off work, and people always look forward to them. But Christmas and Thanksgiving are holidays where people very often feel stressed or miserable. So their bad mood makes them less honest.

The other thing Feldman believes affects how honest people are is the morale in an office. When employees like their boss and like their job, then the office is more honest. He also thinks that the higher people are promoted, the less honest they are. He reached this conclusion because, over several years, he'd been delivering three baskets of bagels to a company that was on three floors. The top floor was the executive floor, and the lower two floors were people who worked in sales, and service, and administrative employees. Well, it turned out that the least honest floor was the executive floor! It makes you wonder whether maybe these guys got to be executives because they were good at cheating!

But in general, the story of Feldman's bagel business is a really positive one. It's true that some people do steal from him, but the vast majority, even though no one is watching them, are honest.

e Focus on the task and give Sts time to go through 1–5 and read the options.

Play the audio again pausing, if necessary, after each paragraph to give Sts time to choose the right answer. Play the audio again if necessary.

Check answers.

1 c 2 a 3 b 4 c 5 c

Extra support

- If there's time, you could play the audio again while Sts read the audioscript on *page 129*, so they can see what they understood / didn't understand. Translate / explain any new words or phrases.

f Focus on the question and elicit opinions from the class.

5 MINI GRAMMAR *whatever, whenever, etc.*

Focus on the example from the article, *Would you pass the bagel test?*, and on the explanation. Then go through the rules with the class regarding *whatever, whichever,* etc. writing some or all of these examples on the board.

*You can have **whatever** you want.* = It doesn't matter what you want, you can have it.

*He offered me two watches and said I could have **whichever** one I wanted.* = It doesn't matter which one you have.

*I'll buy it **however** expensive it is.* = I'll buy it.

***However** hard I try, I can never remember birthdays.* = It doesn't matter how hard I try, I always forget birthdays.

*I always take my identity card **wherever** I go.* = It doesn't matter where I go, I always take my identity card.

Highlight that *whichever* is used instead of *whatever* when there is a very limited choice, usually two or three.

Focus on the exercise and give Sts time to complete it.

Check answers.

1 wherever	3 Whenever	5 Whatever
2 whoever	4 however	6 whichever

Extra support

- If you think Sts need more practice, you may want to give them the Mini Grammar photocopiable activity now or leave it for later as consolidation or review.

6 VOCABULARY business

a Focus on the task and get Sts, in pairs, to discuss what all the terms mean.

Check answers.

the head = the person in charge (of the company)
a colleague = a person that you work with, especially in a profession or a business
employees = people who are paid to work for someone
a department = a section of a large organization
set up = to create something, to start it
customers = people who buy something

b Tell Sts to go to **Vocabulary Bank *Business*** on *page 162*.

Focus on **1 Verbs and expressions** and get Sts to do **a** individually or in pairs.

5 7))) Now do **b**. Play the audio for Sts to check answers. Practice any words your Sts find difficult to pronounce.

5 7)))
Business
Verbs and expressions
a
1 Although GAP stands for Genuine American Product, most of its clothes are **manufactured** in Asia.
2 In 1989 Pepsi-Cola **launched** a new product called *Pepsi A.M.*, which was aimed at the "breakfast cola drinker." It was an immediate flop.
3 The Spanish airline Iberia **merged** with British Airways in 2011.
4 Apple Inc. is considered one of the best companies in the world for the way they **market** their products.
5 *Prosciutto* is a kind of Italian ham. Two of the best-known kinds are San Daniele and Parma, which are **produced** in the Friuli and Emilia regions of Italy, and are **exported** all over the world.
6 The Royal Bank of Scotland **took over** NatWest Bank in 2000, even though it was in fact a smaller rival.
7 The social media company Facebook **became** the market leader in 2008, and it's still the US's most-used social media website.
8 Zara shops were opened in Spain in 1975, but the company soon **expanded** internationally.
9 Nowadays it is a risk to **set up** a new business. In the US, 20% to 25% of businesses fail in their first year.
10 The cost of living in Iceland is so high because so many food products have to be **imported**.
11 In a boom period, standards of living improve greatly and the economy **grows** quickly.
12 During a recession, many companies **close down** and living standards **drop**.

Now focus on **c** and give Sts time to put the words into the correct column.

5 8))) Now do **d**. Play the audio for Sts to check answers. Practice any words your Sts find difficult to pronounce.

5 8)))
Verbs and expressions
c
do business with, do a job, do market research, do well, do badly

make a deal, make a decision, make an investment, make a loss, make money

Highlight that *a deal* = a business agreement and *make an investment* = to put money into a business with the intention of profiting from the growth of the business.

Now focus on **2 Organizations and people** and get Sts to do **a** and **b** individually or in pairs.

5 9))) Now do **c**. Play the audio for Sts to check answers. Practice any words your Sts find difficult to pronounce.

5 9)))
Organizations and people

Organizations

1 a chain	4 headquarters
2 a business	5 a branch
3 a multinational	

People

1 the staff	5 the CEO
2 a customer	6 the owner
3 a client	7 a manager
4 a colleague	

You might also want to teach the word *worker*, which is often used to describe someone who works in an office or factory, etc. The word *colleague* is synonymous with *co-worker*.

Testing yourself

For **Verbs and expressions a**, Sts can cover the sentences and try to remember them by reading the words in the list. For **c**, they can look at the words in the list and remember if they go with *do* or *make*. For **Organizations and people**, they can cover the definitions and read the words in the lists to see if they can remember their meaning.

Testing a partner

See **Testing a partner** *page 29*.

Tell Sts to go back to the main lesson **9A**.

Extra support

- If you think Sts need more practice, you may want to give them the Vocabulary photocopiable activity at this point or leave it for later as consolidation or review.

c This is an oral vocabulary practice activity. Focus on the questions and give Sts time to do this in pairs.

Check answers.

1 *A customer* is usually used for someone who buys a product (e.g., in a store) or a service (e.g., a meal in a restaurant). *A client* is usually used for someone who pays a professional for a service, e.g., a lawyer or accountant.
2 *A boom* is a sudden increase in trade and economic activity. *A recession* is a difficult time for the economy of a country, when there is less trade and industrial activity than usual and more people are unemployed.
3 *Increase* means to become or to make something greater in amount, number, value, etc. This can be a verb or noun. *Improve* is a verb and means to become better than before.
4 *Rise* is both a verb and a noun. The verb means to come or go upward, to reach a higher level or position. *Fall* is also both a verb and a noun. The verb means to drop down from a higher level to a lower level.
5 *Export a product* means to sell it to another country whereas *import a product* means to buy it from another country.
6 *A manager* is a person who is in charge of running a business, a store, or a similar organization. *An owner* is the person who owns, e.g., the store or the business.

7 PRONUNCIATION & SPEAKING

changing stress on nouns and verbs

a Focus on the **Changing stress on two-syllable nouns and verbs** box and go through it with the class.

Then get the class to practice saying the eight words (*increase*, *decrease*, etc.) both ways, first as a noun then as a verb, e.g., noun: *increase*, verb *increase*.

b Focus on the task and give Sts time to underline the stress on the words in bold.

Get Sts to compare with a partner.

c 5 10 Now play the audio for Sts to check their answers. You could pause after each sentence and elicit the right answers as you go or check answers after you have played the recording.

See underlining in words in **bold** in audioscript 5.10

5 10

1 We're making good **progress** with the report.
2 The new building is **progressing** well.
3 We **export** to customers all over the world.
4 One of our main **exports** is cheese.
5 **A** Can you **refund** me the cost of my ticket?
B Sorry, we don't give **refunds**.
6 Sales have **increased** by 10% this month, so there has been an **increase** in profits.
7 The demand for organic **produce** has grown enormously.
8 Most toys nowadays are **produced** in China.
9 Half the applicants for the job were **rejected**.
10 **Rejects** are sold at a reduced price.

Now get Sts to practice saying the sentences. They could do this individually or in pairs.

Extra support

- You could get Sts to listen and repeat after the audio.

d Focus on questions 1–3. Elicit the correct pronunciation of *exports* and *imported* in 2, and *increased* and *decreased* in 3.

Put Sts in pairs or small groups and get them to discuss the questions, giving as much information as possible.

Monitor and help Sts with any vocabulary they need.

Get some feedback.

8 5 11 SONG *The Truth* ♫

This song was originally made famous by the American rock band Good Charlotte in 2004. For copyright reasons, this is a cover version. If you want to do this song in class, use the photocopiable activity on *page 237*.

5 11

The Truth

So here we are
We are alone
There's weight on your mind
I wanna know
The truth, if this is how you feel
Say it to me
If this was ever real

Chorus
I want the truth from you
Gimme the truth, even if it hurts me
I want the truth from you
Gimme the truth, even if it hurts me
I want the truth

So this is you
You're talking to me
You found a million ways to let me down
So I'm not hurt when you're not around
I was blind
But now I see
This is how you feel
Just say it to me
If this was ever real

Chorus

I know that this will break me
I know that this might make me cry
You gotta say what's on your mind, on your mind
I know that this will hurt me
and break my heart and soul inside
I don't wanna live this lie

I want the truth from you
Gimme the truth, even if it hurts me
I want the truth from you
Gimme the truth, even if it hurts
I don't care no more, no
Just gimme the truth, gimme the truth
'Cause I don't care no more
Gimme the truth
'Cause I don't care no more, no
Just gimme the truth
Gimme the truth (x4)
'Cause I don't care no more, no

G uncountable and plural nouns
V word building: prefixes and suffixes
P word stress with prefixes and suffixes

9B Megacities

Lesson plan

The context of this lesson is big cities.

In the first section of the lesson, Sts read about Tokyo and Mexico City, which are two of the big cities that journalist Andrew Marr visited as part of the BBC documentary series *Megacities*. There is then a vocabulary focus on word building with prefixes and suffixes, and the pronunciation focus is on word stress.

In the second section, Sts listen to a British travel writer for the Lonely Planet guidebook series who talks about his five favorite cities and his personal connection with each. Sts then talk about which of the places mentioned they would like to visit, and their favorite and least favorite cities. This is followed by the grammar focus, where Sts extend their knowledge of uncountable nouns (e.g., *luggage*, *furniture*, etc.) and plural nouns (e.g., *news*, *politics*). The lesson ends with Sts writing a report.

STUDY LINK
- **Workbook** 9B
- **Online Practice**
- **iChecker**

Extra photocopiable activities

- **Grammar** uncountable and plural nouns *page 168*
- **Communicative** Give your opinion! *page 206* (instructions *pages 184–185*)
- **Vocabulary** Word building *page 224* (instructions *page 212*)

Optional lead-in – the quote

- Write the quote at the top of *page 88* on the board (books closed) and the name of the person who said it, or get Sts to open their books and read it.
- You could tell Sts that Rupert Brooke (1887–1915) was an English poet known for his idealistic war poems written during the First World War.
- Ask Sts what they think the quote means and if they agree with it.

1 READING & SPEAKING

a Focus on the task and elicit from the class what a "megacity" is.

Tell Sts to quickly read the introduction of the article to find out.

Check the answer.

A megacity is a city with more than ten million inhabitants.

You may want to tell Sts that the other megacities that Andrew Marr visited were Dhaka in Bangladesh (the world's fastest-growing megacity), London, and Shanghai.

Now put Sts in pairs and get them to list the biggest problems that they think people might have in megacities. Set a time limit of two minutes.

When time is up, elicit some of the problems and write them on the board.

b Now tell Sts to read the whole article to find if the problems they discussed in **a** are mentioned. If so, are they linked to Tokyo (T), Mexico City (MC), both (B), or neither (N)?

Check answers by writing the initials next to the items on the board.

c Focus on the items under the headings, **Tokyo** and **Mexico City**. Tell Sts to read the article again to find out why the items are mentioned.

Put Sts in pairs and get them to answer the questions together.

Check answers.

<u>Tokyo</u>
33 million the population
eight million the number of commuters on the subway every day
a letter from the train company If you are late for work and you say the train was late, you need a letter from the train company as proof.
driving schools Some are on top of buildings.
270 square feet A family of six could live in an apartment of 270 square feet.
the *Hikikomori* inhabitants of Tokyo who don't like living in a megacity and rarely go out
Rent a friend a company that "rents friends" to people who need someone to talk to or to go to a wedding with
the *Hashiriya* a group of men who drive as fast as they can around Tokyo on a Saturday night

<u>Mexico City</u>
taco stands The city is full of them and people meet there to socialize.
Mariachi bands They walk through the streets and squares playing songs for money.
two-and-a-half hours This is how long it can take commuters to drive to and from work during rush hour.
social imbalance There is great wealth and extreme poverty. Because of this it can be a dangerous city.
kidnapping This is very common.
Kevlar In some stores you can buy men's clothes that are made of Kevlar (a bulletproof material).

d Focus on the task and give Sts time to read the ten definitions and then to find the words in the article.

Get Sts to compare with a partner and then check answers.

1 automated	5 alienation	9 poverty
2 unthinkable	6 loneliness	10 homeless
3 unemployment	7 pollution	
4 overcrowded	8 wealth	

Help with any other new vocabulary and encourage Sts to write down any useful new lexis from the article, e.g., *commuters*.

e Put Sts in pairs and get them to discuss the three questions, giving as much information as possible.

Monitor and help while Sts do the task.

Get some feedback. Have Sts raise their hands to find out which city, Tokyo or Mexico City, Sts would choose to live in.

Extra idea

- You could do question 2 as an open-class activity.

2 VOCABULARY

word building: prefixes and suffixes

a Focus on the **Prefixes and suffixes** box and go through it with the class.

Do the questions as an open-class activity. You could elicit the following adjectives ending in *-less*: *careless, useless, penniless*, etc. Highlight that in the Tokyo text the meaning of *friendless* = without friends – the suffix *less* = without. In the Mexico City text, highlight the meaning of *a liveable place* = a place that you are able to live in – the suffix *able* = you can.

Extra challenge

- Before reading the **Prefixes and suffixes** box, ask the class what prefixes and suffixes are and elicit some examples.

b Tell Sts to go to **Vocabulary Bank *Word building*** on *page 163*.

Focus on **1 Prefixes and suffixes that add meaning** and get Sts to do **a** individually or in pairs.

5 12))) Now do **b**. Play the audio for Sts to check answers. Play the audio again, pausing for Sts to repeat. Practice any words your Sts find difficult to pronounce.

5 12)))
Word building
Prefixes and suffixes that add meaning
a
1 **G** overcrowded
2 **C** megacities
3 **D** underdeveloped
4 **B** multicultural
5 **J** subway
6 **H** bilingual
7 **E** monorail
8 **F** autopilot
9 **A** antisocial
10 **K** misunderstood
11 **I** postgraduate

Get Sts to do **c** individually or in pairs.

5 13))) Now do **d**. Play the audio for Sts to check answers. Play the audio again, pausing for Sts to repeat. Practice any words your Sts find difficult to pronounce.

5 13)))
Prefixes and suffixes that add meaning
c
1 **D** homeless hopeless
2 **A** careful useful
3 **C** bullet-proof waterproof
4 **B** unbreakable

Now focus on **2 Nouns formed with suffixes** and go through the **Noun suffixes** box with the class.

Get Sts to do **a** individually or in pairs.

5 14))) Now do **b**. Play the audio for Sts to check answers. Write answers on the board, eliciting the spelling. Play the audio again, pausing for Sts to repeat. Practice any words your Sts find difficult to pronounce.

5 14)))
Nouns formed with suffixes
intention, pollution, population, reduction
entertainment, excitement, government, improvement
coldness, friendliness, ugliness, weakness
absence, convenience, distance, ignorance
racism, terrorism
brotherhood, childhood

Now focus on **3 Nouns that are different words** and go through the **Noun formation with spelling or word change** box with the class.

Get Sts to do **a** individually or in pairs.

5 15))) Now do **b**. Play the audio for Sts to check answers. Write answers on the board, elicit the spelling if necessary. Play the audio again, pausing for Sts to repeat. Practice any words your Sts find difficult to pronounce.

5 15)))
Nouns that are different words

1	lose, loss	6	hot, heat
2	die, death	7	strong, strength
3	succeed, success	8	hungry, hunger
4	think, thought	9	high, height
5	believe, belief	10	long, length

Testing yourself

For **Prefixes and suffixes that add meaning** exercises **a** and **c**, Sts can cover the meanings, look at the sentences and remember the bold prefixes and suffixes. For **Nouns formed with suffixes**, they can cover the chart and remember the nouns in the list. For **Nouns that are different words**, they can cover the column on the left, look at the nouns on the right, and remember the verbs and adjectives.

Testing a partner

See **Testing a partner** *page 29*.

Tell Sts to go back to the main lesson **9B**.

Extra support

- If you think Sts need more practice, you may want to give them the Vocabulary photocopiable activity at this point or leave it for later as consolidation or review.

3 PRONUNCIATION & SPEAKING

word stress with prefixes and suffixes

a Focus on the **Word stress on words with prefixes and suffixes** box and go through it with the class.

Now give Sts time to underline the main stressed syllable in the multisyllable nouns and adjectives in the list. Encourage them to say the word out loud.

Get them to compare with a partner.

Extra support

- Get Sts to do **a** in pairs.

b 5 16 Play the audio for Sts to listen and check.

Check answers and then give Sts time to practice saying the words.

See underlining in audioscript 5.16

5 16

accommodation
antisocial
bilingual
entertainment
government
homeless
loneliness
multicultural
neighborhood
overcrowded
poverty
underdeveloped
unemployment
vandalism

c Put Sts in pairs and get them to discuss the questions about their cities or regions, giving as much information as possible.

Monitor and help if necessary.

Get some feedback.

Extra support

- Do these as open-class questions.

4 LISTENING & SPEAKING

a Do this as an open-class activity. You could also tell the class what you do.

b Focus on the task and ask Sts if they know the Lonely Planet guidebooks and what they think of them. If you have used them yourself, you could tell Sts your opinion of them, too.

Either put Sts in pairs or do this as an open-class activity.

If Sts worked in pairs, elicit some ideas. You could write these on the board, but don't tell Sts if they are right or not.

c 5 17 Tell Sts they are now going to listen to Miles Roddis, the travel writer, talking about each place. They must listen to find out where each photo is and what Miles's personal connection with each place is.

Play the audio once all the way through for Sts to find out what the places are and what his personal connection is to each place.

You could get Sts to compare with a partner before checking answers.

Extra support

- Before playing the audio, go through the audioscript and decide if you need to preteach / check any lexis to help Sts when they listen.

1 Sydney in Australia: His son and family live there.
2 Edinburgh in Scotland: He went there for his honeymoon.
3 Cairo in Egypt: He lived there for five years in the 70s and both his sons were born there.
4 Lucca in Italy: It is the birthplace of Puccini, who is one of Miles's all-time favorite composers.
5 Vientiane in Laos: He went there after finishing university and it was his first experience of living and working outside Western Europe.

5 17

(audioscript in Student Book on *pages 129–130*)

I = interviewer, M = Miles Roddis

I So, Miles, you're going to tell us about your top five cities.
M Yes. It was a difficult question for me because, of course, as a travel writer I've been to so many places. But, in the end, I decided that if I was making a personal choice, they had to be cities that meant something to me personally, that had a personal connection. So, these aren't necessarily big tourist cities, though some of them are, but the cities that are my own personal top five. Incidentally, these five aren't in any particular order.
I So, what's the first one in your top five?
M Well, the first one is Sydney. The personal connection is that my son and his family live there, so, of course, my wife and I have been there quite often and got to know it well. Of course, there are lots of amazing things about Sydney. For one thing, it's a waterfront city, it has the sea all around it; there's wonderful surfing on Bondi beach and plenty of great little bays for sunbathing and swimming. It's also a very cosmopolitan city. Sydneysiders – which is what people from Sydney are called – come from all corners of the world, so, for example, the choice of places to eat is endless. You can find everything from simple soup kitchens to elegant, world-class restaurants, so you can choose to eat Thai, Vietnamese, Greek, Italian, and many, many other kinds of cuisine.
I And your second city?
M My wife and I spent our honeymoon in Edinburgh, so it's always been a special place for me. But I think it's especially exciting during the festival, which happens every August. Of course, there's a fantastic program of music, and dance, and the arts. But what gives the city a special buzz during the festival is "the Fringe." "The Fringe" is a massive alternative festival, and it has literally hundreds of events – comedy, theater, amateur student groups, street entertainers. And of course the pubs stay open until much later than usual during the Festival and that adds to the atmosphere, too. However, it's really hard to get accommodation during the festival, so you need to book well in advance.
I I must say I've never been to the festival, though I've often thought about going. Next year I really have to get there. What about your third city?
M My third city is Cairo. We lived there for five years in the 70s and both our sons were born there, beside the River Nile. People always associate Cairo with the pyramids, and of course they are amazing, but for me the best thing about it is the museums, which are absolutely fantastic. The Egyptian Museum has the world's largest and best collection from Pharaonic times. Then the Coptic museum, which is in the suburb of Al Fustat has the best of Egypt's Christian culture. And the Museum of Islamic Art has a whole lot of exquisite pieces from Muslim times. So if you're someone who likes museums and antiquities, my advice is go to Cairo.

I Oh, I have been to Cairo and I completely agree with you. And your next one?
M For my next one, we're back in Europe in Italy. I've chosen Lucca, in Tuscany. Tuscany's two major tourist towns, Florence and Pisa, are absolutely jam-packed with tourists all year round, but most of them never get to Lucca. You can only really explore it on foot, which is the way I like to move around a town, and in about an hour you can do the four-kilometer circuit all around its Renaissance town walls. These walls are amazing – they're completely intact, and you can peer into people's living rooms as you walk past. Or you can walk from one end of the town to the other along *Via Fillungo*. Also, Lucca is the birthplace of Puccini, who's one of my all-time favorite composers. He played the organ of the town's magnificent cathedral when he was a young man, and there's a wonderful open-air festival every year where they perform his operas at a place called Torre del Lago, which is just nearby.
I And your last city?
M My last city is one that not many people have been to – it's not on the usual tourist route. I'd just finished university and I was curious about the wider world, so I went to Laos in South East Asia. Laos and its capital, Vientiane, were my first experience of living and working outside Western Europe. The Laotians are a lovely, gentle, laid-back people. They taught me to relax. And they showed me how it's quite possible to be happy with very little money. The scenery is spectacular, too. The impressive Mekong River flows far away over the sands in the dry season and speeds by the city like a wide, rushing torrent once the rainy season begins. I remember looking down on it from one of the restaurants along its banks, and feeling that it was sweeping away all my troubles.

d Tell Sts they will now listen to the interview again and this time they must take notes why each place is special.

Play the audio, pausing after each city is mentioned to give Sts time to write.

Play the audio again as necessary and then check answers.

1 Sydney: it is a waterfront city with the sea all around it; there's wonderful surfing and plenty of bays for sunbathing and swimming. It's also a very cosmopolitan city, so there's a wonderful choice of restaurants.
2 Edinburgh: it is especially exciting every August during the festival, when there's a program of music, dance, and the arts. There is also "the Fringe," a massive alternative festival, which has hundreds of events – comedy, theater, amateur student groups, street entertainers. And the pubs stay open until much later than usual during the Festival, which adds to the atmosphere.
3 Cairo: The pyramids are amazing, but the best thing about Cairo is the museums, which are absolutely fantastic.
4 Lucca: It isn't as crowded as nearby Florence and Pisa. You can explore Lucca on foot in about an hour. It is surrounded by Renaissance town walls, which are amazing – they are completely intact and you can peer into people's living rooms as you walk past. Or you can walk from one end of the town to the other along *Via Fillungo*. Nearby there's a wonderful open-air festival every year, where they perform Puccini's operas.
5 Vientiane: The Laotians are lovely people. They showed him how it is possible to be happy with very little money. The scenery is spectacular. The Mekong River is impressive; it flows far away over the sands in the dry season and speeds by the city like a torrent when the rainy season begins.

e 5 18))) Focus on the task and give Sts time to read the extracts from the interview.

Play the audio, pausing after the first extract. Elicit from Sts what they think the word is, how they think it is spelled, and what they think it means.

1 bays (= a part of the ocean, or of a large lake, partly surrounded by a wide curve of the land)

Repeat with the other extracts.

2 endless (= very large in size or amount and seeming to have no end)
3 buzz (= to be full of excitement, activity, etc.)
4 exquisite (= extremely beautiful or carefully made)
5 jam-packed (= very full or crowded)
6 peer (= to look closely or carefully at something, especially when you cannot see it clearly)
7 gentle (= calm and kind; doing things in a quiet and careful way)
8 sweeping away (= to get rid of something completely)

You might want to point out that *jam-packed* is an informal adjective based on the meaning of *jam* as in *traffic jam* (not what you put on toast) and that *to sweep away* is a phrasal verb.

5 18)))
1 ...there's wonderful surfing on Bondi beach and plenty of great little bays for sunbathing and swimming.
2 ...the choice of places to eat is endless.
3 But what gives the city a special buzz during the festival is "the Fringe."
4 And the Museum of Islamic Art has a whole lot of exquisite pieces from Muslim times.
5 Tuscany's two major tourist towns, Florence and Pisa, are absolutely jam-packed with tourists all year round...
6 These walls are amazing – they're completly intact, and you can peer into people's living rooms as you walk past.
7 The Laotians are a lovely, gentle, laid-back people.
8 I remember looking down on it from one of the restaurants along its banks, and feeling that it was sweeping away all my troubles.

Extra support

- If there's time, you could play the audio again while Sts read the audioscript on *pages 129–130*, so they can see what they understood / didn't understand. Translate / explain any new words or phrases.

f Put Sts in small groups of three or four and get them to discuss the questions.

Monitor and help while Sts do the task.

Get feedback. For question 1, you could have Sts raise their hands to show which city is the most / least popular and why.

Extra idea

- Before doing **f**, find out if any Sts have been to any of the five cities Miles Roddis mentioned in the interview. If they have, ask if they agree with him.

5 GRAMMAR uncountable and plural nouns

a Focus on the task. Encourage Sts to use their instinct if they are not sure.

Get Sts to compare with a partner and then check answers. Elicit why the other form is wrong and that these nouns (e.g., *advice*, *weather*, etc.) are uncountable, and so can't be used with *a* or in the plural, although they may not be in Sts' L1.

1 advice
2 some bad weather
3 hard work
4 too much luggage
5 the outskirts are
6 some interesting news

b 5 19 5 20 Tell Sts to go to **Grammar Bank 9B** on *page 149*. Focus on the example sentences and play the audio for Sts to listen to the sentence rhythm. You could also get Sts to repeat the sentences to practice getting the rhythm right. Then go through the rules with the class.

Additional grammar notes

uncountable nouns

- **rules 1 and 2:** Sts will be familiar with the concept of countable (C) and uncountable (U) nouns, especially in the context of food, e.g., *an orange* (C), *some water* (U), etc. However, there are many non-food nouns that are uncountable in English, though they may be countable in Sts' L1, e.g., *information, advice, furniture*. Other uncountable nouns can be confusing because they end in *s* and so would seem to be plural, e.g., *politics, news*, but are uncountable. Here Sts are introduced to the most common nouns of this type and shown to use some of them with *a piece of* to talk about individual items, e.g., *Do you want a piece of toast? I'll give you a piece of advice. Some* can also be used with these words to mean an unspecified amount, e.g., *Do you want some toast? I want to buy some new furniture.*
- Because the list of nouns here is not very long, encourage Sts to learn them by heart.
- **rule 3:** Sts probably already know the different uses of these words passively. Words like this include many materials, and also abstract nouns like *light* and *space*, which are uncountable, but have a different meaning when they are countable. Check that Sts know the difference in meaning between the two forms, e.g.,
business (= general word to describe commercial activity), *a business* (= a company)
paper (= the material), *a paper* (= a newspaper)
light (= the energy from the sun), *a light* (= a lamp)
time (= what is measured in minutes, hours, etc.), *a time* (= an occasion)
space (= where the planets are), *a space* (= an area that is empty)

plural and collective nouns

- **rule 1:** Make sure Sts know the meaning of these words, e.g., *belongings* = things that are yours. Remind Sts that words that can be used with *a pair of* can also be used with *some*. Other words in this group are *jeans, pajamas, pants / shorts, tights, (sun) glasses.*
- **rule 2:** These nouns refer to a group of people but they take a singular verb (except *police*). Other similar words are *orchestra, choir, government, class,* and *army*.

Focus on the exercises and get Sts to do them individually or in pairs.

Check answers, getting Sts to read the full sentences.

a
1 ✗ We had beautiful weather
2 ✗ some beautiful furniture
3 ✓
4 ✗ a pair of scissors
5 ✗ some new pants / a new pair of pants
6 ✓
7 ✓
8 ✗ The homework was
9 ✓
10 ✗ The police are sure

b

1 is	6 a piece of paper
2 ✓	7 some
3 look	8 some
4 works	9 progress
5 ✓	10 an

Tell Sts to go back to the main lesson **9B**.

Extra support

- If you think Sts need more practice, you may want to give them the Grammar photocopiable activity at this point or leave it for later as consolidation or review.

c This is an oral grammar practice activity. You could tell Sts that it is a very popular radio program on the BBC and has been running since 1967.

Focus on the task and go through the rules with the class. Stress that they have to try and keep going for one minute without stopping. If a student hesitates for too long, then he or she is "out" and the next student must continue speaking on the same topic until the minute is up. However, he / she can't just repeat things that the previous person said. Point out to Sts that you will be the time-keeper.

Give Sts a minute to look at all the topics.

Now put Sts in small groups of three or four and get them to decide which order they will go in.

Tell Sts to start and stop them after one minute. Then get the next student in the group to take the next topic. Stop the activity either when Sts have been through all the topics or each student has spoken at least twice. Monitor while Sts are talking and help with the scoring.

Find out who got the most points.

6 WRITING a report

Tell Sts to go to **Writing *A report*** on *page 119.*

a Focus on the report. Highlight that the second paragraph has a heading and tell Sts to read the report and then, in pairs, to think of headings for the other three paragraphs.

Extra support

- Put Sts in pairs and suggest that they begin the headings for 1 and 3 with *When…* and point out that section 4 is different from the first three because it is more general.

Get feedback and write the different suggestions on the board. You could get Sts to vote for the best heading.

Possible headings

1 When you want to eat out cheaply / If you are on a small budget
3 When you are celebrating something / For a special occasion
4 General advice / Things to remember about eating out in New York

b Focus on the task and put Sts in pairs. If you want to challenge your Sts, you could encourage them to do the one about entertainment.

Get Sts to brainstorm useful information for their chosen report by going through points 1–3.

Extra support

- Focus on the first topic, *good places for eating out*, and elicit headings from the class. Write their ideas on the board. Then elicit some information for each heading. Do the same with the second topic, *entertainment in your town*.

c Focus on the **Useful language: talking in general** box and go through it with the class.

Now go through the instructions. Then either get Sts to write the report in class (set a time limit of e.g., 20 minutes) or get them to write at home for homework.

d Sts should check their work for mistakes before turning it in.

COLLOQUIAL ENGLISH

8&9 Talking about advertising

Lesson plan

In the first part of this lesson, the person interviewed is George Tannenbaum, an ad executive, who is one of the best-known copywriters and creative directors in the advertising industry.

In the second part, people are asked whether they are influenced by advertising campaigns and if they think any products should be banned from advertising.

STUDY LINK

- **Workbook** Talking about advertising
- **Online Practice**
- **iChecker**

Testing Program CD-ROM

- **File 9 Quick Test**
- **File 9 Test**

Optional lead-in (books closed)

- Tell Sts that they are going to watch / listen to an interview with a man who makes ads. Write the word JINGLE on the board and elicit / explain that it is a short song or tune that is used in advertising and is easy to remember.
- Elicit from the class any jingles that have been used in their country either now or in the past.

1 VIDEO THE INTERVIEW Part 1

a Books open. Focus on the photo and the biographical information about George Tannenbaum. Either read it out loud or give Sts time to read it.

Focus on the question and do it as an open-class activity.

b 5 21))) Focus on the **Glossary** and go through it with the class.

Now focus on the task and give Sts time to read questions 1–6.

Play the DVD or audio (**Part 1**) once all the way through. Then play it again, pausing as necessary to give Sts time to answer the questions.

You could get Sts to compare with a partner before checking answers.

1 his father's brother / his uncle and his father
2 1984
3 talk when the commercials were on
4 because they get into your head and you can't get them out, and you sometimes hear them several times a day
5 animated cartoons advertising cereal for children
6 Willie trips over a rock every day, so one day Wilhelmina tells him to move it. When he says he can't because it is too big, she says she will do it. Willie says she isn't strong enough, but he is wrong – Wilhelmina eats H. O. Farina, so she is strong.

5 21)))

(audioscript in Student Book on *page 130*)

I = interviewer, G = George Tannenbaum

Part 1

I What first drew you to advertising as a career choice?

G What drew me to advertising was actually, in a weird way, I had no choice, I'm a third generation advertising guy. My father's brother, my uncle, who was 15 years older than he, was in advertising believe it or not in the 1940s in Philadelphia. My father kind of took the baton from him, was in advertising and I grew up with it, so I've been making a living in the business since 1984. It's a long time. It's 30 years.

I Do you still remember any commercials from your childhood?

G So I remember a lot of commercials, you know, growing up in an advertising household as we did, TV was more of a social event in those days, there wasn't a TV in every room, like the family would gather to watch television. And, we were told not to talk, you know, during the commercials, we could talk during the shows, so I grew up kind of watching commercials. I remember a lot of commercials. I bet you most people of my generation would remember a lot of...I feel kind of guilty saying this because they are usually decried as not very creative, but you remember a lot of jingles.

I What do you think makes jingles memorable?

G Among purists in the field, jingles are, you know, laughed at, scoffed at, but God, you remember them. You know they, what do they call them, ear worms? They get into your head and you can't get them out sometimes and you add that to almost everyday exposure six times a day, it's going to get in there. I can do, there was a, you know, there was a, there was a, I could sing one for you, there was a kids hot cereal, a hot cereal for children called H. O. Farina and it was an animated cartoon, it was very rudimentary. If you saw it today, you wouldn't believe it was a nationally broadcast cartoon, and it was a little story of Willie and Wilhelmina, and Willie trips on a rock and he goes, "Every day I trip over that rock, Wilhelmina." And she says, "Move it, Willie." And he says, "Can't, too big." And I bet you I'm getting this word for word if you could find it. And she says, "I will." And he says, "Huh, you're a girl." And she picks it up and then the jingle comes up and it goes "Strong Wilhelmina eats her Farina." Like I said, I probably heard that 500 times, maybe more, when I was growing up because it was, it was every weekend for about eight years.

VIDEO Part 2

5 22))) Focus on the **Glossary** and go through it with the class.

Give Sts time to read notes 1–4 and make sure they know what *an acronym* is. Remind them to only write one or two words in each blank.

Now play the DVD or audio (**Part 2**) once all the way through. Then play it again, pausing as necessary to give Sts time to complete the task.

You could get Sts to compare with a partner before checking answers.

Extra support

- When you play the DVD or audio the second time, pause after each question has been answered and get Sts to compare what they have understood.

1 1 impact 2 communication 3 persuasion
2 **A**ttention, **I**nterest, **D**esire, **A**ction
3 getting impact, (giant) fan
4 incredibly important

5 22

(audioscript in Student Book on *page 130*)

Part 2

I What elements of a commercial are the most important?
G To me, a commercial basically is built in three parts. If you think of it as a pyramid, the top part of the pyramid I would say is impact. I have to intrude upon your life because you are probably working on your computer while you're watching TV or you're doing something, and when I'm talking about a TV commercial, it's the same for a web ad or an app. So you have to get impact, you have to intrude, you have to kind of knock on the door. The second thing is communication, what do you want the person to know. And, and that needs to be clear and precise. And the third thing is the hardest, it's persuasion because you ultimately you are running a commercial to get people to do something, so it's that amalgamation. Another way of talking about it – and this is old school – but there's an acronym that probably comes from the *Mad Men* era that is called AIDA, you know like the opera: Attention, Interest, Desire, Action.
I How do you feel about using celebrities to sell things?
G Sometimes it's a short, using a celebrity is a short cut to uh, intrusion because people pay attention to celebrities. Hopefully, it's a celebrity that has some bearing on the brand. I don't think, if I was working on a depilatory, I'd want to use Tommy Lee Jones, but um, that would just be gross. But, you know, if you find the right person, they can have special, um, special meaning, I think, and we do live in a celebrity culture, and people, you know, their ears perk up when they see a celebrity. So, if you go back to that pyramid I drew, it's a way of getting impact. I'm not a giant fan of it, but sometimes you do things you're not a giant fan of.
I On your website you say, "I can make people laugh." How important is humor in advertising?
G I tend not to be funny in TV commercials, I'm just, partly because I am a kind of cerebral guy and I wind up having to use that more than humor, but I think humor is incredibly important in the business and a lot of the commercials that really resonate with people I think are funny, a lot of the movies, a lot of everything.

VIDEO Part 3

5 23 Focus on the task and give Sts time to read the **Glossary** and sentences 1–5, making sure they understand all the lexis.

Now play the DVD or audio (**Part 3**) once all the way through for Sts to do the task.

Give Sts time to discuss what they understood with a partner.

Then play the DVD or audio again as necessary.

You could get Sts to compare with a partner before checking answers.

Extra support

- When you play the DVD or audio the second time, pause after each question has been answered and get Sts to compare what they have understood.

1 remain important
2 both good and bad ads
3 because they make people feel good about themselves
4 innovative
5 honest and clear

5 23

(audioscript in Student Book on *page 130*)

Part 3

I With all the technology, viral advertising, etc., do you think billboards and TV commercials have had their day?
G Have billboards and TV commercials had their day? You know what, I don't think so. I mean, I can tell you empirically and I can tell you rationally that 75% of all media dollars is spent on broadcast, and I know it's like current to say, "I don't have a TV," or "I never watch TV." but people do. But, the fact is, TV viewership is at an all-time high. So I don't think TV is dead and I don't think billboards will be, you know, something as kind of passé as a billboard will be dead as long as, like, the highways are crowded, because you've got a captive audience, and until we can kind of pixelize ourselves and beam ourselves to work, I think there will be billboards. I mean, they can be effective.
I As a consumer, and obviously as an advertiser, does advertising influence the decisions you make?
G Yeah, you know, I'm very, I'm very susceptible to advertising. I think because I tend to notice it. You know, I think I am very sensitive, er, to, um, I think I'm very sensitive to, um, stuff that isn't true. But when I see something that's well crafted and appeals, I think to both my head and my heart, you know, I think, I think I register those things.
I Is there an existing advertising campaign you wish you'd come up with, and why do you think it is so effective?
G Um. Is there an existing advertising campaign? Yeah, that I wish I did? There's a few. Um, I think the stuff that is being done for Nike just in general for 30 years has been exemplary, you know. They tapped into a mind-set, and they made everyone feel like they were athletic, and and they became kind of the gold standard, and they rarely hit a false note. Same thing with Apple, though people are just stressed in the industry about the latest direction Apple has been taking, which seems less sincere.
I Why do you think the Apple campaign is so effective?
G You know Apple took...I think Apple is effective because they looked at an industry and they said, "Here's what's wrong with the industry, and everything that that industry does we're going to do differently." So that industry, for years and years and years and years, was talking about speeds and feeds, and they were talking about 697 megahertz and 4 megabytes of RAM or gigabytes of RAM, or whatever it is, and Apple just said, "It works." And what they did was to say, "You want to be creative? This machine makes you creative." And they simplified, they simplified, and they were compelling, um, and they never lied, yeah.

Extra support

- If there's time, you could play the audio again while Sts read the audioscripts on *page 130*, so they can see what they understood / didn't understand. Translate / explain any new words or phrases.

VIDEO 2 LOOKING AT LANGUAGE

a **5 24** This exercise focuses on a feature of spoken English that the interviewer illustrates – in this case using idiomatic language. Focus on the **Metaphors and idiomatic expressions** box and go through it.

Focus on the task and give Sts time to read extracts 1–7.

Play the DVD or audio, pausing after each extract to give Sts time to write.

Check answers.

Extra challenge

- Ask Sts if they can remember any of the missing words before they listen to the extracts.

1 ear	3 word	5 day	7 false
2 head	4 perk	6 audience	

5 24

1 You know they, what do they call them, ear worms?
2 They get into your head and you can't get them out sometimes...
3 And I bet you I'm getting this word for word if you could find it.
4 ...we do live in a celebrity culture and people, you know, their ears perk up when they see a celebrity.
5 Have billboards and TV commercials had their day?
6 ...because you've got a captive audience.
7 ...they became kind of the gold standard and they rarely hit a false note.

b Put Sts in pairs and give them time to discuss the meaning of each expression.

Elicit the meaning of each expression.

Help with any vocabulary problems that come up and get feedback from Sts on what parts they found hard to understand and why, e.g., speed of speech, etc.

3 VIDEO ON THE STREET

a **5 25** Focus on the task and then play the DVD or audio once all the way through.

Check the answer.

four of them

5 25

(audioscript in Student Book on *page 130*)
I = interviewer, J = Jeanine, D = Dustin, El = Elvira, Iv = Ivan, Y = Yasuko

Jeanine
I Do you think you're influenced by advertising campaigns?
J Most definitely.
I Is there any product that shouldn't be advertised, in your opinion?
J Alcohol and junk food to children.
I Why should those ads be banned?
J Because it's promoting something that's unhealthy and that, especially junk food for children, when they see it they're very susceptible to the adverts and then they want it immediately, and it's a problem.

Dustin
I Do you think you're influenced by advertising campaigns?
D I am sure I am, probably not consciously, but I'm sure subconsciously.
I Is there any product that shouldn't be advertised, in your opinion? Why should those ads be banned?
D I mean I, I don't care for, for cigarette ads or alcohol ads, but should they be ad..., or should they not be advertised? That is not a decision I should make, so I don't think so.

Elvira
I Do you think you're influenced by advertising campaigns?
E I'm not very influenced by ad campaigns, I'm influenced by reviews.
I Is there any product that shouldn't be advertised, in your opinion? Why should those ads be banned?
E The only thing that comes to mind that should be banned from advertisements is, I think they tend to use the female body, um, inappropriately to sell things and items. That's pretty much the only thing that I can think of.

Ivan
I Do you think you're influenced by advertising campaigns?
Iv I think that everyone is somewhat influenced by advertising campaigns, even on a minor level.
I Is there any product that shouldn't be advertised, in your opinion? Why should those ads be banned?
Iv Perhaps cigarettes shouldn't be advertised because children, um, probably shouldn't be seeing them advertised in a cool or exciting manner.

Yasuko
I Do you think you're influenced by advertising campaigns?
Y I think a lot of people are usually influenced, you know, a little by advertisement, especially because we've, there's so much advertisement on media. And we watch a lot of TV, you know, Internet. I try not to be, I try to research the product on my own using Internet or whatnot, and choose the, and try to choose the best product. Not because of the advertisement.
I Is there any product that shouldn't be advertised, in your opinion? Why should those ads be banned?
Y Advertisements for cigarettes, I think should be banned. Um, I don't think there's anything positive about cigarette smoking, so I think that anything that causes health issues or bad influences or addiction should be banned from being on commercials.

b Focus on the task and give Sts time to read the questions.

Play the DVD or audio again, pausing after each speaker to give Sts time to do the task. Play again as necessary.

Check answers.

Ivan is against ads that can make smoking seem attractive to young people.

Yasuko prefers to do her own research before she buys a product.

Jeanine and Ivan say that they are concerned about young people's health.

Dustin is not sure we should ban the advertising of unhealthy products.

Elvira thinks that women are sometimes exploited in advertising.

c **5 26** This exercises focuses on some colloquial expressions that were used by the speakers. Focus on the phrases and give Sts time to read them.

Play the DVD or audio, pausing after the first phrase and playing it again as necessary. Elicit the missing word and then the meaning of the whole phrase. Repeat for the other four phrases.

See words in **bold** in audioscript 5.26

5 26

1 ...when they see it they're very **susceptible** to the adverts and then they want it immediately and it's a problem.
2 I am sure I am, probably not consciously, but I'm sure **subconsciously**.
3 The only thing that **comes** to **mind** that should be banned from advertisements is...
4 That's **pretty much** the only thing that I can think of.
5 ...so I think that anything that causes health **issues** or bad influences or addiction should be banned from being on commercials.

Extra support

- Tell Sts to go to *page 130* and to look at the audioscript for **ON THE STREET**. Play the DVD or audio again and tell Sts to read and listen at the same time.

Help with any vocabulary problems and get feedback on what parts Sts found hard to understand and why.

4 SPEAKING

Put Sts in pairs and get them to ask and answer the questions, giving as much information as possible.

Monitor and help with vocabulary. Help with any general language problems at the end of the activity.

Get some feedback.

G quantifiers: *all*, *every*, *both*, etc.
V science
P stress in word families

10A The dark side of the moon

Lesson plan

The topic is science.

In the first section of the lesson, Sts give their opinion as to whether some well-known scientific "facts" are true or whether they are myths. Then they listen to an expert to find out. The vocabulary focus is on words related to science, and pronunciation deals with changing stress in word families (e.g., *science*, *scientist*, *scientific*). The first section ends with Sts interviewing each other about science-related issues.

In the second section of the lesson, Sts read about four scientists who suffered in order to make their discoveries. Then the Grammar – review and extension of the use of a variety of quantifiers – is presented through sentences about the four scientists and later practiced in a science quiz.

STUDY LINK
- **Workbook** 10A
- **Online Practice**
- **iChecker**

Extra photocopiable activities
- **Grammar** quantifiers *page 169*
- **Communicative** Science quiz *page 207* (instructions *page 185*)

Optional lead-in – the quote
- Write the quote at the top of *page 94* on the board (books closed) and the name of the person who said it, or get Sts to open their books and read it.
- Elicit / explain the meaning of *exquisitely* (= beautifully, carefully made) and ask Sts if they agree with the quote and why (not).

1 SPEAKING & LISTENING

a Focus on the task, eliciting what *a myth* is.

Put Sts in pairs and get them to discuss each statement, giving their opinion.

Get some feedback, but don't tell Sts if they are right or not. You could ask Sts to raise their hands for each statement and write the results on the board.

b 5 27))) Tell Sts they are now going to listen to a radio program in which a scientist discusses each statement.

Play the audio, pausing after each statement has been mentioned, and elicit whether it is a fact or a myth. At this stage don't elicit why as this is done in **c**.

Extra support
- Before playing the audio, go through the audioscript and decide if you need to preteach / check any lexis to help Sts when they listen.

Find out who got the most correct answers.

1 myth	3 fact	5 myth	7 myth
2 myth	4 myth	6 fact	8 myth

5 27)))
(audioscript in Student Book on *pages 130–131*)

Let's start with the first one about the coin. Many people think that a coin dropped from the top of the Empire State Building, for example, would be traveling so fast that if it hit a person on the ground, it would kill them. However, this just isn't true. Coins are not aerodynamic and they are also relatively small and light, so although a person on the ground would certainly feel the impact, the coin wouldn't kill them. It wouldn't even hurt them very much!

Number two is one of the most popular scientific myths – that we only use ten percent of our brains. Maybe this is because people would like to think that they could be much more intelligent if they were able to find a way to use the other 90%! In fact, neurologists haven't been able to find any area of our brains that isn't being used for something.

Number three. The dark side of the moon? Well, that only exists as the title of a Pink Floyd album. People used to think that there was a side of the moon that was always dark, that never got the sun, but, of course, that isn't true. The sun illuminates every part of the moon at some point during the 24-hour cycle. It is true that there's a side of the moon that we never see, that's to say we always see the same side of the moon, but the other side isn't always dark.

Now number four, the one about rubber tires. A lot of people think that rubber tires on a car will protect you from lightning in the same way that wearing rubber shoes will protect you from an electric shock. Well, it's certainly true that if you're caught in a thunderstorm, it's much safer to be inside a car than outside. But the tires have nothing to do with it. When lightning strikes a car, it's actually the car's metal body that protects the passengers. It acts as a conductor and passes the electrical current right down to the ground.

Number five. Poor old Einstein. Over the years he's often been used as an example to show that you can do very badly at school and still be very successful in life. And people have actually said that he wasn't very good at math or science. But, in fact, records show that the young Albert, as you would expect, got very good grades in math and science.

Number six. Antibiotics don't kill viruses. No, they don't, and it's a waste of time taking them if you have a virus. Antibiotics help your body to kill bacteria, not viruses. What's more, you can't exactly "kill" a virus at all, since a virus is not really alive to begin with. Stick to your doctor's advice and only take antibiotics when he or she specifically prescribes them. The problem is that it's often very hard for a doctor to know if you're suffering from a virus or from a bacterial infection.

Number seven. I love the idea that a full moon can make people go crazy, but I think this is only true for werewolves. For centuries, nearly all cultures have attributed special mystical powers to the full moon, and, in fact, the English word *lunatic*, which can be used to describe a crazy person, comes from the word *lunar*, which means "to do with the moon." But in spite of a lot of scientific research, nobody has found any link at all between the full moon and insanity or crime.

And finally, number eight, are bats really blind? Most English-speaking people probably think that they are because we have the expression in English "as blind as a bat." But it's just not true. In fact, bats can see just as well as humans, even if they don't depend on their sight in the same way. Like dogs, bats rely heavily on other senses like hearing and smell. They have a very advanced sound-based system called echolocation, which allows them to know where they are when they're flying at night. But they can certainly see.

c Put Sts in pairs and get them to discuss what information they can remember from the radio program about each statement.

Then play the audio again, pausing after each statement to give Sts time to write.

Play again if necessary and then check answers.

1 Coins are not aerodynamic and they are relatively small and light, so although a person on the ground would feel the impact, the coin wouldn't kill him. It wouldn't even hurt very much.
2 Neurologists haven't been able to find any area of our brains that isn't being used for something.
3 The sun illuminates every part of the moon at some point during the 24-hour cycle. It is true that there's a side of the moon that we never see, but the other side isn't always dark.
4 If you are caught in a thunderstorm, it is much safer to be inside a car than outside. But the tires have nothing to do with it. When lightning strikes a car, it is the car's metal body that protects the passengers. It acts as a conductor and passes the electrical current right down to the ground.
5 Records show that the young Albert got very good grades in math and science.
6 Antibiotics help your body to kill bacteria, not viruses. You can't exactly "kill" a virus since a virus is not really alive to begin with.
7 In spite of a lot of scientific research, nobody has found any link at all between the full moon and insanity or crime.
8 Bats can see just as well as humans. Like dogs, bats rely heavily on other senses like hearing and smell. They have a very advanced sound-based system called echolocation, which allows them to know where they are when they are flying at night.

Extra support

- If there's time, you could play the audio again while Sts read the audioscript on *pages 130–131*, so they can see what they understood / didn't understand. Translate / explain any new words or phrases.

d Do this as an open-class question. If your Sts can't think of any more, you could elicit / suggest "Lightning never strikes twice in the same place." (Lightning can strike any location more than once. The Empire State Building, for example, gets struck more than a hundred times a year.) and "Food that drops on the floor is safe to eat if you pick it up within five seconds." (Bacteria can attach themselves to your food even if you pick it up immediately.)

2 VOCABULARY & PRONUNCIATION

stress in word families, science

Pronunciation notes

- In some "word families," i.e., groups of words from the same root, the stress is always on the same syllable, e.g., in all the words related to physics (*physical*, *physicist*), the stress is on the first syllable. In others, however, the stress shifts, e.g., *scientist*, *scientific*, and these groups are often problematic.

a Focus on the task and the three extracts from the audio in **1b**. Point out that the first word in the chart (*scientist*) has been done for them. Then elicit which highlighted word is an adjective (*scientific*) and which is a subject (*science*). Write them on the board in columns.

b Now tell Sts to complete the chart for the four other words for people who study or work in a certain area of science (highlight the *-ist* ending).

c 5 28 Play the audio for Sts to listen and check.

! Some Sts may come up with the word *physician*. If they do, explain that this is also related to physics, but does not mean a scientist who studies physics, but is another word for a doctor (They saw this word in **9A**).

See words in audioscript 5.28

Now focus on the **Stress in word families** box and go through it with the class.

Play the audio again, pausing after each word or group of words for Sts to underline the stressed syllables.

Check answers, by writing the words on the board and underlining the stressed syllables.

See underlining in audioscript 5.28

5 28
scientist, scientific, science
chemist, chemical, chemistry
biologist, biological, biology
physicist, physical, physics
geneticist, genetic, genetics

Now elicit in which groups the stress changes.

The adjectives from *science* and *biology* have the stress on a different syllable from the base word.

Extra challenge

- Get Sts to underline the stressed syllables in the words before they listen to the audio. Get feedback and then play the audio to check answers.

d Give Sts time to practice saying the word groups. They could do this individually or in pairs.

Extra support

- Drill the pronunciation with the whole class first and then get them to practice in pairs. You could use the audio to do this.

e Focus on the task and go through the words in the list. Elicit / explain *laboratory*, *theory*, and *guinea pigs* /ˈgɪni pɪgz/.

Give Sts time to complete the sentences.

Get them to compare with a partner.

f 5.29 Play the audio for Sts to listen and check.

Check answers.

1	laboratory
2	discovery
3	theory
4	drugs, tests
5	research, side effects
6	guinea pigs

5.29

1 Scientists carry out experiments in a laboratory.
2 Archimedes made an important discovery in his bathtub.
3 Isaac Newton's experiments proved his theory that gravity existed.
4 Before a pharmaceutical company can sell new drugs, they have to do tests to make sure they are safe.
5 Scientists have to do a lot of research into the possible side effects of new drugs.
6 People can volunteer to be guinea pigs in clinical trials.

Now get Sts to underline the stress on the bold multi-syllable words in 1–6.

Play the audio again, pausing after each sentence.

Check answers.

See underlining in audioscript 5.29

Give Sts time to practice saying the sentences.

3 SPEAKING

The vocabulary from **2e** is now put into practice in this speaking activity.

Focus on the instructions and make sure Sts understand what they have to do.

Put Sts in pairs, **A** and **B**, and give them time to read the questions. Check Sts understand the word *cosmetics* and the phrase *genetically modified food*.

Then get the **A**s to ask the **B**s the questions in the red circles. Encourage the **B**s to answer each question in as much detail as possible. **B**s then asks the **A**s the questions in the blue circles.

Monitor and help, correcting any mispronunciation of the new lexis.

Get feedback from the whole class on some of the questions.

Extra challenge

- Sts could return the questions they answer by saying *What about you?* or if they finish quickly, ask each other the questions that they previously answered.

Extra idea

- Get Sts to choose two or three questions to ask you after they have done the activity.

4 READING

a Focus on the instructions and pictures. Ask Sts if they have heard of any of these scientists.

Set a time limit for Sts to read about them and find out how many were killed by their own experiments or inventions.

Get Sts to compare with a partner and then check answers.

Three (Alexander Bogdanov, Thomas Midgley, and Louis Slotin) died as a result of their experiments or inventions.

b Focus on the task and questions, making sure Sts understand all the lexis in questions 1–8.

Tell Sts to read the extracts again.

Get Sts to compare with a partner and then check answers.

1 C	3 B	5 A, C	7 C
2 B, D	4 D	6 B	8 A

Extra challenge

- Get Sts to cover the extracts and answer the questions from memory.

c 5.30 Focus on the instructions and give Sts time, in pairs, to look at the highlighted words related to science and medicine.

Play the audio, pausing after each word. Practice the pronunciation and then elicit / explain the meaning and ask if the word is similar in Sts' L1.

Write the words on the board and get Sts to tell you the stressed syllable and mark it on the words.

anesthetic /ænəsˈθɛtɪk/
nitrogen /ˈnaɪtrədʒən/
blood transfusion /blʌd trænsˈfyuʒn/
donors /ˈdoʊnərz/
malaria /məˈlɛriə/
tuberculosis /tubərkyəˈloʊsəs/
lead /lɛd/
additive /ˈædətɪv/
polio /ˈpoʊlioʊ/
nuclear /ˈnukliər/
lethal dose /ˈliθl doʊs/

Highlight that the spelling of *lead* is the same as the verb *lead* /lid/, but the pronunciation is different.

5.30

anesthetic, nitrogen, blood transfusion, donors, malaria, tuberculosis, lead, additive, polio, nuclear, lethal dose

Help with any other new vocabulary and encourage Sts to write down any useful new lexis from the article.

5 GRAMMAR quantifiers: *all, every, both,* etc.

a Focus on the instructions. Point out to Sts that they are going to be looking at quantifiers – all of which they probably will have seen before. However, the rules of use will probably be new, although they may instinctively know what sounds right.

Give Sts time to circle the right form and then check answers. If Sts ask why, say that they are now going to the **Grammar Bank** to find out.

1 Both	3 all	5 everything
2 Neither	4 All the	

b 5 31))) 5 32))) 5 33))) Tell Sts to go to **Grammar Bank 10A** on *page 150*. Focus on the example sentences and play the audio for Sts to listen to the sentence rhythm. You could also get Sts to repeat the sentences to practice getting the rhythm right. Then go through the rules with the class.

Additional grammar notes

- Sts will have frequently seen and heard all the quantifiers they learn here and should know what they mean. They should also have an instinct for how to use them correctly. For example, a phrase like *every animals* should *sound* wrong even if they don't know why.
- The rules here have been simplified (i.e., there are some other uses or positions that we haven't referred to). If Sts find the rules a little overwhelming, focus particularly on the examples and encourage them to use their instinct when they do the exercises and are not sure which form to choose.

all / every / most

- You might also want to point out that *all* can sometimes be used without a noun when it is followed by a relative clause, e.g., *I've forgotten all (that) I learned in school / everything (that) I learned in school.*

no, none, any

- Sts should know the difference between *no* and *none*, but the use of *none of* + pronoun / noun and *any* meaning it doesn't matter what / who, etc. may be new. They may still be making mistakes with double negatives (*we haven't got no time*) or using *any* on its own to mean *none*.

both, neither, either

- You may also want to point out that you can use *not* + *either* instead of *neither…nor*, e.g., *Neither Tim nor Andrew can come. Tim can't come and Andrew can't (come) either.* This is also more informal than *neither…nor*, which can sound very formal in spoken English.

Focus on the exercises and get Sts to do them individually or in pairs.

Check answers, getting Sts to read the full sentences.

a

1 Most of	6 any
2 any	7 None
3 Everything	8 Anybody
4 Most	9 neither
5 every	10 no

b
1 Both the kitchen and the bathroom need cleaning.
2 The food wasn't cheap or tasty. / The food was neither cheap nor tasty.
3 ✓
4 The trip was both long and boring.
5 It's either Jane's or Karen's birthday today.
6 ✓
7 Both her aunt and her cousin came to visit. / Her aunt and her cousin both came to visit.
8 We can either walk or take the bus.
9 ✓ (**Or** I have two children, but neither of them looks like me.)
10 My parents love horses, and both of them ride every day.

Tell Sts to go back to the main lesson **10A**.

Extra support

- If you think Sts need more practice, you may want to give them the Grammar photocopiable activity at this point or leave it for later as consolidation or review.

c This is an oral grammar practice activity. Focus on the quiz and give Sts time to do it with a partner. You might want to check Sts know the meaning of some of the words, e.g., *a current*, *intense*, and *a circuit*.

Elicit some ideas from Sts, but <u>don't</u> tell them if they are right or not.

d 5 34))) Play the audio for Sts to listen and check.

Check answers. Find out which pair got the most correct answers.

1 a	3 b	5 b	7 b	9 c
2 c	4 a	6 c	8 c	10 a

5 34)))
1 In direct current, the electrons move in only one direction.
2 Helium gas can be found in both liquid and solid form.
3 Adult giraffes remain standing all day.
4 Of all the water on our planet, hardly any of it is found underground.
5 Snakes eat either other animals or eggs.
6 A diamond can be destroyed only by intense heat.
7 The human brain can continue to live without oxygen for about six minutes.
8 In our solar system, Pluto is no longer considered to be a planet.
9 When we breathe out, some of that air is oxygen.
10 An individual blood cell makes a whole circuit of the body in about 60 seconds.

10B The power of words

Lesson plan

The topic of this final lesson is public speaking.

In the first section, Sts listen to several famous historical speeches. They begin by listening to a program about the controversy surrounding Neil Armstrong's famous words when he stepped on the moon (Did he make a mistake by omitting an indefinite article?). This leads into the Grammar, where Sts review and extend their knowledge of use and non-use of the definite and indefinite articles. They then read extracts from four famous speeches, and listen to the original recordings of three of them and an actress giving Emmeline Pankhurst's speech.

In the second section of the lesson, Sts hear people talking about disasters that have happened to them when speaking in public and read and discuss tips for giving a good presentation. The vocabulary focus is on word pairs, e.g., *ladies and gentlemen*, *now and then*, and in Pronunciation, Sts learn how pausing in the right places and stressing sentences correctly will make them much easier to understand if they are giving a presentation in English. They then have the opportunity to give a short presentation to the class. The lesson ends with the song *World*.

STUDY LINK
- **Workbook** 10B
- **Online Practice**
- **iChecker**

Extra photocopiable activities

- **Grammar** articles *page 170*
  Review: grammar auction *page 171*
- **Communicative** General knowledge quiz *page 208* (instructions *page 185*)
  Review *page 209* (instructions *page 185*)
- **Vocabulary** Review *page 225* (instructions *page 212*)
- **Song** *World* *page 238* (instructions *page 228*)

Optional lead-in – the quote

- Write the quote at the top of *page* 98 on the board (books closed) and the name of the person who said it, or get Sts to open their books and read it.
- You could tell Sts that Gore Vidal (1925–2012) was an American writer known for his essays, novels, screenplays, and plays.
- Ask Sts what they think the quote means. Do they agree with him?

1 GRAMMAR articles

a Do this as an open-class question.

The first man to land on the moon was Neil Armstrong in 1969.

b 5 35 Tell Sts that they are going to hear the original recording of Neil Armstrong speaking from the moon. Warn them that, understandably, the recording is very crackly.

Play the audio for Sts to listen.

Get Sts to compare with a partner and then check answers.

See words in **bold** in audioscript 5.35

5 35
Neil Armstrong original recording
That's one **small** step for **man**, one giant leap for **mankind**.

Now get Sts to look at questions 1 and 2 with their partner.

Check answers.

1 *a step* = the act of lifting your foot and putting it down in order to walk or move somewhere
a leap = a long or high jump; a sudden large change or increase in something
2 *mankind* = all humans, thought about as one large group; the human race

c 5 36 Tell Sts they are going to listen to an interview about the moon landing. Focus on the three questions they need to answer and make sure they know the meaning of *controversy*.

Play the audio once all the way through for Sts to listen.

Get Sts to compare with a partner and then if necessary, play the audio again.

Check answers.

The controversy is whether he said "one small step for man" or "one small step for a man." The version without *a* doesn't really make sense.
"One small step for **a** man" means one small step for an individual human being.
"One small step for man" means one small step for all men, i.e., the human race (which is the same as *mankind*).
It proved him right.

5 36

(audioscript in Student Book on *page 131*)

H = host, J = James

H When Neil Armstrong became the first man to walk on the moon on July 20th, 1969, a global audience of 500 million people was watching and listening. As he climbed down the steps from the spacecraft and stepped onto the moon, they heard him say, "That's one small step for man, one giant leap for mankind." It seemed like the perfect quote for such a momentous occasion. But from the moment he said it, people have argued about whether Armstrong got his lines wrong and made a mistake. James, tell us about it.

J Well, Armstrong always said that he wrote those words himself, which became some of the most famous and memorable words in history, during the time between landing on the moon and actually stepping out of the capsule onto the moon. That was almost seven hours.

H And so what is the controversy about what Armstrong said when he stepped down the ladder onto the moon?

J The question is, did he say, "one small step for man" or "one small step for a man." That's to say, did he use the indefinite article or not? It's just a little word, but there's a big difference in meaning.
Armstrong always insisted that he wrote "one small step for a man, one giant leap for mankind." Of course, this would have been a meaningful sentence. If you say "a man," then it clearly means that this was one small step for an individual man, that is, himself, but one giant leap for mankind, that's to say, men and women in general. But what everybody actually heard was, "One small step for man, one giant leap for mankind," with no indefinite article, and that sentence means, "One small step for people in general, one giant leap for people in general." And that doesn't really make sense.

H So, did he just get the line wrong when he said it?

J Well, Armstrong himself was never sure if he actually said what he wrote. In his biography *First Man*, he told the author James Hansen, "I must admit that it doesn't sound like the word *a* is there. On the other hand, certainly the *a* was intended, because that's the only way it makes sense." He always regretted that there had been so much confusion about it.
But almost four decades later, Armstrong was proved to be right. Peter Shann Ford, an Australian computer expert, used very hi-tech sound techniques to analyze his sentence, and he discovered that the *a* was said by Armstrong. It's just that he said it so quickly that you couldn't hear it on the recording that was broadcast to the world on July 20th, 1969.

H Was Armstrong relieved to hear this?

J Yes, he was. I think it meant a lot to him to know that he didn't make a mistake.

d Tell Sts they are going to listen to the interview again and this time they need to answer questions 1–6. Give Sts time to read the questions.

Play the audio once all the way through for Sts to listen.

Get Sts to compare with a partner and then, if necessary, play the audio again.

Check answers.

1 during the time (almost seven hours) between landing on the moon and actually stepping out of the capsule onto the moon
2 He says he wrote, "That's one small step for a man...."
3 Because that sentence means, "one small step for people in general, one giant leap for people in general."
4 He thought he said, "one small step for a man...."
5 He is an Australian computer expert, who used very hi-tech sound techniques to analyze Armstrong's sentence. He discovered that, in fact, Armstrong did say ***a** man*, but he said it so quickly that you can only hear it with special sound equipment.
6 He felt relieved.

e Focus on the task and make it clear to Sts that the mistakes all have to do with using or not using the indefinite article *a* / *an* or the definite article *the*.

Give Sts time to do the task.

Get Sts to compare with a partner and then check answers.

1 the US ✓
2 a shy boy ✓, ~~the~~ books and ~~the~~ music
3 at the university ✓
4 the first man ✓, **the** moon
5 by people all over the world ✓
6 **an** astronaut, the US navy ✓
7 ~~the~~ autographs
8 ~~the~~ Armstrong's hair

f 5 37 5 38 5 39 Tell Sts to go to **Grammar Bank 10B** on *page 151*. Focus on the example sentences and play the audio for Sts to listen to the sentence rhythm. You could also get Sts to repeat the sentences to practice getting the rhythm right. Then go through the rules with the class.

Additional grammar notes

- Sts should be familiar with the basic rules for using articles, but this is an area that can be very difficult for some nationalities who don't have articles in their L1. The basic rules are reviewed here, as well as introducing Sts to new areas, such as the use of articles with institutions, e.g., college, and with geographical and other place names, e.g., streets, hotels, etc.

basic rules: *a* / *an* / *the*, no article

- **rule 2:** (non-use of the definite article when generalizing) is an area where Sts often make mistakes, e.g., ~~*The*~~ *men are better at parking...*

institutions

- The use and non-use of *the* with *church*, *college*, and *school* is a tricky point, but with a clear rule. It will help to give Sts other examples, e.g.,
  I'm going to high school (= I am a student there)
  NOT *... going to* ~~*the*~~ *high school.*
  The high school is in the center of town. (= we are talking about the buildings).
- Other words that are used like this are *court*, *mosque* / *synagogue* (and other places of worship).

more rules: geographical names

- The number of rules here, most of which are new for Sts, may seem overwhelming. Emphasize, however, that Sts should already have a good instinct for whether they need to use *the* or not, and also that the easiest way to internalize the rules is by learning and remembering a clear example, e.g., *Fifth Avenue*, ***the** River Nile*, ***the** Mediterranean Sea*, *(Mount) Everest*, ***the** Andes*, etc.

Focus on the exercises and get Sts to do them individually or in pairs.

Check answers, getting Sts to read the full sentences.

a				
1 –	3 –	5 The	7 the	9 a
2 The	4 –	6 –	8 –	10 the
b				
1 –, the	3 the	5 –, the	7 the	9 the
2 the	4 The	6 the	8 the	10 –

Tell Sts to go back to the main lesson **10B**.

Extra support

- If you think Sts need more practice, you may want to give them the Grammar photocopiable activity at this point or leave it for later as consolidation or review.

g Put Sts in pairs, **A** and **B**, preferably face to face. Tell them to go to **Communication *Geography true or false***, **A** on *page 108*, **B** on *page 111*.

Go through the instructions and make sure Sts know what they have to do.

When Sts have completed their sentences, check answers using the key below. Don't read out the sentences, just tell them where articles are necessary and which ones.

A	B
1 The, the, the	1 The, the, –
2 –, the	2 The, the, the
3 The, the, –	3 The, the, the
4 –, the	4 The, the, –
5 The, the, –	5 The, –
6 –, –	6 The, the, –, –
7 –, –	7 –, the, the
8 The, –, –	8 –, –

When the activity has finished, you could ask who got the most right answers in each pair.

Tell Sts to go back to the main lesson **10B**.

2 READING

a Tell Sts they are going to read extracts from four famous speeches. Ask Sts to look at the four names and photos, and elicit anything Sts know about these people. Don't worry if Sts don't know some of the people as each extract has a short introduction.

Focus on the summaries 1–4, making sure Sts understand all the lexis, e.g., *starve* and *racial*.

Now give Sts time to read the information about the four speakers and the extracts, and match them to the summaries.

Get Sts to compare with a partner and then check answers.

1 BO	2 EP	3 WC	4 NM

Extra support

- Before checking answers to **a**, you could check Sts have understood by asking them a few questions about each speaker, e.g.,
  Who was Emmeline Pankhurst?
  What were the suffragettes fighting for?
  What did the women in prison do to try and be let free?, etc.

b Now tell Sts to read the extracts again and find words or phrases for the definitions.

Get Sts to compare with a partner and then check answers.

Emmeline Pankhurst
1 hunger strike
2 (you are) at death's door
3 the authorities
4 sacred

Winston Churchill
1 go on
2 growing
3 surrender

Nelson Mandela
1 cherished
2 if needs be

Barack Obama
1 withstand
2 a cynic
3 a reality check
4 creed

Help with any other new vocabulary and encourage Sts to write down any useful new lexis from the article.

c Do this as an open-class question and make sure Sts understand *inspirational*.

Elicit opinions from the class.

d **5 40** Tell Sts that they are now going to hear historical recordings of three of the speeches (i.e., delivered by the people themselves) and an actress who played Emmeline Pankhurst in a radio play giving her speech.

Play the audio once all the way through for Sts to listen.

Either elicit opinions from the class or put Sts in pairs and get them to discuss the two questions.

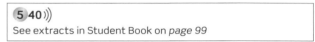

5 40
See extracts in Student Book on *page 99*

Finally, you could ask who they think is the best / most charismatic speaker.

Extra idea

- Ask Sts who they think are (or were) charismatic speakers from their country or foreign speakers that they have heard giving speeches, e.g., on TV.

3 LISTENING & SPEAKING

a Either get Sts to answer the questions in pairs and get feedback, or do them as an open-class activity and elicit Sts' experiences. If you have a story of your own, tell it to the class.

b Focus on the article, *Presentation Disasters!*, and give Sts time to read the article.

Check the answer.

The speaker should have remembered to get to know as much as possible about his / her audience beforehand (tip 3).

c **5 41** Focus on the task and the chart. Tell Sts that the first time they listen they only need to find out what the disaster was (the first column). Before Sts start, get them to copy the chart into their notebooks, so they have more space to write.

Play the audio, pausing after each speaker to give Sts time to write.

You could get Sts to compare with a partner before checking answers.

Extra support

- Before playing the audio, go through the audioscript and decide if you need to preteach / check any lexis to help Sts when they listen.

Speaker 1	The speaker only spoke English and his audience only spoke Chinese.
Speaker 2	The speaker arrived a little late. He went into the women's bathroom by mistake and had to wait a while to get out. He was nearly late for the talk.
Speaker 3	The equipment she needed – a video player – wouldn't work at first.
Speaker 4	Her skirt fell down as she was speaking.

5 41

(audioscript in Student Book on *page 131*)

1 **Man**

I was doing a tour of Asia where I was giving a presentation about database programs. I assumed the audiences would understand English – the organizers knew that I couldn't speak Chinese – and I knew they would be familiar with the, um, with the technical language of the products I was going to talk about, which were dBase and Clipper.

Well, for most of the tour the talks seemed to go extremely well; there were big audiences and the venues were great. The questions I was asked by the audience at the end of the talks showed that, um, everyone had really understood what I was saying.

When we arrived in the penultimate city, whose name I'm not going to mention, I started my session as I usually did with a few questions to get to know something about the audience. So, first I asked them, "How many of you use dBase?" I raised my own hand, because I use it myself and pretty much the whole audience raised their hands. So then I asked, "How many of you here use Clipper?" And, once again, pretty much 100% of the audience raised their hands. This was extremely unusual – in fact, almost impossible. With a sinking feeling, I then asked, "How many of you want to be an astronaut?" and I watched as everyone's hands went up. I might as well have been speaking to a group of aliens – as it turned out, most of the audience spoke Chinese and only Chinese. But I could see that two or three people in the audience spoke English, because they were practically rolling on the floor laughing.

2 **Man**

I was giving a talk in Hungary to a group of about 200 English teachers. I got to the place where I was giving the talk a little bit late, only about ten minutes before I was supposed to start. I rushed to the room and saw that everything was set up and most of the audience was already waiting and I told the organizers that I just needed to quickly go to the bathroom and then I would start. They pointed me in the right direction, but when I got to the bathroom, I saw that there were two doors with words on them in Hungarian, but no signs. I looked at the words and decided that one of them must be the men's room and I went in and went into a cubicle. Suddenly I heard voices of other people coming in – but, to my horror, they were women's voices, and I realized that I had guessed wrongly and had gone into the women's room. I guessed that these women must be teachers coming to my talk, so there was no way I could open the door and come out. I waited and waited, getting more and more stressed by the minute and worrying about being late to start my talk. After about five minutes or so, everything went quiet and I was able to rush out and go back to the room where the audience was waiting for me to start as it was already five minutes past the start time. Thank goodness nobody saw me...

3 **Woman**

My very first ever presentation was at a conference for English teachers around 1988. I wanted to show the audience some good ideas for using video in the classroom. I explained one of the ideas and then I went to turn on the video player and nothing happened... and then again... nothing...and again. By this time I was so stressed and annoyed that in the end I said, "OK, if it doesn't work this time, I'm leaving," ...and I really meant it. Amazingly, almost as if it had heard me, it worked. I never forgot that talk and it taught me to never rely 100% on technology in a presentation.

4 **Woman**

Some years ago, I had to do a presentation to a group of construction workers about health and safety at work. When I was getting dressed that morning, I put on a silk skirt, and as I was fastening it, the button at the waist broke. I didn't bother to change, because the skirt had a zipper, and anyway I was in a hurry.

During the presentation, as I walked backward and forward across the stage, I started to feel something silky hit the back of my ankles. My skirt was falling down! The audience was absolutely entranced – and not by what I was saying. I quickly pulled it up and said, "Now that I have your attention..." The audience roared with laughter and one of them shouted out, "I thought that was part of your presentation!" I felt terribly embarrassed, and I could hear my mother's voice in my ear saying, "You should always wear nice underwear, in case you are ever in an accident." I managed to finish my presentation and I rushed outside and started to shake. That audience may never remember a thing I said, but I'm sure they won't forget me.

d Tell Sts they are going to listen to the audio again and this time they need to complete the next column (*How and why it happened*) as they listen.

Play the audio, pausing after each speaker to give Sts time to write.

Finally, tell Sts to look at their answers and decide which of the top ten tips the speaker should have remembered.

You could get Sts to compare with a partner before checking answers.

Speaker 1	He was doing a tour of Asia and he assumed the audiences would understand English because the organizers knew that he couldn't speak Chinese. Tip 3
Speaker 2	There were two doors with words on them in Hungarian, but no signs. He didn't speak Hungarian, so he looked at the words and decided that one of them was the men's room and he went in. Tip 5
Speaker 3	She wanted to show the audience some good ideas for using video in the classroom, but the video player wouldn't work. She hadn't checked the equipment before the talk. Tip 6
Speaker 4	When she was getting dressed, she put on a silk skirt and as she was fastening it, the button at the waist broke. She didn't bother to change, because the skirt had a zipper and she was in a hurry. As she walked backward and forward across the stage, her skirt fell down. Tip 4

Extra support

- If there's time, you could play the audio again while Sts read the audioscript on *page 131*, so they can see what they understood / didn't understand. Translate / explain any new words or phrases.

e Do this in pairs, small groups, or as an open-class activity. If you have ever been to a presentation where something went badly wrong or if you have experienced your own disastrous presentation, you could tell the class about it.

4 VOCABULARY collocation: word pairs

a Focus on the **Word pairs** box and go through it with the class.

Focus on the questions and elicit the equivalent expressions in the Sts' languages and ask them which order the words come in.

b Focus on the instructions. Do one with the class. Ask Sts which word (from circle B) often goes with *pepper* (from circle A) and elicit *salt*. Then ask Sts if we say *salt and pepper* or *pepper and salt*, and elicit that it is the former.

Sts then continue matching the pairs. Don't check answers yet.

c Focus on the task and get Sts to do it individually or in pairs. Sts should know most of these or be able to guess them.

Extra support

- Get Sts to do **b** and **c** in pairs.

d  5 42 Play the audio for Sts to listen and check their answers to **b** and **c**.

Check answers.

See words pairs in audioscript 5.42

5 42

b
salt and pepper
peanut butter and jelly
bread and butter
thunder and lightning
knife and fork
bed and breakfast
peace and quiet
backward and forward

c
right or wrong
now or never
more or less
sooner or later
all or nothing
once or twice
dead or alive

Elicit / explain that in these word pairs *and* is usually pronounced /ən/.
Then give Sts time to practice saying the phrases. You could use the audio to do this.

Extra idea

- You could get Sts to test each other by saying the first word from each pair for the partner to complete the expression, e.g., **A** (book open) *peanut butter* **B** (book closed) *and jelly*. Make sure they switch roles.

e Tell Sts that they are now going to look at some more word pairs that are idioms. Focus on the task and give Sts time to match the idioms and meanings.

Check answers and make sure Sts are clear about the meaning of these idioms.

1 C	3 F	5 E	7 B
2 G	4 H	6 A	8 D

Then tell Sts to cover sentences 1–8 and call out in random order the phrases in A–H to prompt the idiom. Alternatively, you could get Sts to do this in pairs.

f This exercise recycles some of the expressions Sts have just learned. Focus on the sentences and give Sts time to complete them.

Check answers.

1 now and then	6 Sooner or later
2 now or never	7 More or less
3 black and white	8 law and order
4 safe and sound	9 sick and tired
5 peace and quiet	10 thunder and lightning

Extra idea

- You could do this in pairs or small groups as a timed race.

5 PRONUNCIATION & SPEAKING
pausing and sentence stress

a **5 43** Focus on the instructions and elicit / explain that *a chunk* is a reasonable amount of something, e.g., *a chunk of cheese*. Highlight that there will always be a pause after periods and commas, but that there are sometimes more pauses that help the listener to follow what is being said. Point out the first pause that has already been marked.

Play the audio once all the way through for Sts just to listen.

Then play it again and get Sts to mark the pauses.

Get Sts to compare with a partner and then play the audio again.

Check answers.

See the pause marks in audioscript 5.43

5 43

Good afternoon everyone / and thank you for coming. / I'm going to talk to you today / about one of my hobbies, / collecting adult comics. / Since I was a child / I've been crazy about comics / and comic books. / I started reading Spider-Man and Superman / when I was seven or eight. / Later, / when I was a teenager, / some friends at school / introduced me to Manga, / which are Japanese comics. / I've been collecting them now / for about five years / and I'm also learning to draw them.

Extra challenge

- Play the audio again, pausing after each sentence for Sts to underline the stressed words. See underlining in audioscript 5.43.

b Get Sts in pairs to practice reading the speech, making the right pauses and trying to get a good rhythm.

Extra support

- Play the audio again and get Sts to listen and repeat at the same time. Then put them in pairs to practice again.

c Focus on the instructions. Set a time limit for Sts to prepare their presentation, and monitor and help with vocabulary. Encourage Sts to make a plan and write notes rather than writing the presentation out in full.

! If you know that some of your Sts will be nervous about giving a presentation, tell them now that they won't be doing it in front of the whole class, but in small groups.

Extra support

- Less confident / proficient Sts might want to write up their presentation at home and learn it before doing the presentation in the following class.

d When Sts are ready to give their presentations, focus on the **Giving a presentation** box and go through it with the class.

Now divide Sts into groups of three or four to give the presentations to each other. Remind them of the question and answer session after each presentation.

Try to listen to as many Sts as possible and to give positive feedback to the whole class because this may be one of the most challenging speaking activities that they have done.

Extra idea

- If you have a video camera, you could film some or all of the presentations to show later, provided Sts feel comfortable with this.

6 5 44)) SONG *World* ♫

This song was originally made famous by the American singer Five for Fighting in 2006. For copyright reasons, this is a cover version. If you want to do this song in class, use the photocopiable activity on *page 238*.

5 44))

World

Got a package full of wishes
A time machine, a magic wand
A globe made out of gold

No instructions or commandments
Laws of gravity or indecisions to uphold

Printed on the box I see
ACME's Build-a-World-to-Be
Take a chance, grab a piece
Help me to believe it

Chorus
What kind of world do you want?
Think anything
Let's start at the start
Build a masterpiece
Be careful what you wish for
History starts now...

Should there be people or peoples?
Money, funny pedestals for fools who never pay
Raise your army, choose your steeple
Don't be shy, the satellites can look the other way

Lose the earthquakes, keep the faults
Fill the oceans without the salt
Let every man own his own hand
Can you dig it, baby?

Chorus

Sunlight's on the bridge
Sunlight's on the way
Tomorrow's calling
There's more to this than love

What kind of world do you want?
What kind of world do you want?
What kind of world do you want?
Think anything
Let's start at the start
Build a masterpiece, yeah

History starts now
Starts now

Be careful what you wish for
Start now

Now

Extra idea

- Before doing the **Review and Check** lesson, you could give Sts one or all of the final three photocopiable activities (Grammar, Communicative, and Vocabulary), which include questions to review all the grammar points and lexis they studied in this level.

9&10 Review and Check

For instructions on how to use these pages see *page 39*.

Testing Program CD-ROM

- **File 10 Quick Test**
- **File 10 Test**
- **Files 6–10 Progress Test**
- **End-of-course Test**

GRAMMAR

1 b	6 b	11 c
2 c	7 a	12 b
3 a	8 c	13 a
4 c	9 a	14 b
5 c	10 c	15 a

VOCABULARY

a
1 genetics
2 scientific
3 neighborhood
4 loneliness
5 death

b
1 overpopulated
2 mispronounced
3 multinational
4 autobiography
5 underpaid

c
1 loss
2 start up
3 leader
4 launch
5 branches
6 staff
7 rise
8 side
9 carry
10 guinea

d
1 quiet
2 sound
3 later
4 order
5 never

PRONUNCIATION

a
1 neighborhood
2 prove
3 research
4 launch
5 colleague

b
1 biological
2 physicist
3 multicultural
4 increase
5 manufacture

CAN YOU UNDERSTAND THIS TEXT?

a Billy Ray Harris feels surprised and sad.

b
1 b	3 a	5 a	7 a	9 c
2 c	4 c	6 c	8 b	10 b

c Get Sts to compare their five words with a partner and practice pronouncing each word.

VIDEO CAN YOU UNDERSTAND THIS MOVIE?

5 45

1 fabrication
2 idea
3 printing
4 complex
5 layers
6 faster / cheaper
7 younger
8 designer / inventor

5 45 Available as MP3 on CD1

A short movie on digital design

My name is Austin. I'm the co-founder of 3D NYC Lab, which is a digital design and fabrication studio based in Brooklyn, New York. We design things, we make things, and we help other people with an idea realize that idea into a physical, tangible thing. Sometimes an individual or a hobbyist or an entrepreneur or designer in New York might come to us and have an idea for something and not know how to actually make it. So what we would do is help by putting that in the computer. And then using a technology like 3D printing to make that into a real thing. Definitely, the use cases in, in, um, 3D printing you're seeing everywhere from not only the design world. But to artists and, and sculptors. The great thing about 3D printing is that you can make incredibly complex things that would be really expensive or difficult to do otherwise. And the other reason is, more people have access to tools that allow them to be inventors or designers. Every idea starts as, as a digital design in the computer. What the computer's going to do is take that and slice it horizontally layer by layer – in tiny, tiny layers. And what the printer will do is build one layer at a time. So, do one, maybe move a half a millimeter up, and then do another one. And then the end process, you end up with a finished object. I think the, there could be really exciting things in the future of integrating electric conductivity into the materials, so we might be able to print electronics next. Beyond that, what you're going to see is an overall improvement in all the different aspects that aren't perfect about it now. Which, I think, the prints will get faster, and the machines will get cheaper, and then the quality will rise. What really excites me about the future of 3D printing is actually younger and younger students becoming very skilled at the digital design tools. So what that means is, if printers are more available, that anyone can become a designer. And anyone can become an inventor. So it's possible that, you know, some student tinkering around in his garage with a 3D printer can invent the next light bulb, or the next great invention.

Photocopiable activities

Contents

Photocopiable material

- There is a **Grammar activity** for each main (A and B) lesson of the Student Book.
- There is a **Mini Grammar activity** for every Mini grammar item in the Student Book.
- There is a **Communicative activity** for each main lesson of the Student Book.
- There is a **Vocabulary activity** for each section of the Vocabulary Bank in the Student Book.
- There is a **Song activity** for every File of the Student Book, in either lesson A or B. The recording of the song can be found on the relevant part of the Class CDs.

Using extra activities in mixed-ability classes

Some teachers have classes with a very wide range of levels, where some students finish Student Book activities much more quickly than others. You could give these fast-finishers a photocopiable activity (Grammar, Vocabulary, or Communicative) while you help the slower students. Alternatively, some teachers might want to give faster students extra oral practice with a Communicative activity while slower students consolidate their knowledge with an extra Grammar activity.

Tips for using Grammar activities

The Grammar activities are designed to give students extra practice in the main grammar point from each lesson. How you use these activities depends on the needs and abilities of your students and time you have available. They can be used in the lesson if you think your entire class would benefit from the extra practice, or you could assign them as homework for some or all of your students.

- All of the activities start with a writing stage. If you use the activities in class, get students to work individually or in pairs. Allow students to compare before checking the answers.
- The activities have an **Activation** section that gives students a chance to practice the language either by testing their memories, or gives freer practice to produce the target language. If you are using the activities in class, students can work in pairs and test their partner. If you assign them for homework, encourage students to use this stage to test themselves.
- If students are having trouble with any of the activities, make sure they refer to the relevant Grammar Bank in the Student Book.
- Make sure that students keep their copies of the activities and that they review any difficult areas regularly. Encourage them to go back to activities and cover and test themselves. This will help with their review.

Grammar activity answers

Introduction

2 decided to move 3 is five / five years old 4 who are 5 the oldest / eldest child 6 He used to be 7 in charge of 8 to meet 9 I've been learning 10 went to 11 as a teacher 12 very hard work / a very hard job 13 had improved 14 to be able to speak 15 good at reading 16 is good enough 17 have very little 18 I'd learn

1A question formation

a 1 Who paid for it?
2 Do you know who that woman is over there?
3 Where are they going on their honeymoon? How long are they going for?
4 Who did Tony come with? Why did she leave him?
5 How long have Matt and Claire known each other? Where did they meet? Who told you that?

b 2 Do you know why Sarah didn't come to the wedding?
3 Do you know if / whether that tall woman over there is Claire's mother?
4 Do you remember what Molly's husband does?
5 Do you have any idea if / whether I can get a taxi after midnight?
6 Do you remember if / whether Claire's sister got married here?
7 Do you think they'll be happy?
8 Do you know where they put our coats?

1B auxiliary verbs

a 2 do 3 isn't 4 Have 5 aren't 6 do 7 Is 8 will

b 2 am 3 are 4 do / did 5 Did 6 did 7 Couldn't 8 do 9 can't

2A present perfect simple and continuous

a 2 Have you been eating 3 haven't had 4 haven't wanted 5 Have you been having / Have you had 6 've taken 7 Have you been working 8 have been 9 've been getting 10 haven't been sleeping 11 've been overworking 12 've just been promoted

b 2 Have you ever been injured... 3 have you been coming... 4 have you missed 5 have you been living / have you lived 6 Have you ever studied

2B adjectives

a 2 The French 3 homeless people 4 Japanese girl 5 ✓ 6 The Spanish 7 the poor 8 ✓ 9 The Chinese 10 The young

b 2 blue denim 3 awful modern 4 big dark 5 long black silk 6 beautiful old wooden 7 small black leather 8 delicious Thai 9 short curly brown 10 new striped

3A narrative tenses

a 1 hadn't noticed, had stopped
2 had been (carefully) saving, had been concentrating, had been watching, had (only) been looking
3 was leaving, was happening, were looking

b 2 asked 3 mentioned 4 had been looking 5 had accused / accused 6 had searched / searched 7 made 8 had said 9 jumped up 10 made 11 had never seen 12 drove 13 parked 14 had taken place 15 came 16 started 17 had never stolen 18 made 19 found 20 had stopped 21 were watching

3B adverbs and adverbial phrases

a 2 do you really mean that; were absolutely awful
3 Minnesota played well
4 Unfortunately, Minnesota never plays well
5 was incredibly lucky
6 do you ever have
7 To be honest, Minnesota was very lucky
8 was extremely lucky
9 Personally, I thought both teams played badly; Minnesota was a little better, especially in the second half
10 New England next, so let's see how they do there

b 2 slowly 3 quickly 4 earlier that day 5 obviously 6 actually 7 angrily 8 a little 9 badly 10 incredibly 11 here 12 always 13 well 14 naturally 15 in fifteen minutes

4A future perfect and continuous

a 1 won't be thinking
2 'll (still) be working; 'll have been promoted
3 will have left
4 won't be using
5 won't have gone; 'll (still) be watching
6 'll have graduated; 'll be looking for
7 won't have had
8 Will (you) be coming
9 Will (you) be picking me up
10 will (they) have visited
11 'll have finished; 'll be celebrating
12 won't have saved

4B conditionals, future time clauses

a **2** a and b **3** a **4** b **5** b **6** c **7** a and c **8** a and b **9** a **10** c **11** b **12** a and c **13** b and c **14** a and b **15** c

5A unreal conditionals

a **2** had put; would have tasted / would taste
3 found; be
4 wouldn't have gotten; 'd taken
5 were; wouldn't swim
6 wouldn't have left; hadn't fallen
7 hadn't used; wouldn't have found
8 'd buy; could
9 would have gone; hadn't been
10 didn't (both) work; wouldn't be able to
11 would have bought; 'd known
12 wouldn't be; got

5B structures after *wish*

a **2** wouldn't borrow **3** would stop raining **4** would let **5** would do **6** wouldn't make **7** would clean **8** wouldn't wear

b **2** hadn't told **3** were / was **4** had **5** earned **6** had tried on **7** hadn't shouted **8** wasn't

6A gerunds and infinitives

a **2** to see **3** go out **4** to take **5** not stay **6** working **7** to wear **8** live **9** laughing **10** to finish **11** seeing **12** not to tell **13** work **14** seeing **15** to help **16** waiting **17** to park **18** speaking **19** getting up / to get up **20** not come **21** spending **22** to give

b **2** not to be **3** changing **4** meeting **5** arriving **6** to review **7** to tell **8** turning

6B *used to, be used to, get used to*

a **2** get used to **3** usually **4** was used to being able **5** used to be **6** usually go

b **2** 'm used to **3** get used to **4** used to **5** usually **6** get used to **7** 'm used to **8** get used to **9** get used to **10** used to

c **2** being **3** seeing **4** stay up **5** enjoying

7A past modals

a **2** might have broken **3** must have left **4** must have turned the oven on **5** couldn't have drunk **6** might not have seen **7** must have worked **8** couldn't have finished **9** might not have been able to get / might not have gotten **10** must have turned it off

b **2** shouldn't have used **3** shouldn't have broken up **4** should have come **5** should have waited **6** should have kept **7** should have told **8** shouldn't have worn

7B verbs of the senses

a **2** smells **3** smells as if (like) **4** smells like **5** feels **6** feels like **7** feels as if (like) **8** feels **9** tastes **10** tastes like **11** tastes as if (like) **12** tastes **13** look as if (like) **14** look **15** look as if (like) **16** look **17** look like **18** look **19** sounds **20** sounds **21** sounds as if (like) **22** sound like

8A the passive

a **2** have been stolen **3** are being interrogated **4** was being driven **5** were discovered, was stopped **6** be taken **7** are caught **8** has been vandalized **9** had been broken **10** are going to / will be robbed **11** to be sent

b **2** is thought that **3** is said to **4** are understood to **5** is expected that **6** are thought to

8B reporting verbs

a **1** to give **2** to come **3** having / having had **4** not going / not having gone **5** to tell; breaking **6** going **7** not to leave **8** making

b **2** promised to clean
3 apologized for forgetting
4 advised (his father) to keep
5 suggested trying
6 admitted eating
7 invited (me) to come
8 blamed (us) for losing

9A clauses of contrast and purpose

a **2** j **3** h **4** i **5** f **6** e **7** a **8** c **9** d **10** b

b **2** A lot of companies have reduced staff numbers in order to save money.
3 Despite the long flight / Despite the fact the flight was long, she felt great when she arrived in New York.
4 Nick didn't tell Louisa the truth so as not to hurt her feelings.
5 I bought the shoes even though they were ridiculously expensive.
6 The company has a big market share in spite of doing very little advertising / in spite of the fact that they do very little advertising.
7 They had to leave the hotel early so that they wouldn't miss their train.
8 She didn't get the job though she was a strong candidate.

9B uncountable and plural nouns

a **2** some jeans **3** says **4** have **5** is **6** some **7** some **8** equipment **9** business **10** staff **11** is **12** is **13** experience **14** advice **15** some **16** some **17** those **18** them **19** the **20** homework **21** trash

10A quantifiers

a 2 either of them; both
3 everything
4 all day; any
5 They all passed.
6 any; every
7 all of the research; all of
8 nor; Both; neither of them

b **2** Neither **3** Every **4** All **5** Most of **6** no **7** anyone **8** Most **9** all **10** both **11** every **12** None of

10B articles

a **2** the **3** – **4** an **5** the **6** The **7** the **8** – **9** The **10** – **11** – **12** an **13** The **14** the **15** the **16** a **17** The **18** – **19** the **20** – **21** – **22** the **23** the **24** – **25** the **26** the **27** – **28** a **29** – **30** the **31** the **32** the **33** – **34** the **35** – **36** the **37** the

Review Grammar auction

Instructions

Sts review the main grammar points of the book by playing a game where, in pairs, they have to bid to try to "buy" correct sentences. Copy one sheet per pair.

- Put Sts in pairs. Give each pair the list of 20 sentences. Elicit what an auction is = a sale where things are sold to the person who offers the most money. Explain that Sts have 1,000 dollars. They have a list of sentences, some of which are correct and some incorrect. They bid to "buy" as many correct sentences as they can. Bids start at 50, the next bid is 100, then 150, etc. Sts must record on their sheet how much they have spent on a sentence, in order to calculate how much money they have left. The pair that buys the most correct sentences is the winner.
- Start with the first sentence and invite bids. Make the activity more fun by using typical language of an auctioneer, e.g., *How much will you bid for this fantastic sentence? 50 dollars, 100? Do I hear 150? Going, going, gone to Marc and Andrea for 150 dollars.*
- When you have "sold" all the sentences, go through each one eliciting whether it is correct or not, and what the mistake is. Then find out who bought the most correct sentences.

1 ✓
2 ✗ Her name's Marta, isn't it?
3 ✓
4 ✗ She has beautiful long dark hair.
5 ✓
6 ✗ I like classical music very much.
7 ✓
8 ✓
9 ✗ I would have enjoyed the movie more if it hadn't had subtitles.
10 ✗ I wish I had more free time! / I wish I could have more free time!
11 ✗ It's getting late. We'd better go now.
12 ✓
13 ✗ He couldn't have seen you or he would have said hello.
14 ✗ It looks like / as if it's going to rain.
15 ✗ The missing man is thought to be from Miami.
16 ✓
17 ✗ Lilly is going to the hospital this afternoon to visit her husband.
18 ✗ I need to buy some new furniture for my living room.
19 ✓
20 ✗ The man was sent to prison for ten years.

GRAMMAR introduction

a Read about Erin. Then correct the **bold** phrases 1–18.

My name's Erin and I'm from Chicago. I was born there and [1]**I have lived there** until I was 14. Then my family [2]**decided move** to Seattle, and that's where I live now.

I'm divorced and I have a son named Jacob, who [3]**is five years.** He spends weekdays with me and weekends with his father. I have two brothers, [4]**which are** both studying at college. I am [5]**the older child** in the family. My mother works in a bank and my father is retired. [6]**He use to be** a business consultant.

I work for a big clothing company. I am [7]**on charge of** foreign suppliers. All of my customers speak English, but sometimes I travel to other countries such as Mexico and Japan [8]**for to meet** suppliers.

[9]**I am learning** Japanese for about nine years. I studied it in high school and college, and then after school, I spent eight weeks in Japan. During the day, I [10]**was going to** Japanese classes, and in the evening, I worked [11]**like a teacher** in a small English-language school. It was [12]**a very hard work**. When I came home, my Japanese [13]**has improved** a lot, but that was a few years ago, and I've forgotten a lot since then. My main aim this year is [14]**to be able speak** more fluently and to improve my writing. I think I am very [15]**good at read** in Japanese. As soon as my level of Japanese [16]**will be good enough**, I'll go back to Japan, but this time for a vacation!

I [17]**have very few** free time, but when I can, I go horse back riding. If I had more time, [18]**I'll learn** another language, maybe Spanish or French.

1 *I lived there*
2 ______
3 ______
4 ______
5 ______
6 ______
7 ______
8 ______
9 ______
10 ______
11 ______
12 ______
13 ______
14 ______
15 ______
16 ______
17 ______
18 ______

activation

b Write a similar text about yourself, in five paragraphs. Include the following information:

- where you live
- your family
- what you do
- how long you've been learning English and why
- what you do in your free time

American English File 2nd edition Teacher's Book 4 Photocopiable © Oxford University Press 2014

1A GRAMMAR question formation

a Complete the questions.

1 **A** I don't like her dress.
B What *don't you like* about it?
A The style. I think it's awful.
B It must have cost a fortune though.
A Yes. Who ________ ________ it?
B Her grandparents paid. It was a wedding present.

2 **A** Do you know ________ ________ ________ ________ over there?
B That woman there? I think she's Claire's cousin.
A Her hairstyle is very old-fashioned!

3 **A** Where ________ ________ ________ on their honeymoon?
B On an African safari, I think.
A How ________ ________ ________ going ________?
B Three weeks!

4 **A** Who ________ Tony ________ ________?
B Nobody. He came on his own. His girlfriend left him last month.
A Why ________ ________ ________ him?
B I think she moved to another country.

5 **A** ________ long ________ Matt and Claire ________ each other?
B For about a year, I think.
A Where ________ ________ ________?
B Someone told me they met on an online dating site.
A Online dating? Who ________ ________ that?
B I think Alex told me. He's Matt's best friend.

b Change the direct questions to indirect questions.

1 "Where are the bathrooms?" — "Could you tell me *where the bathrooms are*?"
2 "Why didn't Sarah come to the wedding?" — "Do you know ________________?"
3 "Is that tall woman over there Claire's mother?" — "Do you know ________________?"
4 "What does Molly's husband do?" — "Do you remember ________________?"
5 "Can I get a taxi after midnight?" — "Do you have any idea ________________?"
6 "Did Claire's sister get married here?" — "Do you remember ________________?"
7 "Will they be happy?" — "Do you think ________________?"
8 "Where did they put our coats?" — "Do you know ________________?"

activation

c Work with a partner. Write two direct and two indirect questions to find out something you didn't know about your partner. Ask for more information.

 Photocopiable © Oxford University Press 2014

1B GRAMMAR auxiliary verbs

a Circle the correct answer.

A Hello.

B Good morning. Are you here for an interview, too?

A Yes. They say it's a good company to work for, [1]***don't*** / ***doesn't*** / ***do*** they?

B Yes, they [2]***do*** / ***are*** / ***don't*** say that.

A By the way, I'm Andreas Kourkoulos.

B That's a Greek name, [3]***is*** / ***does*** / ***isn't*** it?

A Yes. I'm from Athens, but I've been living in New York for the past two years.

B [4]***Do*** / ***Are*** / ***Have*** you? I've got a friend who lives there. Anyway, I'm Beatriz Flores, from Buenos Aires, in Argentina.

A Nice to meet you.

B You're a little nervous, [5]***are*** / ***don't*** / ***aren't*** you?

A A little. Don't you get nervous before interviews?

B Not really. I [6]***am*** / ***will*** / ***do*** get nervous before exams, but not interviews. What time is it now?

A 2:30. My interview's at 2:45.

B [7]***Is*** / ***Has*** / ***Does*** it? Mine's at 3 o'clock. We won't have to wait much longer, [8]***have*** / ***will*** / ***do*** we?

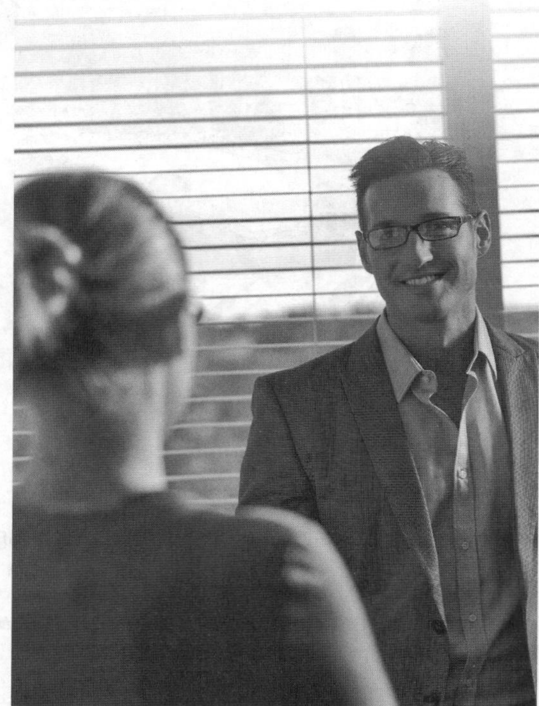

b Complete the next part of the dialogue with auxiliary verbs.

A Are you hungry?

B No, I'm not.

A Neither [1]*am* I, but I wouldn't mind a coffee.

B Me too. Where are you staying, by the way?

A At the Holiday Hotel.

B Ah, so [2]__________ I. The rooms aren't very nice, [3]__________ they?

A No, they aren't. But I [4]__________ like the restaurant. I had a good meal there last night.

B [5]__________ you? Are you working right now?

A No, I resigned last week.

B Why? Didn't you like your job?

A Oh, I [6]__________ like the job, but, to be honest, I couldn't stand my boss!

B [7]__________ you? I get along with my boss, but I think I need a new challenge.

A So [8]__________ I. Ah, it's your turn now. Good luck, Beatriz.

B Thanks. I'll go to the cafe on the corner when I finish.

A OK. And we can compare notes, [9]__________ we?

activation

c Practice the dialogues in **a** and **b** with a partner. Try to use the correct rhythm and intonation.

American English File 2nd edition Teacher's Book 4 Photocopiable © Oxford University Press 2014

2A GRAMMAR present perfect simple and continuous

a Complete the dialogue with the verbs in parentheses in the present perfect simple or continuous. Sometimes both tenses are possible.

DOCTOR So, what seems to be the problem?

PATIENT Well, for about a week now I [1] *'ve been feeling* very dizzy. I even thought I was going to faint once or twice. (**feel**)

DOCTOR I see. [2] ______________ as usual? (**you** / **eat**)

PATIENT Well, to tell you the truth I [3] ______________ much of an appetite recently. I'm just not hungry. (**not have**)

DOCTOR You need to eat regularly, you know, even if you're not hungry.

PATIENT I know, but I [4] ______________ to eat anything recently. (**not want**).

DOCTOR Hmm. Any other symptoms? [5] ______________ headaches or any other aches or pains? (**you** / **have**)

PATIENT Well, I [6] ______________ my blood pressure three times this week, and it's a little bit high. (**take**)

DOCTOR I'll check that in a minute. [7] ______________ harder than usual? (**you** / **work**)

PATIENT Yes, I suppose I have. This is a very important time of the year for us and things [8] ______________ incredibly busy recently. I [9] ______________ home very late, and to be honest, I [10] ______________ very well for the last few days. (**be**, **get**, **not sleep**)

DOCTOR I think you [11] ______________. I want you to take a week off work and have a complete rest. (**overwork**)

PATIENT I couldn't possibly take a week off right now. I [12] ______________ to head of the department. (**just** / **be promote**).

DOCTOR Well, I'm afraid they'll just have to manage without you. You can't take risks with your health.

b Write questions with either the present perfect simple or continuous.

1 How long *have* you *had* your phone? (**have**)
2 __________ you ever __________ in an accident? (**be injure**)
3 How long __________ you __________ to this school? (**come**)
4 How many classes __________ you __________ this year? (**miss**)
5 How long __________ you __________ in your current home? (**live**)
6 __________ you ever __________ abroad? (**study**)

activation

c Work with a partner. Ask and answer the questions in **b**. Ask your partner for more information.

American English File 2nd edition Teacher's Book 4 Photocopiable © Oxford University Press 2014

2B GRAMMAR adjectives

a Circle the correct form. Check (✓) if both phrases are correct.

1 *The unemployed* | *Unemployed people* can apply to do these training courses free of charge. ✓
2 *The French* | *The Frenchs* are very proud of their language and culture.
3 There are a lot of *homeless* | *homeless people* sleeping on the streets at night.
4 I met a very nice *Japanese* | *Japanese girl* in Chicago. She was really friendly.
5 *The rich* | *Rich people* always live in the best part of a city.
6 *The Spanish* | *Spanish* are now famous for their world-class restaurants.
7 "President, a lot of people say that your government just doesn't care about *poor* | *the poor*."
8 Don't talk like that – you should show more respect for *elderly people* | *the elderly*.
9 *The Chinese* | *The Chineses* invented paper.
10 *The young* | *Young* are finding it very difficult to buy their first apartment or house.

b Complete the sentences with the adjectives in parentheses in the correct order. Use your instinct if you are not sure.

1 **A** Can I help you?
B Yes, I'm looking for some *stylish high-heeled* sandals. (**high-heeled** / **stylish**)

2 **A** Did you see either of the robbers?
B It all happened so fast. I saw a young man wearing a ______________ jacket running out of the restaurant. (**denim** / **blue**)

3 **A** Your granddaughter's boyfriend is a rock musician, isn't he, Mrs. Jones?
B Yes, he is, but I can't stand the ______________ music he plays! (**modern** / **awful**)

4 **A** Your son looks very much like you – he has your ______________ eyes. (**dark** / **big**)
B Do you think so? I think he looks more like my husband.

5 **A** Are you looking for something?
B Yes. I've lost a ______________ scarf. Have you seen it? (**silk** / **long** / **black**)

6 **A** We used to live in a ______________ house near the river. (**wooden** / **beautiful** / **old**)
B How nice. It must have been really peaceful.

7 **A** I just arrived on the flight from Mexico City, but my suitcase hasn't arrived.
B Can you describe it?
A It's a ______________ case. (**black** / **leather** / **small**)

8 **A** Ever since Simon came back from Bangkok he's been cooking me ______________ curries. (**delicious** / **Thai**)
B Lucky you! I love curries.

9 **A** What does Adam's wife look like?
B She's very slim and she has ______________ hair. (**brown** / **curly** / **short**)

10 **A** I'm going to wear my ______________ shirt to the party. (**new** / **striped**)
B Good idea. It really looks good on you.

activation

c Describe three items that you own, e.g., clothes, a car, a guitar, etc., using two or three adjectives in the correct order. Use the frame to help you.

item	adjectives	description
bag	*beautiful, leather, brown*	*I have a beautiful brown leather bag that I bought in Italy last summer.*

American English File 2nd edition Teacher's Book 4 Photocopiable © Oxford University Press 2014

3A GRAMMAR narrative tenses

a Read the first part of the story and find examples of each tense below.

1 the past perfect *had ended* ____________ ____________

2 the past perfect continuous ____________ ____________ ____________ ____________

3 the past continuous ____________ ____________ ____________ ____________

The most embarrassing moment of my life (Richard, Austin)

Part 1

When I was about nine years old, I used to go to the movies every Saturday morning – in those days it was very popular. After the movie had ended, I would go to a toy shop and look at model planes and trains, and sometimes I bought them with the money that I had been carefully saving. One day after the movie, I went to a big department store to look at the model planes they had. I didn't buy anything, but as I was leaving a very large man grabbed my arm violently and accused me of shoplifting. The man said that he was a store detective. Because I had been concentrating on the toys, I hadn't noticed that he had been watching me. He made me empty my pockets and he went through my coat, searching for stolen goods, even though I told him very clearly that I had only been looking. Of course he didn't find anything, but by this time several people had stopped to see what was happening. I felt very embarrassed and humiliated that so many people were looking at me, and I was very glad to leave the store when it was all over.

b Complete the second part of the story with the correct form of the verbs in parentheses: simple past, past continuous, past perfect, or past perfect continuous.

Part 2

An hour or so later, when I [1] *was having* (**have**) lunch with my family at home, my father [2] ____________ (**ask**) me about the movie. I then [3] ____________ (**mention**) that I [4] ____________ (**look**) at toys in a department store when a store detective [5] ____________ (**accuse**) me of shoplifting and [6] ____________ (**search**) me in the middle of the store. My father [7] ____________ (**make**) me repeat what I [8] ____________ (**say**), and then immediately [9] ____________ (**jump up**) from the table. Without either of us having finished our lunch, he [10] ____________ (**make**) me get in the car. I [11] ____________ (**never see**) my father so angry! He [12] ____________ (**drive**) quickly to the store, [13] ____________ (**park**) outside, and took me to where the incident [14] ____________ (**take place**). He then demanded to see the manager and the store detective. When the manager [15] ____________ (**come**), my father [16] ____________ (**start**) shouting at him and he told him that I [17] ____________ (**never steal**) anything in my life. He [18] ____________ (**make**) the manager and store detective apologize to me for having accused me of shoplifting and for embarrassing me. But the thing is, I [19] ____________ (**find**) this scene even more embarrassing than the first one, especially because I could see that a lot of customers [20] ____________ (**stop**) and [21] ____________ (**watch**) us!

activation

c Work with a partner.

Student A: Cover the text. Try to remember what happened to Richard in Part 1.

Student B: Cover the text. Try to remember what happened to Richard in Part 2.

3B GRAMMAR adverbs and adverbial phrases

a Put the adverbs in the best place in the dialogue.

GARY So, what did you think of the game?

CRAIG [1]Even though they lost, I think San Francisco played *well* again *tonight*. (**well** / **tonight**)

JOHN [2]Craig, do you mean that? (**really**) I thought they were awful. (**absolutely**)

CRAIG [3]I suppose you think Minnesota played. (**well**)

JOHN [4]No, I don't. Minnesota plays these days. (**unfortunately** / **never** / **well**) But they deserved to win.

CRAIG [5]But you must admit that Minnesota was lucky. (**incredibly**)

GARY [6]Craig, do you have anything good to say about Minnesota? (**ever**)

JOHN [7]Minnesota was lucky with their second touch down. (**very** / **to be honest**)

CRAIG [8]Come on, John, Minnesota was lucky with both the first and second touch downs! (**extremely**)

GARY [9]I thought both teams played (**personally** / **badly**), but at the end of the day, Craig, I'd say Minnesota was better in the second half. (**a little** / **especially**)

JOHN [10]Well, Minnesota is playing New England, so let's see how they do. (**next** / **there**)

b Complete the dialogue with the correct adverbs from the list.

~~absolutely~~ actually always angrily a little badly earlier that day here in 15 minutes incredibly naturally obviously quickly slowly well

DIRECTOR Jason, that was [1]*absolutely* marvelous, but you've got to get to the center of the stage.

JASON But I have to wait for Tanya to finish her line and she's doing it too [2]__________.

TANYA Well, I could try saying it more [3]__________ if you want me to.

DIRECTOR Yes, could you? Now, Jason, remember when Tanya tells you she's going to marry Henry, you know about it, because you heard them talking in the park [4]__________, so you aren't at all surprised.

JASON Well, [5]__________ I know about it, but I thought maybe I should pretend at first that I didn't know.

DIRECTOR No, we want to see your emotion! You reacted very calmly, but [6]__________ you're not a calm person at all. I want you to react [7]__________, OK? Now the next scene. Sally, you were great. But, when you've finished reading Tanya's letter, when you're on the last couple of lines, pause [8]__________ and look up at the audience. Let them feel how [9]__________ you've been treated by her.

SALLY Do you want me to cry? I am [10]__________ good at crying.

DIRECTOR Not [11]__________, not in this scene. Look out at the audience.

TANYA Can I just ask why you [12]__________ ask me to play horrible characters?

DIRECTOR Because you do it so [13]__________, darling. It just comes [14]__________ to you. OK everyone, take a break and come back [15]__________.

activation

c Write five sentences using the adverbs. Then compare your ideas with a partner.

1 gradually __________
2 incredibly __________
3 fortunately __________
4 sadly __________
5 intelligently __________

American English File 2nd edition Teacher's Book 4 Photocopiable © Oxford University Press 2014

4A GRAMMAR future perfect and continuous

a Complete the dialogues with the verbs in parentheses in the future perfect or future continuous.

1 **A** I'm really looking forward to our trip to Paris on Friday.
B Me, too! This time tomorrow we*'ll be getting on* (**get on**) the plane, and we __________ (**not think**) about work!

2 **A** Do you think you __________ still __________ (**work**) here in ten years?
B Probably. But I hope I __________ (**be promoted**) to head of the department by then.

3 **A** Why are you walking so fast?
B If we don't hurry, by the time we get to the station, the train __________ (**leave**).

4 **A** Oh, no! My car won't start, and I need to pick up a friend at the airport.
B You can borrow mine. I __________ (**not use**) it today.

5 **A** Do you think it's too late to call Hilary?
B No, it's only 11 o'clock. Knowing her, she __________ (**not go**) to bed yet. She __________ still __________ (**watch**) TV.

6 **A** Is this your son's final year at college?
B Yes, by this time next year he __________ (**graduate**), and he __________ (**look for**) for a job.

7 **A** Shall I make some soup or something for your parents when they arrive?
B Good idea! They'll be starving because they __________ (**not have**) time for lunch.

8 **A** __________ you __________ (**come**) with us to see the new Bond movie tonight?
B Sorry, I'd love to, but I still have lots of work to do.

9 **A** What time does your plane land?
B At seven in the morning. __________ you __________ (**pick me up**) from the airport?
A Of course. I always do!

10 **A** Mark and Paul are traveling around Asia. They've already been to China and Thailand.
B Wow! How many countries __________ they __________ (**visit**) by the time they get back home?

11 **A** I'm sick of all these exams.
B Yes, but just think – we __________ (**finish**) them all by Friday, we __________ (**celebrate**)!

12 **A** Tim's going to South Africa next month, isn't he?
B No, he's decided to wait until July. He __________ (**not save**) enough money until then.

activation

b Write **one** thing that you will …

1 be doing tomorrow afternoon.
2 have done by the end of next week.
3 have done a year from now.

c Work with a partner. Compare your sentences. Ask for more information.

4B GRAMMAR conditionals and future time clauses

a Circle the correct answer. Sometimes two answers are possible.

1 I'll have my cell phone with me ______.
- **a** in case you need to call me
- **b** in case you'll need to call me
- **c** in case you've needed to call me

2 Call him as soon as ______ that report.
- **a** you finish
- **b** you've finished
- **c** you'll finish

3 I'll play soccer with you when ______.
- **a** I've had my dinner
- **b** I'll have my dinner
- **c** I have my dinner

4 I'm not going to go to the party unless ______.
- **a** you'll go too
- **b** you go too
- **c** you've gone too

5 Could you get me some milk if ______?
- **a** you'll go to the store
- **b** you go to the store
- **c** you're going to the store

6 If the weather ______, we'll go for a walk.
- **a** will have improved
- **b** will improve
- **c** improves

7 I won't tell my boss I'm leaving ______.
- **a** until I find a new job
- **b** until I'm finding a new job
- **c** until I've found a new job

8 If I don't have breakfast, ______.
- **a** I'll be hungry all morning
- **b** I'm hungry all morning
- **c** I'll be being hungry all morning

9 Please come in quietly because ______.
- **a** we'll be sleeping when you arrive
- **b** we'll sleep when you arrive
- **c** we're sleeping when you arrive

10 Take a jacket in case ______ later.
- **a** it'll have got cold
- **b** it's getting cold
- **c** it gets cold

11 Their flight was delayed, so they ______ back until after midnight.
- **a** 'll be
- **b** won't be
- **c** 'll have been

12 We're going to have a picnic tomorrow unless ______.
- **a** it rains
- **b** it will be raining
- **c** it's raining

13 I ______ book our flights until we've found a hotel.
- **a** don't
- **b** am not going to
- **c** won't

14 If you want to improve your spoken English, ______.
- **a** you'll have to practice
- **b** you have to practice
- **c** you've had to practice

15 Come and say goodbye tomorrow ______.
- **a** before you'll leave
- **b** before you've left
- **c** before you leave

15

11–15 Excellent. You can use conditionals and future time clauses very well.
8–10 Good. But check the rules in the Grammar Bank (Student Book *page139*) for any questions that you got wrong.
0–7 This is difficult for you. Read the rules in the Grammar Bank again (Student Book *page139*). Then ask your teacher for another photocopy and do the exercise again at home.

activation

b Complete the sentences with your own ideas. Then compare your ideas with a partner.

1 As soon as I get home, I ______________________.
2 If I don't have time for breakfast ______________________.
3 I'm not going to buy a new phone until ______________________.
4 When my English is better ______________________.
5 I'll stay in tonight unless ______________________.
6 I always ______________ in case ______________.

American English File 2nd edition Teacher's Book 4 Photocopiable © Oxford University Press 2014

5A GRAMMAR unreal conditionals

a Complete the sentences with the correct form of the verbs in parentheses, using second or third conditionals.

1 They met in Paris at a conference.

If they *hadn't gone* to the conference in Paris, they *wouldn't have met*. (**not go** / **not meet**)

2 The curry is a little tasteless. I should have put more spices in it.

If I __________ more spices in the curry, it __________ better. (**put** / **taste**)

3 I'm not very happy in my current job. Maybe I should quit and look for another.

If I __________ another job, I might __________ happier. (**find** / **be**)

4 We got wet because you wouldn't take the bus. You wanted to walk.

We __________ wet if we __________ the bus. (**not get** / **take**)

5 Don't swim in that river; there might be crocodiles.

If I __________ you, I __________ in that river because there might be crocodiles. (**be** / **not swim**)

6 Laura fell in love with Tom. She left Liam.

Laura __________ Liam if she __________ in love with Tom. (**not leave** / **not fall**)

7 He used the stolen credit card at a hotel, so the police found him.

If he __________ the stolen credit card at a hotel, the police __________ him. (**not use** / **not find**)

8 They don't have enough money to buy a new car.

They __________ a new car if they __________ afford one. (**buy** / **can**)

9 We didn't go on the Ferris wheel because the line was too long.

We __________ on the Ferris wheel, if the line __________ so long. (**go** / **not be**)

10 My husband and I both work, so we can pay all the bills.

If we __________, we __________ to pay all the bills. (**not work** / **not be able**)

11 I didn't know you wanted to go to the concert. I didn't buy you a ticket.

I __________ you a ticket if I __________ that you wanted to go to the concert. (**buy** / **know**)

12 Nicola is overweight because she doesn't get any exercise.

Nicola __________ so overweight if she __________ some exercise. (**be** / **get**)

activation

b Cover the sentences. Look at the pictures and try to remember the sentences.

5B GRAMMAR structures after *wish*

a Complete the sentences with *would* / *wouldn't* and a verb from the list.

~~leave~~ let clean stop raining do not borrow not make not wear

Rachel

1 I wish my mom *would leave* me alone! She's always interfering with what I do.

2 I wish my brother ________ my things. He never puts them back.

Rachel

Frankie

3 I wish it ________! Then we could go out and play baseball.

4 I wish mom and dad ________ me have a dog. Then I could take him for walks.

Frankie

Mr. Taylor

5 I wish the kids ________ their homework without me having to help them.

6 I wish my wife ________ me eat salad every day. I'd rather have fries and a burger!

Mr. Taylor

Mrs. Taylor

7 I wish the children ________ their bedrooms. Then I wouldn't have to do it!

8 I wish my husband ________ that old jacket! He looks awful in it.

Mrs. Taylor

b Complete the sentences with a verb from the list in the simple past or past perfect.

be earn have ~~not argue~~ not be not shout not tell try on

1 **Rachel:** I wish I *hadn't argued* with Lilly and Sophie. Now I have no one to go out with.

2 **Rachel:** I wish I ________ mom and dad about my grades. Now they're worried I won't get into college.

3 **Frankie:** I wish I ________ taller. Then I could be on the basketball team.

4 **Frankie:** I wish I ________ the latest version of this game. The one I've got is two years old!

5 **Mr. Taylor:** I wish we ________ more money. Then we could have a bigger house.

6 **Mr. Taylor:** I wish I ________ these pants before buying them. They're too tight.

7 **Mrs. Taylor:** I wish I ________ at my boss yesterday. Now he won't promote me.

8 **Mrs. Taylor:** I wish everything ________ so expensive. Then we could save for a vacation.

activation

c Write three sentences beginning *I wish*: one with simple past, one with past perfect, and one with person + *would*.

American English File 2nd edition Teacher's Book 4 Photocopiable © Oxford University Press 2014

6A GRAMMAR gerunds and infinitives

a Complete the sentences with the verbs in parentheses in the infinitive (with or without *to*) or the gerund (-ing).

1 I learned *to speak* French when I was in school. (**speak**)
2 Would you like __________ a movie tonight? (**see**)
3 Laura's mother lets her __________ when she wants. (**go out**)
4 I can't afford __________ a vacation this year. (**take**)
5 It's getting late. We'd better __________ much longer. (**not stay**)
6 I'm going to keep on __________ until 8:00 tonight. (**work**)
7 What are you planning __________ to the party? (**wear**)
8 Would you rather __________ in the country or in a town? (**live**)
9 I couldn't help __________ when my brother fell off his bicycle. (**laugh**)
10 Did you manage __________ the report before the meeting? (**finish**)
11 We're really looking forward to __________ you again. (**see**)
12 If I tell you a secret, do you promise __________ anybody? (**not tell**)
13 My boss made me __________ late last night. (**work**)
14 Since I've moved abroad I really miss __________ my friends. (**see**)
15 Would you like me __________ you with the dinner? (**help**)
16 I don't mind __________. I'm not in a hurry. (**wait**)
17 Sorry, you aren't allowed __________ here. (**park**)
18 We need to practice __________ before the oral exam. (**speak**)
19 I like __________ early in the morning in the summer. (**get up**)
20 Monica might __________ tomorrow. She's sick. (**not come**)
21 I love __________ time with my grandparents. (**spend**)
22 Will you be able __________ me a ride to work tomorrow? (**give**)

b Complete the sentences with the verbs in parentheses in the gerund or the infinitive with *to*.

1 You forgot *to buy* the milk. (**buy**)
2 Could you try __________ late tomorrow? (**not be**)
3 The sheets on this bed are dirty. They need __________. (**change**)
4 Don't you remember __________ his wife at the company party? (**meet**)
5 I'll never forget __________ in New York for the first time. (**arrive**)
6 I think you need __________ the irregular verbs. (**review**)
7 Did you remember __________ James about the meeting tomorrow? (**tell**)
8 If the computer doesn't work, try __________ it off and on again. (**turn**)

25–30	**Excellent.** You can use gerunds and infinitives very well.
16–24	**Very good.** But check the rules in the **Grammar Bank** (Student Book *page142*) for any questions that you got wrong.
0–15	**This is difficult for you.** Read the rules in the **Grammar Bank** again (Student Book *page142*). Then ask your teacher for another photocopy and do the exercise again at home.

activation

c Write sentences that are true for you, using the prompts. Compare your ideas with a partner. Ask him / her for more details.

1 something you learned to do when you were a child
2 something your parents didn't let you do when you were younger
3 a place you remember visiting
4 a person you enjoy spending time with
5 something you often forget to do
6 something that you try not to do

6B GRAMMAR *used to, be used to, get used to*

a Circle the correct form.

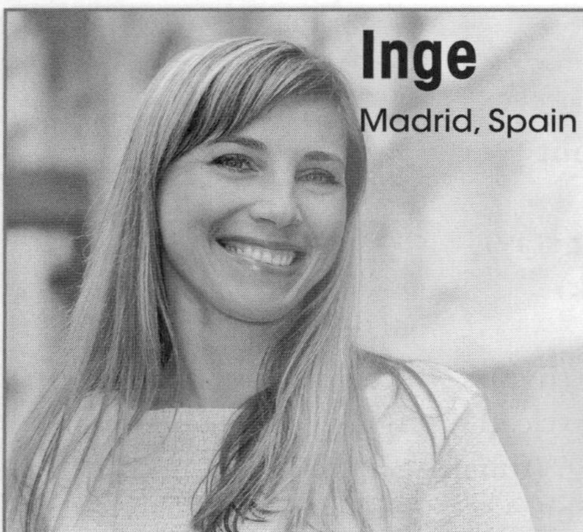

Inge
Madrid, Spain

I come from Germany, and I [1]**used to live / am used to living** in the north, in Hamburg, but then I moved to Madrid about five years ago. I had to [2]**be used to / get used to** having lunch very late, at about 2:00 p.m., and dinner as late as 9:00 or 10:00 p.m. I love the weather in Spain – there are more sunny days and it's a lot warmer. In Germany, things [3]**usually / use to** happen exactly on time, but here things are much more relaxed. I like that, too. The only thing I really miss is the bread! I [4]**was used to being able / was used to be able** to choose from between 20 or 30 different kinds of bread, but here it's more like two or three, and white, not whole wheat. And sometimes I have problems with noisy neighbors, especially at night. That never [5]**used to be / was used to being** a problem in Hamburg. People there [6]**usually go / are used to going** to bed earlier.

b Complete the text with *used to*, *am used to*, *get used to*, or *usually*.

Jeremy
São Paulo, Brazil

I [1]*used to* live in St Louis, Missouri, but I married a Brazilian woman and now I live in San Paulo, Brazil. I've been here for six years now, so I [2]__________ the lifestyle. Life is more hectic here than in Missouri. Brazilian people socialize more than the people do where I grew up, and I really enjoy that. I had to [3]__________ eating lots of rice and beans with spicy chili sauce, which you can find everywhere in San Paulo. In the US, I [4]__________ eat spicy food once or twice a month, and now I [5]__________ have it once or twice a week! I also had to [6]__________ the big city traffic. There can be traffic jams on the highways for miles. But now I [7]__________ taking the subways and buses. I can take public transportation anywhere I need to go. It was also very hard for me to [8]__________ the dialect they speak in San Paulo. I still sometimes have to ask people to repeat things. The only thing I can't [9]__________ are the sports. I know, soccer is supposed to be the best sport in the world, but I miss baseball! In the US, I [10]__________ play soccer, but it was baseball season I really loved. Still, I do enjoy a good soccer game, and Brazil is a very exciting place to be a soccer fan!

c Complete the text with a verb from the list in the correct form.

Neil and Shirley
New York City, US

be enjoy stay up ~~live~~ see

We used to [1]*live* in England, but we've been living in New York City, since 2010. We're used to [2]__________ here now, but at first it was quite hard. In England, we lived in the country, and when we first moved into our apartment in New York, I just couldn't get used to [3]__________ cars and buildings instead of trees, but now it's not a problem. We love the energy of the city. Although we speak the same language, there are still some things here that are strange. People here usually [4]__________ really late. The streets are still busy well past midnight, which we still haven't gotten used to. Summer doesn't feel right either – I haven't gotten used to [5]__________ blue sky and sunny days, rather than our rainy English weather!

activation

d Complete the sentences with information about your life. Compare your answers with a partner.

1 I usually ____________________.
2 I used to ____________________.
3 I'm used to ____________________.
4 I'm not used to ____________________.
5 It's difficult to get used to ____________________.
6 I didn't use to ____________________.

 Photocopiable © Oxford University Press 2014

7A GRAMMAR past modals

a Complete the dialogues. Rewrite the phrases in parentheses using *might (not) have*, *must have*, or *couldn't have* + past participle.

1 A Why is there so much traffic today?
B I don't know. There *must have been* an accident. (**Maybe there was**)

2 A Can you move your leg?
B No, it hurts too much. I think I __________ it. (**Maybe I have broken it**)

3 A Look! The gate's open and the dog has gone.
B Oh, no! We __________ it open when we went out. (**I'm sure we left it open**)

4 A Oh, no, the cake's burning!
B You __________ too high. (**You definitely turned the oven on**)

5 A I can't find the milk. We __________ it all. (**I'm sure we didn't drink it**)
B Yes, you're right. It must be in there somewhere.

6 A Where's Jeremy? He should be here.
B He __________ the email about the meeting. (**Maybe he didn't see**)

7 A Ellen passed all her exams with high grades!
B Wow! She __________ really hard. (**I'm sure she worked**)

8 A Mom, I'm going to play soccer now.
B What? You __________ all of your homework. (**It's impossible you've finished**)

9 A We didn't see Dan and Sarah at the concert.
B They __________ tickets. I think the concert was sold out. (**Maybe they weren't able to get**)

10 A I called you earlier, but I got your voicemail.
B Sorry. I __________ by mistake. (**I'm sure I turned it off**)

b Complete the sentences with *should* / *shouldn't have* and the past participle of a verb from the list.

break up come keep ~~take~~ tell use wait wear

1 We're lost. I knew we *should have taken* the second exit at the rotary!
2 This tastes really spicy. You __________ so much chili.
3 You __________ with James. He was such a nice guy.
4 The concert was amazing. You __________ with us.
5 Jim's already gone? I don't believe it – he __________ for us.
6 I'm afraid we can't exchange the jacket now. You __________ the receipt.
7 You __________ us that you were in the hospital. We would have visited you.
8 I __________ these jeans. They really don't look good on me.

activation

c Write **four** dialogues of two lines using *must have*, *might have*, *could(n't) have*, and *should(n't)*.

7B GRAMMAR verbs of the senses

a Complete the dialogue with *smells*, *smells like*, or *smells as if*.

Customer	I'm looking for a perfume for my wife that [1] *smells* nice and fresh.
Assistant	What about this one? It [2] ___________ very flowery.
Customer	No, I don't like it. It [3] ___________ it's for an older woman.
Assistant	Try this one then – it's called "Paris."
Customer	That's very nice. It [4] ___________ roses.

Complete the dialogue with *feels*, *feels like*, or *feels as if*.

Assistant	It's very good quality and it [5] ___________ very smooth. Touch it and see.
Tourist	Hmm, yes. It [6] ___________ silk. Is it silk?
Assistant	No, it's cotton, but it [7] ___________ it's made of silk.
Tourist	The material [8] ___________ very soft. I like it.

Complete the dialogue with *tastes*, *tastes like*, or *tastes as if*.

Woman 1	Try a piece of this. It [9] ___________ delicious.
Woman 2	Mmm. This one [10] ___________ the cakes my grandma used to make.
Woman 1	It's very nice. It [11] ___________ there's a little bit of orange in there.
Woman 2	That's right! And it [12] ___________ much better than the store-bought cakes.

Complete the dialogue with *look*, *look like*, or *look as if*.

Woman	You shouldn't have said you wanted to come if you didn't.
Man	Why do you say that?
Woman	You [13] ___________ you are totally bored.
Man	I did want to come. It's just that they all [14] ___________ fine to me.
Woman	Even the ones that make me [15] ___________ I'm 60 years old?
Man	OK, those ones do [16] ___________ a little old fashioned.
Woman	And these ones that [17] ___________ something a 13-year-old would wear?
Man	They [18] ___________ OK to me.
Woman	Oh, you're so helpful.

Complete the dialogue with *sound(s)*, *sound(s) like*, or *sound(s) as if*.

Engineer	Wait! You're coming in too soon. It [19] ___________ wrong.
Guitarist	It [20] ___________ fine to me.
Engineer	No, it [21] ___________ you're rushing in.
Guitarist	Well, how should it sound?
Engineer	It should [22] ___________ an early 80s rock band, remember?

activation

b Practice the dialogues with a partner. Then cover the dialogues and try to act them out from memory.

American English File 2nd edition Teacher's Book 4 Photocopiable © Oxford University Press 2014

8A GRAMMAR the passive

a Complete the sentences by putting the verbs in parentheses into the correct form of the passive.

1 Three men were arrested this evening and *will be questioned* by police tomorrow morning. (**question**)
2 Oh, no. My bike isn't here! It must __________. (**steal**)
3 Right now, three suspects __________ by the police. (**interrogate**)
4 The accident happened because the car __________ at 120 mph. (**drive**)
5 The fake goods __________ when the truck __________ at the border. (**discover, stop**)
6 Strong measures must __________ to reduce the amount of crime in the city. (**take**)
7 People who __________ shoplifting often turn out to have some kind of psychological problem. (**catch**)
8 The town hall __________ again – someone has painted graffiti over the walls. It's the third time this year. (**vandalize**)
9 As soon as we got home we could see that the kitchen window __________ and that there were two men in the living room. (**break**)
10 Police are worried that a lot of tourists __________ next weekend during the carnival. (**rob**)
11 In the past, people used __________ to prison for speaking out against the government. (**send**)

b Complete the newspaper report with the verbs in parentheses in the passive. Add any other necessary words, e.g., *to* or *that*.

Investigation after neighborhood incident

Police have begun an inquiry after a fight broke out between several people on North Street, in Baltimore.
The fight [1] *is believed to* (**believe**) have started in the early hours of Friday morning at an address near the corner of North Street. It [2] __________ (**think**) the fight started after a car was damaged by one of the men.
At least one of the men involved [3] __________ (**say**) have been armed. Three men remain in the hospital and are being treated for injuries, which [4] __________ (**understand**) be the result of the fight.
It [5] __________ (**expect**) one man will be released from the hospital later today.

Five men, who [6] __________ (**think**) be from the Washington DC area, and are aged between 21 and 32, have been arrested. The police are asking anyone who witnessed the incident to contact them urgently. All information will be treated confidentially.

activation

c Choose one of the headlines below and write a short news article in about 100 words.

- Vandals attack cars in supermarket parking lot
- Two men escape from prison van
- Armed men steal $50,000 from post office
- Robbery at town center jeweler's
- Mugger finally caught

8B GRAMMAR reporting verbs

a Complete each sentence with the correct form of the verb in parentheses.

1 A Remind me _to book_ a taxi to the airport. (**book**)
  B We don't need one, Andy's offered ________ us a ride. (**give**)
2 A Hi, Tom. I'm surprised to see you here. I didn't think you liked opera.
  B I don't, but Camila persuaded me ________ tonight. (**come**)
3 A Have the police found the men that robbed the supermarket?
  B Apparently, they've arrested one man, but he denies ________ anything to do with it. (**have**)
4 A I've always regretted ________ to college when I was younger. (**not go**)
  B Well, it's never too late. Why don't you apply?
5 A Have the kids been arguing again? Chen's really upset, but he refuses ________ me why. (**tell**)
  B Oh, Harry's accused Chen of ________ one of his toys, and now they aren't speaking to each other. (**break**)
6 A Where are you going on vacation this year?
  B We haven't decided yet. Keiko suggested ________ on a cruise, but I always get seasick. (**go**)
7 A Someone broke into the car and stole my laptop while I was in the supermarket.
  B I warned you ________ it in the car. Have you reported it to the police? (**not leave**)
8 A There's a funny smell in the kitchen.
  B That's because your dad insisted on ________ curry for dinner and he burned it. (**make**)

b Complete the sentences using the reporting verb in parentheses and a verb from the list.

come ~~cook~~ eat forget keep lose clean try

1 Adam _offered to cook_ dinner for everyone. (**offer**)
2 Andy ________________ his room at the weekend. (**promise**)
3 Sofia ________________ to call. (**apologize**)
4 Bill ________________ his father ________________ all of his money in the bank. (**advise**)
5 Kathy ________________ the new pizza place. (**suggest**)
6 Amir ________________ all of the chocolates. (**admit**)
7 Mike ________________ me ________________ to the theater with him. (**invite**)
8 Jamie ________________ us ________________ the game. (**blame**)

activation

c Think of a time when you…

- received some good advice. _My sister advised me to take a class to improve my computer skills._
- apologized to someone.
- offered to help someone.
- made a suggestion.
- were blamed for something you didn't do.
- regretted something you did / didn't do.

Make sentences using reported speech. Then compare your sentences with your partner.

American English File 2nd edition Teacher's Book 4 Photocopiable © Oxford University Press 2014

9A GRAMMAR clauses of contrast and purpose

a Match 1–10 with a–j to make complete sentences.

1 [g] They went to Boston for…
2 [ ] She flew to São Paulo to…
3 [ ] Although Josh played really well,…
4 [ ] We downloaded a travel app so that…
5 [ ] Despite losing the first set,…
6 [ ] Even though I wasn't feeling very well,…
7 [ ] I took a taxi so as not to…
8 [ ] He went for a walk in spite of…
9 [ ] We left early in order to…
10 [ ] The men went out fishing in spite of…

a be late.
b the rough water.
c the fact that it was raining.
d avoid the traffic.
e I still went to work.
f she won the match.
g ~~a weekend break.~~
h he lost in the end.
i we would know the best things to see.
j visit her brother.

b Rewrite the sentences using the words in parentheses so that both sentences mean the same.

1 In spite of the cold weather, the barbecue was a success. (although)
Although the weather was cold, the barbecue was a success.

2 A lot of companies have reduced staff numbers so that they can save money. (in order to)
______________________________.

3 Even though the flight was long, she felt great when she arrived in New York. (despite)
______________________________.

4 Nick didn't tell Louisa the truth because he didn't want to hurt her feelings. (so as)
______________________________.

5 I bought the shoes in spite of the fact they were ridiculously expensive. (even though)
______________________________.

6 The company has a big market share even though they do very little advertising. (in spite of)
______________________________.

7 They had to leave the hotel early. If not, they would have missed their train. (so that)
______________________________.

8 She didn't get the job in spite of being a strong candidate. (though)
______________________________.

activation

c Complete the sentences with your own ideas. Then compare your ideas with a partner.

1 Sara is learning English so that *she can get a job in the US*.
2 My husband isn't making very good progress in English even though ______________.
3 Nicola watches movies in English to ______________.
4 Jan passed his English test despite ______________.
5 Our English teacher took us to New York for the weekend so that ______________.

d Write two true sentences about yourself and learning English. Use expressions of contrast and purpose. Then compare your ideas with a partner.

 Photocopiable © Oxford University Press 2014

9B GRAMMAR uncountable and plural nouns

a Circle the correct option.

1

Daniel! Bertha! I want to see you out of your [1]**pajama / pajamas** and in [2]**a jeans / some jeans** and a T-shirt in two minutes – OK? Your breakfast is on the table. The news [3]**says / say** there's been an accident and the police [4]**has / have** closed the highway. The traffic [5]**is / are** sure to be bad, so hurry up!

2

OK, everybody, listen, I have [6]**a / some** very good news. You'll remember that we did [7]**a / some** research about new sports [8]**equipment / equipments** for Central Arenas. Well, we're going to be doing [9]**a business / business** with them! We'll be organizing a party for the [10]**staff / staffs** to celebrate.

3

So, Kevin, Economics [11]**is / are** what you did in college, and athletics [12]**is / are** what you spend your time doing on the weekend. But tell me about the work [13]**experience / experiences** you had this summer? What practical skills did you learn that you could you bring to this company?

4

I know what you're going to say, doctor. You're going to give me some [14]**advices / advice** about reducing stress, and tell me to take [15]**a / some** homeopathic medicine when I need to. But I read [16]**an / some** information on the Internet which said it didn't really help.

5

Bertha put [17]**that / those** scissors down – you could hurt yourself with [18]**it / them**, or scratch [19]**a / the** furniture. Have you finished your [20]**homework / homeworks**? Good, then come and help me. Daniel, stop writing and take the [21]**trash / trashes** out.

activation

b Choose four nouns from the list and write a sentence using each one. Compare your sentences with a partner.

advice cabin crew furniture information police politics trash staff

American English File 2nd edition Teacher's Book 4 Photocopiable © Oxford University Press 2014

10A GRAMMAR quantifiers

a Circle the correct form.

1 A How did the trip to the science museum go?
B It was fine. **Most** / **Most of** the students enjoyed it.

2 A What subject do you like best – physics or chemistry?
B I don't like **either of them** / **both of them**. They're **either** / **both** boring!

3 A How often do you use the library?
B Hardly ever. I can find **everything** / **all** on the Internet.

4 A When can I see you to discuss my science project?
B I'll be in my office **all day** / **every day** today. Come **any** / **all** time.

5 A How did your students do on the biology test?
B Not too badly. **They passed all.** / **They all passed.**

6 A We don't do **any** / **no** experiments in our chemistry class.
B You don't? We do something hands-on in **every** / **all** class.

7 A Did you do **all research** / **all of the research** yourself?
B Yes, I did **all** / **all of** it myself.

8 A Neither my mother **or** / **nor** father went to college.
B Really? **Both** / **Either** my parents studied law, but **either of them** / **neither of them** worked as lawyers.

b Complete the sentences with words from the list.

~~all~~ all all anyone both every every
most most of neither no none of

		quantifiers
1	Not ______ birds can fly.	*all*
2	______ kiwis nor penguins can fly.	______
3	______ country in South America, except Bolivia and Paraguay, has a coastline.	______
4	______ cars nowadays are fitted with seatbelts in the front and the back.	______
5	______ the students in my class, about 80%, live very close to the school.	______
6	There are ______ wild tigers in Africa. Some can still be found in parts of Asia.	______
7	In Ireland, ______ who is 18 or over can vote in an election.	______
8	______ Canadians speak English as their first language (77%), but some speak French.	______
9	Nocturnal animals are animals that sleep ______ day and hunt for food at night.	______
10	Alexander Graham Bell and Elisha Gray ______ invented the telephone at the same time.	______
11	The subways in New York City run ______ day of the year, including major holidays.	______
12	______ the people who survived the sinking of the Titanic are still alive today. The last survivor, Millvina Dean, died in 2009.	______

activation

c Cover the **quantifiers** column in **b**. Work with a partner and try to remember the missing words in each sentence.

10B GRAMMAR articles

a Complete the sentences with *a*, *an*, *the*, or – (no article).

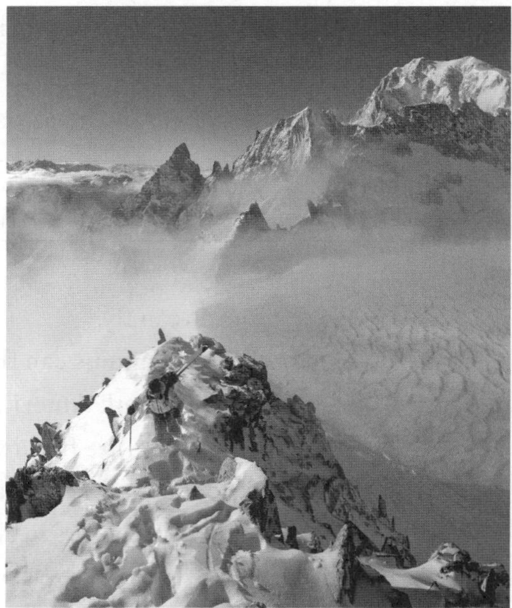

1 [1]*The* Kremlin is probably [2]_____ most famous building in [3]_____ Moscow.

2 James had [4]_____ accident while he was skiing in Austria and now he's in [5]_____ hospital.

3 [6]_____ first state in [7]_____ US where [8]_____ women could vote was Wyoming.

4 [9]_____ population of [10]_____ South Africa is approximately 47 million.

5 I went to [11]_____ college the year after I finished high school. First, I worked as [12]_____ English teacher in Seoul.

6 [13]_____ River Ebro in Spain flows into [14]_____ Mediterranean Sea.

7 We couldn't visit [15]_____ village church yesterday because there was [16]_____ wedding taking place.

8 [17]_____ quickest way to get around in New York is by [18]_____ taxi or by taking [19]_____ subway.

9 [20]_____ Lake Superior, in [21]_____ Canada, is [22]_____ biggest lake in [23]_____ world.

10 I'm not usually frightened of [24]_____ spiders, but [25]_____ spiders in [26]_____ zoo were enormous!

11 The man was sent to [27]_____ prison for eight years for robbing [28]_____ bank in Boston.

12 I love eating at [29]_____ Mario's. I think it's the best pizza restaurant in the city.

13 Whenever I'm in Seattle, I take [30]_____ bus to [31]_____ Science Museum and spend the morning looking around.

14 We spent our honeymoon in Morocco and camped in [32]_____ Sahara Desert for two nights.

15 My sister doesn't usually like [33]_____ heights, but she managed to climb to the top of [34]_____ Eiffel Tower.

16 [35]_____ Mont Blanc is [36]_____ highest mountain in [37]_____ Alps.

28–37 Excellent. You can use articles very well.
10–27 Good. But check the rules in the Grammar Bank (Student Book *page151*) for any questions that you got wrong.
0–9 This is difficult for you. Read the rules in the Grammar Bank (Student Book *page151*). Then ask your teacher for another photocopy and do the exercise again at home.

activation

b Write two paragraphs about your country and city or town. Include the following information:

Your country:
- Where is it?
- What are the most important geographical features, e.g., mountains, lakes, rivers, etc.?

Your city or town:
- Where is it?
- What are the most important buildings, tourist sites, stores, etc.?

American English File 2nd edition Teacher's Book 4 Photocopiable © Oxford University Press 2014

Review GRAMMAR AUCTION

Sentences	Price
1 Can you tell me what time it is?	______
2 Her name's Marta, isn't she?	______
3 How long have you been taking driving lessons?	______
4 She has long beautiful dark hair.	______
5 The accident happened because the driver had been drinking.	______
6 I like very much classical music.	______
7 This time tomorrow we'll have finished all our exams.	______
8 Are you going to tell them the news when they're having dinner?	______
9 I would have enjoyed the movie more if it wouldn't have had subtitles.	______
10 I wish I would have more free time!	______
11 It's getting late. We'd better to go now.	______
12 I'm not used to getting up so early.	______
13 He mustn't have seen you or he would have said hello.	______
14 It looks like if it's going to rain.	______
15 The missing man is thought that he is from Miami.	______
16 Nick insisted on paying for the meal.	______
17 Lilly is going to the hospital this afternoon for to visit her husband.	______
18 I need to buy some new furnitures for my living room.	______
19 You can have either the chocolate or vanilla ice cream. Not both.	______
20 The man was sent to the prison for ten years.	______

Mini Grammar Activity Answers

1B *the...the...* + comparatives

a **2** a **3** g **4** b **5** d **6** f **7** e **8** c

b **2** The bigger a car is, the more gasoline it uses.
3 The older you get, the wiser you become.
4 The more things people have, the more they want.
5 The hotter the weather is, the more you need to drink.
6 The more you know her, the less you like her.
7 The more slowly you cook it, the better it'll taste.
8 The more work we do now, the less we'll have to do tomorrow.

3A *so / such...that*

a **2** such a **3** so many **4** such **5** so many **6** so **7** such a **8** such **9** so much **10** so

b **2** It was such a bad movie (that) we left after half an hour.
3 The food was so disgusting (that) nobody could eat it.
4 He made so many mistakes (that) the boss fired him.
5 It was such beautiful music (that) everyone stopped to listen.
6 They were such good seats (that) we had a perfect view.
7 There was so much traffic (that) we missed our flight.
8 Joe ate so many cookies (that) he felt sick.

7A *would rather*

a **2** would rather not see **3** Would you rather have **4** would rather stay **5** would rather not do **6** would (you) rather have **7** Would (you) rather go **8** would rather not go out

b **2** I'd rather not go shopping today.
3 Would Karen rather work for herself or for a company?
4 Would you rather get takeout or go out for dinner?
5 Hamish would rather not work at night...
6 I'd rather not see my in-laws so often…

7B *as*

a **2** f **3** h **4** c **5** g **6** i **7** a **8** j **9** d **10** e

b **2** as **3** like **4** like **5** as **6** as **7** as **8** like

8A *have something done*

a **2** She's having her hair washed.
3 She's having her hair cut.
4 She's having her hair dried.
5 She's having her hair curled.

b **2** had my portrait painted
3 having my photo taken
4 are having our kitchen redecorated
5 have your blood pressure checked
6 had your fortune told
7 'm having my car fixed / 'm going to have my car fixed
8 to have my watch repaired
9 have the big tree cut down
10 have our house repainted
11 have the brakes tested
12 had a lot of new furniture delivered

9A *whatever, whenever,* etc.

a **2** Whenever **3** Whoever **4** however **5** whatever **6** wherever **7** Whenever **8** however **9** whichever **10** Whoever **11** whichever **12** wherever

b **2** b **3** a **4** d **5** c

1B MINI GRAMMAR *the...the...* + comparatives

a Match 1–8 with a–h to make complete sentences.

1 [*h*] The more dangerous the sport,...
2 [ ] The longer I waited,...
3 [ ] The more hours you do in this job,...
4 [ ] The younger you are,...
5 [ ] The older you are,...
6 [ ] The later we leave,...
7 [ ] The longer I stay in bed,...
8 [ ] The faster you drive,...

a the angrier I got.
b the easier it is to learn something.
c the more likely you are to have an accident.
d the harder it is to make new friends.
e the worse I feel.
f the more traffic there will be.
g the more you earn.
h ~~the more I enjoy it.~~

b Rewrite the sentences using *The...the...* + a comparative.

1 If we start soon we'll finish soon. *The sooner we start, the sooner we'll finish.*
2 If a car is big it uses a lot of gasoline. ______
3 When you get old you become wise. ______
4 If people have a lot of things, they want more. ______
5 If the weather is hot you need to drink more. ______
6 When you know her more you like her less. ______
7 If you cook it slowly, it'll taste good. ______
8 If we do a lot of work now, we'll have less to do tomorrow. ______

activation

c Complete the sentences with your own ideas. Then compare your ideas with a partner.

1 The more you practice your English, *the better you will get.*
2 The sooner I finish these exercises, ______.
3 The more exercise you get, ______.
4 The colder the weather is, ______.
5 The more free time I have, ______.

 Photocopiable © Oxford University Press 2014

3A MINI GRAMMAR *so / such...that*

a Complete the sentences with *so, such, so much / many,* or *such a.*

1 My briefcase is <u>*so*</u> heavy (that) I can barely pick it up.
2 It was __________ small airport (that) there were only two flights per day.
3 There were __________ people at the airport (that) we couldn't see my cousin.
4 It was __________ awful weather (that) we couldn't leave the hotel.
5 I bought __________ souvenirs in Mexico (that) I had to buy another bag.
6 The staff at the first hotel were __________ unfriendly (that) we decided not to stay there.
7 The receptionist was __________ rude man (that) most people complained to the owner.
8 They were __________ cheap tickets (that) we decided to buy them.
9 I ate __________ food at the barbecue (that) I had to lie down.
10 The service at the restaurant was __________ good (that) I left a big tip.

b Rewrite the sentences using *so, such, so much / many,* or *such a.*

1 I played badly. I lost 6–0, 6–0.
I played <u>*so badly (that) I lost 6–0, 6–0*</u>.
2 The movie was very bad. We left after half an hour.
It was ______________________________.
3 The food was disgusting. Nobody could eat it.
The food ______________________________.
4 He made a lot of mistakes. The boss fired him.
He made ______________________________.
5 The music was beautiful. Everyone stopped to listen.
It was ______________________________.
6 They were good seats. We had a perfect view.
They were ______________________________.
7 There was a lot of traffic. We missed our flight.
There was ______________________________.
8 Joe ate a lot of cookies. He felt sick.
Joe ate ______________________________.

activation

c Complete the sentences with your own ideas. Then compare your ideas with a partner.

1 It was such a hot day (that) ______________________________
______________________________.
2 She has so many clothes (that) ______________________________
______________________________.
3 I have so much work (that) ______________________________
______________________________.
4 We were so tired (that) ______________________________
______________________________.
5 They were playing such loud music (that) ______________________________
______________________________.

American English File 2nd edition Teacher's Book 4 Photocopiable © Oxford University Press 2014

7A MINI GRAMMAR *would rather*

a Complete the sentences with *would rather* and a verb from the list.

go have (x2) not do not go out not see stay ~~walk~~

1 Would you *rather walk* or go by car tonight?
2 I'm not going to the party because I ______________ my ex-boyfriend.
3 ______________ meat or fish for lunch?
4 I ______________ in a hotel than go camping this summer.
5 Most of the students ______________ homework, but they have to do it.
6 Where ______________ you ______________ lunch today, at home or at a restaurant?
7 ______________ you ______________ to the movies tomorrow instead of this evening?
8 I ______________ tonight because I'm feeling very tired.

b Rewrite the sentences using *would rather*.

1 I'd prefer to stay at home tonight. I'm exhausted.
I'd rather stay at home tonight.
2 I'd prefer not to go shopping today. The stores will be really crowded.
____.
3 Would Karen prefer to work for herself or for a company?
____?
4 Would you prefer to get takeout or go out for dinner?
____?
5 Hamish would prefer not to work at night, but he doesn't have any choice.
____.
6 I'd prefer not to see my in-laws so often, but they live nearby.
____.

activation

c Ask a partner the questions.

1 Would you rather go on vacation with friends or with your family? Why?
2 Would you rather work at home or in an office? Why?
3 Would you rather live in your town or somewhere else? Why?
4 Would you rather be an only child or have brothers and sisters? Why?

7B MINI GRAMMAR *as*

a Match 1–10 to a–j to make complete sentences.

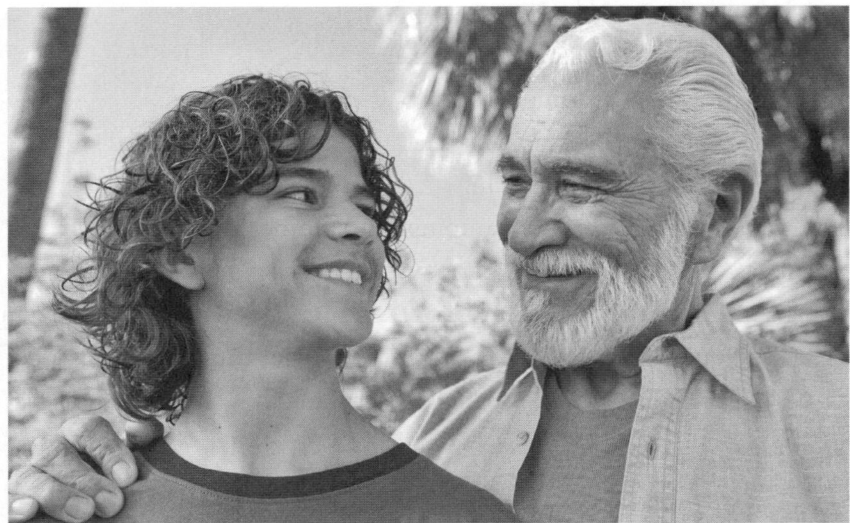

1 [b] You're nearly as tall...
2 [ ] The burglar was arrested...
3 [ ] He's very well known...
4 [ ] We'll have to use this scarf...
5 [ ] I didn't go and see that movie...
6 [ ] Because I wasn't feeling well...
7 [ ] The pasta tasted awful...
8 [ ] Turn the light off...
9 [ ] I never read that newspaper...
10 [ ] As I was coming here...

a as if it had been cooked for too long.
b ~~as me.~~
c as a bandage.
d because it's too biased.
e I met an old friend.
f just as he was leaving the house.
g because the reviews were awful.
h as a composer and conductor.
i I didn't go to work.
j as you leave.

b Complete the sentences with *like* or *as*.

1 This tastes *like* chicken, or is it turkey?
2 My brother works __________ a freelance journalist.
3 Tim looks __________ his father. They have the same mouth and nose.
4 That sounds __________ thunder. Do you think it's going to rain?
5 It isn't as cold __________ yesterday.
6 When I was camping, I had to use my sweater __________ a pillow.
7 You sound __________ if you are very tired.
8 I'm not sure what it is, but it smells __________ gasoline.

activation

c Complete the sentences with your own ideas. Then compare your ideas with a partner.

1 As I was coming out of the movies, *I met an old friend*.
2 I won't be able to go away this weekend because __________________________.
3 I haven't heard the weather forecast, but it looks as if __________________________.
4 I would love to work as __________________________.
5 I'm not as __________________ as my __________________.

American English File 2nd edition Teacher's Book 4 Photocopiable © Oxford University Press 2014

8A MINI GRAMMAR *have something done*

a Look at the pictures. What are these people having done?

straight

1 *She's having her hair straightened.*

wash

2 ______________________

cut

3 ______________________

dry

4 ______________________

curl

5 ______________________

b Complete the sentences with the correct form of *have*, the past participle, and the words in parentheses.

1 I need *to have my suit cleaned* before my cousin's wedding. (suit / clean)
2 When we were in Paris, I ______________ by a street artist. (my portrait / paint)
3 I absolutely hate ______________. I always look awful! (my photo / take)
4 We ______________ right now. (our kitchen / redecorate)
5 If you are feeling dizzy, you should ______________. (blood pressure / check)
6 Have you ever ______________? (your fortune / tell)
7 I ______________ tomorrow. Could you give me a ride to work? (my car / fix)
8 I need ______________ – it's not working well. (my watch / repair)
9 They had to ______________ in their yard. It was damaged in a storm. (the big tree / cut down)
10 We usually ______________ every five years. (our house / repaint)
11 I almost couldn't stop in time at the traffic lights today. I must ______________ tomorrow. (brakes / test)
12 Our neighbors ______________ yesterday. (a lot of new furniture / deliver)

activation

c Work with a partner. Ask and answer the questions.

1 Where do you have your hair cut?
2 Do you mind having your photo taken?
3 When was the last time you had your blood pressure checked?
4 How often do you have your eyes tested?
5 Have you ever had your portrait painted? If not, would you like to?

9A MINI GRAMMAR *whatever, whenever*, etc.

a Complete the sentences with *whatever, whichever, whoever, whenever, however*, or *wherever*.

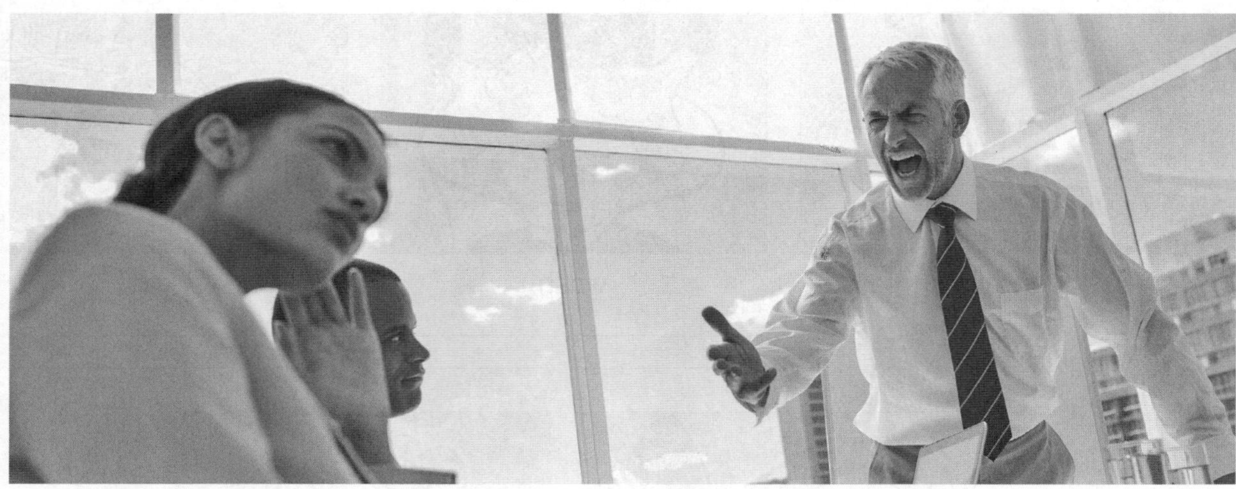

1 *Whatever* I do, my boss always finds something wrong with it.
2 __________ I see Naila, she's always in a good mood.
3 __________ broke the window must come and see me after school.
4 I'm lucky. I never put on weight __________ much I eat.
5 We've decided that we are going to go __________ happens.
6 In Thailand, people were really friendly to us __________ we went.
7 __________ I go to New York on business, I always try to see a show on Broadway.
8 I never seem to get better at tennis __________ much I practice.
9 I like both desserts, so you have __________ one you want and I'll have the other one.
10 __________ said, "It's better to be poor, but happy" was wrong!
11 We could fly or take a train to Prague, __________ is quicker.
12 I'm sure the police will find the murderer, __________ he's hiding.

b Match 1–5 to a–e to make complete sentences.

1 [*e*] I am happy to cook or go out. We'll do…
2 [ ] Whenever you have a problem,…
3 [ ] The theme park is open every day,…
4 [ ] I am going to finish this today…
5 [ ] Whoever borrowed my jacket without asking…

a whatever the weather.
b you can come and see me.
c is in big trouble!
d however long it takes.
e whichever you prefer.

activation

c Complete the sentences with your own ideas. Then compare your ideas with a partner.

1 I'll always love you, whatever *you do*.
2 However rich people are, __________.
3 You must come and see me whenever __________.
4 Let's buy this one or that one, whichever __________.
5 Wherever you go in the world, you'll always find __________.
6 You can invite whoever __________.

 Photocopiable © Oxford University Press 2014

Communicative activity instructions

Tips for using Communicative activities

We have suggested the ideal number of copies for each activity. However, you can often manage with fewer, e.g., one copy per pair instead of one per student.

When Sts are working in pairs, if possible get them to sit face to face. This will encourage them to really talk to each other, and also means they can't see each other's sheet.

If your class doesn't divide up into pairs or groups, get two Sts to share one role, or get one student to monitor, help, and correct.

Extra idea

- If some Sts finish early, they can switch roles and do the activity again, or you could get them to write some of the sentences from the activity.

Introduction Tell me about it

A pairwork activity

Sts write information about themselves. They then exchange papers with a partner and ask each other to explain the information. This is a two-page activity. Copy one page of questions and "snakes" (A and B) per student.

Language
General review of *American English File 3* grammar and vocabulary

- Put Sts in pairs, **A** and **B**, and give each student a sheet (**A** or **B**). Focus on a–c.
- Give Sts five minutes to write answers in the appropriate spaces. When they have finished, tell Sts to fold the paper in half.
- Now get Sts to exchange "snakes." Demonstrate the activity by taking a "snake" from a student and asking him / her *Why did you write...?* Ask follow-up questions, to continue the conversation.
- Sts now do the activity in pairs. Make it clear to them they have different instructions, and stress that they can ask about the information in any order. Monitor and help where necessary. Stop the activity when most Sts have asked about all their partner's information.

1A Ask me a question

A semi-controlled speaking activity

Sts practice question formation. Copy one sheet per student.

Language
Question formation

- Give out the copies. Tell Sts they have five minutes in pairs to decide what the missing words are for each question. They must **NOT** write the missing words in.
- Check answers.

Your home
1 Where **do you** live?
2 How long **have you** lived there?
3 Who **do you** live **with**?
4 What **do you** like most about your home?
5 Is **there** anything you **don't** like about your neighborhood? Why not?

Getting around
1 How **do you** usually get **to** work (or school)?
2 How long **does it** take?
3 **Do you** drive? **What** car **do you drive**?
4 **How** often **do** you **use** public transportation?
5 **What's** the best way **to** get **around** your town / city?

Free time
1 What **do you** enjoy doing in your free time?
2 **What kind** / **type** of music **do you** listen **to**?
3 How **often do you** go out during the week?
4 **What** sport(s) **do you** like playing?
5 **How much** time do you spend on social network sites every day?

Lifestyle
1 How **much** tea or coffee **do you** drink **a** day?
2 **How many** hours **do you** sleep at night?
3 What **do you** do **to** relax?
4 What do **you** do **to** keep healthy?
5 What **was** the last live event you went **to**?

Travel
1 What's **the most** beautiful place you**'ve** / **have ever** been to?
2 Where **are** you going **to go** for your next vacation?
3 **Do you** think it's better **to** travel alone **or** with other people?
4 **Do you** prefer taking vacations **at** home or abroad?
5 Have **you ever** been **to** an English-speaking country?

Family
1 **How many** people **are** there in your immediate family?
2 **Who** in your family **do you** most like talking **to**?
3 **Who do you** prefer spending time **with**? Family **or** friends?
4 How much **do you** know **about** your family tree?
5 When **was the** last time all **your** family did something together?

Childhood and school
1 Where **were you** born?
2 Which high **school did** / **do you** go **to**?
3 What **was** / **is your** best / worst subject?
4 **Have you** ever cheated on a test? **Did you** get caught?
5 What **did you** want **to** be when you were a child?

A male or female relative
1 What's **his** / **her name**?
2 How old **is he** / **she**?
3 What **does he** / **she** do?
4 What **does he** / **she** look **like**?
5 What**'s** / **is he** / **she** like?

- Sts continue choosing topics and asking and answering the questions until you feel the activity has gone on for long enough.
- Get feedback from a few pairs.
- If a pair has finished early, get them to try another topic.

1B The Island

A psychological test and free-speaking activity

Sts use their imagination to describe an experience they have on an island. They interpret each other's descriptions.

Copy one sheet per student and cut into two separate pieces: **The story** and **The interpretation**.

> **Language**
> Simple present (narrative):
> *It's a cold island. It makes me feel afraid. I start to look around me slowly.*
> *The .... the* + comparatives: *The darker the forest is, the more negative you feel about your life.*
> Vocabulary: personality

- Tell Sts that they are going to use their imagination to describe an experience they have on an island. They will describe the situation to each other, and then ask their partner to imagine the details.
- Put Sts in pairs, ideally facing each other, and give out just **the story** part, not **the interpretation**, and give them time to read it.
- Tell **As** to put their sheet face down. They have to answer **B's** questions about the island in as much detail as they can. **B** begins by reading the introduction to **A** (*"You are traveling on a boat. There is a terrible storm..."*) and then asks **A** the questions and notes **A's** answers.
- When **B** has finished, they change roles: **B** turns the sheet over, **A** asks all the questions, and takes notes of his / her answers.
- When both Sts have described their island to each other, tell Sts that this was a psychological personality test and that now they are going to interpret each other's answers. Give out the other half of the photocopied sheet: **The interpretation**.
- Give Sts time to read the interpretation and then tell them to take turns using the information to interpret their partner's answers. Encourage them to do this in as imaginative a way as possible.
- Get some quick feedback from pairs to find out if Sts agreed with the interpretation of their personality.

2A Doctor, doctor

Two role-plays

Sts take the parts of doctor / patient and review the grammar and vocabulary of the lesson. Copy one sheet per pair and cut into **A** and **B**.

> **Language**
> Present perfect: *How long have you been feeling like this?*
> Vocabulary: illness and medicine

- Put Sts in pairs, **A** and **B**, ideally facing each other. Give out the sheets. **Make sure Sts can't see each other's sheets.** If you have odd numbers, make one pair a three and have two **As** (or take part in the role-play yourself).

Extra support

- You could preteach / check the meaning and pronunciation of *alternative medicine* = non-traditional medicine; *acupuncture* = a way of treating illness or stopping pain by inserting thin needles into the body; *diagnosis* = what a doctor thinks is wrong with a patient; *homeopathy* = a system of treating diseases or conditions using very small amounts of the substance that causes the disease or condition.

- Give Sts time to read the instructions for Role-play 1. Sts should think about their role and what they are going to say. Encourage the patients and doctors to be as imaginative and inventive as possible in their questions and answers. Tell the patients they can invent a new persona (age, job, etc.).
- When Sts are ready, tell the **Bs** to begin. Give Sts time to act out the role-play. While they do this, move around the class monitoring and noting anything you might want to draw their attention to afterward.
- Repeat the process for Role-play 2, but with **A** starting. If a pair finishes early, get them to repeat the role-play, but changing roles.
- Finally, get feedback from some pairs on what the outcome of the patient / doctor conversation was.

2B Spot the difference

A pairwork information gap activity

Sts describe their pictures to each other to find twelve differences between them. Copy one sheet per pair and cut into **A** and **B**.

> **Language**
> Adjective order: *She's wearing a pair of high-heeled leather sandals.*
> *He's a tall, thin man.*
> Vocabulary: clothes and appearance

- Put Sts in pairs, **A** and **B**, ideally facing each other, and give out the sheets. **Make sure Sts can't see each other's sheets.**
- Focus on the instructions and explain that they both have a very similar picture, but there are twelve differences.
- Now get **A** to start by describing the first person on the left (*My first person is a man. He's very short and fat, and he has short, dark hair.*). **B** should listen, and ask questions if necessary, to see if there are any differences. Then **B** describes the next person.
- Sts continue in pairs. When they've described all the people and found the differences, they can finally show each other the pictures to check.
- Check the differences, correcting any mistakes with adjective order.

1 In **A** man 1 is wearing a plain black, sleeveless T-shirt; in **B** it's a short-sleeved T-shirt.
2 In **A** man 1 is wearing a baseball cap backwards; in **B** it's on the right way.
3 In **A** woman 2 is wearing a dark, striped jacket; in **B** it's dark and plain.
4 In **A** woman 2 has dark shoulder length hair; in **B** it's short.
5 In **A** man 3 is wearing a pair of tight, black cycling shorts; in **B** they're loose, black shorts.
6 In **A** man 3 is wearing patterned socks; in **B** the socks are plain.
7 In **A** woman 4 is wearing knee-high boots; in **B** they're ankle high.
8 In **A** woman 4 is wearing a sweater with a collar; in **B** the sweater has no collar.
9 In **A** man 5 is wearing jeans with holes in the knees; in **B** he's wearing jeans without holes.
10 In **A** man 5 is wearing a belt; in B he's not wearing a belt.
11 In **A** woman 6 is wearing a short knit cardigan; in **B** she's wearing a long knit cardigan.
12 In **A** woman 6 is wearing a long scarf; in **B** she's wearing a long scarf with a pattern of flowers on it.

3A Talk about it

A group-work activity

Sts are dealt cards with prompts for anecdotes. They plan what they are going to say. Copy and cut up one set of cards per group of three.

Language
Narrative tenses: simple past, past continuous, past perfect (simple and continuous)

- Put Sts in groups of three and give each group a set of cards. They must each choose two that they can talk about. Set a time limit, e.g., two minutes, for Sts to plan what they are going to say. Help Sts with the vocabulary they need.

Extra support

- Sts may want to make notes on their cards to help them tell their anecdotes.

- Suggest that each student starts with "*I'm going to tell you about a time when….*" Then Sts take turns telling their first anecdote. Monitor, help, and take notes of any misuse of narrative tenses to check at the end.
- If there is time, let each student tell three anecdotes.
- Get feedback to find out if there were any unusual / interesting stories.

Non-cut alternative

- Make one copy per pair. Put Sts into pairs and give them a few minutes to read through the cards. Tell Sts to choose two anecdotes each to tell each other. Give them a few minutes to plan what they are going to say. They then tell alternate anecdotes.

3B Tell the story

A groupwork activity

Sts describe pictures to each other and then put them in the right order to make a story. Copy one cut-up sheet per group of four.

Language
Adverbs
Narrative tenses review
Linkers

- Cut up the sheet into four strips with two pictures on each. Put Sts into groups of four. Shuffle the strips, and give Sts one each.

Extra idea

- If you have a group of three or a pair, give one or both Sts two strips.

- Tell Sts that the pictures they have tell a story. Sts have to describe their two pictures to the rest of the group (without letting them see them), and decide which order the strips go in. Tell Sts the adverbs on the picture will later be used for telling the story.
- Monitor while Sts describe their pictures. When they have finished, tell them to look at the four strips and decide if their order is right.
- Check Sts have the strips in the right order. Now tell Sts to tell the story using narrative tenses and the adverbs on each picture.
- Finally, get feedback by getting students from different groups to tell the story picture by picture.

1 obviously
2 all night
3 unfortunately
4 incredibly
5 five minutes later
6 two weeks later
7 immediately
8 In the end

Extra idea

- As a follow-up activity, get Sts to write the story in pairs.

Non-cut alternative

- Make one copy per group. Sts work together to tell the story, using all the adverbs and narrative tenses. Ask one / two groups to tell their story during feedback.

4A In 20 years

A groupwork activity

Sts review the two new future tenses by discussing predictions.

Language
Will be + gerund
Will have + past participle
It's already happening
I think it's very unlikely
will probably/definitely happen

- Put Sts into groups of three and give out the sheets. Go through the predictions and make sure Sts understand them all. Sts then discuss each one in turn and decide if they think it will happen, and if they think it will be a good thing. They then take a group vote before making a decision and moving onto the next prediction.

Extra support

- Discuss the first prediction with the whole class, eliciting opinions and giving your own opinion.

- Stop the activity when Sts have discussed all the predictions or when you think it has gone on for long enough. Get feedback from different groups, and find out which prediction Sts think is the most positive and which is the most negative.

4B Finish the sentences

A groupwork activity

Sts race to complete sentences. Copy and cut up one sheet per groups of four or five.

Language
Future time clauses

- Put Sts into groups. Give each group a set of cards, either face down or in an envelope. Ask a volunteer in each group to take notes.
- Each group picks up a card, and together they decide on a way to correctly finish the sentence. Then the note-taker writes out the sentence and takes it to the teacher who checks if it is correct. If it's correct, their group scores a point. If not, they must re-write it.
- Set a time limit, e.g., ten minutes. When the time is up, the group with the most points wins.

Extra idea

- You could do this as a competition between pairs. Give one sheet to each pair. The pair who makes the most sentences within a time limit wins.

Non-cut alternative

- Copy one sheet per pair. Set a time limit for the pair to write continuations of the sentences. When the time is up, check answers. The pair with the most correct continuations wins.

5A What would you do?

A free-speaking activity

Sts read about some extreme situations and have to choose the correct answer.

Copy one sheet per student and cut into two separate pieces: **What would you do** and **The answers**.

Language
Second conditional: *What would you do?*

- Tell Sts that they are going to look at some difficult situations and at the end of the activity, they'll find out what they should do.
- Put Sts in groups of four and give out a sheet to each group (just the **What would you do** part, not **The answers**). Give them time to read it.
- Ask Sts to discuss and agree on what the best thing to do in each situation would be. Encourage them to give as much information as possible.
- When Sts have answered the questions, hand out **The answers**. Sts read through the answers and see if they knew any of the answers.
- Get some quick feedback from the groups to find out which Sts might know what to do in each situation.

5B Wishes

A pairwork activity

Sts write their wishes in circles. They then exchange circles with a partner, and ask each other to explain the information. **This is a two-page activity**. Copy an **A** and a **B** page for each pair.

Language
wish + simple past, *would* or past perfect

- Put Sts in pairs, **A** and **B**, and give each student their corresponding sheet.
- Focus on **a** and the instructions for the circles. Point out that they each have different instructions for what to write. Make it clear that Sts should just write words in the circles, not sentences with *wish*, e.g., in **A's** circle 1, he / she should write a celebrity's name – not *I wish I could meet George Clooney*.
- Give Sts five minutes to write the answers in at least seven circles. When they have finished, focus on **b** and **c**, and tell them to fold their sheet in half (or tear off the instructions).
- Now get Sts to exchange circles. Demonstrate the activity by taking a copy from one student and asking him / her *Why did you write...?* And elicit: *Because I wish...* Ask follow-up questions to continue the conversation.
- Sts now do the activity in pairs. Tell Sts that they can ask about the information in any order. Monitor and help where necessary, correcting any errors Sts make using *wish* during feedback.

6A Gerund or infinitive?

A pairwork activity

Sts complete questions with gerunds or infinitives and then ask the questions to each other. Copy one sheet per pair and cut into **A** and **B**.

Language
Verbs + gerund or infinitive (with or without *to*)

- Put Sts in pairs, **A** and **B**, and give out the sheets. Focus on instruction **a** and explain that Sts should write in the **Verb** column on the right (not in the sentences). Give Sts time to write the verbs in, and then check answers – first **A's** and then **B's**. See key on next page.
- Focus on instruction **b**. Tell Sts to fold their sheet on the fold line, so they cannot see the verbs in the **Verb** column, and to remember the right form of the bold verb in parentheses. **A** asks **B** the questions, and then **B** asks **A** his / her questions. Encourage Sts to react to what their partner says, and ask for more information when they can.
- Monitor and correct any mistakes with gerunds and infinitives. Finally, get feedback on some of the more interesting answers.

A	B
1 living	1 having
2 speaking	2 to fix
3 to like	3 to assemble / assembling
4 doing	4 emigrating
5 eating	5 read
6 doing	6 doing
7 to worry	7 meeting
8 play	8 eating
9 to do	9 learn
10 to visit	10 studying
11 getting	11 watching
12 watching	12 to spend

6B *usually, used to, get used to*

A pairwork activity

Sts practice asking and talking about things people used to do, usually do, or could / couldn't get used to doing. Copy one sheet per pair and cut into **A** and **B**.

> **Language**
> *Did you use to...?*
> *Do you usually...?*
> *Do you think you could get used to...?*

- Put Sts into pairs, **A** and **B**, and give out the sheets. Focus on the instruction **a** and on the three questions forms. Highlight that for each prompt Sts must use the most appropriate question form. Ask an **A** student to ask the first question: *Do you usually read everything on a tablet?* Then elicit **B's** first question: *Did you use to have a favorite toy?*
- Remind Sts that after *get used to* they will need to use the gerund and highlight that the *get used to* questions need to be about something their partner doesn't already do.

Extra support

- You could elicit all the possible questions for each category before moving to the next stage.

- In pairs, Sts take turns to ask and answer the questions. Remind them that the "questioner" should show interest and ask follow-up questions wherever possible.
- Get some feedback from individual pairs.

7A Guess my verb

A groupwork activity

Sts practice using past modals by trying to guess their partner's sentences. Copy one sheet per pair and cut into **A** and **B**.

> **Language**
> Past modals: *He may have gotten lost, He couldn't have seen you, He shouldn't have done it, etc.*

- Put Sts in pairs **A** and **B**, and give out the sheets. If possible, sit **A** and **B** face to face so that they can't see each other's sheet.
- Demonstrate the activity by writing (secretly) on a piece of paper in big letters: *Jack didn't come to my party last night. He must have forgotten.* Then write the same sentences on the board like this: *Jack didn't come to my party last night. He must have* __________, and get Sts to suggest ways of finishing the sentence.
- Highlight that there are often several possibilities but they have to guess the ending you have on the piece of paper. If they say a correct sentence (but not your original ending) say, "Try again!" When they guess correctly say, "That's right." Finally, show them the sentence you wrote on the piece of paper.
- Focus on the instructions and ask Sts to look at their sentences. Explain that half of their sentences have blanks, and that the missing words are ***have* + a verb phrase**. Where **A** has sentence blanks, **B** has the completed sentence and vice versa. The aim of the activity is for Sts to figure out the missing verbs by making guesses. They should try guessing until they say the exact phrase their partner has. Remind Sts they have a maximum of three guesses. If the guess is almost right, e.g., they say *gone home early* rather than *left early,* then Sts can help each other.
- Give Sts a few minutes to read their sentences and try to think of possible verbs to fill their blanks.
- Student **A** begins by trying to guess the missing verbs in his / her first sentence. Emphasize that when Sts make their guesses, they should say the whole sentence. If the verb is wrong, **B** should say: *Try again*, and **A** has another guess. When **A** correctly guesses the missing verbs, he / she writes it in the blank.
- Now **B** tries to guess his / her first verbs, etc.

Extra challenge

- At the end of the activity, you could get Sts to turn over the sheets and try to recall the verbs by reading out the sentences one by one. Get them to say "blank" or make a noise where the missing verbs are, and let the class call them out.

7B Spot the difference

A pairwork information gap activity

Sts describe their pictures to each other to find nine differences between them. Copy one sheet per pair and cut into **A** and **B**.

> **Language**
> Present continuous: *She's typing with her right hand.*
> Vocabulary: clothes and appearance: *She's wearing jeans.*
> Verbs describing body language: *She's staring angrily.*

- Put Sts in pairs, **A** and **B**, ideally facing each other and give out the sheets. Make sure Sts can't see each other's sheets.
- Focus on the instructions and explain that they both have a very similar picture, but there are nine differences.
- Now get **A** to start by describing the first person on the left (*My first person is a woman. She looks nervous and biting her nails.*) **B** should listen, and ask questions, to find out if there are any differences. If there is a difference, both Sts should write them down.
- Sts continue in pairs. When they've described all the people and found the differences, they can finally show each other the pictures to check.
- Check the differences.

From left to right
1 Woman 1: In **A** she is biting her nails; In **B** she is biting a pencil.
2 Woman 2: In **A** she is leaning forward; In **B** she is sitting up.
3 Woman 3: In **A** her legs aren't crossed; in **B** her legs are crossed at the ankles.
4 Woman 3: In **A** she is facing forward, but looking at the man on the phone out of the corner of her eye; in **B** she is looking at the man on the phone and frowning.
5 Man 1: In **A** he's making a fist with his left hand; In **B** he is scratching his head with his left hand.
6 Woman 4: In **A** she has her arms crossed across her chest; in **B** she's stretching, you can see the palms of both her hands.
7 Woman 4: In **A** she is asleep; in **B** she is awake.
8 Man 2: In **A** he is asleep; in **B** he's staring to his left.
9 Man 2: In **A** he has his arm around his wife. His right hand is on her shoulder; in **B** both his hands are behind his head, his elbows are raised.

8A Good laws?

A group speaking activity

Sts read about laws in different countries and discuss whether they think they are good or not. They then invent some new laws they would like to see introduced in their own countries. Copy one sheet per group.

Language
Passive (all forms)
Vocabulary: crime and punishment

- Focus on the instructions and go through them. Emphasize that all these laws are real laws. Tell the Sts to read the two laws about animals and set a time limit for Sts to discuss them (you can adjust the time limit as necessary if Sts have a lot to say). When the time is up, tell them to now think of a new law related to animals. Monitor while Sts are talking, helping with vocabulary. Repeat the process for the other topics.
- Finally, get each group to explain their new law to the class. Get the other Sts to vote if they think it is a good law.

8B TV political debate

A roleplay

Sts discuss political ideas. Copy one sheet per group of four Sts and cut into **A** & **B**, and **C** & **D**.

Language
Reporting verbs: *We promise to give free Internet access to all.*
Vocabulary: media

- Divide the class into groups of four. Ideally, Sts **A** and **B** should sit opposite **C** and **D**. If you have an odd number, you could have two Sts representing one political party and only one representing the other. Go through the instructions with Sts. Highlight that they have to **first** decide how to defend their own policies, and **second** how to attack the opposition's policies.
- Set Sts a time limit for them to prepare for the debate. Monitor and help with vocabulary. Stress that Sts are playing the role of politicians and it doesn't matter if they don't personally agree with the policies they have to defend.
- Set the scene by reminding them that it's a live TV debate the day before elections, and it's the politicians' last chance to convince viewers to vote for them.
- Sts now have their debate. **A** and **B** begin by introducing their first policy and the reasons. **C** and **D** then try to attack the policy giving reasons. Then **C** and **D** introduce their first policy.
- When Sts have debated all the policies, ask Sts which ones they think would be a good idea in their country and why.

9A Tell me about...

A pairwork speaking activity

Sts complete circles and then use the information to talk about each of the things in the circles. Copy and cut one sheet per pair.

Language
Vocabulary: clauses of contrast and purpose, e.g., *in spite of, in order to*, etc.

- Focus on instruction **b**. Sts take turns asking each other *What did you write in circle 1? Why*? Encourage Sts to ask for more information to get a small conversation going, e.g.,

B What did you write in circle 1?
A Thailand
B Why?
A Because it's a country I'd like to visit in order to try the cuisine.
B How did you discover Thai food? etc.

- When they have finished asking about what they have written in all the circles, get some feedback from the class.

9B Give your opinion!

A group board game

Sts review countable and uncountable nouns by trying to talk for a minute about their opinion on different statements. Copy one sheet per three or four Sts. The emphasis of the activity is fluency, but the teacher and Sts should also watch out for mistakes with the target language.

Language
Vocabulary: countable and plural nouns

- Put Sts into groups of three or four players. Each group needs markers, e.g., small pieces of paper or small coins, and a dice. If you don't have a dice, Sts could toss a coin. Heads = move one, tails = move two.

- Explain the rules of the game: when a player lands on a speaking square, he / she must talk for one minute on that subject. If they land on a blank square, their turn is over and the next person plays. If Sts land on a square with a statement, they must then talk for one minute about the topic on that square. They should first read out the statement, and then say what they think. Ask someone in each group to monitor the time. Before Sts start, remind them that the main emphasis of the activity is fluency. However, both teacher and Sts should watch out for mistakes with the target language.
- If Sts successfully speak for one minute about the subject, they can keep their marker where it is. If they "dry up" before the minute is up, they must move their marker back to the last square it was on. The winner is the first St in each group to reach the end of the board.
- When everyone has finished, highlight any common or important errors with the target language and get Sts to provide the correct answers in feedback.

10A Science quiz

A quiz about natural sciences

Sts review quantifiers by doing a true / false science quiz. Copy one sheet per pair.

Language
Quantifiers: *each, all, neither,* etc.
Vocabulary: animal vocabulary

- Put Sts in pairs **A** and **B**, and give out the sheets.
- Focus on instruction **a**. Give Sts time, e.g., five minutes, to circle the correct quantifier.
- Check answers. First **A's** and then **B's**.

A	B
1 Most	1 both
2 All the	2 no
3 all	3 Every
4 None	4 Most
5 anything	5 Both
6 either	6 any
7 any	7 nor

- Tell Sts to read the information again and ask them to remember the explanation for each question.
- Focus on **b**. **A** can ask all his / her questions first.
- Encourage them to try and give an explanation for their answers and to use their own words when giving the explanation for a wrong answer.
- At the end of the activity, see who got the most answers right.

10B General knowledge quiz

A quiz on a range of subjects

Sts review articles by completing quiz questions, answering them in pairs. Copy one sheet per pair.

Language
Definite and indefinite articles

- Put Sts in pairs **A** and **B** and give out the sheets.
- Focus on instruction **a** and set a time limit for Sts to complete the questions. Check answers.

1 – 2 the / the 3 a 4 the 5 the / the 6 – 7 –
8 the / the 9 the / the 10 – / – 11 the 12 – / – 13 the
14 a 15 a 16 the / the 17 – / the 18 the / the 19 a / –
20 the 21 – 22 a / an 23 the / a 24 the 25 – / –

- Focus on instruction **b**. Set a time limit, e.g., five minutes, for Sts to try to answer as many questions as possible.
- When the time is up, check answers, making sure Sts use the article correctly in their answers, and see which pair had most correct answers.

1 Kenya, Uganda, Tanzania
2 Buzz Aldrin
3 4
4 Indian Ocean
5 Mont Blanc
6 25
7 Blue for Caucasian babies, gray or brown for babies of African or Asian descent
8 The Bald Eagle
9 "W" on a "QWERTY" keyboard, "P" on an "AZERTY" keyboard. NB. You may wish to check the keyboard type used in your country, because there are sometimes national differences.
10 dogs
11 Neptune
12 The most common answer amongst researchers in this area is that there are slightly more men than women.
13 50
14 apple
15 5
16 Aries
17 New Zealand
18 Yuri Gagarin
19 Switzerland
20 The Great Wall of China
21 corn
22 no – it's an arachnid
23 orange
24 Russia
25 light

Review

Questions to review vocabulary, verb forms, and tenses

Sts ask each other questions about the main vocabulary areas from *American English File 4, Second Edition,* using a range of tenses and verb forms from Files 1–10. This could be used as a final "pre-test" review. Alternatively, it could be used as an oral exam. Copy and cut up one set of cards per pair.

Language
Grammar and vocabulary of the course

- Sts work in pairs or groups. Give each pair / group a set of cards. Sts take turns choosing a card and talk to their partners about the topic on the card, using the prompts. Encourage Sts to ask follow-up questions. Monitor, help, and correct.

Non-cut alternative

- Give one sheet to each pair of Sts. They take turns asking their partner questions on one topic. They continue until they have used up all their topics.

COMMUNICATIVE Tell me about it

Student A Instructions

a Read the instructions and write your answers in the correct place.

In the snake's head, write your first name.
In number 2, write the name of a cafe or restaurant you often go to.
In number 3, write the name of the last movie you really enjoyed.
In number 4, write the place you went to on your last vacation.
In number 5, write the name of an app you use a lot.
In number 6, write the number of years you've been living in this town.
In number 7, write your favorite day of the week.
In number 8, write a date that is important for you.
In number 9, write the name of the person in your family you get along with best.
In number 10, write two things you like doing in your free time.

b Exchange charts with **B**. Ask **B** to explain the information in his / her snake. Ask for more information.

Why did you write "4"?

Because I've been learning English for 4 years.

c Explain your answers to **B**.

Where did you study before?

FOLD

Student A Chart

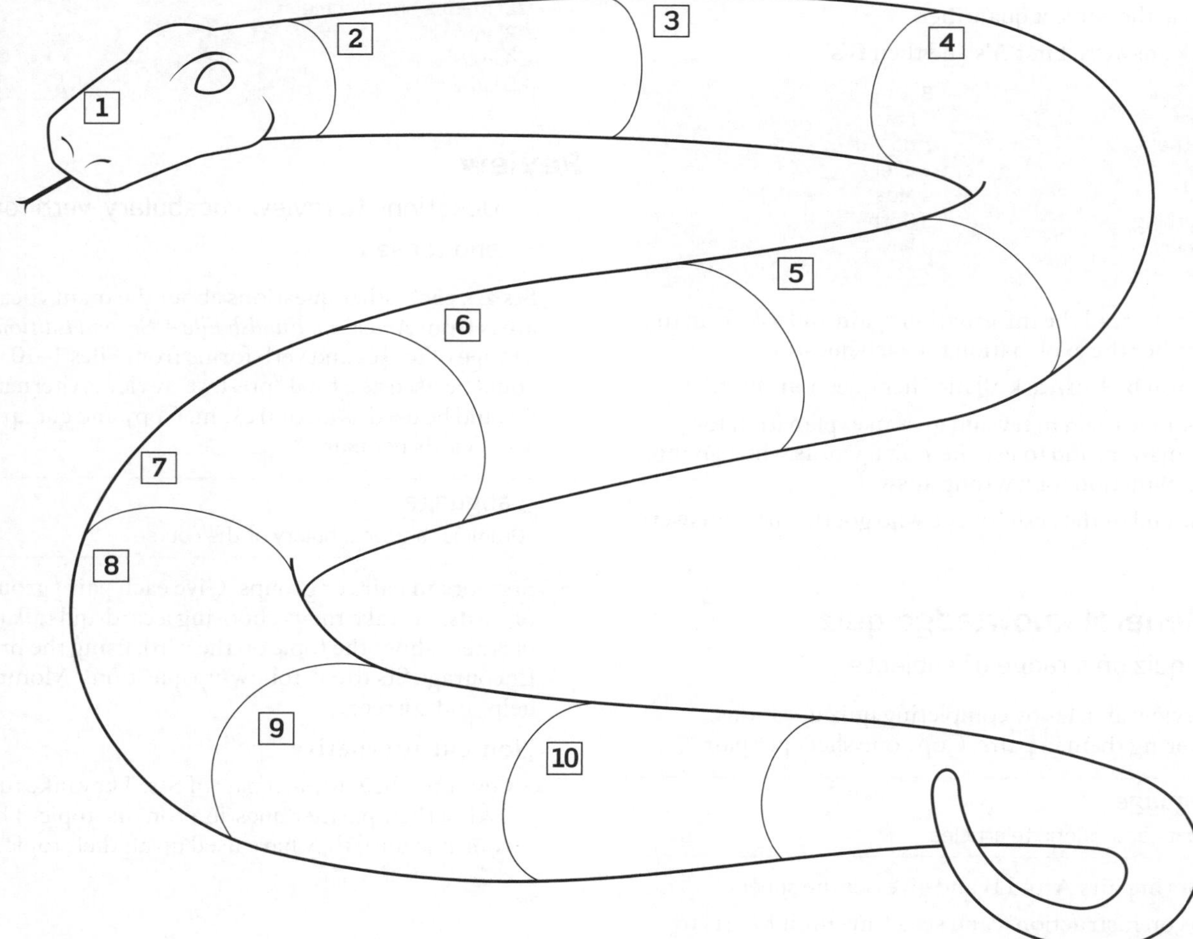

American English File 2nd edition Teacher's Book 4 Photocopiable © Oxford University Press 2014

COMMUNICATIVE Tell me about it

Student B Instructions

a Read the instructions and write your answers in the correct place.

In the snake's head, write your first name.
In number 2, write the number of years you've been learning English.
In number 3, write your favorite food or drink.
In number 4, write the name of a website you've used to improve your English.
In number 5, write the last new gadget you bought.
In number 6, write the name of a TV show you've been watching recently.
In number 7, write the name of the game you play most on your phone or computer.
In number 8, write a number that is important to you in some way.
In number 9, write the name of a sport you like watching or playing.
In number 10, write the name of your oldest friend.

b Exchange charts with **A**. Ask **A** to explain the information in his / her snake. Ask for more information.

Why did you write Starbucks?

Because I often go there for coffee.

c Explain your answers to **A**.

Why do you like it?

FOLD

Student B Chart

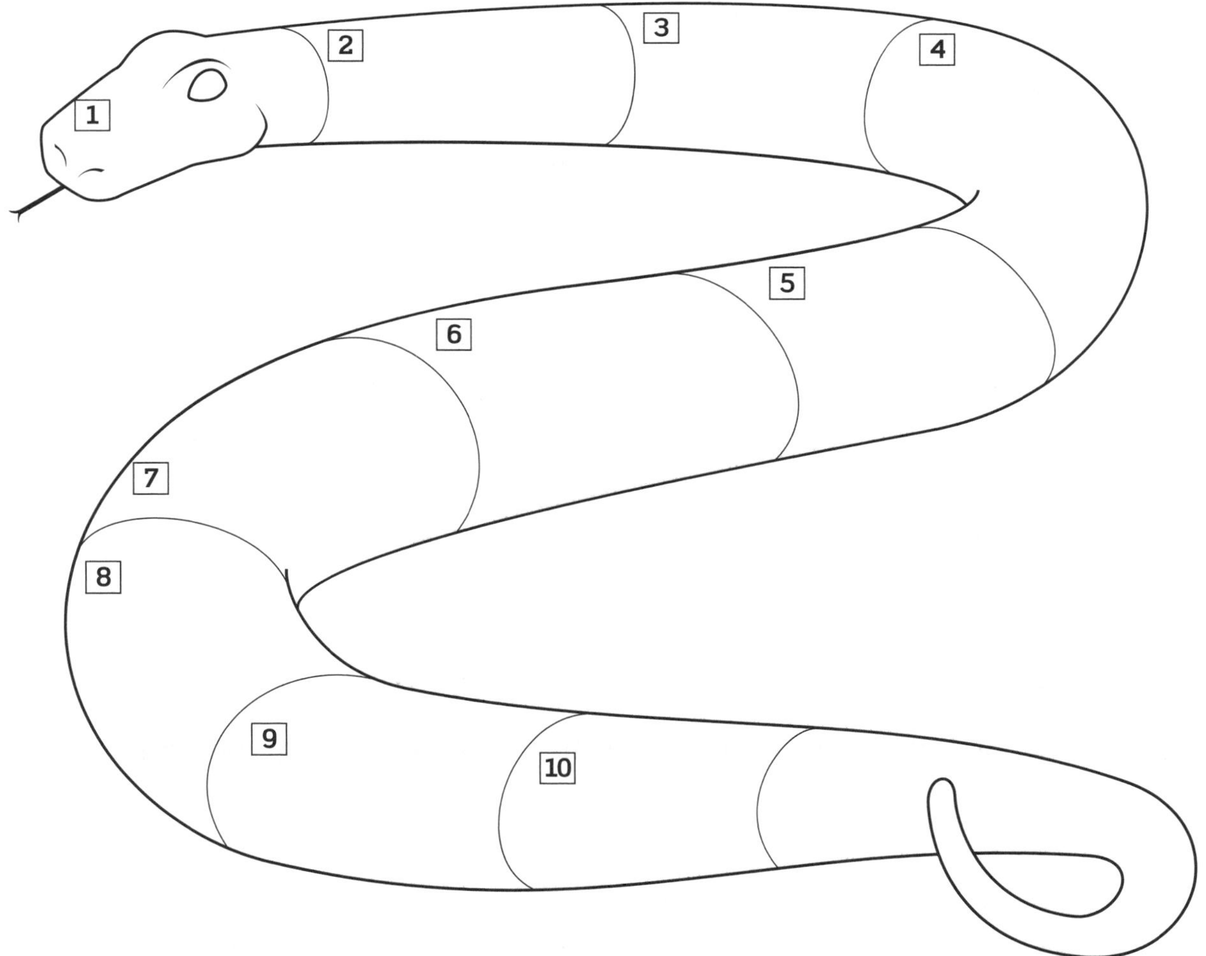

1A COMMUNICATIVE Ask me a question

a In pairs, read the questions and think about what the missing words are. Don't write them in.

b Choose a topic. Interview your partner. Ask for more information.

Your home

1 Where ■ ■ live?
2 How long ■ ■ lived there?
3 Who ■ ■ live ■?
4 What ■ ■ like most about your home?
5 Is ■ anything you ■ like about your neighborhood? Why not?

Getting around

1 How ■ ■ usually get ■ work (or school)?
2 How long ■ ■ take?
3 ■ ■ drive? ■ car ■ ■ ■?
4 ■ often ■ you ■ public transportation?
5 ■ the best way ■ get ■ your town / city?

Free time

1 What ■ ■ enjoy doing in your free time?
2 ■ ■ of music ■ ■ listen ■?
3 How ■ ■ ■ go out during the week?
4 ■ sport(s) ■ ■ like playing?
5 ■ ■ time do you spend on social network sites every day?

Lifestyle

1 How ■ tea or coffee ■ ■ drink ■ day?
2 ■ ■ hours ■ ■ sleep at night?
3 What ■ ■ do ■ relax?
4 What do ■ do ■ keep healthy?
5 What ■ the last live event you went ■?

Travel

1 What's ■ ■ beautiful place you ■ ■ been to?
2 Where ■ you going ■ ■ for your next vacation?
3 ■ ■ think it's better ■ travel alone ■ with other people?
4 ■ ■ prefer taking vacations ■ home or abroad?
5 Have ■ ■ been ■ an English-speaking country?

Family

1 ■ ■ people ■ there in your immediate family?
2 ■ in your family ■ ■ most like talking ■?
3 ■ ■ ■ prefer spending time ■? Family ■ friends?
4 How much ■ ■ know ■ your family tree?
5 When ■ ■ last time all ■ family did something together?

Childhood and school

1 Where ■ ■ born?
2 Which high ■ ■ ■ go ■?
3 What ■ ■ best / worst subject?
4 ■ ■ ever cheated on a test? ■ ■ get caught?
5 What ■ ■ want ■ be when you were a child?

A male or female relative (e.g., brother, nephew, aunt, grandmother)

1 ■ ■ name?
2 How old ■ ■?
3 ■ ■ ■ do?
4 ■ ■ ■ look ■? (appearance)
5 ■ ■ ■ like? (personality)

American English File 2nd edition Teacher's Book 4 Photocopiable © Oxford University Press 2014

The story

1 You are traveling on a boat. There is a terrible storm and the boat starts sinking. You are thrown into the water and lose consciousness. When you next open your eyes, you're lying on the beach of a small island. **Describe the island in as much detail as you can.**
- Where is it?
- What's it like? (vegetation, etc.)
- What's the weather like?

2 You get up and discover that you aren't injured. **Describe what you are wearing.**
- What are you wearing on your feet?
- What are you wearing on your top / bottom half?

3 **What do you decide to do first?**
- Look for other possible survivors?
- Look for food or water?
- Make a shelter or fire?

4 You walk up a nearby hill and you can see that there is a clearing in the middle of the island and what looks like water. You decide to try and find the clearing, but to get there, you need to walk through a forest. **Describe the forest in detail and how you'll get to the middle of the island.**
- Is it easy / difficult to get through the forest?
- Is there a path?
- Is it dark or light?

5 You reach the middle of the island and you see a house. You look through the windows. **Describe the house in detail**.
- What's it like inside and outside?

6 You continue walking until you come to a lake. **Describe the lake and what you do, and why.**
- Do you immediately jump in and go for a swim?
- Do you walk around it?
- Do you get into the water slowly?

The interpretation

1 **the island =** where in the world you would ideally like to live. Did you see palm trees and tropical vegetation? Was it hot? If so, you'd probably like to live in a warm, tropical climate, etc.

2 **the clothes =** how you feel about style. The more elaborate the clothes you describe, the more important outward appearances are to you.

3 **actions =** the action you do first shows what your priorities are in life, e.g., if you decide to look for other survivors, this probably means that you're a caring person who tends to think of other people. If you choose to look for food or water first, this could mean that you're someone who is quite independent. If you decide to make a shelter or fire, it may mean that you're a practical person who tries to solve problems in a logical way.

4 **the forest =** the way you see life. If the forest is easy to get through and there's a clear path, then this could mean that your life is well-planned and organized. You know exactly what you want to do and how to achieve it. If there's no path marked and you have to cut your way through the vegetation to make one, this could indicate that you are a person who sees life as a mystery and you live each day as it unfolds. The darker the forest is, the more negative you feel about the way your life is going.

5 **the house** = what you expect from life. If you describe a very simple, basic house, this could mean that your needs in life are equally simple. If you describe a big, luxurious house, this probably means that you would like to have a more extravagant life style.

6 **the lake =** your attitude to love and relationships. If you walk around the lake but don't go into the water this could mean that you are not ready to commit yourself in a relationship. If you go into the lake, this could show the way you deal with new relationships. Do you jump in head first (you're a risk taker) or do you walk into the lake very slowly and carefully?

American English File 2nd edition Teacher's Book 4 Photocopiable © Oxford University Press 2014

2A COMMUNICATIVE Doctor, doctor

A Role-play 1

You're a family doctor. B is your patient.

You've just finished medical school, and today is your first day in this office. You feel very enthusiastic! In medical school, they taught you to find out as much as you can about a patient when you first meet them. You're a great believer in alternative medicine like homeopathy and acupuncture. You really believe that some conditions can be better treated using alternative remedies, e.g., hypnotherapy for people with phobias or weight problems.

- Find out as much information as you can about the patient, e.g., age, job, family life, previous illnesses, operations, etc.
- Ask the reason for today's visit. Find out how long he / she's had this problem.
- You don't like the medicine the patient usually takes, Calmozone. You prefer a natural, homeopathic one called Tranquilium.

B will start.

Role-play 2

You're a patient. B is your family doctor.

You know your doctor very well because you make an appointment to see him / her at least once a week. You're a favorite patient! You think of him / her as a friend and that's why you call him / her by his / her first name (Chris) and not Dr. Jones.

- Today, you've made an appointment with the doctor because you've got some very strange symptoms (decide what they are), and you're convinced that you have a problem with your heart. You want the doctor to take you seriously and agree with what you think is the problem.
- Explain all your symptoms to the doctor.
- Ask the doctor to check your blood pressure and take your pulse.
- Tell him / her that you'd like to see a specialist. Be prepared to argue with him / her if necessary.

You start the conversation.
Hi, Chris. How are you?

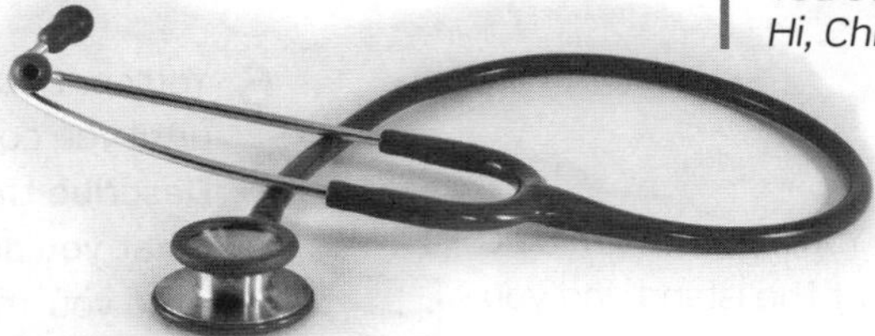

B Role-play 1

You're a patient. A is your family doctor.

You haven't been to the doctor's office for about a year, so you're really surprised to see that you have a new family doctor. He / she's very young! What experience does he / she have? You'd known your previous doctor all your life. He knew all about your fear of flying and was very sympathetic to the problem. You're going on vacation next week – by plane. Your old doctor always prescribed Calmozone, a tablet which relaxes you when you fly. If you take two before the plane takes off, you don't feel nervous. You know what you want – Calmozone! If you don't get it, you can't go on vacation. You aren't very convinced by alternative remedies, especially hypnotherapy and homeopathy!

- Answer any questions the doctor asks you. Explain the reason for today's visit.
- Ask the doctor to prescribe Calmozone and explain why you need it.
- Only accept an alternative remedy you feel completely happy with.

You start the conversation.
Good morning, doctor. You're new, aren't you?

Role-play 2

You're a family doctor. A is your patient.

You're fed up and exhausted! The insurance spending cuts mean that today you've worked for eight hours on your own in the office and there's still paperwork to do. You want to go home! Unfortunately, you have one more patient to see and he /she is a nightmare! He / she comes to see you at least once a week, always with a different problem. You think he / she is a hypochondriac. For some reason, this patient always calls you by your first name. You hate that!

- Ask him / her not to call you by your first name. Ask him / her to call you Dr. Jones.
- Ask him / her what his / her symptoms are (this week!) and how long he / she has had them.
- Give your diagnosis (decide what you think) and decide what medication (if any) to prescribe. You don't think he / she needs to see a specialist.

A will start.

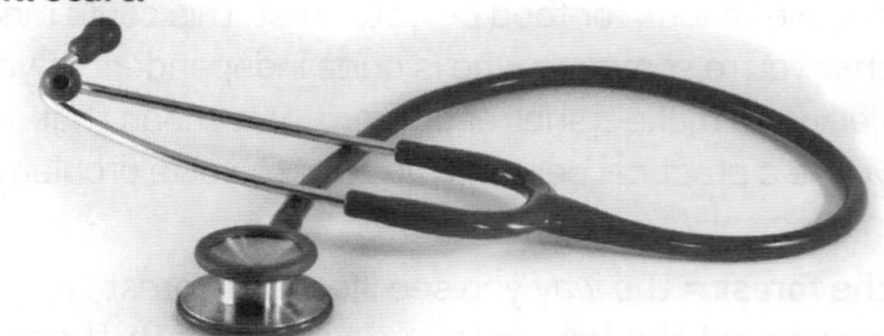

American English File 2nd edition Teacher's Book 4 Photocopiable © Oxford University Press 2014

2B COMMUNICATIVE Spot the difference

Student A

Student B

3A COMMUNICATIVE Talk about it

something you wanted for a long time and that you recently bought

- What exactly did you get?
- Why had you wanted it for so long?
- Did you do any research before you got it? How?
- Where did you get it?
- Have you been using it much since you got it?

a time you went for an interview for a job or class

- What job / class was it for?
- Where had you found out about the job / class?
- How did you feel before the interview?
- Were there any questions you found hard to answer? What were they?
- Did you get the job / get into the class?

a time you had a really bad restaurant meal

- When / Where did you have it? Who with?
- Why had you decided to go to this particular restaurant?
- Why was the meal so bad?
- Were you or any of the other people sick afterwards?
- Did you complain? If not, why not?

a time when someone stole something from you (or someone you know)

- What was taken?
- What had you been doing just before it was stolen?
- How did you feel after you realized it had been stolen?
- Did you call the police? Were they helpful?
- Did you ever get it back?

a time when you overslept and missed something important

- What important thing were you going to do that day?
- Did you go to bed very late the night before? Why?
- Did you set an alarm?
- How late did you wake up? What did you do?
- What happened in the end?

a time when your parents were very angry with you about something

- How old were you?
- Why did they get angry? What had you done / been doing?
- How did your parents find out?
- Did they punish you? How?
- Have you parents forgotten about it?

a time you met or were very close to a celebrity

- When did it happen?
- Where were you?
- What were you doing?
- Which celebrity did you see?
- What was he / she doing there?
- Did you speak to him / her? What about?
- Did you take a photo of him / her?

a time you won something

- What was it?
- When? Where? How old were you?
- Were you expecting to win?
- How did you feel when you realized you'd won?
- Did you celebrate? What did you do?

a vacation you didn't enjoy

- Where / when was it?
- Who went?
- Had you been there before?
- What did you do there?
- Why didn't you enjoy it? Did you ever go there again?

American English File 2nd edition Teacher's Book 4 Photocopiable © Oxford University Press 2014

3B COMMUNICATIVE Tell the story

4A COMMUNICATIVE In 20 years

Discuss each prediction with your group. Decide:

a if you think it will happen

b if you think it will be a good thing

1 People will be mostly reading print books again and e-readers will have declined in popularity.

2 The number of people learning foreign languages will have fallen because apps will translate everything simultaneously.

3 The idea of a retirement age will have disappeared and people will be working until 70 and beyond.

4 We will only be eating laboratory produced meat products, e.g., synthetic hamburgers.

5 Bikes will have replaced the car as the main form of private transportation in towns and cities.

6 People will have stopped using social networking sites like Facebook and Twitter and returned to face to face communication.

7 The teaching of spelling and punctuation will have stopped in schools because people will be using text correctors for everything they write.

8 We will be mainly watching movies with computer animated actors who will have replaced human actors.

9 Fewer people will be getting married and the birth rate will have dropped even further.

10 We will be seeing many more womens' sports on TV because it will have greatly increased in popularity.

11 Life expectancy will have gone down in the developed world because of unhealthy eating habits.

12 It won't be necessary for anyone to learn to drive because we'll be using self-driving cars.

American English File 2nd edition Teacher's Book 4 Photocopiable © Oxford University Press 2014

4B COMMUNICATIVE Finish the sentences

As soon as we arrive at the hotel...	Continue taking the antibiotics **until**...
What are you going to do **when**...	Don't disturb the boss **unless**...
I'll give you a call **after**...	Let's take the GPS **in case**...
I'll do the dishes **if**...	I'm going to buy a motorcycle **as soon as**...
I'm sure your husband will understand **if**...	We'll be having a barbecue tomorrow **unless**...
Shh! Don't make a noise **in case**...	**Unless** you hurry up...
We could go for a walk **after**...	**If** his wife has told him to do it, ...
We must say goodbye to Louise **before**...	We need to book the vacation soon **in case**...
If you're not feeling better tomorrow...	We're going to celebrate **when**...
You might get an electric shock **if**...	I won't be able to start cooking dinner **until**...

 Photocopiable © Oxford University Press 2014

What would you do?

1

You're driving your car along a road by a river. Suddenly your brakes fail on a curve and you can't stop your car from going into the water. What would you do?

2

You're skiing on your own high in the mountains when you suddenly hear a very loud noise behind you. It's an avalanche! What would you do?

3

You're walking in a forest near where you live when suddenly you feel a terrible pain in your leg. You've been bitten by a snake that you think is poisonous. What would you do?

4

You're camping in a forest, and decide to go for a walk. Suddenly, you come face to face with a black bear. It looks ready to attack you! What would you do?

5

You're at home and there's a tornado warning. What would you do?

6

You're swimming in the ocean when you see the dark fin of a shark approaching you. What would you do?

The answers

1 As soon as you hit the water, open the window. This allows water to come in and equalize the pressure so that you can open the door. If you can't open the window or break it, wait until the water reaches your head and hold your breath. When the pressure is equal inside and outside the car, you'll be able to open the door.

2 You must try to stay on top of the snow by using a swimming action. Avalanches tend to occur in areas with new snow on sunny afternoons.

3 Wash the bite with soap and water as soon as you can. Keep the area where the bite is lower than your heart. Wrap a bandage tightly around your leg above the bite to help slow the poison until you can get medical help. Don't suck out the poison and don't tie the bandage too tight.

4 Lie still and be quiet. An attack by a mother bear often ends when the person stops fighting. Don't run or climb a tree because a bear can run much faster than you, and is an expert at climbing trees. If you lie still and the bear still attacks you, try to scare it away by hitting it with anything you can find. Try to aim for the eyes or nose if possible.

5 Go to an underground shelter if possible, or if not, go to the first floor of your home, to the room closest to the middle of the house. Get under a sturdy piece of furniture.

6 If the shark attacks you, try to hit the shark in the eyes, which is the area most sensitive to pain.

American English File 2nd edition Teacher's Book 4 Photocopiable © Oxford University Press 2014

5B COMMUNICATIVE Wishes A

Student A

a Write something in at least seven of your circles.

Circle 1: a well-known person you wish you could meet or could have met
Circle 2: a new gadget you wish you had
Circle 3: a name you wish your parents had called you (instead of the one they gave you)
Circle 4: something you wish the local government would do to improve your town / city
Circle 5: a concert or sporting event you wish you'd been able to go to
Circle 6: something you wish people wouldn't do at the movie theater
Circle 7: an activity you wish you didn't have to do every day
Circle 8: a language (other than English) you wish you could speak
Circle 9: something you wish you had learned to do when you were younger
Circle 10: something you wish you hadn't spent money on

b Give your sheet to **B**. He / She will ask you to explain what you have written.

c Ask **B** to explain what he / she has written.

Why did you write Modern Family in circle 1?

Because I wish they would make more shows of it. I love it.

FOLD

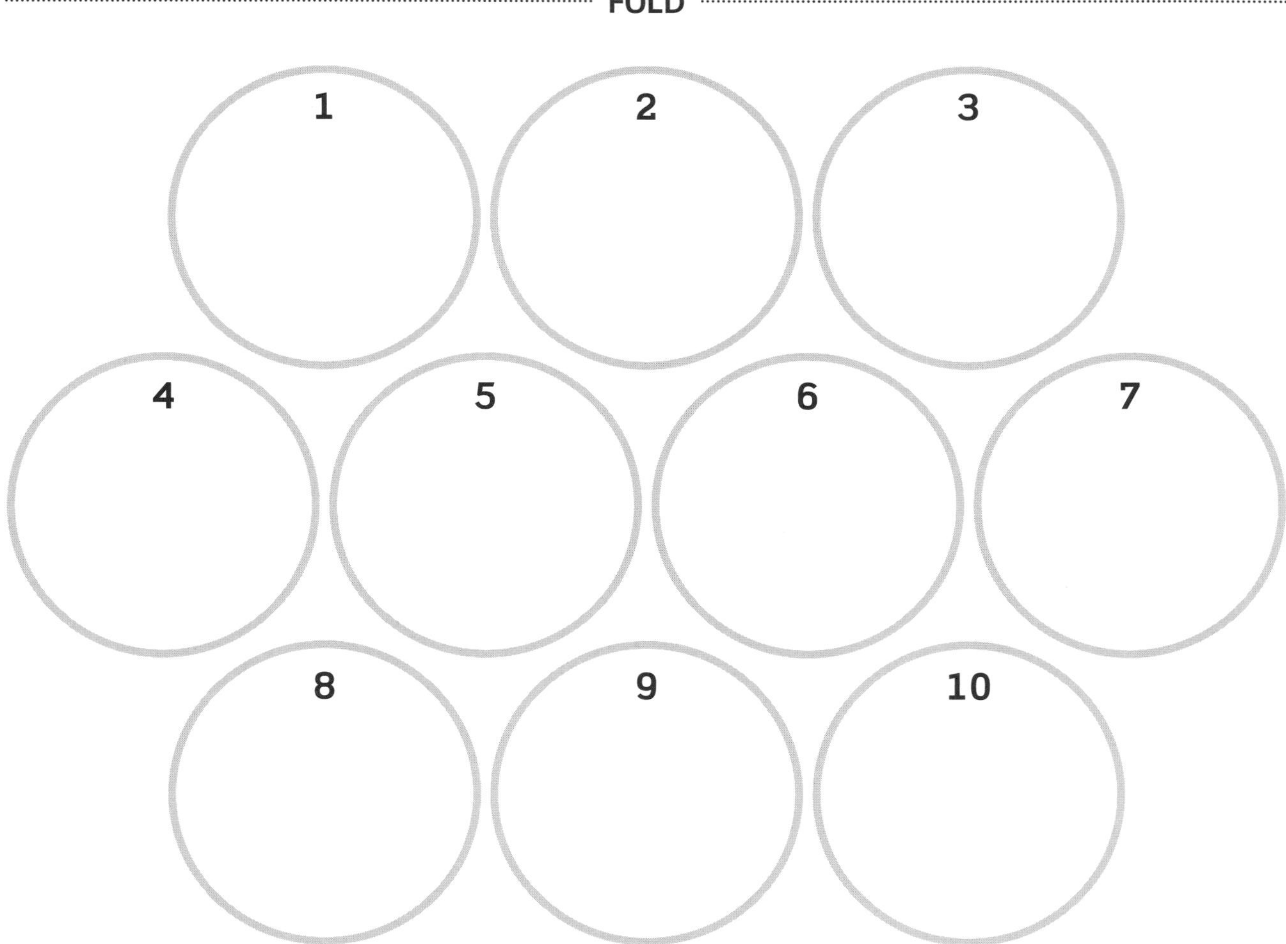

5B COMMUNICATIVE Wishes B

Student B

a Write something in at least seven of your circles.

Circle 1: a TV drama or comedy you wish they had made more shows of
Circle 2: something you wish drivers or bike riders would or wouldn't do
Circle 3: somebody you wish you could see more often
Circle 4: somewhere you wish you had a house or apartment
Circle 5: a free-time activity you wish you had more time to do
Circle 6: a group or singer you wish would come and play in your city
Circle 7: something you wish hadn't been invented
Circle 8: something you wish people wouldn't do on social networking sites
Circle 9: something annoying you wish someone in your family wouldn't do
Circle 10: something you wish you had learned to do when you were younger

b Give your sheet to **A**. He / She will ask you to explain what you have written.

c Ask **A** to explain what he / she has written.

Why did you write Salvador Dali in circle 1?

Because I wish I had met him. He was a great artist.

FOLD

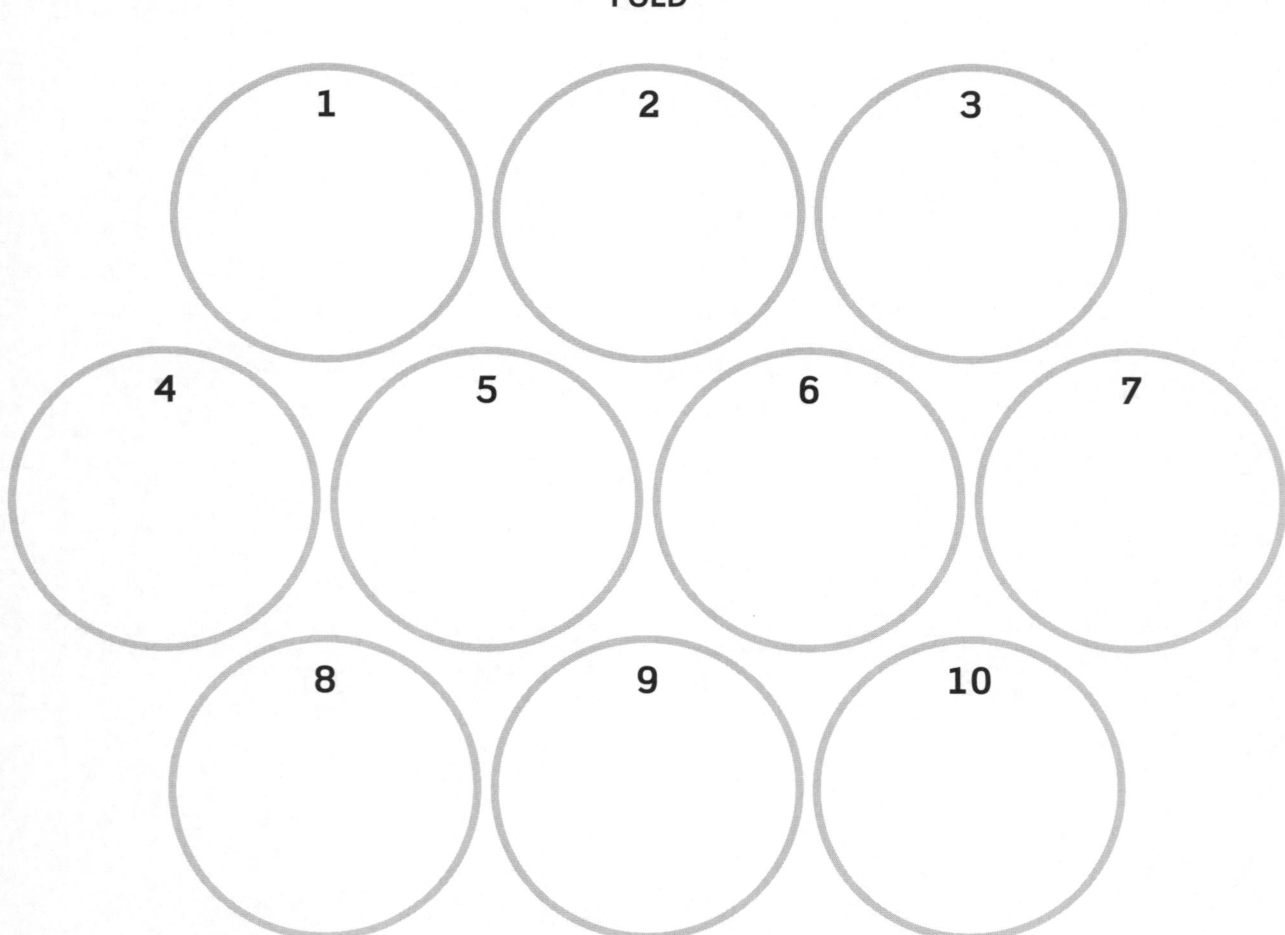

American English File 2nd edition Teacher's Book 4 Photocopiable © Oxford University Press 2014

6A COMMUNICATIVE Gerund or infinitive?

Student A

a Complete the **verb** column with the correct form of the verbs in parentheses.

b Ask your partner the questions in **a**.

c Answer **B**'s questions.

		Verb
1	Could you manage ___ for a week without your phone? (**live**)	___
2	Do you ever get the chance to practice ___ English outside class? (**speak**)	___
3	If you really hated your friend's partner, would you pretend ___ him / her? (**like**)	___
4	Is there any kind of housework you can't stand ___ ? (**do**)	___
5	Would you ever risk ___ something which was past its sell-by-date? (**eat**)	___
6	Is there anything that you think you ought to give up ___ ? (**do**)	___
7	What kind of things do you tend ___ about? (**worry**)	___
8	Did your parents let you ___ on the street when you were a child? (**play**)	___
9	Do you sometimes forget ___ things or do you have a good memory? (**do**)	___
10	Is there a city or country that you'd really like ___ ? (**visit**)	___
11	Are there any apps you'd recommend ___ ? (**get**)	___
12	Is there a TV show you can't help ___ even though you don't think it's very good? (**watch**)	___

FOLD

Student B

a Complete the verb column with the correct form of the verbs in parentheses.

b Ask your partner the questions in **a**.

c Answer **A**'s questions.

		Verb
1	Do you think it's worth ___ a yearly medical check up? (**have**)	___
2	Is there anything that you really need ___ in your house or apartment? (**fix**)	___
3	Have you ever tried ___ build-it-yourself furniture? (**assemble**)	___
4	Can you imagine ___ to another country? (**emigrate**)	___
5	Would you rather ___ an e-book or a paper book? (**read**)	___
6	Are there any jobs in the house that you don't mind ___ ? (**do**)	___
7	Do you remember ___ your best friend for the first time? (**meet**)	___
8	Have you ever had to stop ___ a type of food because you were told it wasn't good for you? (**eat**)	___
9	Did your parents ever make you ___ something you really didn't enjoy? (**learn**)	___
10	Do you think that you'll continue ___ English next year? (**study**)	___
11	Is there a movie you're looking forward to ___ at the theater? (**watch**)	___
12	Would you prefer ___ a week on the beach or a week in the country? (**spend**)	___

FOLD

6B COMMUNICATIVE *usually, used to, get used to*

Student A

a Complete the questions with verb phrases from the list on the right. You don't need to use all the phrases.

Do you usually ______________________?

______________________?

______________________?

Did you use to ______________________?

______________________?

______________________?

Do you think you could get used to ______________________?

______________________?

______________________?

b Ask **B** the questions.

c Answer **B**'s questions.

(read) the news online

(study) in the evenings or at night

(share) a bedroom with a brother or sister

(eat) a lot of sweets when you were a child

(cook) for yourself

(watch) cartoons on TV when you were young

(buy) books and music online

(live) in the UK or the US

(cheat) on tests in school

(go) to bed before midnight

(not eat) meat

(take) only two weeks vacation a year

Student B

a Complete the questions with verb phrases from the list on the right. You don't need to use all the phrases.

Do you usually ______________________?

______________________?

______________________?

Did you use to ______________________?

______________________?

______________________?

Do you think you could get used to ______________________?

______________________?

______________________?

b Answer **A**'s questions.

c Ask **A** your questions.

(have) a favorite toy

(ride a bike) to work or school

(get up) at 5:30 every morning

(listen) to music in the car

(celebrate) your birthday

(live) on your own

(read) *Harry Potter* when you were a child

(drive) on the right

(live) without having access to the Internet

(watch) TV in the morning

(hate) a particular food or drink when you were a child

(go) to the hair salon more than twice a month

American English File 2nd edition Teacher's Book 4 Photocopiable © Oxford University Press 2014

7A COMMUNICATIVE Guess my verb

Student A

a) Complete the bold sentences in a natural way using *have* and a verb phrase.

b) Read sentence 1 to **B**, who has the completed sentence. If you say what **B** has, he / she will say "*That's right,*" if not he / she will say "*Try again.*" You can have a maximum of three guesses.

c) If all your three endings are different from what **B** has, **B** will tell you his / her sentence.

1 **Greg's really late. He may ___________.**
2 I didn't know they didn't accept credit cards. We should have brought some cash.
3 **You couldn't ___________. You only started it yesterday and it's got over 600 pages!**
4 Maria looks so tired. She couldn't have slept very well last night.
5 **You should ___________ last night. We had a great time!**
6 Nobody's answering the phone at the Town Hall. They might have left early.
7 **Ellie always calls me on my birthday, but this year she didn't. She must ___________.**
8 I don't have my wallet with me! I must have left it at home.
9 **My neighbor just bought a really expensive new car. She might ___________!**
10 It's your own fault you got sunburned! You ought to have put on sunscreen.
11 **It's OK to call them. It's only 10:00 They couldn't ___________.**
12 The cat got into the kitchen last night! You must have left the window open.
13 **Have you seen Kathy's huge engagement ring? It must ___________!**
14 They couldn't have gone out. Their car's outside.
15 **I've got a stomachache. I shouldn't ___________.**
16 Michelle isn't in her office. She may have gone home. She wasn't feeling very well.

Student B

a) Complete the bold sentences in a natural way using *have* and a verb phrase.

b) **A** is going to invent an ending for 1. He / She has three turns to try to say exactly what you have written. If all **A's** three endings are different from what you have, tell **A** the sentence.

c) Now read sentence 2 to **A**, who has the completed sentence. If you say what **A** has, he / she will say "*That's right,*" if not, he / she will say "*Try again.*" You can have a maximum of three guesses.

1 Greg's really late. He may have gotten lost.
2 **I didn't know they didn't accept credit cards. We should ___________.**
3 You couldn't have finished that book. You only started it yesterday and it's got over 600 pages!
4 **Maria looks so tired. She couldn't ___________ last night.**
5 You should have come with us last night. We had a great time!
6 **Nobody's answering the phone at the Town Hall. They might ___________.**
7 Ellie always calls me on my birthday, but this year she didn't. She must have forgotten.
8 **I don't have my wallet with me! I must ___________.**
9 My neighbor just bought a really expensive new car. She might have won the lottery!
10 **It's your own fault you got sunburned! You ought to ___________.**
11 It's OK to call them. It's only 10:00. They couldn't have gone to bed yet.
12 **The cat got into the kitchen last night! You must ___________.**
13 Have you seen Kathy's huge engagement ring? It must have cost a fortune!
14 **They couldn't ___________. Their car's outside.**
15 I've got a stomachache. I shouldn't have eaten so much.
16 **Michelle isn't in her office. She may ___________. She wasn't feeling very well.**

7B COMMUNICATIVE Spot the difference

Student A

Student B

American English File 2nd edition Teacher's Book 4 Photocopiable © Oxford University Press 2014

8A COMMUNICATIVE Good laws?

a Read about some existing laws in different countries. In pairs or small groups, discuss whether you think each law is a good one, and whether you would like to have it in your country.

b For each section, write one new law that you would like to see introduced in your country.

Animals

1 Poland
If you have a dog, it must always wear a muzzle and be kept on a leash when you take it for walks.

2 China
Dog owners in Beijing must be content with a small dog. No dogs over 13.7 inches tall are allowed in the city.

3 New law

____

____________________________________.

On the road

1 Germany
People who want to get a driver's license have to do a first-aid training course. They must also carry a first-aid kit in their cars.

2 Spain
Car drivers are not allowed to wear flip-flops while driving.

3 New law

____

____________________________________.

On the street

1 Iceland
Teenagers between 13-16 are not allowed to be outdoors after 10:00 at night unless they are on their way home from a recognized event organized by a school, sports team, or youth group. During the summer months, they can be outdoors for two hours longer.

2 US
It is illegal to throw a banana peel (or any trash) on the ground.

3 New law

____

____________________________________.

The environment

1 Norway
When you buy a bottle or a can of something to drink, you have to pay a deposit. When the bottle or can is empty, you take it back to a recycling center where your deposit is refunded.

2 Mexico
There is a complete ban on free plastic bags in Mexico City. Customers are charged if they want them, and the bags must be biodegradable.

3 New law

____

____________________________________.

Food and health

1 Brazil
All Brazilian public school students are given one free meal at school every day. 70% of this food has to be fresh, and the other 30% must come from local family farmers.

2 Japan
There is a special tax on food or drinks that the government considers to be unhealthy. People who want to buy these things have to pay a lot more than they would for healthier options.

3 New law

____

____________________________________.

 Photocopiable © Oxford University Press 2014

8B COMMUNICATIVE TV political debate

A & B

You're the leaders of a local political party. Tonight you're going to appear "live" on TV in a face-to-face debate with the leaders of the opposing party.

a Prepare some ideas to defend your six policies before the interview. Think of reasons that explain why your policies are good ideas. Take notes. Add one new policy of your own.

b Now prepare some other ideas to "attack" your opponents' policies. Think of reasons that explain why the other party's policies aren't good ideas. Take notes.

c Sit opposite **C & D** and take turns presenting and debating your policies.

Your party's policies

- To ban all dogs from the town center
- To close the town center to traffic on Saturday mornings from 9:00 a.m. – 1:00 p.m.
- To promote tourism in the town by organizing a big sporting event (decide which)
- To introduce large fines for people who download music or movies from the Internet without paying
- To ban fast-food restaurants near all schools and universities
- ____________________

Your opponents' policies

- To ban bicycles from all main roads
- To make it mandatory for everyone to vote in local elections
- To make tourists pay a tax when they come into the country
- To make cafes and restaurants in the town center close before 11:00 p.m. during the week
- To give free Internet access to all homes and mobile devices
- ____________________

C & D

You're the leaders of a local political party. Tonight you're going to appear "live" on TV in a face-to-face debate with the leaders of the opposing party.

a Prepare some ideas to defend your six policies before the interview. Think of reasons that explain why your policies are good ideas. Take notes. Add a new policy of your own.

b Now prepare some other ideas to "attack" your opponents' policies. Think of reasons that explain why the other party's policies aren't good ideas. Take notes.

c Sit opposite **A & B** and take turns presenting and debating your policies.

Your party's policies

- To ban bicycles from all main roads
- To make it mandatory for everyone to vote in local elections
- To make tourists pay a tax when they come into the country
- To make cafes and restaurants in the town center close before 11:00 p.m. during the week
- To give free Internet access to all homes and mobile devices
- ____________________

Your opponents' policies

- To ban all dogs from the town center
- To close the town center to traffic on Saturday mornings from 9:00 a.m. – 1:00 p.m.
- To promote tourism in the town by organizing a big sporting event (decide which)
- To introduce large fines for people who download music or movies from the Internet without paying
- To ban fast-food restaurants near all schools and universities
- ____________________

American English File 2nd edition Teacher's Book 4 Photocopiable © Oxford University Press 2014

9A COMMUNICATIVE Tell me about...

Student A

a Look at the circles. Try and write something in at least six of them.

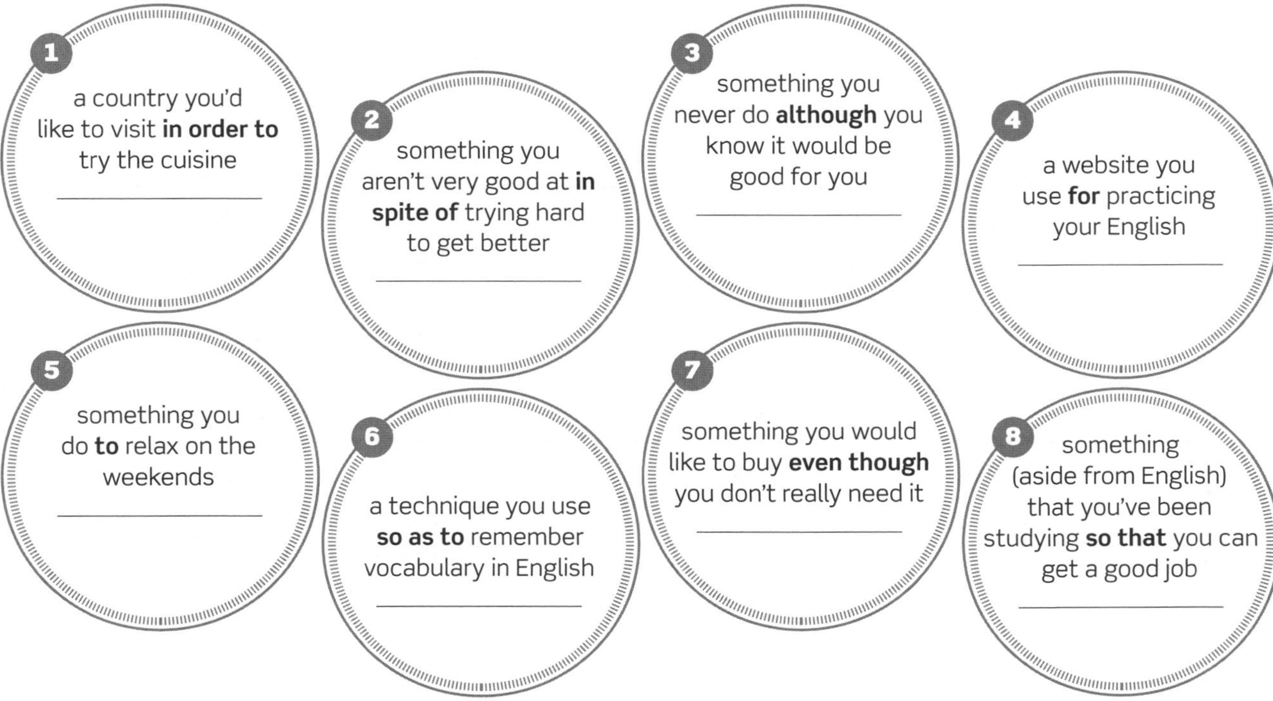

1 a country you'd like to visit **in order to** try the cuisine
2 something you aren't very good at **in spite of** trying hard to get better
3 something you never do **although** you know it would be good for you
4 a website you use **for** practicing your English
5 something you do **to** relax on the weekends
6 a technique you use **so as to** remember vocabulary in English
7 something you would like to buy **even though** you don't really need it
8 something (aside from English) that you've been studying **so that** you can get a good job

b Ask student **B** what he / she wrote in circle 1, and why.

Student B

a Look at the circles. Try and write something in at least six of them.

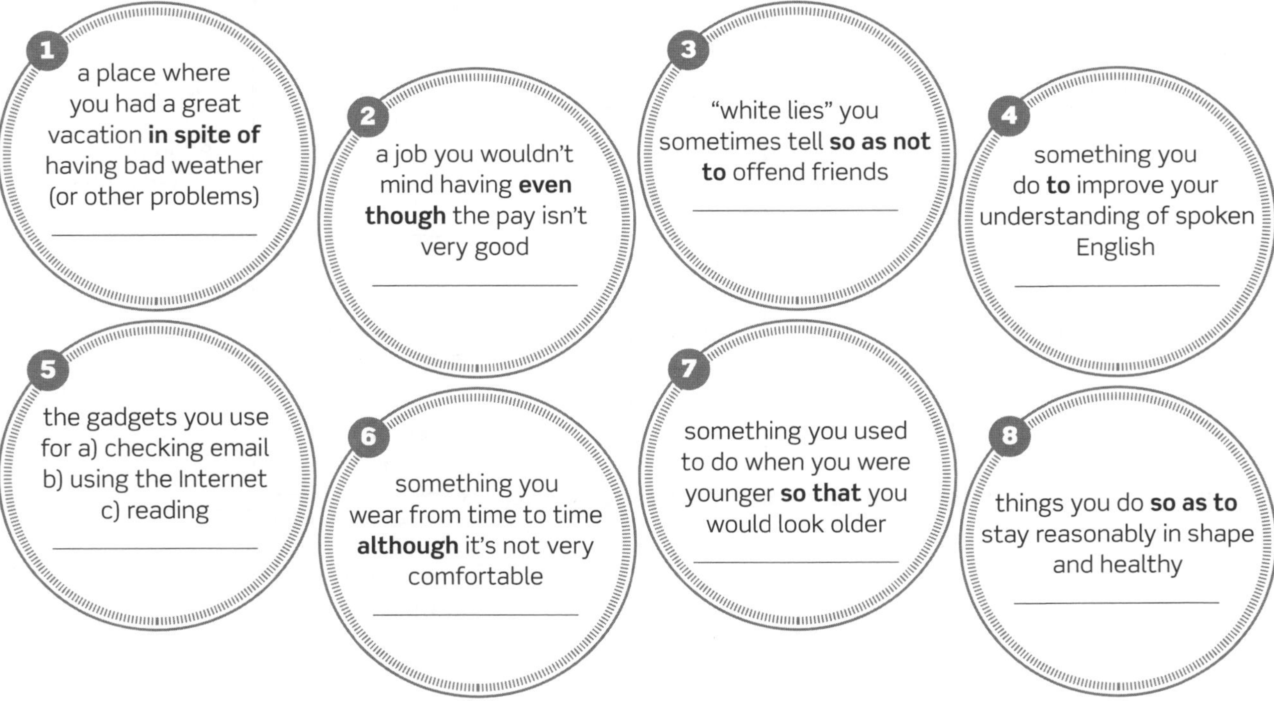

1 a place where you had a great vacation **in spite of** having bad weather (or other problems)
2 a job you wouldn't mind having **even though** the pay isn't very good
3 "white lies" you sometimes tell **so as not to** offend friends
4 something you do **to** improve your understanding of spoken English
5 the gadgets you use for a) checking email b) using the Internet c) reading
6 something you wear from time to time **although** it's not very comfortable
7 something you used to do when you were younger **so that** you would look older
8 things you do **so as to** stay reasonably in shape and healthy

b Ask student **A** what he / she wrote in circle 1, and why.

9B COMMUNICATIVE Give your opinion!

1 START >	**2** GO FORWARD SEVEN SPACES »	**3**		
4 Friends are better at giving **advice** than family.	**5** GO FORWARD THREE SPACES «	**6** The **weather** is a major influence on a country's economy and lifestyle.	**7** The best place to go for a vacation is somewhere with **beautiful** scenery.	**8** Children's **behavior** today is much worse than it was in the past.
9 Children today have too much **homework**.	**10** You should never travel without booking **accommodations** in advance.	**11** GO FORWARD TWO SPACES »	**12** The **clothes** people wear can tell you a lot about them.	**13** The most useful subjects to study in school are **economics** and **business**.
14 The best way of measuring students' **progress** is through tests.	**15** GO FORWARD TWO SPACES «	**16** The most important things to consider if you are buying or renting a house are the amount of **light** and **space**.	**17** The **police** should not be allowed to carry **arms**.	**18** Most of the **news** on TV is not worth watching.
19 GO FORWARD SIX SPACES »	**20** Parents should teach their children good **manners**. It's not the teacher's job.	**21** GO FORWARD TWO SPACES »	**22** If you want to get **information** about an illness, the worst place to look is the Internet.	**23** Hotel and restaurant **staff** in my country are usually neither friendly nor efficient.
24 GO FORWARD ONE SPACE «	**25** All uniforms should be unisex, with **shorts** or **pants** for both men and women.	**26** GO FORWARD FOUR SPACES «	**27** Modern **furniture** is usually less comfortable than old-fashioned **furniture**.	**28**
29	**30** FINISH			

American English File 2nd edition Teacher's Book 4 Photocopiable © Oxford University Press 2014

10A COMMUNICATIVE Science quiz

Student A Science quiz

a Read the sentences. Circle the correct quantifier, and read the answers so that you can re-tell them from memory.

b Read your sentences to **B**, and ask if they are true or false. If **B** is wrong, tell him / her the answer, and give him / her the explanation.

c Listen to **B**'s sentences and say whether they are true or false. If you can, say why.

1 ***Most / Most of* thunderstorms happen at night.**
(False. Most happen late afternoon because the ground and air are warmest at that time of day. This heat fuels the storms. But thunderstorms can happen any time of the day if the conditions are right.)

2 ***All the / All* bones in our body continue to grow until we are 16 and then they stop growing.**
(False. Our bones continue growing until we are around 20.)

3 **12% of *every / all* humans that have ever been born are alive at this very moment.**
(True. The total human population today is around seven billion. Scientist estimate that 57 billion people have existed since humans first evolved 200,000 years ago.)

4 ***No / None* of the footprints or tire marks made on the moon are still visible today.**
(False. Footprints from the astronauts who landed on the moon in 1969 could be there forever because there is no wind to blow them away.)

5 **A snake can't see *anything / nothing* if both its eyes are closed.**
(False. It can see through its eyelids.)

6 **A newborn shark doesn't swim close to *either / neither* of its parents.**
(True. As soon as it's born, it swims away so that the mother doesn't eat it.)

7 **Whales don't have *any / no* teeth.**
(False. The whole family is divided into two types: toothed whales such as dolphins, and baleen whales that have a "filter feeder" instead of teeth, e.g., blue whales.)

Student B Science quiz

a Read the sentences. Circle the correct quantifier, and read the answers so that you can re-tell them from memory.

b Listen to **A**'s sentences and say whether they are true or false. If you can, say why.

c Read your sentences to **A**. Choose the correct quantifier. Ask if they are true or false. If **A** is wrong, tell him / her the answer.

1 **If a child's parents *the both / both* have blue eyes, it is impossible for the child to have brown eyes.**
(False. It is not common, but it is possible for the child to have brown eyes if both parents carry the brown-eye gene.)

2 **Almost *no / none* wild birds sing during the summer.**
(True. Birds usually sing during spring and early summer to establish a territory and attract a mate. By the middle of summer, most birds have already mated, so there is no need for them to sing.)

3 ***Every / All the* time we sneeze, our heart stops for one second.**
(False. Although it feels as if our heart stops for a very short period, it doesn't, it's just a change in pressure in our chests.)

4 ***Most / Most of* fruit and vegetables (but not all) contain vitamin C.**
(False. All fruit and vegetables contain some vitamin C. Among those containing the highest amounts are citrus fruits, kiwi fruit, broccoli, and green and red peppers.)

5 ***Both / Both of* men and women who are left-handed live longer than people who are right-handed.**
(False. Although some studies showed that right-handed people live longer, the figures were in fact misinterpreted. There is no connection between right- or left-handed and life span.)

6 **Children grow more quickly in the summer than in *any / no* other season.**
(False. Children grow in "spurts" or stages, and grow very slightly more in spring than any other season.)

7 **Neither dogs *or / nor* cats should be given cow's milk to drink.**
(True. Neither of them have systems that can break down lactose, a chemical found in some types of milk. They should only be given water to drink.)

10B COMMUNICATIVE General knowledge quiz

a Complete the questions with *a*, *an*, *the* or – (nothing) where necessary.

b In pairs, see how many questions you can answer.

1. **What country is _____ Lake Victoria in?**
2. Who was _____ second person to walk on _____ moon?
3. **How many strings does _____ bass guitar have?**
4. In which ocean can you find _____ Seychelles?
5. **What's _____ highest mountain in _____ Alps?**
6. What is _____ 50% of 50?
7. **What color are _____ babies' eyes at birth?**
8. Which bird is _____ symbol of _____ US?
9. **What letter is on _____ right of _____ "O" on a keyboard?**
10. Which animals were domesticated first, _____ cats or _____ dogs?
11. **Which planet in our solar system is furthest from _____ sun?**
12. Who are more numerous in the world, _____ men or _____ women ?
13. **How many states are there in _____ US?**
14. What type of fruit is _____ Granny Smith?
15. **How many players can be on the court in _____ basketball team?**
16. What is _____ first sign of _____ zodiac?
17. **Which nation first gave _____ women _____ right to vote?**
18. What was _____ name of _____ first man to be sent into space?
19. **Which European country hasn't fought in _____ war since _____ 1815?**
20. What is _____ largest man-made structure on Earth?
21. **What vegetable are _____ tortillas often made from?**
22. Is _____ spider _____ insect?
23. **What color is _____ black box flight recorder on _____ plane?**
24. What country does _____ Volga River flow through?
25. **Which travels faster _____ light or _____ sound?**

American English File 2nd edition Teacher's Book 4 Photocopiable © Oxford University Press 2014

COMMUNICATIVE REVIEW

1 Personalities

Tell your partner about two of the following people:
- somebody you know who is very bad-tempered
- somebody you know who is incredibly absentminded
- somebody you know who is extremely big-headed
- somebody you know who is rather tight-fisted
- somebody you know who is a bit two-faced

2 Your style

- Do you have a lot of clothes that you never wear?
- Do you prefer wearing plain or patterned clothes?
- Do you consider yourself to be trendy?
- What's your favorite items of clothing?
- Where do you tend to buy most of your clothes? Why?
- Do you ever buy clothes online?

3 Your town

- In which part of your town / city do you live? (in the center, on the outskirts, etc.)
- What do you like best / least about your neighborhood?
- Are there any famous landmarks or sights in your town?
- Are there any problems with...?
  a homeless people b pollution c crime
- If you had to choose one adjective to describe your town, what would it be?
- Are you happy living there or would you like to move?

4 Your health

Tell your partner about a time when you or someone you know...
- needed stitches.
- fainted.
- had food poisoning.
- choked on something.
- had an allergic reaction to something.
- twisted their ankle.

5 Music

- When and where do you usually listen to music?
- What kind of music do you listen to?
- Did your parents listen to a lot of music when you were growing up? What kind?
- Is your taste in music similar in any way to your parents'?
- Do you tend to have friends who share your musical tastes?
- If you could be a world-class musician, what instrument would you choose to play?

6 The media

- How up-to-date are you with what's going on in the world?
- Where do you usually get the news from?
- Do you think news reporting in your country is objective or biased?
- What's the biggest story in the news right now?
- What kind of reviews do you usually read? Are you influenced by them?

7 Feelings

Tell your partner about a time you felt...
- really disappointed about something.
- a little homesick.
- very grateful for something someone did for you.
- proud because of something a friend or family member did.
- frightened before you had to do something.

8 The weather

Tell your partner about...
- the kind of weather you enjoy.
- the kind of weather you hate.
- the most extreme weather you have ever experienced.
- a vacation or trip that was a disaster because of the weather.

9 Crime and punishment

- What are the most common crimes in your town / city?
- Have you or someone you know ever been the victim of a crime?
- What would you do to reduce crime?
- Have you or someone you know ever been on a jury?
- Do you enjoy...?
  reading detective novels
  watching TV crime shows

10 Advertising

Talk about...
- an ad (or TV commercial) you love.
- an ad that really irritates you.
- a brand that has a memorable logo or slogan.
- an ad that made you buy something.

 Photocopiable © Oxford University Press 2014

Vocabulary activity instructions

2A Illnesses and injuries

A pairwork vocabulary race

Sts race to think of answers to questions. Copy one sheet per student or per pair.

Vocabulary
Illnesses and injuries

- Put Sts in pairs and give out the sheets to individual Sts or pairs. Set a time limit, but give Sts more time if you can see that they need it. Tell Sts that they have to read the question or definition and write down the answers.
- Check answers. Make sure Sts are pronouncing the words and phrases correctly.

2 blood pressure 3 sunburn 4 painkillers 5 get over
6 sniff / sneeze, cough 7 allergic reaction 8 lie down
9 faint; pass out; come around 10 flu 11 bleed
12 twisted, sprained 13 burn 14 bandage
15 food poisoning 16 choke 17 swollen
18 vomit, throw up

2B Clothes and fashion

A crossword

Sts read the definitions and write the answers into the crossword. Copy one sheet per student or per pair.

Vocabulary
Clothes and fashion

- Give out the sheets to individual Sts or to pairs. Make sure Sts understand the difference between across and down. Set a time limit, e.g., five minutes, to fill in their words.
- When they've finished, they can compare their answers with a partner.
- Check answers. Make sure Sts are pronouncing the words and phrases correctly.

Across: 4 suede 5 checked 6 trendy 7 cardigan
9 sleeveless 12 hooded 14 dress up 15 fit 16 denim

Down: 1 match 2 scarf 3 get dressed 4 sandals
8 tight 10 scruffy 11 wool 13 try on

3A Air travel

An alphabet race

Sts read the sentences and fill them in with the correct word. Copy one sheet per student or per pair.

Vocabulary
air travel

- Give out the sheets to individual Sts or to pairs and set a time limit, e.g., five minutes.
- Highlight that each word begins with a different letter of the alphabet. You may want to give Sts a little longer than five minutes, or until at least one pair has finished.
- If they did the activity individually, get them to compare with a partner before checking answers.

B boarding pass C check-in D domestic E excess
F fill in G gate H height I illegal J jet lag L long haul
M metal N noisy / naughty O online P pick up Q quickly
R runway S security T turbulence U unpack V visa
W wait

3B Adverbs and adverbial phrases

A vocabulary completion and discrimination activity

Sts complete the sentences with the correct adverb / adverbial phrase. Copy one sheet per student or per pair.

Vocabulary
Adverbs and adverbial phrases

- Give out the sheets to individual Sts or to pairs. Focus on 1 Confusing adverbs and adverbial phrases. Give Sts a time limit, e.g., five minutes to write the missing adverb / adverbial phrase in 1.
- If Sts did the activity individually, get them to compare their answers before you check them. Make sure Sts are pronouncing the words and phrases correctly.

1 Confusing adverbs and adverbial phrases
2 ever 3 hardly 4 specially 5 in the end 6 even
7 near 8 late 9 nearly 10 lately 11 at the end
12 hard 13 yet 14 at the moment 15 still 16 actually

- Now focus on 2 Comment adverbs, and set a time limit for Sts to choose the correct one.
- Check answers. Make sure Sts are pronouncing the words and phrases correctly.

2 Comment adverbs
1 apparently 2 obviously 3 basically 4 eventually
5 Ideally 6 gradually 7 in fact 8 anyway

4A The weather

An information gap activity

Sts define words / phrases to help their partner complete a crossword. Copy one sheet per pair and cut into **A** and **B**.

Vocabulary
Weather

- Put Sts in pairs, **A** and **B**, ideally face to face, and give out the sheets. Make sure that Sts can't see each other's sheets. Explain that **A** and **B** have the same crossword, but with different words missing. They have to describe / define words to each other to complete their crosswords.
- Give Sts a minute to read their instructions. If Sts don't know what a word means, they can look it up in Vocabulary Bank *Weather* on *page* 156.
- Sts take turns asking each other for their missing words. Their partner must define / describe the word until the other student is able to write it in his / her crossword. Sts should help each other with clues if necessary.
- Monitor and make sure Sts are pronouncing the words and phrases correctly.
- When Sts have finished, they should compare their crosswords to make sure they have the same words and have spelled them correctly.

5A Feelings

A vocabulary discrimination activity

Sts circle the correct adjective. Copy one sheet per student or per pair.

Vocabulary
Adjectives of feeling

- Give out the sheets to individual Sts or to pairs and set a time limit.
- Focus on the instructions and give Sts time to circle the right word in each pair.
- If they did the activity individually, get them to compare with a partner before checking answers.
- Make sure Sts are pronouncing the words and phrases correctly.

2 upset 3 thrilled 4 exhausted 5 lonely 6 scared stiff 7 overwhelmed 8 terrified 9 proud 10 relieved 11 confused 12 stunned 13 devastated 14 fed up with 15 guilty 16 desperate 17 offended 18 disappointed

7A Verbs often confused

A vocabulary discrimination activity

Sts circle the right word. Copy one sheet per student or per pair.

Vocabulary
Verbs that are often confused

- Give out the sheets to individual Sts or to pairs, and set a time limit.
- Focus on the instructions and give Sts time to circle the right word in each pair.
- If they did the activity individually, get them to compare with a partner before checking answers.
- Make sure Sts are pronouncing the words and phrases correctly.

2 advise 3 refuses 4 discuss 5 warned 6 denied 7 lying 8 preventing 9 robbed 10 avoid 11 realizes 12 seems 13 laid 14 beat 15 matter 16 notice 17 mind 18 stole 19 win 20 risen 21 arguing 22 raising

7B The body

A pairwork activity race

Sts read a series of clues and write the words. Copy one sheet per student or per pair.

Vocabulary
The body

- Put Sts in pairs and give out the sheets to individual Sts or to pairs. Set a time limit. Tell Sts that they have to write as many words as they can within the time limit.
- The pair who completes all the words correctly is the winner.
- Check answers. Make sure Sts are pronouncing the words and phrases correctly.

2 brush your teeth 3 heart 4 suck your thumb 5 lungs 6 waist 7 fist 8 shrug your shoulders 9 wink 10 blow your nose 11 raise your eyebrows 12 yawn 13 hug 14 wave 15 shake hands 16 nod your head 17 elbow 18 stare 19 stretch 20 frown

8A Crime and punishment

Alphabet quiz

Sts read the sentences and fill them in with the correct word. Copy one sheet per student or per pair.

Vocabulary
Crime and punishment

- Give out the sheets to individual Sts or to pairs and set a five-minute time limit.
- Highlight that each word begins with a different letter of the alphabet. You may want to give Sts a little longer than five minutes, until at least one pair has finished.
- If they did the activity individually, get them to compare with a partner before checking answers. Make sure Sts are pronouncing the words and phrases correctly.

B burglar C committed D dealer E evidence F fraud G guilty H hacker I innocent J jury K kidnapped L let M mugger O offense P pickpockets Q question R robberies S stalker T theft V verdict W witnesses

8B The media

Vocabulary race

Sts read definitions and write the answers into the spaces. Copy one sheet per student or per pair.

Vocabulary
The media

- Give out the sheets to individual Sts or to pairs.
- Focus on the instructions and point out that most of the missing letters are consonants. Set a time limit for Sts to complete the words.
- Check answers. Make sure Sts are pronouncing the words and phrases correctly.

2 headline 3 objective 4 journalist 5 paparazzi 6 wed 7 freelance 8 censored 9 advice columnist 10 accurate 11 split 12 critic 13 commentator 14 host 15 editor

9A Business

An information gap activity

Sts define words / phrases to help their partner complete a crossword. Copy one sheet per pair and cut into **A** and **B**.

Vocabulary
Business

- Put Sts in pairs, **A** and **B**, ideally face to face, and give out the sheets. Make sure that Sts can't see each other's sheets. Explain that **A** and **B** have the same crossword, but with different words missing. They have to describe / define words to each other to complete their crosswords.
- Give Sts a minute to read their instructions. If Sts don't know what a word means, they can look it up in **Vocabulary Bank** *Business* on *page 162*.
- Sts take turns asking each other for their missing words. Their partner must define / describe the word until the other student is able to write it in his / her crossword.
- When Sts have finished, they should compare their crosswords to make sure they have the same words and have spelled them correctly.

9B Word building

A fill-in-the-blanks activity

Sts complete sentences by adding suffixes / prefixes to a given word. Copy one sheet per student or per pair.

Vocabulary
Prefixes, suffixes, irregular nouns

- Give out the sheets to individual Sts or to pairs. Focus on the instructions and on the three sections. Set a time limit.
- Give Sts time to write in the words.
- If they did the activity individually, get them to compare with a partner before checking answers. Make sure Sts are pronouncing the words and phrases correctly.

Prefix: 2 underpaid 3 multimillionaire 4 subtitled 5 monolingual 6 autobiographies 7 antivirus 8 misunderstood 9 postwar 10 megabyte

Suffix: 1 comfortable 2 sleepless 3 cheerful 4 recognizable 5 terrorism 6 improvement 7 inflation 8 weakness 9 elegance 10 childproof

Irregular: 1 heat 2 loss 3 height 4 death 5 Hunger 6 success

Review

A pairwork card game

Sts define words / phrases for their partner to guess. Copy and cut up one set of cards per pair.

Vocabulary
Review from Files 1-10

- Give each pair a set of cards face down. Demonstrate by taking a card, telling Sts what the word group is, and defining the first word for the class to guess.
- Sts continue in pairs, picking a card, saying the topic, and describing the words and expressions on it for the other student to guess. Remind Sts that they shouldn't use the word itself in the definition. They should try to take no longer than two minutes per card.

Non-cut alternative

- **Put Sts in pairs. Copy one sheet per pair and cut it down the middle. Give A and B each half, and continue as above.**

2A VOCABULARY Illnesses and injuries

Vocabulary race

Work with a partner. Complete the words as quickly as you can.

1 Three parts of your body that we use with "ache."
e*ar*ache , **s***tomach*ache, **t***ooth*ache

2 Something that can be high, often because of stress or bad diet.
bl________ **pr**________

3 Something you could get on the beach if you're not careful.
s________

4 What you should take if you have a headache, e.g., aspirin or ibuprofen.
p________**s**

5 A phrasal verb that means to recover from an illness.
g________ **o**________ an illness

6 When you have a cold you
sn________ and **c**________.

7 A condition when something you eat or breathe can make you feel ill. You should take antihistamines.
an **a**________ **r**________

8 You should do this when you feel unwell or tired.
l________ **d**________ (on a sofa)

9 A verb and a phrasal verb that mean to become unconscious, and a phrasal verb that means to become conscious again.
f________; **p**________ **o**________; **c**________ **r**________

10 An infectious illness like a very bad cold that causes fever, pain, and weakness.
fl________

11 If you cut your finger with a sharp object,
it will **bl**________ .

12 Two ways of describing an injury that can happen to your ankle.
A **tw**________ ankle, a **spr**________ ankle

13 This can happen if you drop very hot liquid on yourself.
You **b**________ yourself.

14 Something you should put on a small cut.
A **b**________

15 You might get this if you eat food that is past its sell-by date.
f________ **p**________

16 This can happen to you if a piece of food gets stuck in your throat.
You might **ch**________.

17 Adjective to describe a part of your body that has gotten bigger because of an injury.
a **sw**________ (finger)

18 Two verbs that mean to be sick.
v________, **thr**________ **u**________

 Photocopiable © Oxford University Press 2014

2B VOCABULARY Clothes and fashion

Crossword

Look at the clues and fill in the crossword.

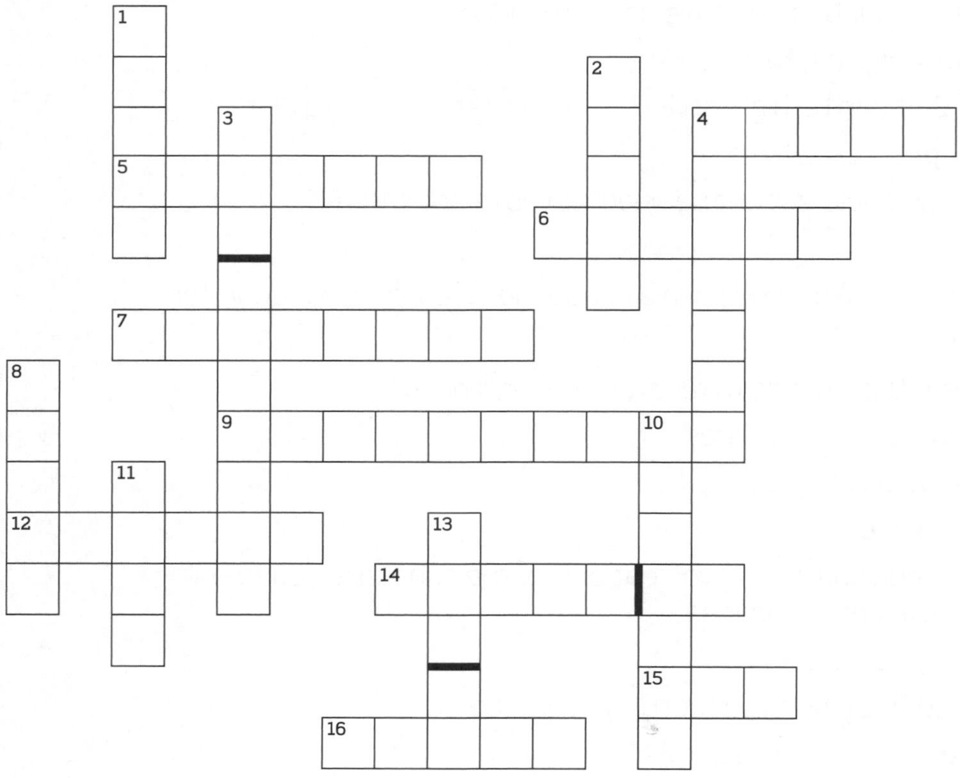

Across →

4 a type of soft leather with a surface like velvet on one side
5 something with a pattern of squares, usually in two colors
6 an informal synonym for *fashionable*
7 an item of clothing similar to a sweater, but with buttons down the front
9 an adjective that describes a top without arms
12 an adjective describing, e.g., a jacket or sweatshirt that has a part that covers the head
14 a phrasal verb that means to put on clothes that are more formal and elegant than those you usually wear
15 a verb that means to be the right shape and size for somebody
16 a type of material that is usually blue and often used for making jeans

Down ↓

1 a verb we use when a piece of clothing combines well with another
2 you wear one around your neck for warmth or decoration
3 a verb that means the same as "put on your clothes"
4 light, open shoes that are worn in warm weather
8 an adjective that describes when clothes fit closely to your body
10 a word to describe a person whose hair / clothes / appearance is messy or dirty
11 the material that comes from a sheep or goat
13 a phrasal verb – you usually do this with clothes before you buy them

American English File 2nd edition Teacher's Book 4 Photocopiable © Oxford University Press 2014

3A VOCABULARY Air travel

Alphabet race

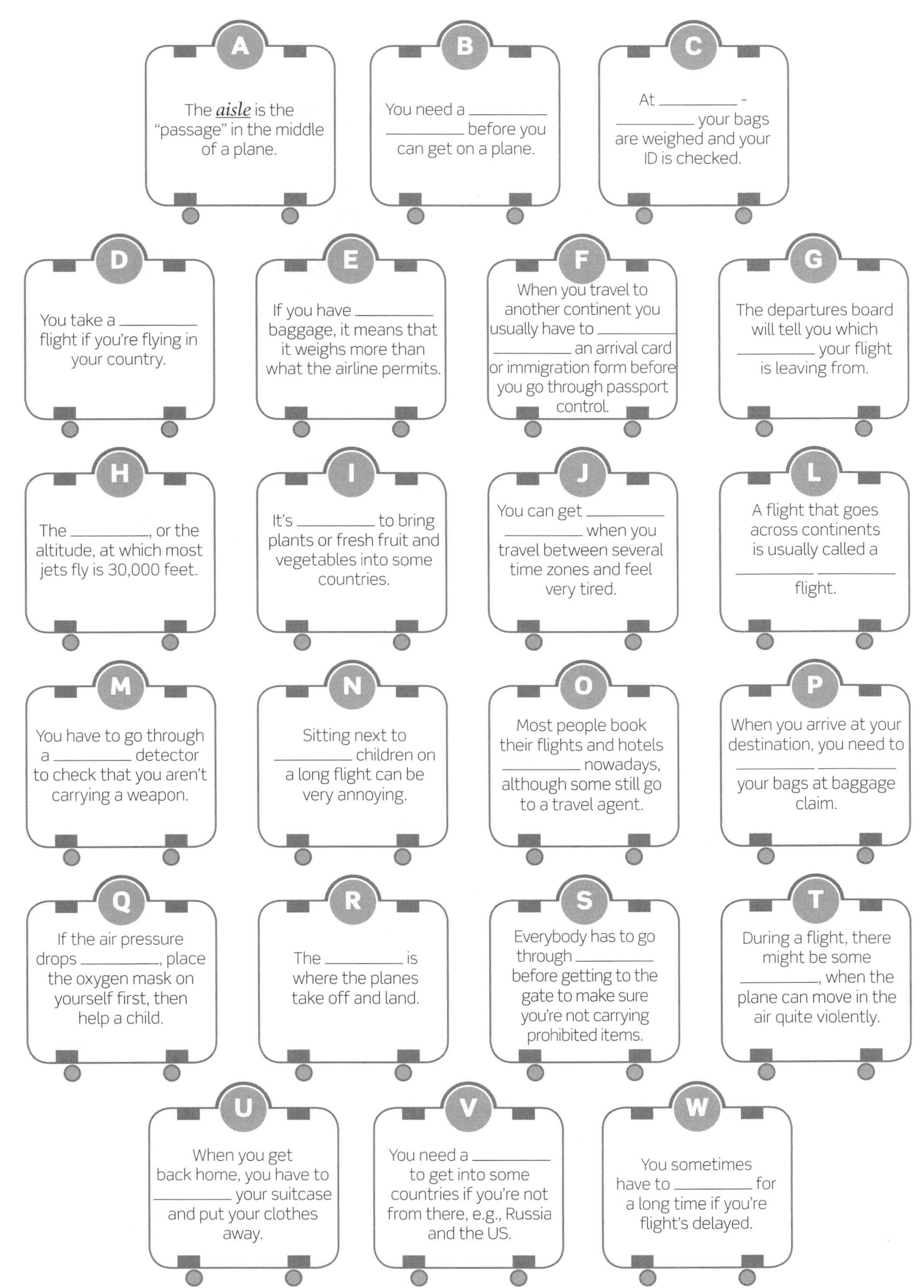

A
The *aisle* is the "passage" in the middle of a plane.
B
You need a __________ __________ before you can get on a plane.
C
At __________ - __________ your bags are weighed and your ID is checked.
D
You take a __________ flight if you're flying in your country.
E
If you have __________ baggage, it means that it weighs more than what the airline permits.
F
When you travel to another continent you usually have to __________ __________ an arrival card or immigration form before you go through passport control.
G
The departures board will tell you which __________ your flight is leaving from.
H
The __________, or the altitude, at which most jets fly is 30,000 feet.
I
It's __________ to bring plants or fresh fruit and vegetables into some countries.
J
You can get __________ __________ when you travel between several time zones and feel very tired.
L
A flight that goes across continents is usually called a __________ __________ flight.
M
You have to go through a __________ detector to check that you aren't carrying a weapon.
N
Sitting next to __________ children on a long flight can be very annoying.
O
Most people book their flights and hotels __________ nowadays, although some still go to a travel agent.
P
When you arrive at your destination, you need to __________ __________ your bags at baggage claim.
Q
If the air pressure drops __________, place the oxygen mask on yourself first, then help a child.
R
The __________ is where the planes take off and land.
S
Everybody has to go through __________ before getting to the gate to make sure you're not carrying prohibited items.
T
During a flight, there might be some __________, when the plane can move in the air quite violently.
U
When you get back home, you have to __________ your suitcase and put your clothes away.
V
You need a __________ to get into some countries if you're not from there, e.g., Russia and the US.
W
You sometimes have to __________ for a long time if you're flight's delayed.

 Photocopiable © Oxford University Press 2014

3B VOCABULARY Adverbs and adverbial phrases

1 Confusing adverbs and adverbial phrases

Complete the sentences with the correct adverb or adverbial phrase.

1 I love all chocolate, **e**_specially_ dark chocolate.
2 Have you **e**________ failed an exam?
3 Paul **h**________ eats anything and that's probably why he's so thin.
4 This pen has been **s**________ designed to write on a tablet. It doesn't work on regular paper.
5 The weather was so bad that **i**________ ________ ________ we decided not to go away for the weekend.
6 Jake's son is so rude. He didn't **e**________ say thank you for the birthday present.
7 They're building a highway **n**________ my house. The noise is terrible.
8 Penny's never on time. She's always **l**________.
9 I can't believe that I've been a teacher for **n**________ 25 years now!
10 Sally hasn't been feeling very well **l**________, so she's going to make an appointment to see her doctor.

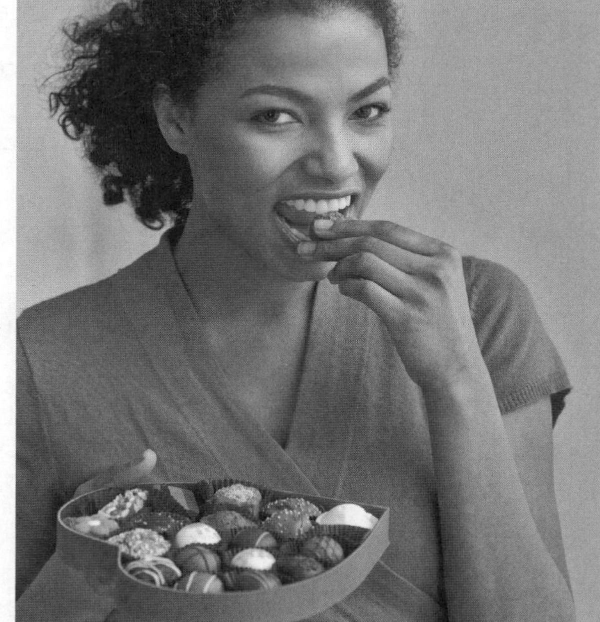

11 I'll pay you back **a**________ ________ ________ of the month.
12 Sara works really **h**________, but her boss won't give her a promotion.
13 Oh, don't go **y**________! Stay for a little longer.
14 I'm afraid Mr. Green can't take calls **a**________ ________ ________. He's in a meeting.
15 We **s**________ haven't decided where to go on vacation this summer. We've been talking about it for weeks!
16 Her dress looks really expensive, but **a**________ it was very inexpensive.

2 Comment adverbs

Circle the correct adverb or adverbial phrase.

1 I thought my boss was retiring next year, but **apparently** / **eventually** she wants to continue working until she's 70!
2 Mark's unemployed, so **gradually** / **obviously** he doesn't have much money to spend on going out.
3 I won't give you the details now, but **ideally** / **basically** the plan's very simple.
4 After looking for his cell phone all morning, my son **eventually** / **obviously** found it under the sofa!
5 **Ideally** / **Gradually**, you should wash wool by hand because that way there's less chance it will shrink.
6 I've been learning French for ages, and **anyway** / **gradually** I'm starting to feel more confident.
7 Rosie's looking absolutely fantastic, but **ideally** / **in fact** she's been sick for the last three months.
8 It's too bad you couldn't come to the concert with us, but **anyway** / **apparently** I don't think you'd have enjoyed it.

American English File 2nd edition Teacher's Book 4 Photocopiable © Oxford University Press 2014

4A VOCABULARY The weather

Student A

a. Look at your crossword and make sure you know the meaning of all the words you have.

b. Now ask **B** to define a word for you. Ask for example, *What's 3 down? What's 5 across?* Write the word in.

c. Now **B** will ask you to define a word.

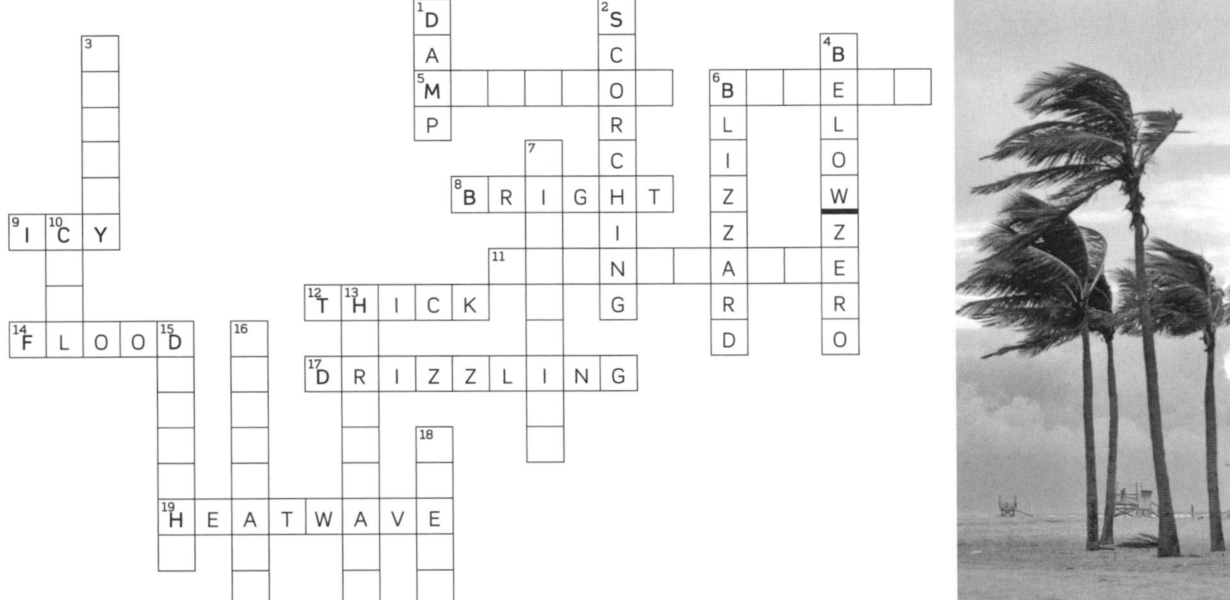

Student B

a. Look at your crossword and make sure you know the meaning of all the words you have.

b. Now **A** will ask you to define a word.

c. Now ask **A** to define a word for you. Ask for example, *What's 1 down? What's 8 across?* Write the word in.

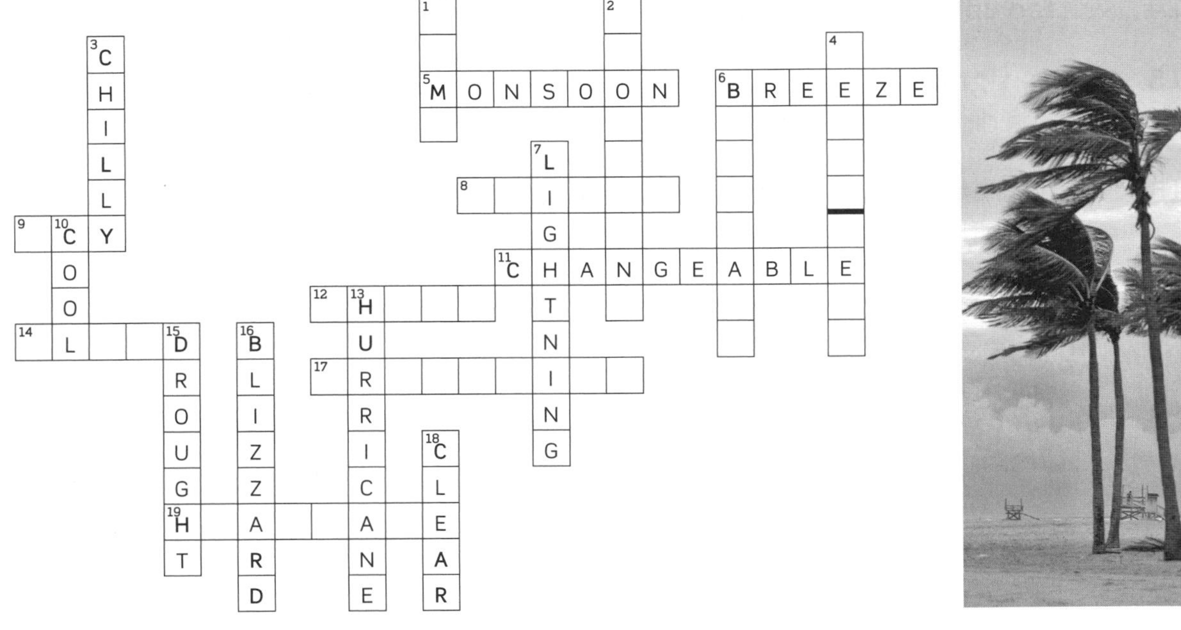

5A VOCABULARY Feelings

Circle the correct word.

1 You look a little **down** / **disappointed** today. Is something wrong?

2 Natalie was very **upset** / **relieved** when she found out that her best friend had been lying to her.

3 You could see how **stunned** / **thrilled** Helen was just by looking at the huge smile on her face.

4 It's been a really long day. I'm absolutely **exhausted** / **overjoyed**!

5 Many older people feel **homesick** / **lonely** when their children have left home.

6 **A:** How did you feel when you heard somebody moving around downstairs?
B: I was absolutely **amazed** / **scared stiff**. I was sure it was a burglar.

7 Sue was **overwhelmed** / **devastated** by all the support she got from her friends when her mother was sick.

8 My best friend is afraid of flying and she feels **terrified** / **horrified** every time she boards a plane.

9 My mom was very **delighted** / **proud** when she learned how to swim at the age of 60.

10 The candidate was **disappointed** / **relieved** when the election results came through. She thought she was going to lose.

11 I think Gemma is feeling **upset** / **confused** by all the different advice she is being given.

12 After the bomb exploded, everyone was so **stunned** / **calm** that nobody moved.

13 Mike was **devastated** / **overwhelmed** when Karen left him. She was the love of his life.

14 I am **fed up with** / **upset about** the people I work with. They're always complaining.

15 I felt very **grateful** / **guilty** when I told Susan that I couldn't go to her wedding. I'm sure she didn't believe me.

16 My cousin is starting to feel **desperate** / **delighted** after looking for a job for six months without success.

17 I think Nora was **astonished** / **offended** that I didn't invite her to my party. She's hardly spoken to me since.

18 James was **disappointed** / **thrilled** when he heard that his team wasn't in the playoffs on Saturday.

American English File 2nd edition Teacher's Book 4 Photocopiable © Oxford University Press 2014

7A VOCABULARY Verbs often confused

Choose the right word

Circle the correct word.

1 Have you been sleeping well recently? You **look** / **seem** really pale.

2 The pharmacist can **warn** / **advise** you which is the best medicine to take.

3 When I ask my son what the problem is, he just **denies** / **refuses** to talk about it.

4 Don't you think we need to **argue** / **discuss** this before we make a decision?

5 Emily's boss **warned** / **advised** her that if she was late for work again, she'd lose her job.

6 When the police accused Jim of the crime, he **denied** / **refused** being there that night.

7 I love **laying** / **lying** on the beach with a good book in the summer.

8 What's **preventing** / **avoiding** you from applying for the job? You've got all the right qualifications.

9 I was **robbed** / **stolen** when I took the train home last night.

10 If we leave at about 6:30, we'll be able to **prevent** / **avoid** rush hour.

11 I don't think Marcus **notices** / **realizes** how important it is for me to have my own income.

12 The new boss **looks** / **seems** very friendly, but I don't trust her at all.

13 The vet picked up the dog carefully and **lay** / **laid** it on the bed.

14 Miriam is really good at tennis. I don't think you will be able to **win** / **beat** her.

15 It doesn't **mind** / **matter** if you can't pay me back until next week. I don't need the money right now.

16 Did you **notice** / **realize** how many times Ella checked her phone during dinner?

17 Does Catherine **mind** / **matter** that you can't go to her wedding?

18 Somebody **robbed** / **stole** my wallet when I was taking a photo of Time Square in New York.

19 Who do you think is going to **win** / **beat** the World Series this year?

20 After the floods, the water level of the river has **risen** / **raised** by several inches.

21 My two sisters don't get along. They're always **arguing** / **discussing**.

22 Have you heard? The government is **rising** / **raising** taxes by 2% next month.

7B VOCABULARY The body

The body quiz

1 Women often paint this part of their fingers and toes. *n a i l s*

2 If you don't do this, you might have to go to the dentist.

3 The organ in your chest that sends blood around your body.

4 You might have done this when you were a baby.

5 Without them you can't breathe.

6 A belt usually goes around this.

7 Boxers close their hand and palm to make this before they hit someone.

8 You might do this if you don't know the answer to something.

9 People often do this with one eye to show they're not being serious.

10 You do this with a tissue when you have a cold.

11 A way of showing surprise using a part of your face.

12 When you're bored or tired you open your mouth and do this.

13 Put your arms around someone to show that you like them.

14 Say goodbye using your hand.

15 What two people often do when they meet for the first time.

16 You do this when you agree with someone or something.

17 The part of your body between your upper and lower arm.

18 When you look at something for a long time.

19 You should do this after exercising.

20 Turn the corners of your mouth down to show you aren't pleased.

American English File 2nd edition Teacher's Book 4 Photocopiable © Oxford University Press 2014

8A VOCABULARY Crime and punishment

Alphabet quiz

A The police stopped me and *accused* me of speeding.

B When we got home last night, we discovered that a ________ had broken into our house and stolen our laptops.

C The police still don't know who ________ the crime.

D The name for a person who sells illegal drugs: drug ________.

E There wasn't enough ________ to prove that he was guilty.

F The gang committed ________ by making fake dollar bills.

G The judge found the accused not ________ of the crime.

H I was furious when a ________ used my identity on Twitter.

I I honestly didn't do anything wrong, officer. I'm ________!

J Twelve people make up the members of a ________.

K The gang ________ the businessman and then demanded money for his return.

L When somebody is acquitted of a crime, the police ________ them go.

M A ________ is somebody who attacks or threatens you on the street and tries to steal something from you.

O Another word for a crime is an ________.

P Be careful of ________ when you go into town! They can take your wallet without you noticing.

Q The police wanted to ________ the suspect about his alibi.

R There have been several ________ in this area. Remember to always lock your door!

S A ________ is somebody who watches and follows another person in a frightening way.

T A common crime on the Internet is identity ________.

V Depending on the ________, the accused will either be sentenced or be released.

W Neither of the two ________ were particularly reliable. They both gave completely different descriptions of the mugger!

8B VOCABULARY The media

Vocabulary race

1 A word which means when, e.g., a newspaper shows favor toward a certain group or opinion.

2 The title of a newspaper article, usually printed in big letters. _ E A _ _ I _ E

3 Not influenced by personal opinions or feeling. O _ _ E _ _ I _ E

4 Somebody who writes for a newspaper or magazine. _ O U _ _ A _ I _ _

5 Photographers who follow celebrities and sell the photos they've taken of them. _ A _ A _ A _ _ I

6 A verb used in newspaper headlines that means to marry. _ E _

7 Journalists who sell work to different newspapers, but don't work for any particular one are this. _ _ E E _ A _ _ E

8 If a newspaper article is considered offensive or immoral it might get ______. _ E _ _ O _ E _

9 This kind of journalist can help you with your problems if you write to him / her. A _ V _ _ E C _ L _ M N _ _ T

10 A story that is correct and has the facts right can be described with this adjective. A _ _ U _ A _ E

11 A verb used in headlines which means that a couple has broken up. _ _ _ I _

12 A journalist who expresses opinions about music, books, movies, etc. _ _ I _ I _

13 A person who works on the radio and describes, e.g., a sporting event while it's happening. _ O _ _ E _ _ A _ O _

14 A person who works on TV and interviews people, often for entertainment. H _ _ T

15 This person decides what goes into a newspaper and what shouldn't. E _ I _ O _

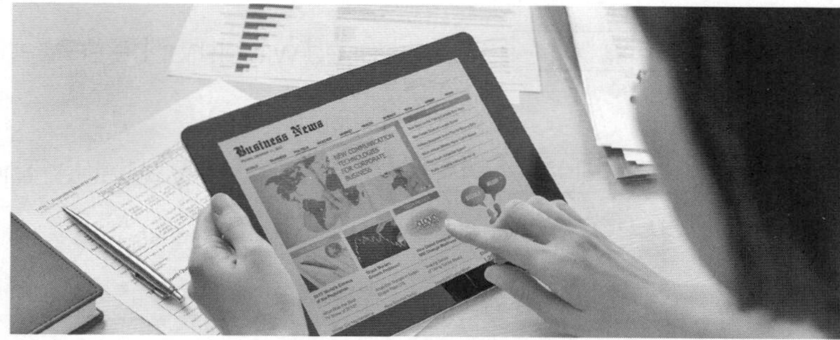

American English File 2nd edition Teacher's Book 4 Photocopiable © Oxford University Press 2014

9A VOCABULARY Business

Student A

a Look at your crossword and make sure you know the meaning of all the words you have.

b Now ask **B** to define a word for you. Ask for example, *What's 2 across? What's 3 down?* Write the word in.

c Now **B** will ask you to define a word.

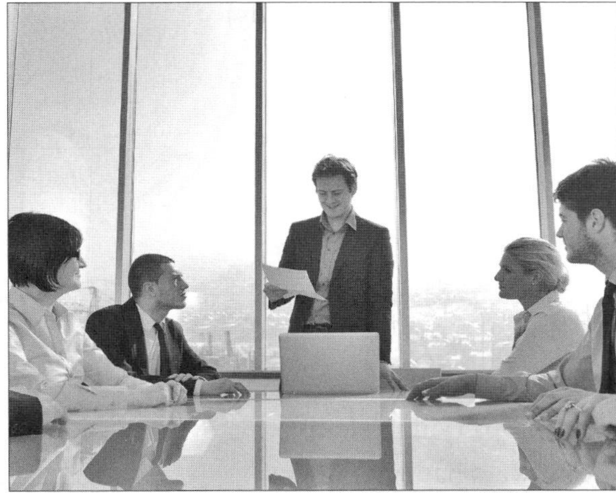

1 MANUFACTURE
2 MULTINATIONAL
5 BRANCH
8 EXPORT
9 MERGE
10 STAFF
11 TAKEOVER
12 CLIENT
16 OWNER
18 CEO

Student B

a Look at your crossword and make sure you know the meaning of all the words you have.

b Now **A** will ask you to define a word.

c Now ask **A** to define a word for you. Ask for example, *What's 1 down? What's 8 across?* Write the word in.

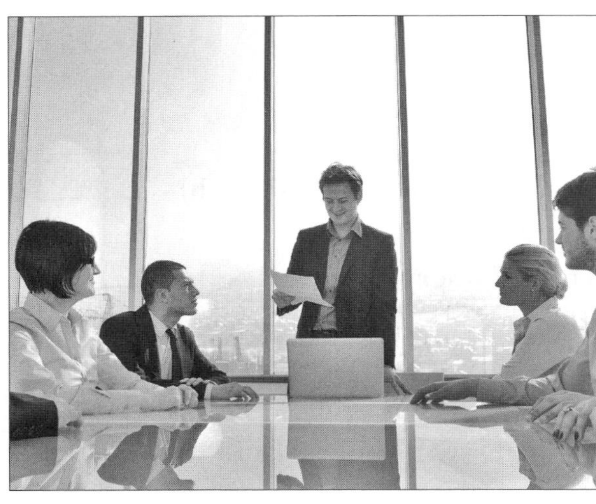

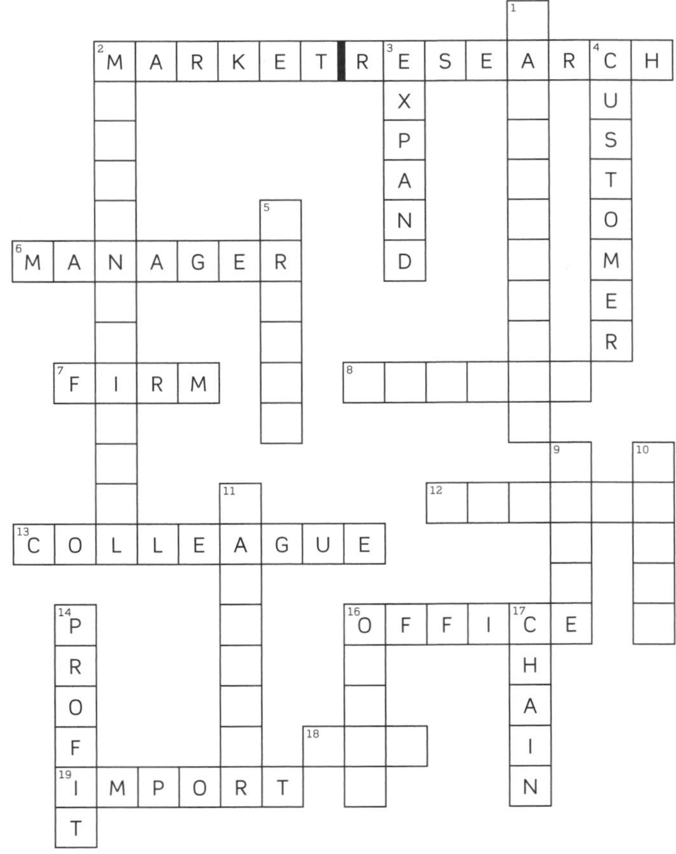

9B VOCABULARY Word building

Complete the column on the right with the correct form of the word in bold.

Add a prefix

1 The bill should have been less than this. I think the waiter has ____ us. (**charged**) *overcharged*
2 Teachers don't earn enough. They're definitely ____ . (**paid**) ______
3 My cousin won a fortune on the lottery. She's a ____ now! (**millionaire**) ______
4 Do you prefer watching a dubbed film or one which is ____ ? (**titled**) ______
5 Is that dictionary ____ or is it French - English? (**lingual**) ______
6 Famous people often write their ____ when they are still quite young. (**biographies**) ______
7 You should always install good ____ software to protect your computer. (**virus**) ______
8 You must have ____ Steve when he gave you the directions. We're lost. (**understood**) ______
9 Much of London was rebuilt in the ____ era. (**war**) ______
10 My first computer only had half a ____ of memory. (**byte**) ______

Add a suffix

1 I like to wear ____ clothes when I'm at home. (**comfort**) ______
2 We had a ____ night last night. The baby just wouldn't stop crying! (**sleep**) ______
3 My mom's one of the most ____ people I know. She's always happy! (**cheer**) ______
4 One of the most easily ____ symptoms of an allergic reaction is a rash. (**recognize**) ______
5 One of the main problems facing governments today is ____ . (**terror**) ______
6 Since Jane's been going to the gym she's noticed a definite ____ in the way she looks and feels. (**improve**) ______
7 The rate of ____ has been very low in my country this year. (**inflate**) ______
8 Martin's biggest ____ is that he can't concentrate for very long. (**weak**) ______
9 Kathy always dresses with such ____ . (**elegant**) ______
10 Medicine bottles have to be ____ so that young children can't open them. (**child**) ______

Irregular nouns

1 Although there's a sauna at my gym, I never use it because I can't stand extreme ____ . (**hot**) ______
2 There are hundreds of weight ____ books on the market right now. Do you think any of them actually work? (**lose**) ______
3 Did you know that the average ____ of a American male is 5 feet, 10 inches? (**high**) ______
4 My mother inherited a lot of money after my grandmother's ____ . (**die**) ______
5 ____ is still a big problem in several African countries. (**hungry**) ______
6 The band's recent tour was a great ____ . (**succeed**) ______

American English File 2nd edition Teacher's Book 4 Photocopiable © Oxford University Press 2014

VOCABULARY Review

Illness and injuries

swollen
food poisoning
to bleed
a blister
flu
an allergic reaction

Clothes and fashion

scruffy
silk
loose
patterned
trendy
to dress up

Air travel

customs
to take off
long-haul flight
jet lag
runway
gate

Weather

a drought
changeable
a heatwave
smog
damp
to pour

Feelings

devastated
relieved
thrilled
shocked
shattered
frightened

Verbs often confused

to expect
to discuss
to deny
to warn
to beat
to remind

The body

an ankle
hips
to wave
to shake hands
to stare
to scratch

Crime and punishment

to steal
a judge
a witness
to bribe
jury
blackmail
hacking

The media

a newscaster
biased
censored
a host
paparazzi
a critic

Word building

overcrowded
homeless
multicultural
bulletproof
neighborhood
bilingual

Business

a multinational
a colleague
a profit
a branch
to do market research
to set up a company

Sleep

to yawn
to snore
to oversleep
insomnia
pillow
blanket

 Photocopiable © Oxford University Press 2014

Song activity instructions

1B Unbelievable

Correcting phrases

Language
Mixed vocabulary

- Give each student a sheet and focus on **a**. Go through the phrases in bold and explain that Sts have to listen and decide if these phrases are right (what the singer sings) or wrong (different).
- The first time they listen, Sts should put a check or an ✗ in column **A**. They shouldn't try to correct the phrases at this stage.
- Check answers (i.e., if the phrases are right or wrong), but don't tell Sts what the right words are.
- Now play the song again. Sts try to correct the wrong phrases. As the song is very fast, pause after every wrong line, to give Sts time to write the correct phrase.
- Let Sts compare with a partner. Replay the song if necessary, and check answers, going through the song line by line.

2 ✓ 3 always asking 4 ✓ 5 talk enough 6 ✓
7 ✓ 8 ✓ 9 leave you 10 ✓ 11 about mine
12 so concerned 13 ✓ 14 ✓ 15 ✓
16 I'd ever known 17 realize 18 ✓ 19 leave you

- Give Sts time to read the song again with the glossary. Help with any other vocabulary problems that come up.
- Tell Sts to read the **Song facts**.
- Finally, if you think your Sts would like to hear the song again, play it to them one more time. If your class likes singing, they can sing along.

2A Just Like a Pill

Listening for extra words

Language
Sentence rhythm

- Give each student a sheet and focus on **a**. Give Sts a couple of minutes to read through the lyrics. Then play the song once or twice as necessary. Check answers.

2 just 3 out 4 great 5 here 6 really 7 real
8 right 9 possibly 10 run 11 get 12 that 13 feel
14 yet 15 very 16 so 17 now

- Now focus on **b**, and get Sts to do it in pairs. Check answers.

1 life support 2 itch 3 middle of nowhere
4 frustrated 5 swear

- Give Sts time to read the song again with the glossary. Help with any other vocabulary problems that come up.
- Tell Sts to read the **Song facts**.
- Finally, if you think Sts would like to hear the song again, play it to them one more time. If your class likes singing, they can sing along.

3A The Airplane Song

Listening for specific words

Language
Mixed vocabulary

- Give each student a sheet and focus on **a.** Highlight that the clue in parentheses will help Sts to decide what the missing words are when they listen.
- Give Sts a minute or so to read through the lyrics once before they listen. Tell them not to worry about the meaning of the song at this stage.
- Play the song once for Sts to try and write the missing words. Get Sts to compare their answers with a partner and then play the song again for them to fill in all the blanks. Play specific lines again as necessary. Then check answers.

2 sweet 3 Friday 4 year 5 extraordinary 6 January
7 messy 8 island 9 lifetime 10 counting 11 chance
12 myself 13 show 14 come home 15 let you go

- Get Sts, in pairs, to read the lyrics with the glossary and to do **b.** Remind them to underline the part of the song where they found the answer. Check answers. Help with any other vocabulary problems that come up.

Possible answers
1 boyfriend / girlfriend or husband / wife
2 The woman has left the man without telling him she was going to. Maybe they'd had an argument; she was fed up.
3 He's in love with her.
4 He'd like her to come back.
5 He promises to "sort himself out," and that he "won't love you and leave you."

- Tell Sts to read the **Song facts**.
- Finally, if you think Sts would like to hear the song again, play it to them one more time. If your class likes singing, they can sing along.

4A Heatwave

Listening for specific words

Language
Mixed vocabulary

- Give each student a sheet. Focus on **a** and give Sts a few minutes in pairs to guess the missing words. Don't check answers at this point.
- Now focus on **b**. Play the song once for Sts to fill in the blanks. Get Sts to compare with a partner, and then play the song again for them to check. Check answers.

2 inside 3 filled 4 heart 5 crying 6 calls 7 flame 8 blood 9 face 10 understand 11 never 12 feeling

- Now focus on **c**. Play the song again while Sts read the lyrics and try and complete the glossary. Then give them a few minutes to compare their answers with a partner.

1 stare 2 tearing (me) apart 3 a devil 4 amazed 5 keep from 6 haze

- Tell Sts to read the **Song facts**.
- Finally, if you think Sts would like to hear the song again, play it to them one more time. If your class likes singing, they can sing along.

5B Same Mistake

Listening for verbs

Language
Common verbs and phrases

- Give each student a sheet and focus on **a**. Give Sts a minute to read through the lyrics. Then play the song once or twice as necessary. Check answers.

2 sleep 3 Walk 4 Look 5 Remember 6 calling 7 screaming 8 Give 9 make 10 meet 11 talk 12 speak 13 buy 14 keep 15 sleep 16 Walk 17 Look 18 Look 19 wonder

- Now focus on **b** and get Sts to do it in pairs. Check answers.

1 my reflection troubles me
2 I'm not calling for a second chance
3 Remember rights that I did wrong
4 maybe someday we will meet
5 Don't buy the promises

- Give Sts time to read the song again. Help with any other vocabulary problems that come up.
- Tell Sts to read the **Song facts**.
- Finally, if you think Sts would like to hear the song again, play it to them one more time. If your class likes singing, they can sing along.

6A Sing

Listening for the correct word / phrase

Language
Mixed vocabulary

- Give each student a sheet and focus on **a**. Play the song once. Sts should write down the word or phrase they hear. Play the song again for Sts to check their answers. Check answers with the whole class, going through the song line by line.

2 needs 3 every 4 voice 5 sell 6 choice 7 shut 8 Living 9 moving 10 Nothing 11 white 12 singer 13 answer 14 get

- Tell Sts to read the **Song facts**.
- Finally, if you think Sts would like to hear the song again, play it to them one more time. If your class likes singing, they can sing along.

7A My Girl

Listening for missing words

Language
Common verbs, rhyming sounds

- Give each student a sheet and focus on **a**. Give Sts a few minutes to read through the lyrics and guess what the missing words are. Elicit some ideas and tell them whether the word they guess is possible, but don't tell them if it's the right one at this stage.

Extra support

- You could go through the bold numbered words and elicit how they are pronounced, to help Sts to guess the missing words.

- Now focus on **b**. Play the song once or twice if necessary. Check answers.

2 me 1 stay 3 heard 4 pain 5 way 6 light 8 unaware 7 weak

- Focus on **c**. Tell Sts to read the song with the glossary and to choose the correct word or phrase in pairs. Help with any other vocabulary problems that come up.

1 mad 2 every now and then 3 take it the wrong way 4 got it straight 5 unaware

- Tell Sts to read the **Song facts**.
- Finally, if you think your Sts would like to hear the song again, play it to them one more time. If your class likes singing, they can sing along.

8B News of the World

Listening for missing words

Language
Prepositions

- Give each student a sheet. Focus on **a** and give Sts a few minutes in pairs to guess the missing prepositions. Don't check answers at this point.
- Now play the song for Sts to fill in the blanks. Get Sts to compare with a partner, and then play the song again for them to check. Check answers.

2 throughout 3 in 4 out 5 on 6 at 7 in 8 out 9 of 10 out 11 through 12 between 13 about

- Now focus on **b**. Play the song again while Sts read the lyrics and try and match the phrases. Then give them a few minutes to compare their answers with a partner. Help with any other vocabulary problems that come up.

1 don't give an inch (NB this is a shortened version of the expression "give them an inch and they'll take a mile")
2 read between the lines
3 our key to the world
4 the gospel truth
5 the goings on
6 day in day out

- Tell Sts to read the **Song facts**.
- Finally, if you think your Sts would like to hear the song again, play it to them one more time. If your class likes singing, they can sing along.

9A The Truth

Listening for wrong words

Language
Mixed vocabulary

- Give each student a sheet and focus on **a**. Go through the phrases in bold and explain that Sts have to listen and decide if these words are right (what the singer sings) or wrong (different from what the singer sings). The first time they listen, Sts just have to put a check or an ✗ in column **A**. They shouldn't try to correct the phrases at this stage.
- Check answers, but don't tell Sts what the right words are.
- Now play the song again and this time Sts have to try to correct the wrong words. Point out that the word he sings sounds more or less the same as the bold word in the lyrics.
- Let Sts compare with a partner and then check answers, going through the song line by line. Help with any other vocabulary problems that come up.

2 ✓ 3 ✗ weight 4 ✓ 5 ✗ how 6 ✗ Say 7 ✗ real 8 ✓ 9 ✗ talking 10 ✗ million 11 ✓ 12 ✓ 13 ✓ 14 ✓ 15 ✗ say 16 ✗ real 17 ✓ 18 ✗ cry 19 ✗ on 20 ✓ 21 ✗ soul 22 ✗ lie

- Tell Sts to read the **Song facts**.
- Finally, if you think your Sts would like to hear the song again, play it to them one more time. If your class likes singing, they can sing along.

10B World

Listening for missing words

Language
Common nouns

- Give each student a sheet and focus on **a**. Give Sts a few minutes to say what they can see in the pictures.
- Now focus on **b**. Play the song once for Sts to write the words in. Get Sts to compare answers with a partner and play the song again if necessary. Check answers

1 package 2 globe 3 box 4 money 5 army 6 satellites 7 earthquakes 8 oceans 9 salt 10 hand 11 bridge

- Tell Sts to read the **Song facts**.
- Finally, if you think your Sts would like to hear the song again, play it to them one more time. If your class likes singing, they can sing along.

1B SONG Unbelievable

a Listen to the song. Are the phrases in **bold** right or wrong? Put a check (✓) or a cross (✗) in column **A**.

b Listen again and correct the wrong phrases in column **B**.

c Read the glossary and lyrics. What kind of problem does the singer have with his partner?

Unbelievable

Verse 1		A	B
You burden me with **your problems**	1	✗	*questions*
You'd have me **tell no lies**	2		
You're **always saying** what it's all about	3		
Don't listen to **my replies**	4		
You say to me I don't **talk too much**	5		
But when I do **I'm a fool**	6		
These times I've spent, I've realized	7		
I'm gonna **shoot through**	8		
And **live with you**	9		

Chorus
The things you say
Your purple prose just give you away
The things you say
You're unbelievable Oh!

Verse 2		A	B
You burden me with **your problems**	10		
By telling me more **about yours**	11		
I'm always **very concerned**	12		
With **the way** you say	13		
You **always have** to stop	14		
Just **think first**	15		
Being one is more than **I'll ever know**	16		
But this time, **I know**	17		
I'm gonna **shoot through**	18		
And **live with you**	19		

Chorus
Seemingly lastless
Don't mean you can't ask us
Pushing down the relative
Bringing out your higher self
Think of the fine times
Pushing down the better few
Instead of bringing out
Just what the world
And everything you're asked to
Brace yourself with the grace of ease
I know this world ain't what it seems

Verse 1 repeated
Chorus x2
You're so unbelievable.

GLOSSARY

brace yourself = prepare yourself for something difficult or unpleasant that's going to happen
burden someone with something = give *someone* the responsibility to listen and sympathize (metaphorically give someone a heavy weight to carry)
shoot through = (*informal*) to leave, especially in order to avoid somebody or something
purple prose = a piece of writing that is exaggerated in style
concerned = worried
lastless = blameless (*Old English word*)
ain't = isn't

SONG FACTS

This song was originally recorded by EMF, an alternative dance band from England who became famous at the beginning of the 90s. Their first single "Unbelievable" reached number 3 in the UK singles chart and number 1 in the US.

2A SONG Just Like a Pill

a Listen to the song and ~~cross out~~ the extra word in each line.

Just Like a Pill

Verse 1

1 I'm lying ~~down~~ here on the floor where you left me
2 I think I just took too much
3 I'm crying out here, what have you done?
4 I thought it would be great fun

Chorus

5 I can't stay here on your life support, there's a shortage in the switch
6 I can't stay on your morphine, 'cos it's really making me itch
7 I said I tried to call the nurse again but she's being a real little witch
8 I think I'll get right outta here, where I can
9 Run just as fast as I possibly can
10 Run to the middle of nowhere
11 Get to the middle of my frustrated fears
12 And I swear that you're just like a pill
13 Instead of making me feel better you keep making me ill
You keep making me ill

Verse 2

14 I haven't moved yet from the spot where you left me
15 This must be a very bad trip
16 All of the other pills, they were so different
17 Maybe I should get some help now

Chorus

b Listen to the song again with the lyrics. Find words in the song which mean the following:

1 a piece of equipment that keeps you alive when you can't breathe
____

2 a feeling on your skin that makes you want to scratch
____

3 an idiom that means a place that is far away from other building or towns
__________ __________ __________

4 annoyed and impatient because you can't do what you want
____

5 say that something is definitely true
____

GLOSSARY

(electrical) shortage = short circuit
'cos = short form of because
morphine = a powerful drug made from opium used to reduce pain
outta = out of
bad trip (*informal*) = a bad experience related to taking drugs

SONG FACTS

This song was originally recorded by American singer Pink in 2002. It was a hit worldwide and Pink's first number 1 hit in the UK. The lyrics of the song are about trying to get out of a difficult relationship, using the metaphor of a patient being in hospital and dependent on the medication and equipment there. It also deals with Pink's own problems with drugs.

American English File 2nd edition Teacher's Book 4 Photocopiable © Oxford University Press 2014

3A SONG The Airplane Song

The Airplane Song

She's a [1] _strawberry_ milkshake (**a type of fruit**)
She's as [2]__________ as a peach (**an adjective**)
But she's ice cold
She never told me she was leaving
She left on a [3]__________ (**a day of the week**)
I went out for the day
And she left for the [4]__________ (**a period of time**)
She never told me she was leaving

Chorus
So get yourself on my aeroplane, 'cos it's been far too long since you went away (x 2)
She's so [5]__________ (**an adjective**)
She left last [6]__________ (**a month**)
And that's the reason I miss you so

She's a [7]__________ creation (**an adjective**)
She hit the road, but the road hit back
Nobody told me you're an [8]__________ (**a place**)
I will wait for a [9]__________ (**a period of time**)
I've been [10]__________ the days since you left one-way (**a verb**)
Nobody reaches her island

Chorus

So give me a [11]__________ (**a noun meaning *opportunity***)
I want you to know
I won't love you and leave you
And then let you go
I need to sort [12]__________ out (**a reflexive pronoun**)
Can somebody [13]__________ me the way? (**a verb**)
And nobody knows the way (x 3)
And nobody knows there's a way
Nobody knows

You gotta give me a chance
And say you'll [14]__________ __________ (**a verb phrase**)
I won't love you and leave you
And then [15]__________ __________ __________ (**an idiom**)
You're always hard on yourself

But nobody knows there's a way
And nobody knows the way (x 3)
And nobody knows there's a way
Nobody knows the right way

Chorus

And get yourself on the aeroplane, 'cos it's been far too long since you went away
Get yourself on the aeroplane, 'cos it's been far too long since you went away (x 6)

a Listen to the song and write the missing words. Use the clues in parentheses to help you.

b Read the lyrics with the glossary and answer the questions.

1 What's the relationship between the singer and the woman?
2 What's happened?
3 How does he feel about her?
4 What would he like her to do?
5 What promises does he make to her?

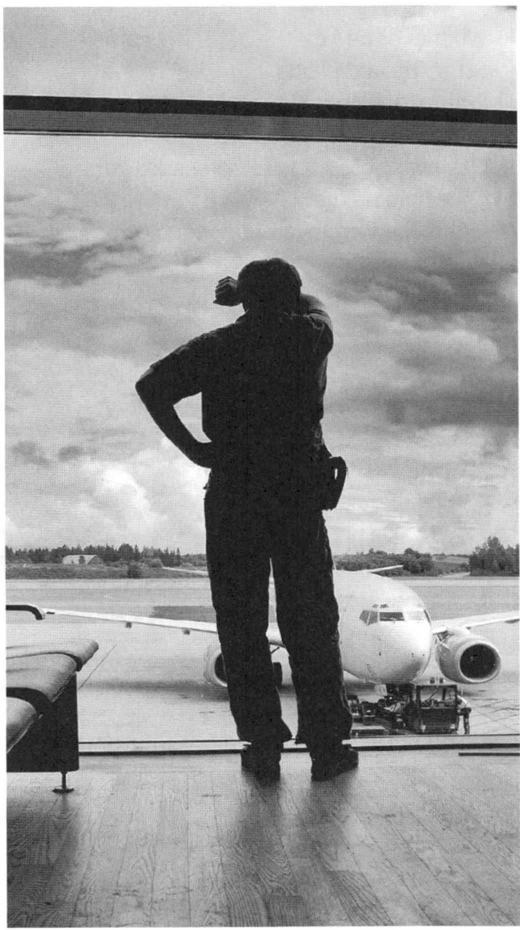

GLOSSARY
hit the road = (*informal*) start a trip
gotta = have got to / have to
sort myself out = to solve my problems

SONG FACTS
This song appears on the 2007 album *Scouting for Girls* and it spent 60 weeks in the UK charts in 2008. This three-piece English band met while they were boy scouts and still in high school.

4A SONG Heatwave

a Look at the song lyrics. With a partner, try to guess some of the missing words.

Heatwave

Whenever I'm [1] **w**_ith_ him
Something [2] **i**________
Starts to burning*
And I'm [3] **f**________ with desire
Could it be a devil in me?
Or is this the way love's supposed to be?

Chorus
It's like a heatwave
Burning in my [4] **h**________
I can't keep from [5] **cr**________
It's tearing me apart

Whenever he [6] **c**________ my name
So softly and plain
Right then, right there, I feel that burning [7] **fl**________
Has high [8] **bl**________ pressure got a hold on me?
Is this the way love's supposed to be?

Chorus

Sometimes I stare in space
Tears all over my [9] **f**________,
I can't explain it, don't [10] **u**________ it,
I ain't [11] **n**________ felt like this before
Now this funny [12] **f**________ has me amazed
Don't know what to do, my head's in a haze
It's like a heatwave.

I feel it burning, right here in my heart,
Don't you know it's like a heatwave

Yeah, don't you know it's like a heatwave?
Burning right here in my heart.

* NB the phrase *to burning* is non-standard

b Listen and complete the words.

c Listen to the song again with the lyrics. Complete the glossary with the highlighted words or phrases.

GLOSSARY

1 ________ = to look at someone / something for a long time
2 ________ = to destroy someone / something completely
3 ________ = an evil spirit
4 ________ = very surprised
5 ________ = to stop yourself (from doing something)
6 ________ = air that is difficult to see through because it contains very small drops of water, especially caused by hot weather

SONG FACTS

This song was the first top ten hit for the Motown group Martha Reeves and the Vandellas in 1963. The original title was "(Love is like a) Heat Wave" and it talks about a teenage girl falling in love for the first time. The song was included in the list of The Rock and Roll Hall of Fame's *500 Songs that Shaped Rock and Roll* and the music magazine *Rolling Stone* included the group in their list of the 100 Greatest Artists of All Time.

American English File 2nd edition Teacher's Book 4 Photocopiable © Oxford University Press 2014

5B SONG Same Mistake

a Listen to the song and fill in the blanks with a verb in the infinitive or + *-ing*.

Same Mistake

Saw the world [1] *turning* in my sheets
And once again I cannot [2]__________
[3]__________ out the door and up the street
[4]__________ at the stars beneath my feet
[5]__________ rights that I did wrong
So here I go

Chorus
I'm not [6]__________ for a second chance
I'm [7]__________ at the top of my voice
[8]__________ me reason but don't give me choice
'cos I'll just [9]__________ the same mistake (again)

And maybe someday we will [10]__________
And maybe [11]__________ and not just [12]__________
Don't [13]__________ the promises
'cos there are no promises I [14]__________
And my reflection troubles me
So here I go

Chorus x 2

Saw the world turning in my sheets
And once again I cannot [15]__________
[16]__________ out the door and up the street
[17]__________ at the stars
[18]__________ at the stars fall down
And [19]__________ where
Did I go wrong?

SONG FACTS

This song was originally recorded by English singer James Blunt on his second studio album *All the Lost Souls*. The song has been used in several TV shows and was played during the trailer and credits for the film *P.S. I love you*. The Spanish flamenco pop singer Melendi has included a version of this song in one of his albums sung in Spanish.

b Listen to the song again with the lyrics. Find the phrases in the song that mean…

1 I don't like what I see in the mirror.
____

2 I don't want another opportunity.
____

3 now I think about the mistakes I made in the past.
____

4 perhaps we'll see each other in the future.
____

5 you shouldn't believe the things I say I'll do.
____

American English File 2nd edition Teacher's Book 4 Photocopiable © Oxford University Press 2014

6A SONG Sing

Listen to the song. Correct all the **bold** words and phrases.

Sing

Sing it out
Boy, you've got to see what [1]**tonight** brings *tomorrow*
Sing it out
Girl, you got to be what tomorrow [2]**brings** ________
For [3]**each** time that they want to count
you out ________
Use your [4]**head** every single time you
open up your mouth ________

Chorus
Sing it for the boys
Sing it for the girls
Every time that you lose it sing it for the world
Sing it from the heart
Sing it till you're nuts
Sing it out for the ones that'll hate your guts
Sing it for the deaf
Sing it for the blind
Sing about everyone that you left behind
Sing it for the world
Sing it for the world

Sing it out
Boy, they're gonna [5]**say** what tomorrow
means ________
Sing it out
Girl, before they kill what tomorrow brings
You've got to make a [6]**noise** ________
If the music drowns you out
And raise your voice
Every single time they try and [7]**close**
your mouth ________

Chorus

Cleaned up, corporation progress
Dying in the process
Children that can talk about it
[8]**Leaving** on the railways ________
People [9]**shooting** sideways ________
Sell it till your last days
Buy yourself the motivation ________
Generation [10]**Nobody**
Nothing but a dead scene
Product of a [11]**wild** dream ________
I am not the [12]**person** that you wanted ________
But a dancer
I refuse to [13]**reply** ________
Talk about the past, sir
And rooting for the ones who want to
[14]**go** away ________
Keep running!

Chorus

We've got to see what tomorrow brings
Sing it for the world
Sing it for the world
Girl, you've got to be what tomorrow needs
Sing it for the world
Sing it for the world

SONG FACTS

This song, by the American band My Chemical Romance, was the second best-selling rock song of 2011 in the UK. In 2011, the group released a new version of "Sing" called "SING" *for Japan* in support of those affected by the 2011 Tohuku earthquake and tsunami. A version of the song was featured in the second season of the TV show *Glee*.

GLOSSARY
rooting for = supporting

American English File 2nd edition Teacher's Book 4 Photocopiable © Oxford University Press 2014

7A SONG My Girl

a Look at blanks 1–8 in the lyrics. With a partner, try to guess some of the missing words. Each missing word rhymes with the word in **bold** that has the same number.

My Girl

My girl's mad at me
I didn't wanna see the film tonight
I found it hard to [1]**say**
She thought I'd had enough of her
Why can't she [2]**see**
She's lovely to [2] _me_?
But I like to [1]________ in
And watch TV on my own
Every now and then

My girl's mad at me
Been on the telephone for an hour
We hardly said a [3]**word**
I tried and tried but I could not be [3]________
Why can't I [4]**explain**?
Why do I feel this [4]________?
'Cos everything I [5]**say**
She doesn't understand
She doesn't realize
She takes it all the wrong [5]________

My girl's mad at me
We argued just the other [6]**night**
I thought we'd got it straight
We talked and talked until it was [6]________
I thought we'd agreed
I thought we'd talked it out
Now when I try to [7]**speak**
She says that I don't [8]**care**
She says I'm [8]________
And now she says I'm [7]________

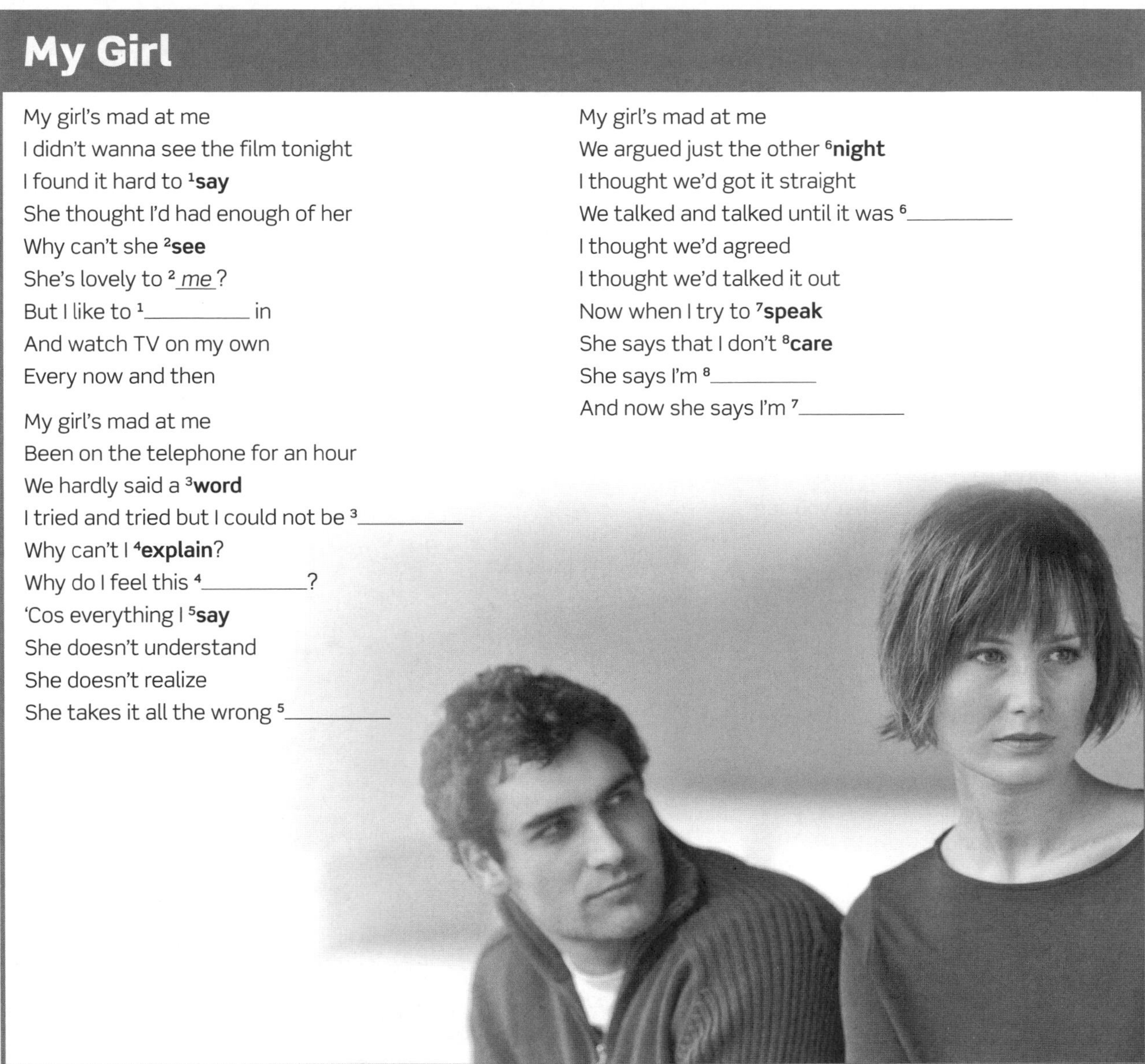

b Listen to the song and complete the missing words.

c Read the Glossary. Find words or phrases in the song which mean the following:

GLOSSARY

1 very angry ________
2 occasionally ________ ________ ________ ________
3 misunderstand and take offense ________ ________ ________ ________ ________
4 clarify a situation ________ ________ ________
5 not know about something ________

SONG FACTS

"My Girl" was originally recorded by the British band Madness and got to number 3 in the UK singles charts in 1979. It was written by the band's keyboard player Mike Barson and is about the relationship he was having with his girlfriend at the time, Kerstin Rodgers, who is now a well-known chef.

8B SONG News of the World

a Listen to the song and fill in the blanks with a preposition.

News of the World

Punk rock
Power pop

I read [1] *about* the things that happen [2] __________ the world
Don't believe [3] __________ everything you see or hear
The neighbours talk
Day in day [4] __________
About **the goings** [5] __________
They tell us what they want
They **don't give an inch**

Look [6] __________ the pictures taken by the cameras
They cannot lie
The truth is [7] __________ what you see
Not what you read
Little men tapping things [8] __________
Points [9] __________ view
Remember their views
Are not **the gospel truth**

Don't believe it all
Find [10] __________ for yourself
Check before you spread
News of the world
News of the world

Never doubt
Never ask
Never moan
Never search
Never find
Never know
News of the world
News of the world

Each morning **our key to the world** comes [11] __________ the door
More than often it's just a comic, not much more
Don't take it too serious – not many do
Read [12] __________ **the lines** and you'll find the truth

Read all [13] __________ it (x2)
News of the world (x2)

b Listen again and read the lyrics. Match the **bold** phrases to their meaning.

1 refuse to change your position or opinion ______________________
2 look for meaning in something that hasn't been said or written openly ______________________
3 a metaphor for a newspaper ______________________
4 idiom meaning the complete truth ______________________
5 activities or events that are strange, surprising, or dishonest ______________________
6 all the time ______________________

GLOSSARY

comic = a magazine, especially for children, that tells stories through pictures
moan = complain about something in a way that other people find annoying

SONG FACTS

This song was a hit for British group The Jam in 1978. The lyrics are advice the band gave to readers about the British tabloid newspaper *News of the World*, encouraging them not to believe everything they read in it. The *News of the World* stopped publishing in 2011 because of controversy over illegal phone hacking.

American English File 2nd edition Teacher's Book 4 Photocopiable © Oxford University Press 2014

9A SONG The Truth

a Listen to the song. Some of the phrases in **bold** are right, and some are wrong. Check (✓) the right phrases or put a cross (✗) for the wrong ones in column A.

b Listen again and correct the wrong phrases in column **B**.

The Truth

		A	B
So **here** we are	1	✓	
We are **alone**	2		
There's **pain** on your mind	3		
I wanna **know**	4		
The truth, if this is **what** you feel	5		
Sell it to me	6		
If this was ever **right**	7		

Chorus

I want the truth from you
Gimme the truth, even if it hurts me
I want the truth from you
Gimme the truth, even if it hurts me
I want the truth

		A	B
So **this** is you	8		
You're **walking** to me	9		
You found a **billion** ways to let me down	10		
So I'm not **hurt** when you're not around	11		
I was **blind**	12		
But now I **see**	13		
This is how you **feel**	14		
Just **sell** it to me	15		
If this was ever **right**	16		

Chorus

		A	B
I know that this will **break** me	17		
I know that this might make me **die**	18		
You gotta say what's **in** your mind (x2)	19		
I know that this will **hurt** me	20		
and break my heart and **so** inside	21		
I don't wanna live this **time**	22		

Chorus

I don't care no more, no
Just gimme the truth, gimme the truth
'Cos I don't care no more
Gimme the truth
'Cos I don't care no more, no
Just gimme the truth
Gimme the truth (x 4)
'Cos I don't care no more, no

GLOSSARY

gimme = give me
let somebody down = fail to help somebody in a way that they'd expected
no more = any more
soul = the spiritual part of a person believed to exist after death
wanna = want to

SONG FACTS

"The Truth" was recorded in 2004 by Good Charlotte, an American punk-pop band. The song is from their third album, *The Chronicles of Life and Death*, which sold 2 million copies. The band has supported animal rights campaigns, but in 2013 they promoted Kentucky Fried Chicken in a series of ads that disappointed many of their fans.

10B SONG World

a Look at the pictures. With a partner, decide what you think they are.

1 
2 
3 
4 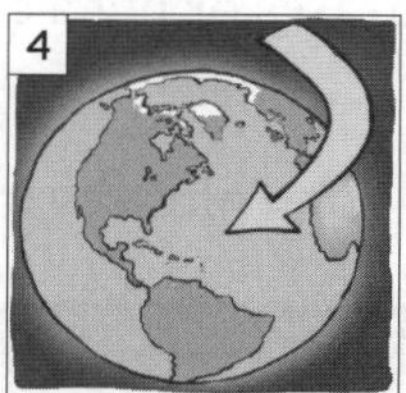
5 
6 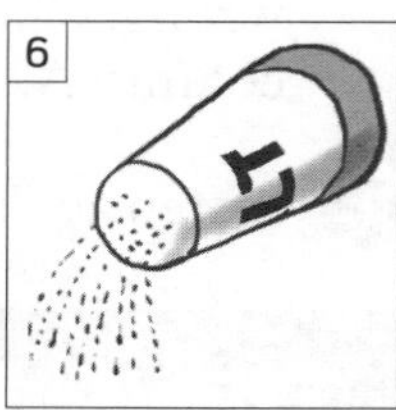
7 
8 
9 
10 
11 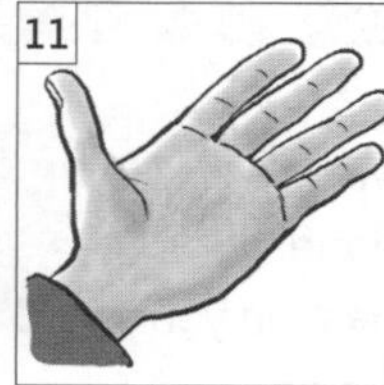

b Listen and complete the song. The missing words are all illustrated in **a**.

World

Got a [1] _package_ full of wishes
A time machine, a magic wand
A [2]__________ made out of gold.

No instructions or commandments
Laws of gravity or indecisions to uphold

Printed on the [3]__________ I see
ACME's *Build-a-World-to-be*
Take a chance, grab a piece
Help me to believe it

Chorus
What kind of world do you want?
Think anything
Let's start at the start
Build a masterpiece
Be careful what you wish for
History starts now...

Should there be people or peoples?
[4]__________, funny pedestals for fools who never pay
Raise your [5]__________, choose your steeple
Don't be shy, the [6]__________ can look the other way

Lose the [7]__________, keep the faults
Fill the [8]__________ without the [9]__________
Let every man own his own [10]__________
Can you dig it, baby?

Chorus

Sunlight's on the [11]__________
Sunlight's on the way
Tomorrow's calling
There's more to this than love

Chorus

SONG FACTS

This song was originally recorded in 2006 by Five for Fighting, the stage name of American singer – songwriter John Ondrasik. The name Five for Fighting is an expression used in hockey (which he used to play) when a player receives a five-minute penalty for fighting. The song was used by the History Channel in an ad for the TV network.

GLOSSARY

uphold = support something you believe to be right and make sure that it continues to exist
ACME = imaginary name of a company first used in a cartoon
can you dig it? = do you like it?
grab = to take something or somebody with your hand suddenly, firmly, or roughly
choose your steeple = choose your religion
steeple = a tall pointed tower on the roof of a church
faults = a place where there is a problem in the layers of rock in the Earth's crust

American English File 2nd edition Teacher's Book 4 Photocopiable © Oxford University Press 2014

Workbook answer key

1A

1 GRAMMAR

a 3 Where do you usually go on vacation?
4 ✓
5 What happened at the meeting yesterday?
6 ✓
7 How long have you been learning English?
8 ✓
9 Can you tell me where the bathroom is?
10 Who are you waiting for?

b 2 where the elevator is
3 where we parked the car
4 if / whether there are any tickets left for the concert tonight
5 what time the game starts
6 when Anna's birthday is

c 2 Who cooks in your family?
3 How long did you spend in Brazil last summer?
4 Do you know who's going to the party tonight? / Do you know who's going to go to the party tonight?
5 Can you remember where I left my keys? / Do you remember where I left my keys?
6 What makes you angry?
7 Who drank the milk I left in the refrigerator? / Who has drunk the milk I left in the refrigerator?
8 How long does it take to get to Boston from here?

2 READING & VOCABULARY

a 1 D
2 E
3 B
4 A
5 C

b 1 inexcusable
2 focused
3 nerve-racking
4 blunders
5 stumped
6 by heart
7 side-tracked
8 sip
9 can't stand
10 fiddle

3 PRONUNCIATION

a 2 Which college
3 Have you ever worked
4 What are your ambitions
5 Would you like to work
6 How many languages

4 LISTENING

a He's successful.

b 2 talking too much

c 1 subway, on foot / he walked
2 three months
3 modern languages
4 hotel, a month
5 three
6 Japan
7 make phone reservations
8 right skills

1B

1 READING

a sports

b 1 b
2 a
3 c
4 c
5 a

2 VOCABULARY

a 2 well-balanced
3 good-tempered
4 narrow-minded
5 self-centered
6 two-faced
7 open-minded
8 strong-willed
9 tight-fisted
10 big-headed

3 MINI GRAMMAR

a 2 more gadgets, lazier
3 later, angrier
4 more I practice, better
5 colder, more clothes
6 more exercise, stronger

4 GRAMMAR

a 2 do I, would I
3 haven't, do
4 aren't you, have you
5 will, won't you
6 could you, have I
7 did I, was I
8 are you, do

6 LISTENING

a 1 Ages
2 spirits
3 Egypt
4 power
5 Middle Ages
6 trees
7 great plague
8 sneezing

Colloquial English

Talking about... interviews

1 LOOKING AT LANGUAGE

2 say
3 begin
4 fill out
5 show
6 buy
7 answer
8 end
9 check
10 see

2 READING

a 1 T
2 F
3 F
4 T
5 T
6 F
7 T
8 F
9 F
10 T

2A

1 READING

a 1 B
2 E
3 A
4 C

b 2 T
3 F
4 F
5 T

2 VOCABULARY

a 2 faint
3 sneeze
4 hurt
5 cut
6 be sick
7 burn
8 choke

b 2 blood pressure
3 allergic reaction
4 sprained
5 sore throat
6 food poisoning

c Across:
5 antihistamine
6 ointment
Down:
2 antibiotics
3 painkillers
4 stitches

3 GRAMMAR

a 2 hasn't started yet
3 Have you ever had
4 I just washed
5 since
6 for
7 has been
8 have only known

b 2 have had / 've had
3 have been / 've been
4 have been writing / 've been writing
5 have moved out / 've moved out
6 have been living / 've been living
7 have already unpacked / 've already unpacked
8 have broken up / 've broken up
9 has been traveling / 's been traveling
10 haven't managed
11 have met / 've met
12 have been seeing / 've been seeing
13 have had / 've had

4 PRONUNCIATION

a 2 specialist
3 finger
4 stomach
5 couch
6 negative

c 2 allergic
3 diarrhea
4 dizzy
5 headache
6 medicine
7 swollen
8 temperature
9 vomit
10 unconscious

5 LISTENING

a, b Speaker 1: press a towel on the wound, stitches
Speaker 2: a broken leg; put snow around the leg
Speaker 3: her friend hit her head and lost consciousness; put her on her side, use coats to keep her warm
Speaker 4: a nosebleed; pinch the soft part of the nose
Speaker 5: her friend was choking; hit her hard on the back

2B

1 GRAMMAR

a 2 The Japanese
3 The Vietnamese
4 The Swiss
5 The Portuguese
6 The English
7 The Scottish
8 The French

b 2 the unemployed
3 the injured
4 the disabled
5 the rich
6 the blind
7 The young
8 the elderly

c 2 ✓
3 some white leather pants
4 some trendy purple glasses
5 ✓
6 his new gray Armani suit
7 ✓
8 scruffy old jeans

2 READING

a 1 ✗
2 ✗
3 ✓
4 ✓
5 ✗

b 1 b
2 c
3 a
4 a
5 b
6 b

c 1 mainstream
2 image
3 accessories
4 vintage clothes
5 needle and thread
6 bothered
7 aversion
8 independent
9 vegans
10 foodie

3 VOCABULARY

a 2 cotton
3 lace
4 leather
5 linen
6 silk
7 suede
8 velvet

b 2 long-sleeved
3 silk
4 loose
5 patterned

c 2 dress up
3 hang up
4 fit
5 suits
6 get changed
7 go with
8 get undressed

4 PRONUNCIATION

a 2 cotton
3 striped
4 shorts
5 leather
6 cheap

5 LISTENING

a She's optimistic.

b 1 F
2 F
3 T
4 F
5 F

3A

1 READING

a D

b 1 D
2 A
3 E
4 B

c 1 turn up
2 hold
3 option
4 disruptions
5 scheduled
6 shift
7 disembark

2 VOCABULARY

a 2 runway
3 departures
4 onetime
5 delayed
6 cart
7 arrivals
8 crew

b 2 check-in
3 aisle
4 security
5 flight
6 took off
7 turbulence
8 pick up

3 MINI GRAMMAR

2 such a
3 such a long
4 so
5 so much
6 such

4 GRAMMAR

a 2 had been waiting
3 had been sitting
4 had picked up
5 had been standing
6 hadn't taken off

b 2 arrived
3 left
4 went
5 got
6 looked
7 had already checked in
8 were waiting
9 had given
10 called
11 had already gone
12 had been waiting

5 PRONUNCIATION

a 2 sang
3 paid
4 met
5 cut
6 woke
7 told
8 flew
9 stood
10 said

6 LISTENING

a 2 Hong Kong
3 Manila
4 Palau

b 1 a
2 b
3 b
4 c
5 a
6 c

3B

1 READING

a C Haruki Murakami

b 1 C
2 B
3 D
4 A

c 1 by hand
2 fill it up
3 grab
4 constructive
5 distractions
6 state of mind

2 GRAMMAR

a 2 ✓
3 ✓
4 badly
5 hard
6 ✓
7 happily
8 well

b 2 My daughter is hardly ever sick.
3 His parents are retiring next year.
4 The boy was extremely rude to his teacher.
5 My brother eats very poorly.
6 Apparently, James is getting divorced.
7 I would have never thought you were thirty.

c 2 Although she studies a lot, she hardly ever goes to the library.
3 Unfortunately, I crashed my new car last week.
4 Ideally, we should leave early tomorrow.
5 I can hardly understand a word when people speak English quickly.
6 My brother almost forgot his girlfriend's birthday yesterday.
7 Surprisingly, it didn't rain at all while we were in Seattle.
8 We're incredibly tired because we went to bed late last night.

3 VOCABULARY

2 lately
3 especially
4 nearly
5 yet
6 hardly
7 ever
8 near
9 even
10 specially
11 right now
12 at the end

4 PRONUNCIATION

a **Stress on 1st syllable:** absolutely; definitely; fortunately; obviously
Stress on 2nd syllable: apparently; eventually; immediately; incredibly; successfully; surprisingly
Stress on 3rd syllable: insecurely

5 LISTENING

a Speakers 2 and 3

b **Speaker 1:** on the beach or by the pool
Speaker 2: historical novels; on public transportation
Speaker 3: academic books and web pages; in his room or at the library
Speaker 4: detective stories; at the gym
Speaker 5: children's stories, in bed

Colloquial English

Talking about… books

1 LOOKING AT LANGUAGE

2 actually
3 sort of
4 mean
5 you know
6 Well

2 READING

a 2 Fewer
3 more
4 on the high street
5 more
6 less
7 an individual
8 printed books

4A

1 READING

a D

b 1 b
2 a
3 c
4 a
5 c

c 1 off the grid
2 impact
3 tax
4 given off
5 environmentally friendly
6 drastic
7 deliberate
8 in reality

2 VOCABULARY

a 2 settled
3 damp
4 thunder
5 breeze

b 2 changeable
3 flood
4 hail
5 heavy
6 drought
7 monsoon
8 lightning
9 humid

c 2 e
3 a
4 d
5 c
6 b
7 g
8 f

3 GRAMMAR

a 2 will have had
3 will take
4 will be having
5 will be studying
6 will buy

b 2 will be flying
3 will have taken / 'll have taken
4 will have read / 'll have read
5 will be playing / 'll be playing
6 will have built / 'll have built
7 will have finished / 'll have finished
8 will be driving / 'll be driving
9 will have stopped
10 Will you be going

4 PRONUNCIATION

a breeze, heat wave
showers, drought
warm, pouring
flood, thunder
bright, lightning

5 LISTENING

a A thunderstorm

b 1 Australia
2 Because paragliders have no engine.
3 -58°F
4 hailstones the size of oranges
5 lightning
6 about half an hour
7 200 feet from where she had taken off
8 an hour
9 China
10 No, he didn't.

4B

1 READING

a 1 B
2 D
3 A
4 C

b 2 T
3 F
4 T
5 F
6 F
7 F

c 1 behind the wheel
2 respond
3 involved
4 rates
5 not confined to
6 reckless driving
7 backed
8 no matter

2 VOCABULARY

2 seriously
3 part
4 after
5 risks
6 time
7 up
8 advantage
9 account
10 place

3 GRAMMAR

a 2 don't get
3 will go / 'll go
4 doesn't rain
5 are
6 won't move
7 cooks
8 doesn't answer

b 2 are having / will be having lunch
3 'll / will complain / am going to complain
4 won't say
5 'll / will finish
6 am / 'm driving
7 haven't read
8 don't take

c 2 as soon as he arrives
3 unless the traffic
4 in case he forgets
5 before she goes
6 until they get
7 after I do / I've done

4 PRONUNCIATION

a 2 account
3 advantage
4 attitude
5 control
6 decision
7 insurance
8 nightmare
9 risky
10 safety

5 LISTENING

a 1 South Pacific
2 their ankles
3 Bristol
4 were arrested
5 the US
6 Golden Gate Bridge
7 American television
8 too long
9 double

5A

1 READING

a He made a snow cave and drank water from a stream.

b 1 c
2 a
3 b
4 b
5 a

c 1 enthusiasts
2 shortcut
3 alerted
4 stream
5 trail
6 curled up
7 out of bounds
8 make it

2 VOCABULARY

a Across:
4 grateful
6 nervous
7 ashamed
Down:
2 disappointed
3 offended
4 guilty
5 homesick

b 2 bewildered
3 horrified
4 astonished
5 stunned
6 delighted
7 devastated

c 2 sick and tired of
3 down
4 worn out
5 couldn't believe his eyes
6 jumping for joy

3 GRAMMAR

a
2 hadn't taken
3 wouldn't have
4 went
5 would have
6 would have been
7 wouldn't get
8 had known
9 didn't have
10 had stayed

b
2 would have made, had been
3 wouldn't have jumped, had known
4 didn't get, would pass
5 had followed, wouldn't have gotten lost
6 used, wouldn't get
7 would have understood, had read
8 could buy, earned

4 PRONUNCIATION

a Stress on 1st syllable: devastated, horrified
Stress on 2nd syllable: astonished, bewildered, delighted, offended
Stress on 3rd syllable: disappointed, overwhelmed

c
2 depressed (/t/ – the others are /ɪd/)
3 surprised (/d/ – the others are /t/)
4 frustrated (ɪd/ – the others are /d/)
5 stunned (/d/ – the others are /ɪd/)

5 LISTENING

a
1 sleeping
2 smoke alarm
3 the bedroom
4 matches, lighters
5 hot oil
6 close
7 towels
8 nose, mouth
9 cleaner
10 pets, possessions

5B

1 GRAMMAR

a
2 I wish you would wash the dishes.
3 I wish my sister wouldn't borrow my clothes.
4 I wish our neighbors wouldn't park outside our house.
5 I wish my grandma would get a hearing aid.
6 I wish the bus would come.

b
2 my brother wouldn't use my computer
3 you would / you'd help with the housework
4 my son wouldn't stay in bed all day
5 my ex-boyfriend wouldn't call me every day
6 you wouldn't leave the bathroom messy

2 VOCABULARY

2 exhausting
3 stressed
4 infuriates
5 disappointed
6 worrying
7 terrifies
8 delighted
9 frustrates
10 embarrassed
11 annoys
12 inspired

3 READING

a
2 E
3 C
4 B
5 F
6 D

b
2 F
3 F
4 T
5 T
6 F
7 F
8 T

c
1 repeatedly
2 denial
3 flawed
4 simultaneously
5 goals
6 obsessively
7 value
8 come to terms with
9 bewilderment
10 principle

4 GRAMMAR

2 lived
3 had gotten up
4 didn't work
5 had offered
6 could
7 hadn't spent
8 wasn't
9 hadn't eaten
10 had worn

5 PRONUNCIATION

a /d/: amazed, confused, inspired, terrified
/t/: astonished, embarrassed, shocked, stressed
/ɪd/: disappointed, frustrated, infuriated, offended

6 LISTENING

a unwell: D
helpful: M
stubborn: not used
selfish: D
critical: M
insincere: not used

b Ana says that Daniel's mom complains that her cabinets aren't organized.
Ana says that if Daniel's dad isn't happy, then he expects everyone else to make sure that he's all right.

Colloquial English

Talking about... waste

1 LOOKING AT LANGUAGE

2 Amazingly
3 Actually
4 Basically
5 Obviously
6 Sadly
7 strangely

2 READING

a
1 C
2 E
3 B
4 D
5 A

6A

1 READING

a
1 Hearing loss from listening to loud music on MP3 players or at concerts.
2 Around 26 million Americans are affected by the problem.

b
2 T
3 F
4 F
5 T
6 T
7 F
8 F
9 T

c
1 needless to say
2 rolled my eyes
3 uncool
4 assault
5 infuriating
6 it turns out that
7 background noise
8 deteriorate

2 GRAMMAR

a
2 doing
3 listen
4 check
5 seeing
6 to play
7 go out
8 stealing
9 to get

10 buying
11 having to
12 to pass

b 2 climbing
3 to call
4 to send
5 to buy
6 reading
7 ironing
8 spending

3 VOCABULARY

Across:
4 keyboard
7 saxophone
8 drums
10 conductor
11 orchestra

Down:
1 soprano
3 cello
5 bass guitar
6 choir
9 flute

4 PRONUNCIATION

a 2 macchiato
3 chorus
4 fiancé

c 1 photographs
2 architecture, graffiti
3 barista, croissant
4 soprano, microphone
5 ballet, rhythm

5 LISTENING

a C It describes a new treatment for Alzheimer's patients.

b 1 c
2 c
3 a
4 b
5 c

6B

1 GRAMMAR

a 2 driving
3 living
4 used to
5 being
6 working
7 play
8 used to

b 2 gotten used to working
3 not used to having
4 used to wear
5 gotten used to living
6 used to taking care of
7 gotten used to using
8 am not used to sleeping

2 READING

a Yes, they do.

b 1 C
2 F
3 A
4 E
5 B

c 1 outbursts
2 put out
3 mumbled
4 bury
5 comes out with
6 dangle
7 dealing with
8 without restraint
9 recollection
10 absurd

3 VOCABULARY

a 2 oversleep
3 snores
4 sleepy
5 sleeping pills
6 log
7 keeps, awake
8 pillow

b 2 nap
3 insomnia
4 set
5 nightmare
6 jet-lagged
7 yawn
8 fast asleep

4 PRONUNCIATION

b 1 fall, yawn
2 alarm
3 blanket, jet-lagged, nap
4 asleep, insomnia, siesta
5 nightmare

5 LISTENING

a C what we should and shouldn't eat and drink

b 1 caffeine
2 fat
3 late
4 light snack
5 water, bathroom
6 milky drink
7 liquid, quickly

7A

1 GRAMMAR

a 2 might have gone
3 couldn't have seen
4 might have taken
5 couldn't have moved
6 must have done

b 2 should have filled up
3 shouldn't have left
4 shouldn't have bought
5 should have taken
6 should have dressed up
7 should have gone off
8 shouldn't have stayed up

c 2 must have told
3 may have fallen
4 couldn't have been
5 might not have heard
6 must have forgotten
7 may not have had
8 couldn't have seen

2 READING

a 1 People can get very aggressive
2 Stricter controls

b 1 c
2 b
3 c
4 a
5 b

c 2 target
3 getting involved in
4 rage
5 offensive
6 remove
7 lacking
8 threads

3 VOCABULARY

a 2 mind
3 avoid
4 Remind
5 argue
6 seems
7 notice

b 2 expected
3 beat
4 robbed
5 denied
6 lay
7 rose

4 MINI GRAMMAR

2 What would you rather do, stay in or go out?
3 I'd rather not cook tonight if you don't mind.
4 Where would you rather go, Boston or New York?
5 I'd rather walk than take the car.
6 I'd rather not go to the movies if you don't mind.

6 LISTENING

a 1 kitchen
2 mall
3 car
4 kitchen
5 work

b Speaker 1: D
Speaker 2: A
Speaker 3: B
Speaker 4: E
Speaker 5: C

7B

1 GRAMMAR

a 2 looks as if
3 smells
4 tastes like
5 feels like
6 sounds as if
7 tastes as if

b 2 tastes
3 looks like
4 smells as if / smells like
5 sounds like
6 feels
7 looks as if / looks like

2 VOCABULARY

a 2 thigh
3 elbow
4 lungs
5 calf
6 kidneys
7 ankle
8 heart
9 waist
Hidden body part: shoulders

b 2 yawning
3 shook
4 waved
5 combed
6 stare

3 READING

a b nonverbal clues

b 1 T
2 T
3 F
4 F
5 T
6 F
7 T
8 F
9 T
10 F

c 1 misconception
2 presume
3 mask
4 fake
5 white lies
6 fidget
7 give them away
8 genuine

4 MINI GRAMMAR

2 e
3 f
4 b
5 c
6 a

5 PRONUNCIATION

2 thum~~b~~
3 ~~k~~neel
4 pa~~l~~m
5 mus~~c~~le
6 whis~~t~~le

6 LISTENING

a 1 They are both method actors.
2 They have both won an Oscar.

b 1 b
2 b
3 a
4 c
5 a
6 c

Colloquial English

Talking about... acting

1 LOOKING AT LANGUAGE

2 completely
3 tremendously
4 overwhelmingly
5 extraordinarily
6 absolutely
7 fantastically

2 READING

a 1 a
2 d
3 c
4 b
5 b

8A

1 VOCABULARY

a 2 hijacking
3 smuggling
4 forgery
5 vandalism
6 fraud
7 bribery
8 murder

b 2 blackmail, to blackmail
3 drug dealing, drug dealer
4 mugger, to mug
5 terrorism, terrorist
6 theft, thief
7 robber, to rob
8 stalking, to stalk
9 hacking, hacker

c 2 robbery
3 stalker
4 smuggle
5 bribe
6 mugged / robbed
7 hack
8 burglar

d 2 verdict
3 charged
4 court
5 investigating
6 acquitted
7 witnesses
8 fine

2 READING

a 1 E
2 A
3 F
4 B
5 D
6 C

b 1 key in
2 landline
3 purchase
4 require
5 dispose of
6 have access to
7 gather
8 go through

3 GRAMMAR

a 2 had been stolen
3 be caught
4 (be) punished
5 questioned
6 visited
7 was arrested / has just been arrested
8 is being held
9 will be heard / is being heard
10 expect / are expecting
11 be given
12 will be stolen

b 3 is expected to be acquitted
4 are reported to have taken the president's wife
5 thought that the terrorists are hiding somewhere in France
6 known that the suspect is dangerous
7 are reported to have damaged the art gallery
8 said that the police have arrested three men

4 MINI GRAMMAR

2 have our burglar alarm tested
3 have had my car repaired
4 had his house painted
5 will have my rugs cleaned
6 are having a wall built
7 has his apartment cleaned
8 are having our kitchen redesigned

5 PRONUNCIATION

a 2 jury
3 guilty
4 blackmail

6 LISTENING

a Speaker 1: B
Speaker 2: F
Speaker 3: E
Speaker 4: A
Speaker 5: D

b 1 F
2 T
3 T
4 F
5 F

8B

1 GRAMMAR

a 2 eating
3 not to be
4 visiting
5 not to park
6 not telling
7 to take
8 to give
9 to return
10 stealing

b 2 advised him not to leave
3 suggested going
4 offered to make
5 warned us not to park
6 apologized for being
7 invited Sarah to have dinner
8 insisted on going

2 VOCABULARY

a 2 critics
3 newsreader
4 commentator
5 reporter
6 editor
7 anchor
8 freelance journalist
9 advice columnist

b 2 wed
3 quit
4 quiz
5 back
6 hit
7 tabbed
8 bids
9 clash
10 split

3 READING

a 1 B
2 E
3 C
4 G
5 A
6 H
7 D
8 F

b 1 handle
2 a dozen or so
3 smarter
4 from time to time
5 pay raise
6 stay on top of
7 deadline
8 quoted
9 urge

4 PRONUNCIATION

a **Stress on 1st syllable:** offer, promise, threaten
Stress on 2nd syllable: accuse, admit, advise, agree, convince, deny, insist, invite, persuade, refuse, remind, suggest

5 LISTENING

a 1 the weather forecast
2 1987
3 a weather forecaster
4 a hurricane
5 he said there wasn't going to be a hurricane
6 110 miles per hour
7 18
8 15 million
9 in the opening ceremony of the 2012 London Olympic Games
10 on YouTube

9A

1 READING

a 2009: Bernard Madoff
2008: Lou Pearlman
1920s: Charles Ponzi
1880s: Early Ponzi schemers

b 1 A
2 E
3 F
4 D
5 C

c 1 trustworthy
2 pouring in
3 fund
4 flops
5 coupon
6 buck
7 legitimate

2 VOCABULARY

a 2 markets
3 imports
4 exports
5 expanding
6 launch
7 become
8 take over

b 2 makes
3 doing
4 made
5 made
6 doing
7 do
8 make

c Across:
4 chain
6 clients
7 headquarters
Down:
1 multinational
2 branch
4 CEO
5 owner

3 MINI GRAMMAR

2 Whichever
3 whatever
4 whenever
5 whoever
6 however

4 GRAMMAR

a 2 to
3 even though
4 in order to
5 so as not to
6 in spite of
7 despite
8 so that

b 2 in spite of the fact that they don't do any marketing
3 so that they would sell more products
4 so as not to miss my train
5 although I was late

5 PRONUNCIATION

a 2 records
3 increase
4 decrease
5 progress
6 permits
7 produces
8 refunds

b 1 exports
2 records
3 increase
4 decrease
5 progress
6 permits
7 produces
8 refunds

6 LISTENING

a Two – Caller 1 and Caller 5

b 1 F
2 F
3 T
4 F
5 T
6 T
7 F
8 F

9B

1 READING

a b stimulating

b 1 b
2 a
3 b
4 d
5 c

2 VOCABULARY

a 2 post
3 sub
4 mono
5 over, under
6 mega
7 multi
8 bi
9 auto
10 mis

b 2 weakness
3 belief
4 strength
5 height
6 racism
7 convenience
8 brotherhood
9 improvement
10 success

3 GRAMMAR

a 3 ✓
4 ✓
5 a piece of luggage
6 some bad news
7 glass
8 ✓
9 good behavior
10 some paper

b 2 is
3 is
4 is
5 are
6 is
7 is
8 is
9 are
10 are

4 PRONUNCIATION

a **Stress on 1st syllable:** friendliness, government, ignorance, poverty,
Stress on 2nd syllable: bilingual, convenience, excitement, reduction
Stress on 3rd syllable: antisocial, entertainment, overcrowded, unemployment

5 LISTENING

a Speaker 1: Washington, D.C.
Speaker 2: Vancouver
Speaker 3: Buenos Aires
Speaker 4: Melbourne
Speaker 5: Hong Kong

b 1 F
2 C
3 B
4 A
5 E

Colloquial English

Talking about... advertising

1 LOOKING AT LANGUAGE

2 had their day
3 get into your head
4 word for word
5 their ears perk up
6 a captive audience
7 hit a false note

2 READING

a 1 C
2 A
3 D
4 B

b 1 F
2 T
3 T
4 F
5 F
6 F
7 T
8 F

10A

1 GRAMMAR

a 2 ✗ Everybody was
3 ✗ Everything went wrong
4 ✓
5 ✗ All men
6 ✓
7 ✗ Most people
8 ✓

b 2 None
3 any
4 none
5 no
6 Any

c 2 neither
3 either
4 nor
5 Both
6 both
7 Neither

2 VOCABULARY

a 2 chemical
3 biology
4 genetic
5 Physics

b 2 e
3 a
4 b
5 d

c 2 be a guinea pig
3 made, discovery
4 test new drugs
5 prove, theory

3 READING

a 1 C
2 E
3 D
4 A
5 B

b 1 C
2 E
3 D
4 B
5 A
6 D
7 B
8 A
9 E
10 C

c 1 thought up
2 a hole in the market
3 withdrawn
4 sketches
5 spilling
6 mass producing
7 still going strong
8 royalties

4 PRONUNCIATION

2 same syllable (first)
3 same syllable (second)
4 different syllable (experiment, experimental)
5 same syllable (second)
6 same syllable (first)
7 different syllable (scientist, scientific)
8 different syllable (theory, theoretical)

5 LISTENING

a 1 smoke detector (right picture)
2 glasses (bottom left picture)
3 ear thermometer (top left picture)

b 1 poisonous gases
2 level of sensitivity
3 scratch
4 new substance
5 measure the temperature
6 reduce the amount

10B

1 READING

a He didn't go to the ceremony to protest about the treatment of American Indians on TV and in movies, and about what was happening at Wounded Knee.

b 1 c
2 a
3 d
4 b
5 c

2 GRAMMAR

a 2 a
3 —, —
4 —
5 the, the
6 —
7 a
8 —, —

b 2 the
3 The
4 —, the
5 the, —
6 —, the, —
7 The, the
8 The, the

c 3 ✗ gone to prison
4 ✗ at school
5 ✓
6 ✗ at church
7 ✓
8 ✗ in college
9 ✓
10 ✓

3 VOCABULARY

a 2 peace and quiet
3 sooner or later
4 knife and fork
5 bed and breakfast
6 more or less
7 all or nothing
8 salt and pepper
9 now or never
10 once or twice

b 1 ends
2 sick, tired
3 give, take
4 ups, downs
5 law, order
6 safe, sound
7 wait, see
8 now, again

4 PRONUNCIATION

a 2 /ði/
3 /ðə/
4 /ðə/
5 /ðə/
6 /ði/

5 LISTENING

a 1 c
2 b
3 c

b 1 Bertie
2 write with his right hand when he was left-handed
3 his brother, Edward
4 1925
5 by filling his mouth with marbles
6 at his own office
7 10 months
8 because he wanted to marry a divorced American woman
9 his therapist Mr. Logue
10 he called the King "Your Majesty," which he had previously refused to do